The Courage to Love

THE COURAGE TO LOVE

Selected Papers of Edith Weigert, M.D.

by Edith Weigert

New Haven and London, Yale University Press, 1970

Library of Congress catalog card number: 76–105458
Standard book number: 300–01282–9

Designed by Marvin Howard Simmons,
set in Caledonia type,
and printed in the United States of America by
Connecticut Printers, Inc., Hartford, Connecticut.

Distributed in Great Britain, Europe, Asia, and
Africa by Yale University Press Ltd., London; in
Canada by McGill–Queen's University Press, Montreal; and
in Mexico by Centro Interamericano de Libros
Académicos, Mexico City.

To my grandchildren
David and Robbin Weigert

I gratefully acknowledge the editorial and secretarial help of Beatrice Bretzfield, Maria Paasche, and Helga Preuss.

E.W.

Contents

Contents

Introduction

Forty years ago, in 1929, I was an assistant to Dr. Ernest Simmel at the first German psychoanalytic hospital in Berlin-Tegel, after having finished my medical and psychoanalytic training and five years of psychiatric work on the staff of the neuro-psychiatric department of the University Medical School of Berlin. European psychiatry was at that time oriented mainly toward finding the organic, particularly the neurological, basis of mental illness. What psychiatry could offer to chronic mental patients was mainly custodial care. There was a deep dissatisfaction in the psychiatric profession about the lack of understanding for the tragedies of psychopathology in the human condition. Freud's discoveries of the conflicts between the unconscious and conscious mind and his dualistic instinct theory opened up new horizons and kindled hope and enthusiasm in some of the young psychiatrists for a better understanding of psychopathological conflicts and potentialities of rational treatment. But these discoveries also encountered skepticism, resistance, ridicule, and open hostility.

Dr. Simmel's hospital was supported only by private means. It was a hospital with open wards. Thirty patients were psychoanalytically treated by three psychoanalytically trained physicians assisted by two nurses. Sigmund Freud had built up psychoanalytic theory and practice mainly on his experience with voluntary, ambulatory patients. Psychotic patients who needed hospitalization were not accessible to him, since academic careers in university hospitals or leading positions in state hospitals were closed to Jews in antisemitic Austria. Freud, who spent his summer vacations in Simmel's home on the hospital grounds, encouraged Simmel's experiment, but we were aware of great difficulties. Freud himself had treated patients at the borderline between neurosis and psychosis, but these patients had been able to maintain sufficient appearance of conventional adjustment to be suited for ambulatory treatment. In Simmel's open-ward hospital the patients were separated from home base. They were treated with daily psychoanalysis stirring up conflicts which mobilized asocial and antisocial impulses. There were neither the restraints nor the personnel which, in mental institutions with closed wards, prevent patients from acting out dangerous impulses.

I remember a young female patient in this hospital who in fierce agitation felt both driven to, yet inhibited from, murdering a child. She had grown up under inhuman conditions in the slums of Berlin and her thirst for revenge was initially an almost uncontrollable rage. I wrestled with another patient half a night. She wanted to strangle me in glaring fury: "My mother hated me." She transferred her vindictiveness from her mother to me. Yet no murder or suicide occurred in Tegel. The experiment of treating these deeply troubled patients psychoanalytically without restraints was more successful than we had expected. But the hospital went into bankruptcy and was closed due to lack of public funds. The German public and the medical profession closed their eyes to the creative, healing potentialities of psychoanalysis.

Two years later, Hitler's national-socialism came into power. Hitler had suffered from hysterical blindness and had been a psychiatric patient in Heidelberg during the First World War. And yet a majority of the German public, even some of the intelligentsia, followed his fanatic leadership blindly. The spirit of irrational vindictiveness was swept up by a mass hysteria. This vindictiveness was directed by transference to the Jews, the socialists, and communists. Many psychotic patients who could not live up to the Siegfried-ideal of invulnerable virility were put to death. Psychoanalysis went underground. A few psychotherapists committed suicide, among them Dr. George Groddeck. I heard that he insisted he would cure Hitler from his paranoia; his friends stopped him in this dangerous intention. Groddeck, unable to carry out his urgent intention, became paranoid himself in his helplessness. The majority of us emigrated into Anglo-Saxon countries, where we found a generous welcome, more open-minded understanding, and better opportunities for development. (My paper on "Conditions of Organized and Regressive Response to Danger" deals with this historical situation.) The tragic experiences that led to the Second World War convinced us not only that individual psychopathology needs more than moral indignation, but that the disasters of mass hysteria and intranational and international power struggles need deeper psychological studies.

However, this country also is not free from prejudice against the tragic aspects of the human condition in psychoneurotic maladjustment. We encounter resistances in psychoneurotic patients and their relatives. Many patients turn to other medical specialists before they reach the psychiatrist's office. The admirable achievements of natural science and their technical applications in medicine have reduced the dangers of nature that threaten human welfare, but more than fifty percent of the patients that seek help from physicians and hospitals suffer from psychological conflicts that the patients cannot solve alone.

The greatest danger that threatens man is man: "Homo homini lupus" (man is a wolf to man). The ethologists who observe animal behavior tell us that the wolves among themselves are less conflicted and hostile than human beings, since instinctive mechanisms in most animals safeguard not only the survival of the individual but also the survival of the species. (See "Human Ego Functions in the Light of Animal Behavior.")

I found that American psychiatrists are more tolerant of diversity of opinion than Europeans. The American philosopher Alfred North Whitehead said: "The clash of doctrines is not a disaster, it is an opportunity." There was a clash of doctrines between the various schools of psychoanalysis in its early European history. C. G. Jung was a disciple of the Swiss psychiatrist Eugene Bleuler and only partially accepted Freud's ideas. Freud in turn emphatically rejected Jung's monistic libido theory, emphasizing instead the dialectic tension in his dualistic instinct theory which he formulated in various ways: libido versus self-preservation, narcissistic versus object libido, Eros versus Thanatos. Originally Freud saw in the conflicts of the sexual instinct with external forces and the internal authority of the conscience (ego-ideal or superego) the source of human fragmentation and alienation, since this conflict produces repression, denial, projection, introjection and dissociation of the conscious from the unconscious mind. After the First World War, Freud was more inclined to see the greater danger to human integrity in the destructive excesses of the aggressive instinct which he called Thanatos or death instinct. He thus came closer to his former disciple, Alfred Adler, who found in Nietzsche's "will to power," in the human struggle for superiority or evasion into inferiority, the cause of human alienation from his destiny and his fellowmen. Adlerian and Jungian psychologies found only a weak echo in U.S.A. They were absorbed without much controversy.

Freud might not have been so disappointed by his dissenting disciples had he not been exposed to so much hostility in his early career. He needed the support of followers and faithful friends. In spite of philosophic differences Freud maintained a lifelong friendship with the Swiss psychiatrist, Ludwig Binswanger, who introduced phenomenology and existentialism into European psychiatry. Binswanger was not a follower of Freud, but the two men respected each other. Binswanger found the biological frame of the instinct theory too narrow for understanding the imponderabilities in human existence. The biological need for release of sexual tension as well as the need for aggressive self-assertion and expanding growth are by nature beyond good and evil. They can become the wellspring of creativity or lead to collapse in insanity. Binswanger thought there must be a spiritual force, distinct from sexual tension. He called it "Eros héauton auxon"—the self-increasing, ever-productive Eros. This spontaneous force of Eros promotes the individual integrating growth of all his latent potentialities in "the single mode of existence." Eros tames and harmonizes aggressive and competitive impulses in the service of "the plural mode of existence," the social aspect of human existence. In "the dual mode of existence," the intimate relation of man and woman, Eros lifts their mutuality to the level of love.

But the enigmatic source of life energy that ebbs and flows in human existence cannot be grasped in the quantitative terms of natural science, whether we call this energy instinctual or spiritual. Freud was not an orthodox Freudian. He was free to call his instinct theory a mythology. Out of the need for spiritual fellowship, man has created many mythologies, religions and philosophies. Ancient mythologies have become a source of psychological understanding of symbols; they reflect an intuitive grasp of the human condition.

Kierkegaard meditated about the ambivalence of the father-son relation in the saga of Abraham's sacrifice. In a paper in the last part of this book, "Cult and Mythology of the Magna Mater," I have studied the ambivalence in the incestuous mother-son relation. The Oedipus legend which treats the incestuous and competitive trends in the family became a cornerstone of psychoanalytic theory. C. G. Jung has attributed the creation of mythologies to the "Collective Unconscious." The yearning for salvation from existential anxieties and the longing for trust are expressed in all religions that man's imagination has created.

I am trying in these collected papers to build a bridge between my earlier European experience and present-day American psychiatry, between what I learned from Freudian psychoanalysis and the extensions of psychodynamic understanding of psychoses in the United States. I am particularly indebted to Harry Stack Sullivan's lectures and seminars on "Interpersonal Relations." Sullivan saw the greatest harm that man does to man in the damage to self-esteem, particularly in the relatively helpless dependency of the child's development, by overstrictness or overindulgence or other deprivations of self-esteem. Such deprivations elicit the warning signal of anxiety and mobilize automatic defenses against the painful experience of anxiety. These defenses become habits of character formation, more or less incapacitating not only emotions, but also perception, cognition and will. We find the deepest degree of fragmentation of the ego and alienation from interpersonal relations in schizophrenic psychoses. Freud had predicted that the psychoanalytic study of psychoses that was handicapped in Europe would open a deeper understanding of ego-psychology.

Introduction

This prediction came true in this country, due to the works of Paul Federn, Heinz Hartmann and his collaborators, Erik Erikson, and many of the younger generation of psychoanalysts.

Though I have only a reading acquaintance with modern philosophy, I would also like to contribute in these papers to the connection between psychoanalysis and existentialism which was introduced into American psychiatry and psychology by Rollo May and into American theology by Paul Tillich. The forerunners of existentialism, Søren Kierkegaard and Friedrich Nietzsche, could also be called ancestors of psychoanalysis, since their highly sensitized neurotic personalities intuitively anticipated some of the later psychoanalytic discoveries. We find that most of the recent existential philosophers, Karl Jaspers (who was a former psychiatrist), Martin Heidegger, Jean-Paul Sartre, Martin Buber, Gabriel Marcel, and Max Scheler are or were interested in psychoanalysis, and they tried to come to terms with it, even though there was little consensus among themselves due to their different theistic, atheistic, or agnostic orientations.

The ideas of the French philosopher, Jean-Paul Sartre, are most closely related to psychoanalysis, though he rejected the concept of the unconscious. His voluntaristic philosophy presents the life style of average man as that of "bad faith;" to protect himself from his fellowmen he deceives them and deceives himself, denying his authenticity, and not being true to himself. Sartre put his finger on man's propensity to harm his fellowmen, his sadomasochistic disposition. He took this concept over from psychoanalysis, but did not confine it to an early stage of child development, he extended it pessimistically to mankind in general. "L'autrui, c'est l'enfer" ("the other one, that is hell") or "Ote-toi que je m'y mette" ("remove yourself so that I can take your place"). Only "love-free-from-purpose" transcends this struggle for existence. According to Sartre, the need for individual freedom is innate in human existence. Man's freedom is threatened by other men's freedom. Each one tries to curtail or destroy the freedom of others. "Love-free-from-purpose" cannot be forced or institutionalized. It is seldom encountered in purity, since anxieties and enforced defenses against anxieties distort this purity.

Freud was not far removed from Sartre's pessimism concerning the human condition. In spite of his basic biological orientation and disinterest in academic philosophies, he was a philosopher himself, deeply involved in the conflicts of human existence. But he saw these conflicts arising in the long developmental process from infantile dependency to adult maturity. Originally Freud understood anxiety as a product of degenerated, frustrated libido. Later he broadened the concept of libido to mean the innate tendency toward need fulfillment. Anxiety remains a danger signal useful for human survival, since it mobilizes aggressive energies to overcome danger and impending frustrations. The helpless child cannot yet overcome these dangers by himself. He is absolutely dependent on parental care. He finds security only in the symbiotic union with his mother. In this union there is an empathic understanding of needs, a basic trust, trust of the child in the parent, reflected in his smile, trust of the parent in the child's basic goodness. The empathy of emotional contagion grows into the sympathy of mutual acceptance and ever renewed reconciliation. The child outgrows this dependency slowly. He learns to take care of himself gradually and with growing rational competence. Sometimes, when dangers are beyond his competence panic reactions of fury and rage overthrow his equilibrium and he loses control, sometimes he withdraws into defiant pretence of independence. These are magic means to deny unbearable anxieties. But the longing for the absolute dependency and security in the symbiotic union with his mother stays with him throughout life, though mostly outside of conscious awareness.

The adult cannot stand complete loneliness, he continually reaches out for human fellowship. According to Martin Buber he has to shed the defensive armour that has been built up against unbearable anxieties, the mask of conventionality, hypocritical compliance, egocentric concern for his own security. Only when man can be true to himself can he overcome the defenses of the other person and can meet him in an I–Thou encounter that respects the authenticity and truthfulness of both partners. Gabriel Marcel calls this spontaneous trust relation between I and Thou "intersubjectivity." The spontaneity of the I–Thou encounter is endangered by the frustrations of the human condition. Under the pressure of unbearable anxieties the I–Thou relation freezes into an I–It relation in which the other one becomes an It, a thing that can be forced when it does not force you. Force mobilizes increased anxieties and defenses against anxiety. The relation of trust and good faith degenerates into what Sartre calls "bad faith," the master–slave relation of hostile, envious competition or relentless vindictiveness. The goal of trust is seen as an illusion, love as a threat to self-preservation. Even the most intimate opportunity for human trust in the sexual act can be marred by distrust, exploitation, domination and submission. The sexual relation can deteriorate into accusatory, hostile competition.

Even in the so-called normal individual, trust cannot be preserved in its purity. In the transition from what Freud called the pleasure-pain principle to the reality principle of adaptation, Ananke, the Greek goddess of fate, takes a heavy toll that human beings are not always able to pay. In those who make the adjustment seemingly successfully, Heidegger as well as Sartre has discovered self deceptions, hypocrisies, pretended role-playing, outwitting of competition, and as-if performances that try to avoid the disapproval and dangerous rejection of their fellowmen, particularly of those in power and authority. The norms of the culture set up the concepts of right and wrong. The ideals of justice are forceful, sometimes formidable and relentless, not always seasoned by mercy. According to Heidegger, "being-in-the-world" is determined by care (Sorge). "Being thrown into the world," we are concerned about our being, we care for our survival and that of our fellowmen. But this care is fraught with anxieties. Imagination anticipates dangers that may never materialize. The anxiety of guilt feelings stems from the discrepancies between unused human potentialities that are often directed towards unreachable ideals and the imperfections of realization. Man in everyday living shuts his eyes to his anxieties and guilt feelings. He loses himself in being busy or distracted. He forgets about his imperfections, his contingencies, his mortality, the tragic aspects of human existence. Thus he loses, more or less, his authenticity. His conscience is not integrated in his ego, it becomes a heteronomous mechanism, a set of rules imposed from the outside, a cruel, punishing superego. This turns the healthy self-love or benign narcissism into a malignant narcissism. Man is at war with himself.

The section on psychopathology deals with some of the extreme deteriorations of human trust and authenticity. A sense of meaninglessness pervades the existence of these patients. The loss of hope and trust in life is illustrated in some vignettes out of the life history of patients. There are so many variations in individual forms of psychopathology that it is more difficult to delineate diagnoses in psychiatry than in organic medicine. The original causes of psychopathology frequently cannot be removed, they may be based on sensitivities of the constitution, on earlier or later traumatic experiences which have made it more or less unfeasible for the individual to cope with the challenges of life. The strategy of therapy is directed toward the goals of reconciliation with the hardships of life by which the patient has been defeated.

The means for arriving at these goals are described in more detail in the chapter on psychoanalytic technique. Psychoanalysis offers the patient or the research candidate an opportunity to reveal himself in an atmosphere of privileged communication, free from moral prejudice and dangers of rejection. Communication in the form of free associations gives free rein to the expression of the patient's emotions, fears and wishes, dreams and daydreams. Initially, the patient is not free in his communications, he cannot trust, he is tied by resistance against shedding the protective mask of conventionality. Some patients expect to be treated with disapproval and rejection, as they were treated by previous authorities. Other patients try to reestablish a relation of dependency and manipulative submission. They hope to be saved from their anxieties by an idealized parental authority; they project a magic savior role onto the analyst, in whom they are sooner or later disappointed. There develops before the eyes of the patient and his therapist, or participant observer, a transference relation, a repetition of past conflicts, a reliving of childhood anxieties and the habitual defenses against these anxieties which have a compelling, repetitive character. Only when the original anxieties can be fully faced and the conflicts revived can the patient give up the defenses that have become obsolete and unsuited to his adult potentialities. Repetitive conflicts can be faced with a broader choice of alternative decisions.

The psychoanalyst enters into these conflicts via empathy. He feels forced into a countertransference on which he is careful not to act without deliberation. When he is relatively free from repetition compulsion himself he can use his emotional response to the patient's transferences as a source of information about the unconscious roots of anxieties and habitual defenses that have created the patient's insoluble conflicts in the past. The conscience, or superego, of the patient, which sets the goals for the patient's style of life, needs alteration. The cruelty of the child's superego is not autonomous but heteronomous; it is not integrated in the patient's personality, but imposed by external authorities which assault his identity and maintain the helplessly vindictive protest, first against parental authority, later against the hardships of fate. Transiently the psychotherapist can function as an auxiliary superego, which permits a corrective emotional experience. On the basis of true sympathy the patient may regain the trust in life that was repressed or denied. He may regain the courage for a new beginning that reconciles his authenticity—being true to himself—with his potentialities of trust in his significant relations.

Since its early beginnings, psychoanalysis has spread out beyond medicine into the fields of education, social work and sociology, and pastoral counseling. Group therapy, family therapy, and preventive and community psychiatry have developed and asserted considerable influence on the spirit of our time, although not without controversy and misunderstandings. The purity of Freudian psychoanalysis with its potentialities of development is maintained in the training institutes of the Psychoanalytic Association. The training of the psychoanalyst is an arduous task. It depends not only on academic achievements but on character development in the direction of maturity and wisdom of its trainees. The wisdom of maturity cannot be learned by rote nor enforced by institutions and certificates. Like all educational institutions, psychoanalytic training has to wrestle with the dangers of institutionalization and specialization. Psychoanalysts cannot afford to become exclusive specialists. They want to be in touch with the philosophic trends of our times, with the social as well as the individual conflicts of our period in history, not in order to subscribe to one or another philosophy, but to clarify reachable ideals and an autonomous identity which is flexible enough to adapt to the changes in the human condition. Psychoanalysts look at individual trees, philosophers at the whole woods. They supplement each other. European existentialism is on the whole more pessimistic than American pragmatism. Herbert Marcuse spoke recently of a trend towards "desublimation" in our time. Psychoanalysts contribute to a better understanding of the human predicament and of the failures in the pursuit of happiness by following the individual development through the long period of childhood dependency. The fears of the child and habitual defenses against these fears reach into adulthood, even into old age, and, reinforced by hardships of fate, prevent the full development of maturity and wisdom. The vital resources of integration and sublimation are at times at a low ebb. When these resources are not completely obstructed, there occurs ever again a rejuvenation of hope, trust, and love.

PART I

Facing the Human Condition

The Psychoanalytic View
of Human Personality

THE MODERN UNDERSTANDING OF EMOTIONAL ILLNESS

Psychoanalysis is a branch of medicine and psychiatry. At the turn of the century medicine had become divided into many specialties, all of which studied the disturbances of the bodily functions on the basis of physics, chemistry, physiology, anatomy, and pathology, and lost sight of the human personality as a total entity. Psychiatry remained closely linked to the neurological study of the central nervous system, and the neurotic and psychotic disorders which could not be understood as dysfunctions of the nervous system were described and classified, but psychiatry had no access to the understanding and treatment of the causes of these illnesses.

By turning research emphasis from the conscious, rational surface of personality to the unconscious, irrational depth of driving motivations, Freud outgrew the old psychiatry of description and classification. We no longer see the mentally ill person—nor the healthily functioning person—as a static entity, but rather as in a constant process of adaptation to his environment.

In order to understand the failures of adjustment in the individual the student of dynamic psychiatry must know to what standards and social norms the individual has to adjust. Recent anthropological studies have emphasized how much standards and norms are at variance in different societies and even within the same society. A religious ritual may be carelessly neglected by a nonbeliever, while to the arduous adherent the breaking of a religious taboo may cause endless neurotic scruples. The sense of property

Adapted from a lecture presented in Washington, D.C., April 29, 1952; published by the Organizing Committee, for the symposium, Christianity and Modern Man.

varies in different social climates. The respect for the preservation of individual life is not the same in war and in peace, in totalitarian and in democratic societies. Premarital sexual abstinence is highly esteemed in a conservative society, while in the rebellious fringes of this society it may be considered almost as a disgrace. In a cultural milieu in which homosexual behavior is considered a social disgrace, the dawning awareness of homosexual impulses may produce a panic and paranoid reactions. The potentially homosexual person feels like an outcast from society. We do not expect such fatal reactions to homoerotic impulses in a cultural milieu like ancient Greece, in which homosexual behavior is taken for granted.

In the two decades of childhood and adolescence the cultural values and standards of the environment are transmitted to the individual by his family, his parents, and extrafamily authorities.

In the individual there is a trend toward integration or wholeness which, if approximated, is accompanied by a feeling of well-being and subjective freedom. But this feeling of wholeness and freedom is constantly threatened. An external disaster may produce an abnormal state of shock, a disintegrating panic. The reaction of grief to the loss of a beloved person has similarities with the symptoms of a depression or melancholia. In normal sleep the integration of personality is loosened up; in our dreams we are like psychotics, exposed to confused, piecemeal images which Freud has taught us to translate into rational language. The slips and errors of everyday living remind us how easily the integrating control of our behavior is jeopardized by unconscious motivations. The borderline between normal and pathological personality functions is fluid.

With such an understanding we have lost many of the older prejudices that morally devaluated neurotic and psychotic persons, who had to endure the ostracism of their more fortunate fellow men, as well as the misfortune of their illness. In the past, mankind has not been as merciful toward the victims of emotional disorders as toward people who succumbed, in the battle with nature, to an invasion of infectious microorganisms or to external or internal physical injuries.

Psychoanalysis and psychiatry have pointed out that those highly sensitized persons who succumb to the hardships of interpersonal living—the neurotics and psychotics—are not morally inferior, but deserve the respect and sympathetic understanding of their fellows. By their very suffering they contribute to our growing understanding of interpersonal tragedies and, we hope, also to future insight and unmasking of group and mass psychopathology such as war, revolution, class struggle, and national, racial, and religious prejudice. Just as physiology has learned much from pathology, so the study of the psychologically disintegrated person has given us insight into the better integrated functions of the so-called "normal person."

It is true that the reactions to external pressure are far from uniform in human beings. We find some individuals who stand up under seemingly unbearable hardships with surprising equanimity, and others who break down under minimal provocation. Psychologists who had an opportunity to study human behavior in concentration camps found that only a few persons can stand such an amount of terror without distortion of personality.

There are constitutional factors which determine resistance to traumatic experience. We find various degrees of adaptive flexibility. Man is more or less emotionally resistant and adverse to any change—he is by nature conservative—particularly to change which threatens immediate satisfactions or the security of future gratifications. A sudden change from wealth to poverty, from recognition to disgrace, from peace to war, from supporting relations to isolation, may overthrow the emotional equilibrium. But even the more gradual transition from protected childhood to responsible adulthood, from full and active life to the limitations of old age, from the freedom of the bachelor to the obligations of marriage and childraising, may reveal a rigidity, an emotional inertia, which defeats the necessary adaptation to changed life conditions.

However, such rigidity—such lag in emotional adaptability—does not stem only from constitutional, hereditary factors. It is influenced by the early development, by the patterns of conflict solutions in childhood, which acquire the tenacity of habits and interfere with the processes of integration and differentiation. In order

5

to understand human personality from the psychoanalytic point of view, we must study the developmental history and the course of disturbances which interfere with development.

THE GROWTH OF PERSONALITY

Man is distinguished from the animals in that he is born in greater helplessness and must acquire in less than two decades all the tools for dealing with the complexities of human culture in order to be successfully integrated with his fellow men. This process of acculturation is far from being always successful. In particular, emotional maturation frequently cannot keep pace with physiological growth, and failures of adaptation and integration lead to various degrees of dissociation of personality.

Physiological growth depends upon processes of intake and output. Similarly, psychological development is determined by the intertwined processes of introjection and projection, or, if you will, incorporation and differentiation. Sigmund Freud called the need for incorporative intake "libido." Libido is akin to the concept of love, and represents the integrative, constructive principle in living. But the destructive principle is just as necessary for our self-preservation, as well as for the preservation of wholesome relations with others. Man has the need to destroy evil or to rid himself from danger and damage from within and without.

These needs of intake and riddance find expression in the emotions of pleasure and pain. The infant is pleasurably contented when his needs for food, warmth, comfort, and tenderness are gratified by adequate intake; he is pained and anxious when gratification is not forthcoming, or when he is subjected to some external or internal harm. His emotional equilibrium is reestablished only when he gets rid of the disturbing pain, be it hunger, inappropriate temperature, harsh handling, intestinal cramps, etc.

The human infant is helpless and depends for his satisfactions and protection on his family environment. He is the needy recipient of love. His life from the very outset is surrounded by the dangers of death. The survival of the newborn infant would be extremely precarious without mothering care. The revolutionary change from the protection of the mother's womb to outside exist-ence produces a state of emergency in which the nervous system mobilizes all the available bodily functions—blood circulation, respiration, muscle spasms, crying in an uproar of primitive self-assertion—to surmount this initial state of shock.

Such a state of shock is reproduced in later life by any threat to survival, and its approach is then consciously experienced as panic. The propensity toward shock is particularly marked in the early beginning of life because of the helpless dependency of the infant. The tender concern of mother or nurse immediately after birth re-establishes an approximation to the security of the maternal womb. Grave neglect in the mothering function threatens the infant's survival and keeps him on the verge of shock.

THE NEED TO TRUST

Before the child develops any thinking or verbal expression of his emotions he is able to trust, since he experiences without con-sciousness that his needs for survival, growth, and development fit into his parents' needs to give gratification and protection in mutually adaptive, tender cooperation. This trust, this confidence, which precedes all rational thought processes, seems to me to be the matrix or an early manifestation of religious experience. It grows with the growing individual and transcends the boundaries of the early environment; it embraces the universe of the broaden-ing personality. This propensity to trust exists even when the par-ents are not trustworthy. In that case, trust is driven underground, hiding behind defenses; but the propensity to trust cannot be abolished in any human being.

When the tender cooperation between parents and child fails, the danger signal of anxiety appears. Anxiety is a mild form of the aforementioned panic which automatically mobilizes energies to surmount the shock arising from a threat to survival. Anxiety as a danger signal is beneficial, since it mobilizes reserve energies to sur-mount and master emergency. There is no childraising without anxiety. Every step forward into undiscovered territory is loaded with danger and anxiety. For instance, the child makes his first daring attempts to learn to walk; hesitantly he leaves the protective and supportive arms of his mother; he stumbles, bumps his head, seeks protection again in his mother's arms; and cries as if he would never try again.

Much depends on the mother's tender rapport with the child, which helps him to transcend his anxieties. The mother may be excessively anxious herself; such excessive anxiety interferes with her realistic evaluation of danger and with the child's potentialities for dealing with danger; she may retard his development by coddling overprotection, or she may ambitiously push the child ahead because she is impatient and herself needs the proof of gratifying performance. But in spite of such shortcomings, the child learns to walk sooner or later; he surmounts his anxieties, and glee about the newly gained mastery over reality obstacles and helplessness beams all over him and his mother.

The child's confidence and trust increase—confidence in himself, in others, in life. Gradually the child becomes more independent of automatic pleasure-pain reactions; he develops recall and foresight, and gains therewith a consolidation of his ego and his relations in the family. He is better equipped to meet dangers, frustrations, postponement of gratifications; he learns to modify his needs in adapation to available gratifications; and the increasing sense of mastery diminishes his anxieties.

After having stressed the beneficial effect of anxiety as a danger signal, I must point out the detrimental effects of excessive anxiety —dread, or panic—which do not further intra- and interpersonal integration. "Anxiety" stems from the Latin word *angustus,* narrow. The excessively anxious individual is narrowed in his potentialties, hemmed in. If the mobilization of reserve energy does not succeed in surmounting the danger, the human being finds himself in a state of painful helplessness, and automatic riddance reactions of fight or flight become unrealistic and destructive. Anger, rage, fury, hatred tend to avert the danger by sadistic means (destruction); despondency, apathy, exhaustion, stupor tend to avert danger in the opposite direction (that of self-destruction or masochism). Such excessive anxiety reactions are observed where the tender parent–child cooperation fails over a prolonged period or in an excessive degree.

The child may have been unwanted from the start; the parents may not be prepared, preoccupied with their own troubles; they may not have the surplus energies to take on the responsibilities of a youngster. Parents may want the child ardently, but mainly for reasons of their own gratification: to fill the boredom of emotional emptiness, for instance, or to patch up a disharmonious marriage. Under such circumstances the natural rapport of tender cooperation cannot develop optimally. From the outset the child may feel like an outcast, a stranger—for example, he should be a girl and he is a boy, or vice versa.

The child who is unable to fulfill the parents' unrealistic expectations becomes a burden; his needs are not being spontaneously taken care of; and the child suffers an undue amount of frustration and excessive anxiety. A vicious circle arises. The overanxious child arouses parental anxieties, and parental anxieties reinforce the infantile anxieties—sometimes to the degree of panic, since the intimacy between parents and child (and particularly mother and child) leads to an immediate contamination of emotions on the preverbal level, a phenomenon which the psychiatrist calls "empathy."

THE EFFECTS OF PARENTAL ANXIETY

An atmosphere of excessive anxieties interferes with the development of natural trust. The trusting child is needy, but not greedy; he learns to wait, and to conform; he shows great adaptability to what the parents can or cannot offer him. The greedy child is haunted by excessive anxieties; his protesting rage estranges him further from parents who are unable to meet his needs. The child that cannot trust barricades himself behind self-centered defenses of despair, defiance, or sullen detachment.

I said before that there is no childraising without anxieties. In a reasonably harmonious family the growing child is constantly guided by small doses of anxiety which, even before the level of

9

verbal communication, arise from parental gestures of forbiddance. In such gestures, and later in words, the parents express to the child their disapproval of behavior or activities that do not conform to parental ideas of the good child.

These ideas depend largely on the cultural traditions in which the parents were themselves brought up. But we all know that there are great changes and discrepancies in our cultural values. Father and mother may not agree at all in their ideas of the good child—and that is very confusing. One or both parents may adhere to certain cultural values with an unbending strictness which betrays their excessive anxiety; so does a constantly wavering attitude or a parental inability to say no when necessary.

The incorporation of parental expectations forms the so-called "superego," which is nearly identical with the layman's term "conscience." (I want to stress that the conscience develops later than the capacity to trust.) If the parental directions which determine the superego give the child ample room for the development of his potentialities, the child feels good—that is, acceptable to his family and later to his fellow men. He can develop solid self-respect, and to the degree that he can respect himself he can also respect others. He should not remain slavishly dependent on parental or other authorities; an overextended dependency is always a sign that the genuine trust between child and parents, and consequently the self-confidence of the child, have remained underdeveloped.

If there is trust between parents and child—if the child trusts parental guidance, and the parents trust the child's fundamentally constructive potentialties—the imitative, automatically conforming cooperation of the dependent child gradually grows into the capacity to collaborate with self-reliance and mutual respect. The flow of communication, mutual understanding, and flexible adaptation open ever broadening possibilities of integration and development. In this atmosphere of trust the child develops a good conscience, the best guarantee of a progressive maturing process.

If the parental concepts of the good child are contradictory, inconsistent, overrestrictive, or overly permissive (that is, loaded with their own excessive anxieties), the child is not only burdened

with their anxieties by contamination, but conflicts arise between his own natural needs and the instructions of the parents. Under such circumstances, due to his dependency on parental gratifications and protection, the automatically conforming child becomes estranged from his natural needs, which do not find parental approval. These needs go underground; they are dissociated or repressed. That does not mean that such needs disappear; they are expelled only from conscious awareness, and they become foreign bodies excluded from the processes of integration. They remain arrested on the infantile level, and cannot participate in the growth and development of the personality.

Whenever such arrested and repressed needs are stirred up by internal or external causes, the specific anxiety of the superego, or the conscience, awakens. The analyst calls this anxiety "guilt." The superego or conscience is the guardian against such anxiety; it reinforces the defenses of repression and dissociation. It keeps the dangerous needs (dangerous because not approved of) out of sight. But these repressed needs, arrested on a primitive level of development, are like naughty children excluded from the company of adults, hammering at the closed door and importunately demanding readmission. Such disturbing demands for readmission are accompanied by excessive anxieties, and the original needs are distorted into importunate greeds which further estrange the child from the parents, who are annoyed by his greed and importunacy.

While the good conscience is a helpful agent in the process of maturing development, the continually bad conscience is like a stone around a person's neck, retarding and impeding his growth and development. From the psychoanalytic point of view, a bad conscience is a man's—and even more a child's—worst enemy. It is not a sign of inner badness; it is the result of a cruel superego, the tragic consequence of failure of tender cooperation and the repression of trust.

When the parents cannot fulfill the child's needs and the child cannot live up to parental expectations, he turns out to be a burden, a liability, and his bad conscience reflects the frustrated reaction of the parents: "You're just a nuisance, a bad child." On the other hand, parents who feel incapable of meeting their child's

11

needs feel guilty, too. Excessive anxiety and guilt intensify the estrangement between parents and child. In order to atone for guilt feelings and to make up for the missing genuine trust, the parents will frequently, by overprotection or overindulgence, squelch the wholesome aggressive and self-assertive needs of the child.

The child's superego, or conscience, which incorporates the parental expectations and standards, not only represses his asocial and antisocial tendencies (which would not develop in the first place if the child felt warmly accepted and wanted), but it may also exclude healthy, constructive tendencies from integration and development. For instance, the child who from early infancy on has been exposed to an unusual degree of deprivation in his need for tenderness and affection becomes estranged from these basic needs. In the gravely neglected or harshly mistreated child the need for tenderness and affection goes underground, since it has too frequently received a painfully frustrating response. Where, in the growing child, you would expect the expression of a longing for tenderness, you meet with anxiety; and when this anxiety reaches excessive degrees, it elicits those automatic defenses which I have mentioned before: rage, anger, defiance, hostility in the active child; or indifference, boredom, apathy in the more passive, despondent child.

The failure of the tender cooperation between parents and child, together with the burden of excessive anxieties and guilt feelings, condemn the child to a degree of loneliness which leaves him inexperienced in the closeness of interpersonal relations. Even if he learns externally to conform to rules and regulations of conventional behavior, he remains fundamentally lonely; and the thin veneer of acceptable adaptation may easily break down in later life under stress and strain, and a neurosis or psychosis may develop under further duress.

Loneliness and the cruelty of the conscience always go hand in hand. The qualms and shame of a bad conscience lead to withdrawal from company; all energies are concentrated on the inner battle with a relentless conscience, to keep vital needs under repression; and unavoidable experiences of defeat in the attempts

to live up to superhuman standards increase the danger of desertion, ostracism, hopelessness, and despair.

THE RESULTS OF LOSS OF TRUST

There are in the course of development infinite possibilities of regaining original losses of trust. Children frequently have a redeeming influence on their parents. Even embittered or desperate parents who have surrounded themselves with a shell of harshness cannot always resist the emotional appeal of the child, and tender cooperation may be reestablished on any later level. On the other hand, there are hurdles in the various challenging complexities of family life which put tender cooperation and trust to the test.

I mentioned before that the excessively anxious child tries to rid himself of his discomforts by anger, rage, or temper tantrums. But such frank expression of hostility cannot find parental approval, and therefore these hostilities are frequently buried in repression. Repressed anger is often transformed into smouldering resentment, and swallowed hostilities overload the organism with indigestible tensions. Psychological conflicts due to the mobilization of excessive anxieties frequently result in psychosomatic disorders such as impediments of respiration (asthma) or disturbances of the digestive tract. The child who suffers under lack of parental acceptance may capitalize on such psychosomatic disorders because they keep the family at his beck and call. Thus tyrannical power is substituted for trust and tender cooperation.

A similar transformation of genuine needs takes place if the child defiantly accepts the idea that he is incorrigibly bad. He gets a bitter comfort out of pointing out that others are just as bad or worse than he; he gets a false pride out of provoking and bullying others; or he tries to attract attention by specializing in mischievousness, since he cannot get attention in any other way. In this need for despotic power the unhappy, isolated child tries to get rid of his unbearable loneliness and helplessness, which accompany his excessive anxieties. But such despotic power is an unsatisfactory substitute for the missing trust and tenderness. It never fills the bill.

Therefore the greed for despotic power, in children as well as in adults, is characterized by insatiability and compulsion.

A particularly difficult test for tender cooperation in a family is sexual lust. The borderline between primitive sexual excitement and the sublimated experiences of love, affection, and tenderness is fluid. Overindulgent coddling may arouse sexual excitement in both the child and the adult. Primitive sexual needs exist in budding form from early childhood on; they are expressed by curiosity, voyeur wishes, and exhibitionistic and masturbatory activities—which are harmless if they are not frowned upon by the adults. But if the adults are overexcited, or frightened into excessive shame, the child becomes estranged from his natural impulses and tries to repress them; and under the pressure of shame and guilt the sexual impulses become the more intensified and compulsive. They cause particularly painful conflicts if the child suffers from lack of tender gratifications, if he is emotionally isolated, and if trust in his most vital relations to his early environment is wanting.

The child who is not inhibited in his emotional development and who feels secure in his trust in parental love will learn to tame his awakening sexual impulses and the accompanying experiences of rivalry, envy, and jealousy. Even if the child goes through periods of upheaval, he learns to tune down his possessive, monopolizing passions for the sake of the family harmony in which he has his anchors of trust.

The Tragedy of Emotional Isolation

Freud used the Greek tragedy of Oedipus Rex as a symbol of the conflicts that are implied in the child's sexual and aggressive impulses which endanger his adjustment to the family and, if they remain repressed and therefore untamed, his later social adjustment. You may remember that the Oedipus of the Greek tragedy had been a rejected child; his parents had gotten rid of him in infancy because of a prophecy which threatened them that their son would in the future interfere with their selfish interests. The son, who had grown up completely estranged from his parents, unwittingly murdered his father and took his place in the kingdom and in an incestuous relation to his mother. Oedipus Rex in the Greek tragedy falls from the summit of self-righteous pride in his heroic achievements into the abyss of shame and despair when his tragic guilt is revealed.

This is a deep human truth: that the child estranged and uprooted from the nurturing soil of trust can become the victim of passionate conflicts and tragic guilt. Incestuous impulses toward a parent or sibling and murderous impulses against a rival are intensified in the emotionally isolated or overanxious child—in a child who is, for instance, irresponsibly seduced, used for the more or less selfish gratification of an older person, or in any other way deprived of the security of tender cooperation and trust. Under such tragic circumstances the child's preoccupation with sexual lust or murderous impulses can become compulsive and insatiable, since sexual lust (like despotic power) is an absolutely unsatisfactory substitute for the original need for trust.

Feeding problems are a typical bone of contention in a disturbed mother-child relationship. Numerous conflicts are centered upon the education toward cleanliness. If the mother is not in rapport with the child's growing abilities, she may hurry or delay the child unduly in the process of teaching him mastery of the excretory functions. If the tender cooperation fails, conflicts and anxieties arise which prevent the child from learning according to his growing abilities. Irregularities of bowel function or enuresis may result.

If the child feels doomed to failure, the learning of other functions may become seriously impeded. Speech disorders like stammering and stuttering betray a highly negativistic resistance to interpersonal communication. Later school progress can be blocked emotionally to a degree that defects in intelligence are incorrectly assumed.

The Effects in Adulthood

Such compulsive preoccupations are threatened by intense disapproval, and therefore they are also driven underground into repression or dissociation. But such attempts at riddance do not extinguish the guilt feelings. Like the automatic safety valve of anxiety, the warning signal of guilt can become oversensitized toward needs and impulses from which the individual feels estranged and therefore threatened by their mere emergence. Under the pressure of an intransigent superego the whole area of sex becomes indicted, but the anxious tensions of guilt increase sexual excitement and temptation. Under the threat of an intransigent conscience a child's lonely experiments in masturbation, which are in themselves a harmless release of tension, become linked up with sadistic fantasies of rebellion and defiance or masochistic fantasies of drastic punishing atonement; and these cruel fantasies increase the feelings of guilt. In this way sexual excitement is divorced from the integrating experience of trust and tenderness.

And the shadows of distrust fall on the later experiments in sexual companionship. Only a sexual partnership that integrates sexual lust with respect, tender consideration, and trust can lift the ban of indictment from sexual activities. For the person with a rigidly intransigent superego the sexual partner frequently remains an accomplice in guilt, more hated than loved—hated since he or she leads into hideous temptation, and he or she mobilizes excessive anxiety and guilt. This makes both partners egocentric, possessive, and exploitative. Instead of providing integrative gratification, the relation is marred by the chilling frigidity of a casual conquest or the slavish dependency of a humiliating addiction.

On the other hand, the natural intimacy of sexual contacts provides the potentialities of spontaneous recovery from loneliness and moral ostracism, when the barriers of shame, excessive anxiety, and guilt can be transcended and the obstructed resources of genuine trust can be reopened.

Returning to the development of the child, we see that the child who cannot trust parental love naturally feels threatened by the arrival of a brother or sister rival. Adjustment to the growing family is complicated by envious competition. The more excessive a child's anxiety, the more importunate is his bid for exclusive possession. The self-defeating claim for despotic power gains in importance in proportion to the degree of failure of the trust in friendly sharing and participation.

The child with a cruel superego, lowered in his self-esteem, is frequently very doubtful about his fitness in competition, which looks merciless to him or her. The overanxious boy is called a sissy. (Hamlet felt that his conscience made a coward out of him.) Withdrawal from competition further lowers the self-confidence of the boy or man who is ridiculed as effeminate. Even if a man overcompensates by pretended toughness, his doubt of his manliness may accompany him far into adulthood. Likewise a girl who distrusts her future value as a woman, her capacity to win a male partner, to bear and rear children, may evade such painful doubts by playing the role of the tomboy or by withdrawing into defiant independence. In heated competition with her male contemporaries, more interested in the prestige of conquest than in the trustworthy depth of a relation, she defeats herself in most natural needs under the pressure of a punishing conscience.

The world of the "as if," of fantasies and daydreams, is a natural playground for the child's testing and probing imagination, and it remains the testing ground for adult planning and striving. But if the growing child does not dare to branch out, to widen his horizon, because of arresting excessive anxieties and lack of trust, this world of imagination becomes an isolating refuge haunted by nightmares of anxiety. Excessive daydreaming of a superman's perfection, of heroic achievements, or of perfect love is substituted for real experiments in living in the process of cooperative adaptation to others. The child remains self-centered and lonely.

The nearer he approaches adulthood the greater the discrepancies between the inexpensive victories of his self-centered fantasies and the defeats in real living with others. He does not dare to expose his pretentious ambitions to honest competition with his compeers. He cannot run the risk of losing or of revealing real incompetence.

Since he finds that his self-centered, ambitious claims antagonize others, he may learn to outwit and to cheat, to win by hook or by crook. But such hypocrisy, the product of excessive anxiety, does not open up trust or increase self-respect. A fundamentally lonely existence becomes the more barren, dull, and boring the more the aspirations of fantasy are solely spent in pretense. Nor can such loneliness be dissipated by flight into meaningless overactivity. The person who is isolated by repression of trust fails to learn that which makes life really meaningful—namely, spontaneous participation and devotion to someone or something outside himself.

OUR YEARNING FOR RECONCILIATION AND PEACE

I said before that on any level of human development the blocked resources of trust may spontaneously open up again. This is an experience totally beyond human efforts of the intellect or of the will; it is an experience which the religious person humbly accepts as the grace of God. Neither the psychoanalyst nor any other human being can produce this redeeming experience, but the analyst may be able to contribute to the removal of impediments of moral and religious self-deceit and hypocrisy, the outgrowth of an intolerant conscience, an intransigent superego. I do not consider deceit or hypocrisy primary needs; they are a defense, like the claim for despotic power, or lust.

In moral and religious hypocrisy we recognize the vestiges of a yearning for peace and reconciliation with the ultimate power, the ground of existence revealed in destiny. But the approach to this ultimate authority is laden with the same excessive anxieties and distrust as the helpless child experiences in the relation to powerful parental authority which he does not dare to trust. The excessively anxious child tries to ward off nightmarish dangers by prayer or by other propitiating or atoning gestures. He tries to win the powers of goodness over onto his side in order to avoid desertion, punishment, and the accompanying excessive anxieties. He tries to fight off the black magic by a protective white magic. We recognize in the black magic the hated punishing parent; while the protective, comforting power represents the good, approving, and rewarding parent.

If his hope for genuine trust has become dissociated, given up in despair, the child—and the child in man—will substitute for trust the magic weapon of deceit in order to transform the dangerous punishing authority into a good and rewarding authority. Parents can be outwitted and placated by "as if" performances, apologetic gestures, going through the motions. The child learns the art of hypocrisy; he gets away with murder; he pursues selfish, not permissible purposes secretly, avoiding the disapproval of authority. He appears good and obedient, and often reaches a pseudopeace with a powerful authority.

By such defiant obedience the child—and the child in man— perpetuates the conflict between obedience and rebellion in relation to authority, as well as in relation to destiny. Though the hypocrite appears good, he does not feel good deep in his heart. The repressed longing for real peace and reconciliation, which seems out of reach, keeps him restless and unsatisfied.

To a greater or lesser degree we are all easily deceived by our own deceitful manipulations of authority. Nothing is more difficult than to be honest with oneself. We are accustomed from childhood on to think in terms of good and bad, black and white. It is important for our sense of prestige and security that we be on the good side; therefore we try desperately to justify ourselves, sometimes by rationalizing argumentation. In such stubborn insistence on self-justification lie the roots of a paranoid development with its ideas of grandiosity and persecution. We all become identified with the role that we play. We really believe in our hypocritical goodness, our self-righteousness, even sometimes in our saintliness.

But this hypocritical conforming adaptation for the sake of opportunistic rewards absorbs an enormous amount of energy and separates us even further from spontaneous sources of trust; how can we learn to trust if we really trust only our hypocritical manipulations of authority, our defenses against excessive anxiety? In adulthood we remain tied to an appalling number of obsessional rituals and devices that stem from childhood days; we remain preoccupied with the unconscious elaboration of the most complicated devices to gain rewards and to avoid punishment.

But, deceived by our own deceit, we frequently are not able to see through our own complex maneuvers, which are sometimes quite enigmatic on the level of consciousness. Whether we are adherents of a church or profess secularized forms of ethical standards, everybody in our culture is more or less restricted in his spontaneity and creativeness by defensive distortions of original needs, and our system of nonspontaneous adaptation is fraught with compulsion and deep-seated anxieties.

If we are fortunate we may be able to carry our precarious equilibrium through our lifetime, and feel quite complacent about our so-called normal adjustment. But under emotional stress and strain this precarious equilibrium may break down, with symptoms of regression to infantile patterns of behavior, distortions of reality, depressions, free floating or localized anxieties, and the like.

Such intense emotional suffering forces us to review the complexities of our development, and to withdraw from the bustle of distracting activities. As neurotic or psychotic patients we may have to go through the hell of human misery, sometimes reaching out for help by dramatizing this very misery, sometimes withdrawing from all human contact or from trust in life itself. Self-accusation and self-condemnation are signs of our conflicts with destiny. Reassurance does not provide any comfort, though we may cry for it in abject infantile despondency.

Self-punishment plays an enormous role in all psychoneuroses, as if there were an unconscious belief that by self-torture and punishment and suffering we could force a reconciliation with the ground of existence, as a child tries to bribe parental approval. But such reconciliation cannot be forced. Sometimes in the depths of despair a flash of insight breaks through the shells of repressions and defensive distortions and shows, not to our heads but to our hearts, that what we are most deeply estranged from is trust.

THE FUNCTION OF THE PSYCHOTHERAPIST

At this point you will ask me what the psychotherapist can do to prepare for the recovery of the psychoneurotic patient—after I have made it, I hope, sufficiently clear that I share the conviction of the French physician who said about his treatment of a patient, "Je le pansai, Dieu le guérit" ("I treated him, God cured him").

I have tried to convey that psychoneurotic suffering is due to arrested emotional development in childhood. No human parents are so ideal, so free themselves, that they could protect their children completely from being tied by such chains. The psychoneurotic adult is bound to repeat in all subsequent interpersonal relations the original conflicts which arrested his development. This repetition tends to maintain the old repressions and the habitual patterns of substitution, as for instance despotic power substituting for repressed affection. This form of repetition compulsion is called "transference" by the analyst. An important lever in psychoanalytic work is this transference—the tendency of the patient to carry over into the relation with the therapist who offers to help him the crippling conflicts with significant persons of his childhood.

We have only a very limited and distorted knowledge of ourselves because of early adaptation patterns and the restrictive influence of the superego, the conscience, which excludes from awareness impulses and needs that caused disapproval by authority and therewith excessive anxiety. It is extremely difficult to extricate oneself from one's self-deceptions, particularly in a period of history which, like our present epoch, leaves us so little opportunity for serious meditation. Psychoneurotic suffering and its therapy lead modern man into meditation.

The method of free associations is intended to free the communications of the analysand from conventional patterns of logical thinking and to open up the floodgates of repressed emotions. The analysand can only gradually arrive at greater frankness. At the start, in accordance with his repetition compulsion, he expects from his therapist the same parental disapproval which had caused his repressions, and he meets the therapist with the old anxieties and the old weapons of defense. The more intelligent the patient, the subtler are his defenses. The analysand fights to preserve his comforting daydreams, illusions of grandeur, claims and entitlements of childhood, which should shield him from frightening new experiences.

Frequently the patient tries ardently to seduce the therapist into a conspiracy of repetition; he prompts him to provide the same substitute gratifications which the patient got as a child from the outwitted parent. He tries to manipulate the therapist, to involve him in a power struggle, to repeat with him the never-ending conflict of obedience and rebellion.

The analysand expects magical help, and if he is frustrated in his infantile demands he may break out into anger and rage. By this he may unconsciously intimidate the doctor and thus circumvent the reliving of painful old anxieties, overwhelming for him in childhood, but which he may face today in companionship with his therapist with better chances of mastering them. Because of the old habit of distrust, however, the analysand may withdraw into sulking passivity, apathy, or despondency.

The great opportunity for profitable change in psychoanalysis is given by the fact that the therapist is *not* father or mother or any other anxiety-arousing authority of the past; that he does *not* get involved in transference repetition; and that when he gets transitorily involved in sympathetic identification, he returns to reality and actuality and regains his benevolent neutrality, which keeps him from overindulgence as well as from moralistic prohibition. The therapist refrains from false reassurances as well as from disapproval, though the patient would like to use him as an auxiliary conscience which would spare him the conflicts of his own responsible decisions.

Ideally, the therapist should not allow himself to be flattered, bribed, or irritated, for he should give the patient an opportunity to relive the old anxieties and to find a more constructive way out of them. The habitually diffident and distrustful patient feels compelled to test the doctor out; and it is too bad if the doctor is pretentious, condescending, or artificial, for thus he loses his usefulness for the patient. Only genuine respect and spontaneous warmth for the patient may dispel his excessive fears of being rejected, forsaken, overpowered, or exploited.

Thus the psychoanalyst needs a lot of life experience to see through the patient's intricate network of illusions, self-deceptions, and distortions, by which he maintains his precarious equilibrium.

You will understand how important it is that the analyst before he starts in his difficult work undergo a successful analysis of himself, with repetition if he gets stale, to discover his blind spots, to free his potentialities from repression and compulsion. He must gain the maturity, the spontaneity, the objectivity, and the tolerance which encourage the patient to give up his childhood ties, to dare to experiment, and to share in the relation, freed from transference repetition, the broadening experience of spontaneous collaboration.

Sexuality and Love

In this paper I want to follow in general lines the development of sexuality and love through childhood, adolescence, and adulthood and compare the various psychoanalytic points of view with the existentialist's approach.

Freud in his younger days had built his psychological system on a biological basis in which the instincts which do not appear in manifest behavior and action are inferred as sources of psychic energy. While C. G. Jung recognized only one monistic source of psychic energy, libido, Freud maintained the dualism of instincts in three formulations: (1) libido versus self-preservation, (2) narcissistic versus object libido, and (3) libido or Eros versus Thanatos or death instinct. In his dualistic formulations libido remained constant, but its instinctual counterpart changed. In the course of this development of basic concepts libido, the source of sexual energy, was used as synonym of love, which in the wide variety of its manifestations builds up the individual personality and maintains the individual life anchored in its significant relations against the powers of dissociation and destruction.

In various psychoanalytic schools there are differences of opinion about the destructive power: does it stem from the inside of the individual, as the school of Melanie Klein assumes,[1] where processes of dissociation, projection, and introjection are believed to manifest themselves from the very beginning of life, or are the destructive energies only mobilized in defense of life against the

Reprinted by permission from *Review of Existential Psychology and Psychiatry*, 3, no. 2 (1966):125–32.
1. Melanie Klein, Paula Heimann, Susan Isaacs, and Joan Riviere, *Developments in Psycho-Analysis* (London: Hogarth, 1952).

24

onslaught of external dangers, against frustration and isolation? In the existentialist psychiatry, the biological theory of instincts has been considered as too narrow a basis for the comprehension of human existence or *Dasein*. Heidegger in his recent book on Nietzsche[2] has reemphasized Nietzsche's "will to power" as the basic force of life, the primary affect of becoming, fulfilling living potentialities of body, soul, and spirit beyond the status quo of mere self-preservation, encompassing the creative forces of development as well as the destructive forces of decay. "To imprint on this becoming the character of Being, that is the highest will to power," says Nietzsche. The human being is, according to this philosophic approach, not in the first line, consciously or unconsciously directed toward pleasure and avoidance of pain. The will to power is directed toward fulfillment of destiny, growth, and broadening development. Pain can be endured for the higher goals of becoming. The nearer the human being approaches his destiny the more joy he experiences; a slackening or exhaustion of the will to power is accompanied by affects of fear, distress, and despair.

The will to power manifests itself in the child's growth and development, in the parents' loving care as well as the child's budding love of the parent, total love, not partial object libido. The give and take in this relation is not equal but fits into the direction of fulfillment of destiny of both parent and child. Without the parental loving care the infant would perish, and if the will to power in the child is throttled by fears and defensive concerns of stagnating self-preservation, the growth and development of the child can become seriously hampered; but there is a trend of ever renewed regeneration of the will to power towards the fulfillment of destiny.

THE PARENT-CHILD RELATIONSHIP

However, the love between parent and child is not identical with sexuality, though since Freud's early "Three Essays on the

2. Martin Heidegger, *Nietzsche* (Pfullingen: Guenther Neske, 1961), 1.46 ff.

Theory of Sexuality" there is still a traditional tendency to equate sex and love. H. S. Sullivan insisted that sexuality and love are worlds apart from each other. The child exposed to and exploited by adult sexual seduction is just as imperiled and exposed to anxieties as the deserted and neglected child; and the child that engages intensely in aggressive seduction or in excessive bodily self-stimulation suffers from anxious frustrations in his overall need for loving care. You remember that Freud made a decisive turn in his theoretical formulation of psychosexual development when he discovered that his hysteric patients had not all been victims of adult seduction in childhood, that the child himself harbored sexual fantasies. The myth of infantile innocence was torn, and the polymorph perverse character of infantile sexuality was considered the basis of later overt perversions and repressions covered by neurotic symptomatology and character distortions. Original sin has been rediscovered on the psychobiological plane. Norman Brown has tried to lift the prejudice against infantile perversions in his book *Life Against Death,* and Medard Boss in his book on perversions has pointed out the yearning for a redeeming, integrating love even in the most hideous perversions.[3]

When we consider that sex and love are not identical, when love, specifically parental love, is defined as the overall concern for the child's optimal development, then we might investigate, whether the child's agitated fantasies, his murderous rages as well as his excessive oral greed, his anal defiance reactions, his overreaching competitive ambitions, his possessive incestuous claims and sado-masochistic power operations are not inevitable expressions of ego defense and protest reactions against the lack of security in a family that is unable to provide the loving care for his optimal development.

In more than thirty years of psychoanalytic practice I have gathered patients' memories of infantile sexual experiences emerging during treatment. These experiences are accompanied by an aura of anxious excitement and alienation from the family. In-

3. Norman Brown, *Life against Death,* A Modern Library Paperback (New York: Random House, 1959); Medard Boss, *Meaning and Content of Sexual Perversions,* trans. Liese Lewis Abell, 2d ed. (New York: Grune and Stratton, 1949).

cestuous sexual excitements frequently arise in relation to a parent whose secret seductive exploitation has become uncanny to the child, or in relation to a parent who in his aloofness has become a stranger to the child, leaving the longing for tenderness and security unfulfilled. The angrily threatening or anxiously agitated parent contaminates the child, still embedded partially in symbiotic dependency, with his or her anxieties; the child feels alienated and the anxious excitement mobilizes sadistic or masochistic fantasies by which the child tries to gain magic, manipulative mastery over objects that frustrate his needs. Secretive, solitary lust by sucking, rocking, masturbation becomes the refuge for the lonely child, but since the sexual excitement or any secretive preoccupation with one's own body does not appease anxiety, but mobilizes guilt, the vicious cycle of habit formation intensifies anxiety as well as the addiction to an ineffective comfort. Secretive voyeuristic excitements, accompanied by shame in envious isolation, are very different from the eager curiosity of a child who explores the fascinating areas of bodily functions in confidence that parents or siblings are all for him. The child that exhibits his nudeness with triumphant pride is cheerfully unconflicted, but the child who is estranged from unsympathetic ridiculing adults feels exhibited in a conflict between anxious lust and humiliating shame. The penis envy of the little girl is mostly combined with an anxious excitement that makes her believe, were she only a boy, she would be more lovable, and the passive effeminate boy is afraid that his aggressive masculinity makes him unacceptable in the family.

The multiple perversions of the child seem to me to indicate a lack of trusting security that hampers the child's growing independence and self-reliance. When the development of organizing self-esteem and a reasonably harmonious integration into the family unit fails, the child becomes stymied in the ambivalent struggle between rebellion and submission; his prolonged positive or negative dependency burdens him with an authoritarian conscience, the Freudian superego that either more or less represses the desires for sexual gratification together with the longing for confidence in mutual understanding; or the repressive inner censor may

27

degrade sexual activities to a mechanical device for alleviation of tension. Under these circumstances a partner is envisaged as an object, a means to an egocentric end. There is only room for mutual partnership when the authoritarian conscience can be gradually transformed into an authentic conscience, which gives both partners the freedom of their unique spontaneity.

I have presented the excesses of sexual excitement in childhood as a sign of isolating alienation from the parental family where the child does not find the sympathetic understanding of his emotional needs corresponding to the stage of his development. But I don't want to join the chorus of those accusers who point the finger at the schizophrenogenic mother and make conscientious parents anxious and guilty about their loving care. Where is the parent who could always expel fear by love and prepare the child for the integration into the tragic complexities of a dangerous world without yielding at times to worrisome preoccupations, without escaping sometimes into idealizing illusions? Conscientious parents cannot help but burden their children with the double bind of human insecurity and doubt. The doubts that accompany child training may be expressed in the reiterated phrase of Kierkegaard's Either-Or: "do it and you will repent it, do it not and you will repent it, do it or don't do it and you will repent it."[4] The parent who tries always to be a loving parent forces himself or herself into hypocrisy and unconvincing "as if" performances, and the child is bewildered by the lack of reliable values to direct his behavior. The parents may take the child's experimenting impulsivity as genuine spontaneity, may accept any emotional self-expression as sacrosanct. They set no limits to the child's overreaching egocentricity which remains an ineffective defense against anxiety. Unbridled impulsivity lowers the child's self-respect; he does not learn to take the cues from others which facilitate his navigation into social life.

Love cannot be dictated or enforced. But the intuitive understanding may at any stage of the development spontaneously heal the ruptures of dissociation and alienation, may change the ma-

4. Søren Kierkegaard, *Either-Or*, trans. David F. Swenson and Lilian Marvin Swenson (Princeton University Press, 1944).

levolent transformation into a benevolent corrective experience. According to Melanie Klein, the child can even in his first year of life arrive at a reconciliation with the deserting or the angrily estranged mother by suffering through the labor of mourning and regaining the trust that the mother who destroys his pleasure and permits and inflicts pain can be trusted to return as the loving mother, when desertion and estrangement is not too deep.[5] This tendency toward reparative reintegration is the saving grace in emotional development, and the deepest anxieties are not elicited by withdrawal of pleasure or infliction of pain, but by despair in the reparative power of love.

The psychology professor Harry Harlow, who experimented with rhesus monkeys reared for six months in complete isolation from maternal care, discovered that these isolated animals were completely inept for socialization and indifferent to sexual opportunities, though their intellectual abilities were not impaired.[6] But when these young monkeys during the period of maternal deprivation were permitted to engage in the rough-and-tumble play and tender exchange with their peers they were able to recoup their social and sexual abilities. The human child is much longer dependent on parental care and his emotional development is much slower. Only after the family ties are partially loosened, the preadolescent, as Sullivan has pointed out, encounters the silent miracle of mutual love.[7] He experiences at first, in the chum relation, the wonder of mutuality, the I–Thou encounter, a give-and-take relation that does not force and is not forced, that is as concerned about the welfare of the partner as about his own. The self-centered egocentricity expressed in the French phrase, "Ôte-toi que je m'y mette" ("remove yourself so that I can take your place") changes into the potentialities of creative collaboration. Commitment and loyalty provide a new security to existence, a security

5. Klein et al., pp. 223, 239.

6. Harry Harlow and R. R. Zimmerman, "Affectional Responses in the Infant Monkey," *Science* 130 (1959):421–32.

7. Harry Stack Sullivan, "The Human Organism and Its Necessary Environment," *Conceptions of Modern Psychiatry,* The First William Alanson White Memorial Lectures (reprinted from *Psychiatry* 3 [Feb. 1940] and 8 [May 1945], p. 25.

that has not to be bargained for by self-denial or imposed by awe-inspiring authority. It is understandable that these spontaneous chum relations are at times colored by covert or more or less overt homoerotic emotions, since the partner of the same sex is closer to the child's primary or secondary, defensive narcissism, while the members of the other sex are still intimidatingly distant to the preadolescent. If the isolation and insecurity of the preadolescent are very stringent due to the anxious turmoil of his or her family, he or she may compulsively and possessively cling to the friend, and when homoerotic desires are touched off by the new exclusive intimacy, the preadolescent may be trapped in a dependent and addicted relation that does not meet family and public approval, and therefore his or her precarious self-esteem is lowered even more.

LOVE AND SEX IN THE ADOLESCENT

The crises of adolescence are frequently triggered off by the risks and hazards of heterosexual intimacy. The powerful upsurge of sexual urges breaks down conventional barriers and the safeguards of authoritarian protection. New intense emotional involvements with partners of the opposite sex lift the youngster out of the family ties. While in childhood all vital energies were primarily concentrated on personal growth and development, the powerful surge of sexual energies in adolescence, the longing for heterosexual intimacy opens new horizons, transcending the self. The yearning for love, which Ludwig Binswanger called the dual mode of existence,[8] reveals to the I the Thou of the partner in the light of radiant idealization of all that is beautiful, good, and true. This enthusiasm of heterosexual love makes the lover humble, but also vulnerable, exposed to the risks of desertion and the humiliation of unrequited love. The personality of the adolescent is frequently not yet fortified enough to withstand the impact of this ecstatic encounter, and the disillusionment may throw him back into depressed isolation. In addition, at a time when the adolescent is

8. Ludwig Binswanger, *Grundformen und Erkenntnis Menschlichen Daseins* (Zürich: Max Niehans, 1953).

most open and ready for an ecstatic heterosexual encounter, he is in our culture economically still unsettled, and the intense competition for a place under the sun for himself and to provide for a family demands the sacrifices of an extended training to master the contingencies of I–It relations in the struggle for existence. The selection of the partner in adolescence is therefore still groping, overshadowed by egocentric competitiveness between partners and rivals, ambivalent struggles between fear and love. The competition for the conquest of the most popular girl, for the seduction of the boy in the highest prestige position, mingles into the early romantic experiences the elation of short lived victories and the bitterness of hateful, contemptuous riddance reactions. Even in an enlightened period of birth control, the defiance against traditional prohibitions elicits anxieties, and the overwhelming fear of failure in competition burdens the adolescent's experiences of love frequently with reactions of panic or distress. The adolescent may in self-protection repress his sexual needs to preserve his or her more or less illusional ideals of love, or he may in cynical despair dissociate love from sex and treat sexual activities in Sullivan's words as "indoor sport."

I doubt the wisdom of labeling these conflicts of dissociation in adolescence as psychopathology. These conflicts arise frequently in the best endowed individuals who have difficulties reconciling their emotional needs with the complexities of our culture. Even when these adolescent crises lead to tragic psychotic decompensation, the psychiatrist cannot trace the origin always back to traumatic emotional impoverishment in childhood. On the other hand, the psychotherapist in his practice seldom meets adolescents who in spite of early deprivations navigate through these crises to a fairly satisfactory integration of self-assertion and erotic fulfillment. But such adolescents do exist—they only come more rarely to the psychotherapist's attention.

In older oriental cultures the elders have tried to mitigate the tribulations of passion and romance in adolescent adaptation by eliminating the trials and errors in the choice of the heterosexual partner and by determining the selection of the partner by authoritarian decree, which may or may not be guided by psychological understanding and wisdom. The modern marriage of convenience is a similar attempt at rational simplification. Also, the old-time absolute supremacy of the male, which relegates the female to a role of subservience and protected dependency, represents a simplification of mutual adjustment in the conjugal love relation. All these authoritarian solutions of the adjustment problems in conjugal love are unbearable to the spirit of freedom and independence which entrusts the modern individual, man as well as woman, with his own pursuit of happiness, though this freedom and independence of the modern adult is restricted by constitutional, including hormonal, endowment, the contingencies of early upbringing as well as the complexities of modern living conditions. The conventional mental hygiene ideal that identifies maturity with matrimonial happiness supports the popular belief that happiness can be pursued, and in the eagerness of this pursuit through hypocrisy and "as if" performances the individual may lose sight of the fact that erotic happiness is a gift of grace. The pursuit of happiness in a legalized marital relation may lead to milder or more severe forms of mutual persecution of both partners accusing each other that their happiness did not last, or one of the partners or both may withdraw into the isolation of self-accusation and depression. This alienation splits sexual desire from tender concern or extinguishes the sexual interest.

THE I–THOU ENCOUNTER OF ADULTHOOD

The I–Thou encounter of heteroerotic attraction lifts the individual out of his egocentric boundaries and opens a vista of perfect union and harmony, which has some similarities with the blissful symbiosis of mother and infant. There is a freedom of relaxation and regression in this encounter which hallows the so-called "perverse" arabesques of sexual intimacy as a play of generous abundance. The instant of fulfillment extinguishes self-consciousness which in Hegel's words is an unhappy consciousness; time and space seem to be dissolved in the instant of orgastic encounter. The I and Thou are transparent to each other in a trusting understanding that transcends the words of rational mastery with which we manipulate the world of I-It contingencies.

The delight of the erotic encounter could be hailed by the famous words of Nietzsche: "Alle Lust will Ewigkeit, will tiefe, tiefe Ewigkeit," literally translated: "All lust wants eternity, wants deep, deep eternity." But lust is not identical with the German word *Lust* which embraces a broader meaning. The orgastic delight reflects the spiritual potentialities of a creative happiness, able to integrate body and soul, freedom and necessity. In this encounter the I and the Thou may not only feel their worlds and their destiny in harmony as they are now, but also as what they may become in a future that reaches into eternity.

"Omne animal est triste post coitum" ("all living beings are sad after cohabitation"). The I-Thou encounter of erotic fulfillment is an immediate, instantaneous experience. It does not last. Yet love promises constancy and hopes for permanence. The creative encounter of man and wife is renewed ever again with the glow of memory and the radiance of hope. But the quest for permanence may degenerate into repetition compulsion under the pressure of egocentric anxieties. This is the theme of Goethe's Faust, who similar to Don Juan is defeated by the devil when he orders the instant of fulfillment to stay for ever. The complacency of habituation or the withdrawal into resentful isolation are defenses against the anxieties of loss and desertion. When the trust in spontaneous renewal of I-Thou encounters fades, the willful manipulation of the exigencies in I-It relations becomes shallow and meaningless. The sense of duty may maintain the security of the home, the care for the partner and the children, but an uncompromising either–or morality must gradually erode the creative spontaneity of free encounters, and this erosion splits sexuality from love in a similar estrangement as in the earlier periods of life. The need for security may become a suffocating dependency that paralyzes growth and development when marital partners try to force each other under the pretext of a right that is bolstered by might. The creative freedom of love cannot be maintained by ethical standards alone. The spontaneity of the loving encounter carries man into a religious dimension, into a creative freedom beyond institutionalized religion. This dimension does not condemn but hallows the infantile forms of sexual behavior, since the anxieties that dictate the repetition compulsion can be faced and transcended by the courage of love, in spite of the sadness of separation, the fear of death, helplessness, and despair. The courage to love does not deny the tragedies of human existence in manic flight reactions. The courage to love endures the distress of disillusionment and frustration, faces the anxiety of loneliness in the labor of mourning. The courage to love is inexhaustible in its resources of genuine repentance, repair, and reconciliation, since this courage enables man to trust without rational proof in the dignity and wholeness of the I and the Thou, not as partial objects and means of only sensual, and therefore egocentric, gratification, but this courage trusts in the creative wholeness of the We.

The Nature of Sympathy in
the Art of Psychotherapy

The pioneer work of the psychotherapist has been honored by David Rioch with the words: "No science is better than its art, and a science of human behavior is dependent for its growth on the artists who develop new operations."[1] Frieda Fromm-Reichmann emphasized that the psychotherapist works not only with his rational, but also with his emotional endowment, that he participates in the reliving of the patient's emotional experience. The transmittal of emotional experience is based on a kind of contagion, an immediate grasping, by physiognomic clues, and on the preconscious level, of the emotion of the partner. By this preverbal and preconscious communication the partners of a psychotherapeutic session understand each other without words, and through the overtones of their verbal exchange—the speed, pitch, and rhythm of speech—they transmit emotional nuances to each other which cannot be expressed in rational terms. This participation is called empathy.

But empathy, sometimes considered a neutral between sympathy and antipathy, cannot be free from the values reflected in either, for emotional participation cannot remain neutral. I have come to feel doubtful when I hear, in psychoanalytic discussions, of the cool, detached, mirrorlike, neutral observer who yet participates in the intense emotional conflicts of his patients. I do not suggest, by this doubt, that the therapist should regress to un-

Reprinted by permission from *Psychiatry: Journal for the Study of Interpersonal Processes* 24 (Aug. 1961): 187–96. Copyright 1961 by the William Alanson White Psychiatric Foundation, Inc.

1. David McK. Rioch, "Psychiatry as a Biological Science," *Psychiatry* 18 (1955): 313–21.

critical emotional response, but rather recommend careful self-scrutiny of his own emotional reactions in the treatment situation.

In the long years of my own therapeutic work and supervisory experience, I have found the most constructive understanding growing out of the therapist's sympathy, the positive side of empathy. Sympathy cannot be forced by any form of teachable technique. Antipathy is aroused by signals of anxiety and distress transmitted from one partner to another; its presence throws a sharp flash of light on areas of incompatibility which have to be cleared away before a creative understanding can take place. But most antipathetic reactions on the part of the therapist are of short duration. The commitment and dedication to the work favor sympathy that transcends anxiety and defenses against it. Persistent antipathy, according to my experience, explodes the treatment situation.

It seems worth while to compare what a modern phenomenologist, Max Scheler, has to say about the nature of sympathy and its creative contribution to human understanding. Scheler was a German philosopher and sociologist who died in 1928. His publications found a wide interest in Europe. Only his book, *The Nature of Sympathy*,[2] which is perhaps one of his best, has been translated into English. In spite of serious differences in philosophical approach from his contemporary, Freud, he respected in Freud the genius which could lead to an understanding of man's destiny. Scheler was, like Edmund Husserl, a disciple of Franz Brentano, the same professor of philosophy whose lectures Freud had attended as a student. Brentano overcame the clash of the idealistic philosophy presented by the neo-Kantians and the materialistic philosophy of Jeremy Bentham and John Stuart Mill by stressing human intentionality that distinguishes good and bad, as the intellect distinguishes true and false. Husserl and Scheler, both phenomenologists, demanded that the scientist become aware of his philosophical premises. Phenomenology, out of which the existential philosophy of Heidegger, Jaspers, Sartre, and others

2. Max Scheler, *The Nature of Sympathy,* trans. Peter Heath (New Haven: Yale University Press, 1954).

developed, criticized the scientists of the past for not taking sufficiently into account the relative unpredictability of human intentionality. These scientists of the past saw their ideal in a natural
science that gains domination over nature by establishing the laws
of cause and effect—laws to which inorganic material can be
ideally submitted. But a dynamic understanding of the living organism's history is less accessible to the application of such stable
laws, for it is based on the sympathetic tuning in of the living explorer with his living and—like himself—never quite predictable
partner.

Scheler has much in common with Henri Bergson. Both were
interested in the intuitive understanding of the total personality
through creative vision, and both recognized the religious dimension in this spiritual unification. Bergson was at the end of his life
close to joining the Roman Catholic Church. Scheler was Roman
Catholic during part of his life, but he was always critical of
theological dogmatization, and he moved in his religious development from personal theism to a pantheism strongly influenced by
Eastern philosophies, seeing a connection between the Buddhistic
doctrine and the teaching of Freud.[3] Scheler shared Freud's idea of
sublimation, the guidance and direction of the power stream of the
organic impulses by the spirit and the spiritual will,[4] which represents the creative unity of the total personality. But he raised the
question: What is to start the process of sublimation, unless the
spirit itself is the cause and not the result of sublimation? I shall
present here some ideas stimulated in a psychoanalyst by Scheler's
work on the nature of sympathy.

The understanding of other human beings has always been a
challenge to philosophers. Scheler makes it clear that no synthetic
summation of correctly observed psychological mechanisms can
ever convey an understanding of the total personality. He considers it a root error to assume that the knowledge of self must precede the knowledge of others. Some experiences of understanding
take place in an animal who is able to sense his master's anger or

3. Ibid., pp. xxiv–xxv.
4. Ibid., p. xxviii.

37

tenderness, and in the preverbal child who distinguishes friend or foe from the smile or frown of the person he encounters. These experiences of understanding are prelogical, preceding self-awareness, and not yet supported by any conclusions drawn from analogy. Scheler defines empathy as a form of emotional contagion facilitating identification.[5] Yet empathy is an incomplete and immature understanding of another person, since an emotional response by contagion is not yet consolidated by the integrative process of self-awareness.

Scheler points out that the awakening of self-awareness and self-reflection takes place rather late in individual development. The infant lives in symbiosis with his mother. Because of the long dependency of the human child, he only gradually learns to discriminate between himself and the powerful, unilaterally respected parental authority. Here Scheler's observations have since been supported by Piaget's demonstration that a distinction of the self and the other, mutual respect and moral autonomy, do not fully develop in Western culture before the ninth to twelfth year, the preadolescent period in which Sullivan also observed the first experiences of genuine mutuality, "the quiet miracle of preadolescence."[6]

Previously the child was submerged in the current of collective experience, carried by the emotional waves of the environment, and the vortices of self-awareness in the beginning were few and far between. Similarly, as Lévy-Brühl first demonstrated, the adults of primitive tribes do not show the degree of individuation that man has developed in modern Western culture.[7] Customs such as the vendetta show that the members of a family or a clan feel an insult done to one member as if it were done to all of them, and the choice of a marital partner is not an individual emotional decision, but one in which the whole group participates.

Symbiotic experiences in adulthood are less frequent in West-

5. Ibid., pp. 15, 24 ff.
6. Jean Piaget, *The Moral Judgment of the Child* (London: K. Paul, Trench, Trubner, 1932). Harry Stack Sullivan, *Conceptions of Modern Psychiatry* (New York: Norton, 1953), p. 41.
7. Lucien Lévy-Brühl, *How Natives Think* (London: Allen and Unwin, 1926).

ern culture, although such experiences, as well as withdrawal into defensive autism, are not at all rare in psychopathology. These symbiotic experiences appear, too, in emotionally moved mass meetings, when the highly individualized modern citizens of Western culture may return to the level of collective experience, the loss of rational orientation and susceptibility to emotional contagion sweeping the members of a whole assembly off their feet. Freud, who compared this phenomenon to hysteria and hypnosis, considered it a regression to an earlier phase of libido development, to heteronomous dependency on a parental leader, a leading idea, or a common ego ideal.[8] Heteronomy is characteristic of the child's relation to authority, representing the dependency on laws and orders given by external forces to which the child or the child in man submits without conviction, or against which he rebels without durable effect. Autonomy, on the other hand, represents the integration of the mature personality under the direction of a flexible morality and self-chosen commitment. The existential philosophers point out that a trend of regression from autonomy to heteronomy is widespread in modern mass society.

According to Heidegger, being in the world is from the start a being with others, a caring for others and being cared for by others.[9] From this interwoven state of existence it follows that emotional participation accompanies the givenness of primary relations of belonging and dependency. This emotional participation precedes conceptual and logical thinking. Intuition, therefore, does not need mystical explanations. The world is given to the child first in emotional terms. The earliest cognitive experiences are emotional ones, and to a certain degree man relies on emotional cognition all his life. He listens to what Pascal calls "les raisons du coeur,"[10] which may at times differ from the reasons of rational thought.

Emotional experience discriminates between values from the

8. Sigmund Freud, "Group Psychology and the Analysis of the Ego," in *The Complete Psychological Works of Sigmund Freud,* vol. 18 (London: Hogarth, 1955), pp. 65–143.

9. Martin Heidegger, *Sein und Zeit* (Halle a.d.S.: Niemeyer, 1935).

10. Blaise Pascal, *Pensées* (Paris: P. Hartmann, 1943).

start. One thinks here first of the positive value of pleasure and the negative value of pain. Bodily sensations have, however, a private character; my bodily pain and my bodily pleasure are mine alone.[11] Strong bodily sensations narrow consciousness and may paralyze imagination and communication. Scheler distinguishes the emotionally expressed suffering from the pain itself, pleasurable emotion from pleasurable sensation.[12] He believes that sensations and emotions have different thresholds—a difference which psychoanalytic literature sometimes neglects. Sensations are private, but emotions can be propagated by contagion, and it is this contagion that Scheler calls empathy. Emotions that arise in the context of interpersonal relations, emotions of positive value, such as joy, affection, enthusiasm, and gratitude, or emotions of negative value, such as anxiety, grief, despair, and rage, may contaminate a passive partner and momentarily wipe out the boundaries between him and the other one. But emotions can also be actively shared by a sympathetic partner who is not overwhelmed by the contagion, who is able to evaluate the meaning of the shared emotional experience for the total personality of the partner, not in defensive aloofness, but on the basis of human solidarity. Happiness is enhanced by being shared, and distress diminished by the experience of true sympathy, since true sympathy alleviates anxiety.

I should like here to supplement Scheler's concept of emotional solidarity versus emotional contagion by some psychiatric observations. If a child grows up in a family where emotional solidarity is seriously defective because of heredity, because of an excess of negative emotions, or because of a defensive withdrawal from emotional exchange—and if this alienation is not a transient crisis, but repetitive and continuous—the forsaken child becomes more or less autistic, isolated in the prison of his body, lonely with his uncommunicable bodily sensations of pain and pleasure. The empathic anxiety between mother and child leads into a vicious cycle

11. J. von UexKuell, *Theoretical Biology* (London: Routledge and Kegan Paul, 1926). Von UexKuell considered pain "one of the most powerful indications of one's own body."

12. Scheler, pp. 41, 255.

of mounting distrust and despair, and their beneficial symbiotic union is prematurely broken up. The autism into which the child withdraws stunts his emotional development, for it represents a deterioration of the basic symbiosis out of which both emotional solidarity and individual differentiation develop in healthy circumstances. The self-comforting pleasures of sucking, rocking, or masturbation become frantic. The child is delayed in finding the boundaries of the *I* and the other one. He reaches out for what Mahler and Furer call "corrective symbiotic experience,"[13] but he overvalues the missing symbiosis, and it becomes a threat.

The adult psychotic also reaches out for symbiotic experience, and yet he dreads the loss of defensive boundaries. Rational functions cannot substitute for the gaps in symbiotic experience, but may even interfere with the immediacy and spontaneity of emotional self-expression. Yet in the course of his development the person relies on the rational functions for the sake of security, and he is afraid at times of losing control under the pressure of intense emotions arising out of his own sensations or out of the contagion of others. He may hide his emotions or pretend, for instance, to be cheerful when he is sad, to be indifferent when he is enraged. But conscious or unconscious misrepresentation of emotions is mostly unsuccessful; its forced character becomes apparent to an attentive observer.

When a partner passively succumbs to the contagion of empathy, every emotion carrying a positive or negative value moves him automatically to sympathy or antipathy, to love or hate. Positive emotions are mostly welcome; negative emotions often mobilize movements of defense or escape, repression, isolation, dissociation, or denial. In a state of immaturity or tribal primitivity these reactions are intensely ambivalent, of the all-or-none type, since there is not yet a unified *I* that encounters a unified *you*, that integrates light and shadow, good and bad. An immature partner is passively pulled into the current of alien emotions, and he experiences the echo of his partner's emotions as his own experience.

13. Margaret S. Mahler and Manuel Furer, "Observations on Research Regarding the 'Symbiotic Syndrome' of Infantile Psychosis," *Psychoanalytic Quarterly* 29 (1960): 317–27.

Scheler distinguishes heteropathic identification, in which the immature person is pulled into the wake of his partner's emotions, and idiopathic identification, in which he imposes his own values on the other.[14] Introjection and identification channel emotions into habitual directions, into the powerful currents of traditional adaptation determined by verbally fixed definitions of traditional values. Automatic emotional responses along the lines of traditionally accepted values stand between the passive emotional contagion of empathy and the autonomous emotional decision-making of the mature person.

The autonomy of the mature person overcomes the anxiety of unilateral respect for and dependency on authority and arrives at individuation and the experience of self-esteem. In this process of individuation, Ives Hendrick saw the "instinct of mastery" at work,[15] Karl Buehler the enjoyment of functioning (*Funktionslust*).[16] Goethe saw in this achievement of mastery the highest happiness of human beings. Personality (*Persönlichkeit*) represents the sense of inner unity, the uniqueness of creative integration—unpredictable, created anew in each moment in each new situation. This gift is, of course, losable, but it may be ever so often regained. The tendency toward passive empathy remains a basic disposition to which one returns in times of weakness and decreased defenses. But out of this passivity, the unified, self-respecting personality arises ever anew and encounters the other in creative, mutual understanding.

Scheler does not consider the emotional experience of value to be a merely subjective phenomenon.[17] Decisions on the basis of sympathy and antipathy, love and hate, moving a human being toward or away from the partner who elicits these emotions, are not exclusively the product of slavish obedience to present-day influences or to traditional values. Emotions respond to objects that

---

14. Scheler, p. 131.

15. Ives Hendrick, "Instinct and the Ego during Infancy," *Psychoanalytic Quarterly* 11 (1942): 33–58.

16. Karl Buehler, *Die geistige Entwicklung des Kindes* (Jena: G. Fischer, 1921), pp. 434 ff.

17. Scheler, pp. 195 ff.

carry value as the eye responds to light and the ear to sound. There is a reciprocity between eye and light, ear and sound, between subject and object in the experience of value. Scheler describes a hierarchy of values, differentiated by the increasing participation of intelligence and wisdom in judging them. On the lowest level are the private pleasure-pain values, the determinations of what is agreeable or disagreeable to the individual in his bodily singularity. On the second level Scheler places vital or welfare values that promote life, health, vitality, and social well-being. On the third level he locates the spiritual or cultural values, comprising beauty, justice, and truth. At the summit of this hierarchy Scheler places the sacred values, the values of holiness reflected in the sage or saint who transcends the anxiety evoked by evil in free and loving acceptance of his destiny, his dependence as well as his independence, his aloneness as well as his belonging. On the lowest level, the level of bodily sensations, man is set apart in his individual singularity. On the highest level he transcends the instinctual drivenness of the herd animal as well as the defensive singularity of individuation. But there is the danger that transcendental mysticism may deteriorate into world-denying solipsism.[18]

My experience in psychoanalysis has taught me to be wary of any professed scale of objective values raised by a patient to the rank of absoluteness, for it stems from the rigid heteronomy of an infantile superego. Absolute values can be used to endorse a regime of force and submission to force which contradicts the spontaneity and creative flexibility of love and sympathy. Love cannot be forced. Enforced morality which is not integrated into the individual unity and uniqueness will never inspire the creativeness of love.

Scheler defines love and hate, sympathy and antipathy, not as emotions only, but as movements.[19] Love moves toward the enhancement of value, from the lower to the higher level, and it is a movement in the lover as well as in the beloved. This movement is spontaneous, not compelled by the subtle force of duty. The

18. Ibid. p. 60.
19. Ibid., pp. 195 ff.

lover has a vision not only of what the beloved is, but also of what he can become, and this vision moves the beloved freely in the direction of liberation and unification of the total personality. Hatred moves in the opposite direction, destroying instead of enhancing values. But hatred may destroy deteriorated or heteronomous values and clear the way for the movement of love toward the enhancement of autonomous values.

Sympathy and antipathy, as well as love and hatred in Scheler's terms, are close to Eros and Thanatos in Freud's terminology. Freud sees these movements as the outflow of instinctual energies. But wherever the energy of movement stems from, its directedness seems as important as its source. Eros or love achieves the integration of personality and of the person in his human relations, as long as its fusion with Thanatos prevails over their diffusion. The highest standard of value is not only the preservation of individual life, but the acceptance of man's biological destiny in a broader frame, in the growing richness of communal life. This includes the sacrifice of the single life; it includes death or partial death in human suffering. Without this dying and renewed becoming—Goethe's *Stirb* and *Werde*—maturing growth and community life would not be possible. Freud's "Beyond the Pleasure Principle" describes the triumph of Eros over Thanatos in life, as well as the deep urge of human nature to be delivered from all tensions and strife in the peace of death.[20] Scheler sees in death the ultimate sacrifice which can be rendered without bitterness, if man attains the wisdom of accepting the gift of life with gratitude and his destiny with fortitude.

The physician takes up the challenge of helping the patient in this struggle of life and death, enhancing the potentialities of Eros and strengthening the patient's fortitude in the confrontation with suffering and with the ultimate sacrifice. The active sympathy of the psychotherapist, in differentiation from a passive empathy, is not merely a transference phenomenon; it is a part of this value-enhancing love, capable of envisioning the personality of the pa-

20. Sigmund Freud, "Beyond the Pleasure Principle," in *Complete Psychological Works*, 18:3–64.

tient in his potential wholeness, even though this wholeness may at present be only adumbrated, obscured by a preponderance of destructive processes from which he seeks liberation. Freud used the word love with reserve, since it is so often misused to refer to sentimentality, but he expected that the patient freed from crippling transference would mature to receive and give love. Just as the word love has become misunderstood in more than one sense —a coin deteriorated by usage—the word sympathy also no longer has the ring of a spontaneous emotion. It carries connotations of hypocrisy, sentimentality, blind partiality, or sadomasochistic exploitation. The emotion of sympathy is so strongly suspect that the psychoanalyst has been instructed in his training to free himself from a prejudicial dependency on value systems, to be mirrorlike and directed only by rational intentions. Yet when his emotional attitude toward the patient genuinely transcends the reactions of transference and countertransference, he gains the distance of genuine, spontaneous, respectful sympathy, dedicated to honest concern for the patient's welfare. But it seems to me that he can reach this point only if he gives up the illusion of artificial neutrality and becomes fully aware of his emotional reactions.

Scheler has spoken of a rehabilitation of virtue in an era in which the striving for goodness, truth, and justice has frequently become suspect of hypocrisy and opportunistic adaptation, and traditional values have been debunked. Freud seldom mentioned his own high standards; he quoted Visher's famous words, "das Moralische versteht sich ja von selbst" ("morality can be taken for granted").[21] The longing for goodness, justice, and truth is seldom given weight and meaning as epiphenomena of instinctual drives. The superego, the internal guardian, incorporates the values of the family and the broader community. Every upheaval and change of values represents a loss of solidarity and mobilizes anxiety, since the security of traditional confirmation is shaken. The struggle between solidarity and individuation, dependence and independence, is inevitable, even for a person who has grown up

21. Sigmund Freud, "Zur Technik (Ueber Psychotherapie)" in *Gesammelte Schriften*, vol. 6 (Leipzig Internationaler Psychoanalytischer Verlag, 1925), p. 23.

in a harmonious family setting. It is the tragedy of man to lose his integration in a group ever again; it is his glory that he can regain a form of integration on each level of his life course.

I have encountered in psychoanalytic practice a number of patients who are not able fully to endure the loneliness of individuation. They regard me, the therapist, as an authority. They are anxious to please me, to avoid disagreement with me, but they cannot really trust me. Even a wholehearted endorsement remains suspect to them. Since the original family group was unreliable, they remain skeptical in any interpersonal attachment. The natural solidarity for them is replaced by egocentric, opportunistically calculated adaptation, by role-playing, by adjustment to traditional values, to an other-directed, heteronomous morality. Although these patients are sometimes free of symptoms, their calculated adjustment maneuvers leave them with an insecurity about their identity, and I hear complaints about bitter disappointments in their search for genuine fellowship. This lack cannot be covered over by an active social life or by superficial sexual adventures. The patient longs for a meaningful mutuality, and without it friendships or erotic relations remain unstable, burdened by unfulfilled needs, tensions, and angry explosions. A heteronomous morality, a slavish sense of duty, cannot deal with these conflicts.

One patient who was haunted by marital conflicts complained that he could not stay, in the long run, a slave of unloved duties that did not elicit any genuine dedication from him. He was only slowly responsive to my sympathy, which gradually melted the armor of his harsh Phariseeism, a defense against his own and his mate's spontaneous needs. Sexual frustration was the result, not the cause, of this marital alienation, which in the course of analysis was punctured by upheavals of anxiety. I could show the patient the positive value of these anxieties and outbursts of anger, which indicated an inner revolution, breaking the narrow barriers of a self-righteous morality, aiming at a new understanding, a new meaning. In the light of this new orientation the tensions of the marital relation became a meaningful challenge.

Another patient, in his predicament of inner loneliness, dreaded any emotional experience or self-expression as if it would lead to complete disorganization. When his boss expected him to perform a job, he did not dare to ask for directions. He struggled through his work with mute resentment because his task was over his head, because he got no help, but could not ask for help. He felt neglected by his wife, who drifted away from his mute reproaches. His therapy threatened to bog down in despair, for he dared not ask me for help, either. He had to learn to express his emotional experience, his anxieties as well as his needs, in an atmosphere of true sympathy in order to find out that communication of emotional experience is not a danger but a relief, and that interpersonal conflicts can be solved in the here-and-now situation.

The wife of this patient reacted to his withdrawal with desertion anxieties, insisting that she needed to be loved in order to function. In such cases, understanding sympathy can reinforce the endurance and patience of both marital partners, and I consider it profitable to see the spouse simultaneously or separately. This gives me an opportunity to demonstrate the vicious cycle of mutually aroused anxiety, to clarify that love cannot be demanded out of a need for control, but can best spring up spontaneously, when the anxieties on both sides are tuned down to a more bearable pitch.

True sympathy enables the therapist to look through the patient's false front. It is easy to recognize the deceptions of a bad actor who tries to express emotions that are not really his own. It is more difficult to understand unconscious emotional distortions beyond the volition and grasp of a patient who has become the slave of defensive habits. His false front is a powerful protection against a panic that might transiently overflow his rationalizations and his self-control.

Man is in general better able to understand the other person than to understand himself. As Nietzsche said, "Everybody is most remote to himself."[22] In relation to himself he builds up the strongest barriers of prejudice. He is most aware of his social self, the role that environment and tradition force him to play. As to his

22. Quoted by Scheler, p. 251.

true self, the contents of his genuine emotions, he may be stuck in self-deception. I have to ask my patients repeatedly: "How do you really feel?"

A psychotic patient is particularly distressed by emotional outbursts alien to the stiff artificiality by which he tries to maintain his composure, outbursts which are triggered by the therapist's slight movements of impatience or flickers of defensive condescension. These are outside of the therapist's awareness, but the patient picks them up with the ingenuous sensitivity of contagious empathy. If I cannot admit them, the tenuous rapport with the patient is lost. The patient sees these nonverbal communications of impatience or condescension through the magnifying glass of his anxiety and defensive distrust—remnants of his infantile dependency—which make him feel painfully victimized by powers beyond his control. His infantile dependency and my corresponding therapeutic authority are unbearable to his fragile composure. His sensitive, empathic reactions to failures in my sympathy do not permit him to see me or himself as total personalities in the here-and-now situation. Only when not only the patient, but I, too, become aware of the unobserved movements of separation or intrusion can we gradually establish a mutuality in which therapy works.

An indiscriminating empathy on the part of the therapist would remain ineffective, because he would get involved by contagion in the emotions elicited by the patient's misleading self-expression. Overidentification with the patient, sharing his defenses and his rationalizations, might lead the therapist into a conspiracy with the patient against the world, at worst into a *folie-à-deux* that would not alter the patient's self-alienation. The therapist who empathizes by contagion is usually not firmly established in his own values, so that he has to exploit the patient for the sake of his own deficient self-respect; he may derive a weak comfort from looking down on the patient who is worse off than himself, or he may try to reform him, foisting upon him a social adjustment that leaves him estranged from autonomous values.

True sympathy on the part of the therapist is not compatible with blindness toward values. Every physician is committed to finding out, as much as the progress of science permits, what ails the patient, and how his health can be restored. The higher value toward which he would help the patient move is that of health and maturity, but the inferior value—whether expressed in immaturity or in neurotic or psychotic illness—is not an object of worthlessness to the sympathetic explorer; it reveals the potentialities of growth and recovery, as fever or phagocytosis indicates the pathways of the natural healing process. Similarly, the sympathetic psychotherapist is guided by the patient's complaints, omissions, denials, and trepidations. Only an understanding therapist can create the atmosphere of calm acceptance that loosens the spasms of self-defense. If the therapist had nothing more to offer than detached scientific neutrality, the patient might not feel safe in dropping his defenses, and the therapist might only discover the chains of cause and effect that can be discussed intellectually without any emotional change. The content of what the psychotherapist has to say is not always accepting, confirming, or reassuring. Some of the insights he tries to convey are extremely painful to the patient, painful to his self-esteem, to such a degree that he may transiently lose his hope and trust that he will recover. It is a high achievement of the psychotherapeutic art to convey an insight in the spirit of true sympathy which not only points out the causes of the patient's failures and imposes compulsive duties, but permits the vision of freedom to choose new alternatives. The vision of true sympathy opens new horizons and facilitates attraction toward higher values.

If the therapist and patient are to experience such a liberation, they cannot remain strict adherents of a philosophy of absolute determinism. Both must have some degree of faith in freedom of choice, in the possibility of altering decisions, and some commitment and responsibility in relation to values that have a superpersonal meaning. This responsibility does not represent an arbitrary, egocentric freedom. The responsible person does not decide all by himself, but responds to challenge, demand, question, or request, and his decisions establish a new creative union between request and response.

The request for free associations leaves a broad area of freedom to the patient, but the spoken or unspoken question, "What comes to your mind?," summons the patient to a reevaluation of his intentions. He steps out of the private world of his dreams, fantasies, wishes, and fears into a relation with his partner in psychotherapy. As much as possible he strips off the conventional masks of traditional adjustment, but since most patients are bewildered about their destiny and confused about who they are and where they are going, they try to find an answer in the psychotherapist's unspoken words, in his attitude, in his nonverbal communications. The therapeutic relation reestablishes the lost or impaired experience of solidarity in the identification of the patient with the therapist. However, the therapist is very careful not to give advice or guidance bluntly; he respects the patient's spontaneous search for genuine insight. But the unspoken vision of the patient's liberated potentialties in the mind of the sympathetic therapist is a powerful support that keeps up the courage of the seeking patient, mostly without any spoken words of comfort and support.

One theme in the psychoanalytic work that contributes to the therapeutic change is assisting the patient in the process of learning to endure frustrations. This depends on the freedom of the therapist to offer genuine sympathy to the patient. Frequently, the patient expects from therapy a complete deliverance from all evil. If this were possible, the patient would not receive the stimulus to grow that is provided by responding creatively to anxiety, or receive the constructive insight that comes from sincerely acknowledging guilt. In neurotic patients and to an even greater extent in psychotic patients, one finds a dangerous intolerance of frustrations, and walls of defense against the frustrating aspects of reality. The denial, repression, and dissociation of these tragic aspects of life lead to withdrawal from mutuality to egocentricity, from spontaneity and creativity to heteronomous compulsiveness. To many disturbed patients the challenges of modern living have become overwhelming. They are often richly endowed, yet oversensitive, and they do not find a place in communal living. For them an empathy which is neutral as to values is of no help. The highest value for human beings, the unification of personality, may remain unreachable, simply because they try to exclude limitations, tragedies, doom, and death from their destiny.

Typical are the obsessional patients who try to eliminate dirt and decay from their existence by washing ceremonials, who exclude hostile thoughts by rituals of hypocrisy. One of my obsessional patients was a mother who tried to exclude from her awareness the possibilities of tragedy that might befall her only son. She did not let go a symbiosis with him, unsuitable to his development and directed merely by her egocentric demands. In order to protect the child from contamination, illness, and death she subjected him every day to repeated cleaning and scrubbing maneuvers and deprived him of his freedom to play. These maneuvers made them both miserable with irritations and hostilities which the mother desperately denied. Obviously such techniques to avoid suffering only increase human misery. The exclusion of death deprives life of its meaning, the personality of its wholeness, and human relations of the depth of mutuality.

The great philosophies of world history have recommended various techniques to learn the endurance of suffering. Buddhism teaches the discipline of extinguishing the thirst of desire that chains man to the world of appearance, makes him a victim of suffering, and shackles the freedom of the spirit which unites the individual in himself and with his destiny in the universe. The philosophy of cynicism teaches the blunting of suffering by apathy; hedonism preaches escape from suffering through a one-sided cultivation of the pleasure principle. Biblical philosophy deprives suffering of the sting of meaninglessness by interpreting it as punishment and a means of expiation.

The modern psychiatrist has an opportunity to watch sympathetically the various individual techniques by which his patients try to come to terms with suffering. In the beginning of treatment, the patient frequently, in infantile egocentricity, submits to or rebels against the therapist, whom he sees as a heteronomous authority. He insists with blind gullibility or bitter disillusion on the elimination of suffering. The patient and the therapist may reach in this struggle the frontiers of despair, as Leslie Farber has demonstrated.[23] He described a turning point in treatment when true

23. Leslie H. Farber, "The Therapeutic Despair," *Psychiatry* 21 (1958): 7–20.

sympathy—he called it pity—awakens in the patient. In the course of treatment the patient encounters the therapist more realistically in the mutuality of enduring sympathetic cooperation. The patient recognizes that protesting against adversity, raging blindly against external obstacles and inner limitations, only increases his helplessness and anxiety and cannot achieve a magic transformation of destiny. The greatest achievements in the endurance of suffering are found among those who are committed and dedicated to goals beyond the limits of their egocentricity. Although the security and solidarity of primitive embeddedness are forever lost and the goals of unification remain only partially reachable, the ability to sympathize and to love lifts the person out of his loneliness and suffering under inner and outer limitations. The psychotherapist's sympathy that visualizes the patient's wholeness, despite his various states of confusion and despair, mobilizes his genuine emotions directed toward freedom to encounter also the tragic aspects of his destiny in the spirit of spontaneous responsiveness.

The psychotherapist does not preach his philosophy in words prone to be misleading and misused by hypocritical conformity or self-righteous Phariseeism. He must not underestimate the value of nonverbal, unconscious communication between himself and the patient. Whether the therapist knows it or not, he lives his philosophy. It may radiate warmth and kindle the light of sympathetic understanding, which has an evocative, creative influence on the patient, not only convincing the intellect, but also transforming the heart. A creative response can be found to human suffering, and where suffering remains inevitable it can be experienced in the light of the evangelic paradox: "Whosoever shall seek to save his life shall lose it; and whosoever shall lose his life shall preserve it" (Luke 17:33).

Loneliness and Trust—
Basic Factors of Human Existence

One of the modern developments of psychoanalysis is the emergence of an ego psychology which is concerned not only with instinctual sources of the psychic apparatus, but with the integrative development of the whole person as he transcends present frustrations to open up to future gratifications. Within the frame of classical psychoanalysis, this ego psychology is linked with the names of Hartmann, Kris, and Loewenstein, from a more sociological vantage point with Erikson, and, in dynamic psychiatry, with Sullivan and his theory of interpersonal relations.[1] There are also parallels with the objective observations of the ethologists, who find that instinctual behavior in animals shows a tendency toward concentric hierarchical organization on different levels of maturation, subordinating primitive instincts to more encompassing, goal-directed impulses.

Psychoanalysis, while it also utilizes objective observation, relies largely on introspective reports about emotions that reflect instinctual impulses in subjective experience. If instinctual impulses are concentrated on ego-syntonic and reality-confirming goals, the subjective emotional experience is that of confidence or trust;

Reprinted by permission from *Psychiatry: Journal for the Study of Interpersonal Processes* 23 (May 1960): 121–31. Copyright 1960 by the William Alanson White Psychiatric Foundation, Inc.

1. Heinz Hartmann, Ernst Kris, and Rudolph M. Loewenstein, "Notes on the Theory of Aggression," in *Psychoanalytic Study of the Child*, vols. 3/4, ed. Anna Freud et al. (New York: International Universities Press, 1949), pp. 9–36; Erik Erikson, *Childhood and Society* (New York: Norton, 1950); Harry Stack Sullivan, *The Interpersonal Theory of Psychiatry*, ed. Helen Perry and Mary Gawel (New York: Norton, 1953).

if instinctual impulses are in a state of disorganization and conflict with reality, the subjective experience of anxiety prevails.

But the emotional experience of wholeness is never static; the synthetic function of the ego does not create a closed system. As long as a person lives, he remains—although in varying degrees—open to the future, open to the world as he sees it. The world of his experience, his world and his ego, lives in continuous interchange. He shapes his world, and in turn this world—his reality—shapes his ego. His impulses, his potentialities, aiming into the future, are shaped by processes of disintegration and reintegration, which Freud identified as Thanatos and Eros. Freud's reduction of integrative and disintegrative processes to basic instincts appears to some analysts, however, as an oversimplifying hypothesis. Even Melanie Klein, who uses the term "death instinct" amply, does not see in it a biological force but a subjective experience—the elementary fear of death, the prototype of all anxiety.[2]

From a subjective point of view the complicated exchange between the individual and his world is experienced as more or less pleasurable, or more or less painful. If intolerable pain prevails, the creative process of interchange may be partially interrupted by neurotic or psychotic stagnations. The openness of the individual to the future and to the encompassing world is reflected in the subjective experience of trust; a recoiling from the future and from the embracing world is subjectively experienced as anguished loneliness.

Loneliness is so painful an experience that one seldom hears directly about it. Sullivan and Fromm-Reichmann have pointed out that man escapes automatically from experiences of loneliness, and if he has once looked into this abyss of horror he seldom cares to talk about it. There is deep shame in the experience of loneliness. The first line of defense, therefore, is anxiety. Only in tolerable doses does anxiety stimulate a striving for mastery and useful defense. Excessive anxieties have a disorganizing effect.

In his essay on "Inhibition, Symptom and Anxiety," Freud enumerates three main categories of anxiety as they first emerge

2. Melanie Klein, *Envy and Gratitude* (New York: Basic Books, 1957).

in childhood: first, anxiety due to the threat of desertion by the mother; second, castration anxiety, due to the threat of losing the organ or losing the power of attraction that promises a future reunion with a mother or father substitute; and, third, superego anxiety, due to the threat of being deserted by the superego, to which the ego reacts as if it were forsaken by the powers of fate —"which puts an end to security against every danger."[3]

Anxiety, which is the basic problem of all the neuroses, and is, in higher degrees of intensity, at the root of the functional psychoses, not only announces the deprivation of certain needs, but, more important, is a danger signal of threatening isolation and loss of trust. The person senses, in an anxiety state, the over-all danger of being forsaken, of becoming impotent in the pursuit of happiness, of being delivered to the meaninglessness of existence. Freud's categories of anxiety and their sources in childhood do not exhaust the phenomena of loneliness, but they may be of help in organizing an understanding of the dialectic tension between trust and loneliness—of the ways in which the basic human longing to enter into a relation of trust deals with the fundamental danger of loneliness.

THE THREAT OF DESERTION

The child has experiences of relatedness as well as of loneliness, of satisfaction and over-all contentment as well as of anguish and emptiness. When he is transiently separated from his mother, the trust that she will return, and hence the ability to endure the present frustration, are due to a hope, a faith, that has arisen between mother and child. It is not the achievement of one, or of the other, exclusively; it is a creation of their mutuality.

Similarly, the relation of trust between doctor and patient arises as a joint creation, facilitating the gratification of mutual understanding. The experience of trust starts with an unconscious or

3. Sigmund Freud, "Inhibition, Symptom and Anxiety," *Psychoanalytic Quarterly* 5 (1936): 267.

conscious risk, a dive into uncertainty. There is no guarantee of mutual understanding, and the patient—like the burned child—may recoil from the risk, from the danger of being deserted and misunderstood, which he experienced in the past. He may prefer to avoid the risk, for when he has appealed for help before, he has usually experienced painful frustrations.

Trust, by its very nature, aims at interpersonal truth, but the fear of loneliness recoils from self-revelation as well as from truthful response. When mutual trust fails, egocentric self-concern takes over the search for security—but in vain, since this self-concern cannot provide the security of trust. It separates the partners, in their longing for mutuality, by emerging suspicions. Trust, by its very nature, does not force, does not impose one partner's will on the other; nor does a trusting person give up his own identity to submit to the partner's wishes, blindly, for the sake of peace and harmony. Trust is characterized by a self-revelation that needs neither diplomacy nor hypocrisy, no false appearances for the sake of approval, no clever persuasion or concealment to avoid disapproval.

Even though the partners of a trusting relation—parent and child, or doctor and patient—are different in age, status, and social role, a mutuality of gratification is not only possible, but is the very basis of their trust. Each being true to himself, true to his realistic function in this relation, is therewith true to his partner also; both enter into an unplanned process of creative understanding. Efforts at fraternization, or identifications, busy at wiping out the ego boundaries, are dictated by the fear of desertion and loneliness; they are not part of a relation of trust. In a meaningful relation of trust the partners grant each other freedom. Although the more experienced partner may, at times, have a clearer picture of the goals toward which the other is developing, his trust detaches him from impulses of impatient guidance, since the genuine gratification in this relation is the spontaneity of the creative process that develops between the two. Becoming present and transparent to each other need not be expressed in words. A glance, a gesture, may reveal mutuality of understanding, most gratifying to both of them.

THE THREAT OF CASTRATION

Under the broad title of castration anxiety Freud has collected various manifestations of psychopathology that mar the potentially deepest of all trust relations, adult heterosexual intimacy. The full surrender of the adult man and woman in love to each other, transcending into the future with the overt or covert aim of procreation, can fulfill most completely the yearning for an experience of trust and creative grace. The failures in reaching this creative fulfillment, the shipwrecks of love and marriage, are frequently accompanied by experiences of painful desolation and loneliness.

In tracing back into the patient's childhood the sources of such a failure, one often finds nonacceptance of his own sexual role, along with the manifold imagery of castration anxiety and penis envy, and unbearable resentments of experiences of rejection by either or both his parents. This denial of essential features in his own being exposes the patient to the threats of nonbeing. He is torn by inner conflict, as well as by his repeated failures in interpersonal relations. In psychoanalysis, it is often easier to reawaken the repressed passions of envy, jealousy, murderous rage, and vengeance than the more deeply repressed yearning for a trust and love relation, since the desolate child is more inclined to withdraw into the fortress of defiant loneliness and pretended self-sufficiency than to expose himself to renewed frustration by openly reaching out for confirmation by a relation of trust.

The lonely child can work out powerful compensations. He may learn to master people as he has learned to master the things necessary for his survival. He can, in fact, remain, throughout his whole life, an impressive success in the management of human relations, relatively undisturbed by tormenting anxieties, since he has built up a kind of security by compulsive means, through the brutal or subtle sadomasochistic management of his egocentric need for survival. But this kind of security is more or less brittle and rigid, unyielding to the surprises of fate. It is inaccessible to the spontaneous experience of grace, in which human beings are able to grant each other the freedom of a trusting relation—a freedom that would gradually dissolve the rigidities of egocentric, compulsive defenses.

It is not sufficient that the psychoanalyst works through his patient's disturbances regarding sexual compatibility. A patient can be a Don Juan, successful in sexual performances, and yet inaccessibly lonely in the dimension of trust. Or he may have made a conventional heterosexual adjustment, and still be unaware of his loneliness and longing for trust. On the other hand, a person who finds himself painfully caught in the compulsion of an isolating perversion may be more aware of his loneliness and longing for liberation. Medard Boss, a Swiss psychiatrist, who tries to reconcile existence philosophy with psychoanalysis, has demonstrated that the therapist can discover, even in the most distorted perversions, the basic yearning for love and trust.[4]

But the rediscovery of trust can often be achieved only through the confrontation with the patient's anguish of loneliness. By accepting and enduring the patient's anxieties, the psychotherapist can surmount the patient's defenses, his timidity and diffidence as well as his defensive assaults. But the courage of the therapist must be genuine, for otherwise it is not convincing. The patient has been exposed to many imitations of confidence, hypocritical promises of love, and facsimiles of truth. He himself may ask petulantly for false reassurances as a supply for his defensive narcissism. It is important for the psychoanalyst to be open to the patient's deeply repressed, genuine need for trust, and to try to reach this need, unhampered by preconceived ideas or moralizing prejudice. Emotional involvement or moral prejudice serve the therapist's egocentric claims; only by being unreservedly open to the patient's genuine present needs can he elicit truthful responses and help the patient to discover a renewed relation of trust.

SUPEREGO ANXIETY

Moral prejudice leads me to the third of Freud's categories of anxiety. The fear of moral ostracism and loneliness leads the child,

4. Medard Boss, *Meaning and Content of Sexual Perversions* (New York: Grune & Stratton, 1949).

beginning very early, to conform more or less automatically to the desires of his elders and the moral standards of his environment. If he is not merely a means of egocentric gratification or a pledge of compulsive duty for his parents, if there is a sound balance of closeness and distance, love and respect between them, the child will be able to take over his parents' values in due time, voluntarily, with discrimination, in the light of his own rational and emotional agreement. But if the child is browbeaten into obedience by excessive threats of loneliness in a precarious family situation, he remains secretly rebellious; he incorporates moral values only under pressure and uses them compulsively to cripple his own spontaneous impulses. He may suddenly overthrow this imposed regime, rebelliously indignant about a morality that is foreign to him, but then find himself surrounded by potential enemies, ready to desert and ostracize him. After longstanding habits of submission, he does not yet have the moral courage to be himself, to be unique and spontaneous.

A child loses the sense of direction in his development when he has been unable to live up to his parents' expectations, whether it is because the ideals and values of father and mother are contradictory or mutually exclusive, or because the most influential parent is himself torn by inner contradictions.[5] A mother, out of her own sense of unworthiness, may make insatiable demands for love on the child, yet simultaneously rebuff his need for closeness and love. Or a father may invest the most ambitious expectations in his son, for the sake of vicarious gratification, and yet react to any success of the son with envy and bitterness. If a child cannot gratify his parents' expectations without eliciting guilt feelings, anxiety, or envy in them, he becomes bewildered in his assessment of gratification and frustration as well as in his evaluation of himself as good or bad, and the consolidation of his ego is impaired by doubts about his own identity. Such a loss of identity is particularly characteristic for the schizophrenic development. Allen Wheelis, in his book, *The Quest for Identity*, has pointed out that

5. Bateson, Jackson, Haley, and Weakland have described the situation of contradictory parental injunctions as the "double bind." See their "Toward a Theory of Schizophrenia," *Behavioral Science* 1 (1956): 251–264.

the decline of the superego has contributed to the bewilderment and loss of direction of many people who nowadays turn for help to psychotherapy.[6]

Nobody can survive without some degree of trust in the confirmation of his fellows. A human being who remains isolated, threatened by loneliness, feels the urgent need to justify his existence against the onslaught of the nonself, the horror of nonbeing. All his energies are consumed in the battle of "to be or not to be," a battle that is never won; and this narcissistic concern with self-defense and self-justification increases his isolation and loneliness. In this vicious spiral of anguish, the person who is threatened by loneliness becomes insatiable in his compensatory ambition to rise to heights of perfection, to seek unassailable, absolute values.

Sartre sees this potential striving for godlike omnipotence in all human beings. But there are differences of degree. As long as the person sees his ego ideal at a realistic distance, firing his imagination and stimulating his aspirations, it may have an integrative effect on his personal development as well as on his potentialities for interpersonal relations. But if he is ruled by a relentlessly prohibitive and threatening superego, he may not know how to escape the horrors of loneliness except by desperately trying to be perfect and unassailable. Transient success may nourish his illusion that he can live up to his ideals of perfection and merit the high regard of others, but any failure may easily destroy the illusion and throw him back into the abyss of despair and loneliness. Thus he loses all certainty of self-evaluation, and he is inclined to hate and despise himself, taking the hostile contempt of others for granted. He may try to comfort himself by keeping up appearances, maintaining his prestige in the eyes of the world—his support by the majority; but this does not provide any reliable security.

In this dilemma, a genuine relation of trust offers a sobering reorientation. A relation of trust sets realistic limits to solitary strivings for perfection, since it gratifies the need for acceptance

6. Allen Wheelis, *The Quest for Identity* (New York: Norton, 1958).

and creative response. The illusion of omnipotence and the deceptive adaptation to prestige values become superfluous. A creative understanding dissolves the self-centered guilt feelings which foster a perpetual dependency on majority support. Existential guilt is not dissolved or argued away by the relation of trust, but neither does it remain an isolating failure; it can be faced honestly as a life-damaging event. It is redeemable in so far as it can be experienced in the genuine humility which can grow only in the atmosphere of trust.

The psychotherapist who deals with the guilt feelings of a lonely patient distinguishes between the wounds and scars of a hurt narcissism and existential, realistic guilt. His trust in the revealing truth of a creative relationship prevents him from going astray into personal prejudice or falsifying consolations. His trust stimulates the patient's courage to face his failures squarely, arrive at his own moral decisions, and regain the authenticity he has partially lost in his loneliness.

A relation of trust is not immune to errors and limitations of mutual understanding. But while the lonely person magnifies or minimizes such errors under the pressure of his need for perfection or his fear of desertion, they can be accepted in the light of trust. They delay mutual understanding, but such delay can be endured when the insatiable drive for compensations of loneliness loses its urgency. The psychoanalyst needs all his knowledge of psychopathology and the techniques of his therapy to recognize and dissolve the falsifying and yet revealing transference and countertransference phenomena, as he helps the patient to clear the way for a creative understanding.

THE CONCEPTS OF EXISTENTIAL ANALYSIS

Modern ego psychology has brought psychoanalysts closer to the viewpoint of the existentialist philosophers who have protested against traditional psychology. In spite of great differences among themselves, these existentialist philosophers have in common a subjectivistic, phenomenological approach which recommends them to the serious attention of the psychiatrist. The Swiss psychiatrist, Ludwig Binswanger—a lifelong friend and admirer of Sigmund Freud—has formulated his philosophical anthropology under the influence of such philosophers as Martin Buber, Martin Heidegger, Karl Jaspers, and Jean-Paul Sartre. Among these philosophies, the heroic voluntarism and aggressive nihilism of Sartre are least compatible with psychoanalytic determinism, although he has tried to come to terms with psychoanalytic thinking.

Existential analysis has been introduced to American psychiatry, so far, chiefly by Eugen Kahn's appraisal, by the work of Rollo May and his collaborators, and, in Washington, by the visit of Martin Buber in the spring of 1957.[7] Binswanger's book, *Grundformen und Erkenntnis menschlichen Daseins* (Basic Forms and Understanding of Human Existence), published in 1942,[8] has not yet been translated into English, but May's book introduces the American reader to Binswanger's ideas, and Buber's world of thought has much in common with that of Binswanger. It should, at the same time, be noted that there are interesting parallels between various ideas and theories conceived in this country—such as Sullivan's interpersonal theory, Horney's ideas about self-realization, and Fromm's concept of freedom[9]—and certain of the existentialist ideas and theories, such as Buber's thoughts about the I-Thou relation[10] and Binswanger's concept of the dual mode of existence.

The concepts of existential analysis add a new dimension to psychological understanding. The viewpoint of science splits the subject—the observing physician—from the object—the patient. However, the observed patient is part of a "reality" to which he

7. Eugen Kahn, "An Appraisal of Existential Analysis," *Psychiatric Quarterly* 31 (1957): 417–44; Rollo May, Ernest Angel, and Henri F. Ellenberger, eds., *Existence* (New York: Basic Books, 1958); Martin Buber, "The William Alanson White Memorial Lectures, Fourth Series," *Psychiatry* 20 (1957): 97–129.

8. Ludwig Binswanger, *Grundformen und Erkenntnis menschlichen Daseins* (Zurich: Niehans, 1942).

9. Sullivan, *The Interpersonal Theory of Psychiatry*, ed. Helen Perry and Mary Gawel (New York: Norton, 1953); Karen Harney, *New Ways in Psychoanalysis* (New York: Norton, 1939); Erich Fromm, *Escape from Freedom* (New York: Rinehart, 1941).

10. Martin Buber, *I and Thou* (New York: Scribner, 1958).

is more or less adapted, and which is necessarily influenced by the preferences and values of his own world. The existentially oriented psychiatrist who applies the phenomenological method of observation sees each person—each patient—as "being-in-the-world," in his own world. The psychiatrist's objective observation can be amplified when he enters into the world of the observed patient, remaining, however, as fully aware as possible of his own emotional preferences and aims, resulting from his own egocentric orientation. According to the phenomenological method the investigator should keep his theories and hypotheses in suspense; otherwise, he is in danger of seeing and hearing only that which proves his preconceived ideas.

The psychiatrist is not only in danger of losing his objectivity by his adherence to the necessary guideposts of preconceived ideas, but he is also exposed to emotional contamination by his patient. Sullivan has alerted the psychiatrist to watch himself as participant observer, since his emotional identification might interfere with his objectivity.[11] Emotional participation tends to wipe out the boundaries between the I and the Thou, the doctor and his patient; and the distressed patient may then either escape from the freedom of self-realization, seeking refuge in close identification with and dependency on his therapist, or withdraw into defensive distance. The psychiatrist gains his objectivity by understanding his own emotional responses to the closeness-and-distance maneuvers of his patient.

The merely scientific approach necessarily reduces the object of observation to a thing, an It. In contrast to Thou, It is predictable material, resulting from chains of cause and effect, to be grasped, defined, compared, and demonstrated to other observers. Buber as well as Binswanger considers the scientific approach to human existence the indispensable basis of psychotherapeutic action. But in the course of psychotherapy the strictly determined I-It relation gradually recedes as the potentiality arises for the broader freedom of an I-Thou relation. The encompassing system of Freud, con-

11. Harry Stack Sullivan, *Conceptions of Modern Psychiatry* (New York: Norton, 1953).

structed from the building stones of natural science, gives the therapist method and a valuable map of orientation. Throughout Freud's studies it remains clear, however, that man is a product not only of nature, but also of history. His developmental history implies a certain limited degree of freedom of choice that makes him less predictable than are other objects of scientific exploration.

The psychoanalyst's attention is largely directed toward the past of his patient: How has this person arrived at the present stage of his existence? What causes and effects have built up his symptomatology and his character structure? In the neurotic development, and to an even greater extent in the psychotic development, there are stagnations in the free interchange between the person and his world. Because problems of the past remain unsolved, repetitive agitation appears whenever the danger signal of anxiety indicates that the area of conflict is close again. The patient's recurrent withdrawal from his world, or falsification of his world, has led to pseudorelations with others, and now leads to a pseudorelation with his therapist—a transference relation in which he sees the analyst primarily as a ghost of the past. He cannot yet meet the therapist as a present-day partner; he is inclined to handle him, to manipulate him, like a thing, a possession. Preserving for himself a status quo, the patient tries to make of the therapist an object to be bribed or exploited, used for protection or comfort, for the discharge of revenge or contempt. A patient once said to me, "You are the thing that has to get me well." In such transference maneuvers the therapist is not a Thou, related to an I, to the patient; he is not his real, alive partner, but an It, a thing, a means by which the patient tries to establish a pseudosecurity, to maintain certain defensive stagnations of his past development.

On the basis of his training the psychoanalyst is prepared to be open to his patient's self-revelation, first shedding, as far as possible, the restrictions which any kind of self-absorption imposes on interpersonal relations. But he needs constant vigilance, in order to be fully there, present to his patient—in order to understand him as a subject in his own right, without getting sidetracked by such egocentric aims as vicarious gratification, the achievement of a "success," the justification of his own existence, or the proof of his theories. Such aims interfere with a fully open attention to the patient and with the optimal objectivity of the therapist's understanding.

Not all that occurs between therapist and patient is transference and countertransference. Through the clouds of repetitive self-isolation and obscuring pseudoattachment break the rays of real mutual understanding. The psychoanalyst, as Freud points out, works like a sculptor who removes the layers of encrusting material to free the original Gestalt of the patient, as he can visualize it.[12] The analyst works patiently through layers of resistance, inspired by a vision of the patient as whole, open to the future, open to the world—and, to that extent, less predictable, more unique. This vision of the physician must not be the product of his biased imagination, his egocentric aspirations, for only his purified objectivity can slowly reach the patient's buried potentialities of trust. And this rediscovery of trust can become a turning point in the patient's development, mobilizing the forces of reintegration.

Such a turning point in psychoanalysis leads beyond transference experiences which—whether positively or negatively colored —repeat infantile dissociations, preserve an oppressive loneliness, and thereby delay a development that opens the patient up to his future and to his world. Trust is not merely an emotion; it is a response of the total personality. In adult life trust is experienced as choice, as decision, and as commitment. When a person is relatively free from overwhelming emotions or compulsive defenses, he feels able to give or withhold trust, according to his decision. He chooses those to whom he is close; he differentiates those whom he trusts from his adversaries and from those toward whom he is indifferent. Every human being has a yearning to enter into relations of trust that give free room to the I as well as to the Thou, according to the needs of both in a given situation. If a person has been forced to withdraw from relations of trust under the onslaught of frustrations, he suffers from loneliness, and forever longs

---

12. Sigmund Freud, "Zur Technik (Ueber Psychotherapie)" in *Gesammelte Schriften,* vol. 6 (Leipzig: Internationaler Psychoanalytischer Verlag, 1925), p. 15.

to return into a relation of trust. This indestructible yearning gives psychotherapy a chance. Manifestations of trust and loneliness reach far back into childhood, to the time when the child began to emerge from his original symbiosis with his mother and his separate existence began to dawn on him. In one of his Washington seminars Martin Buber spoke of the child who awakens at night, all alone in a dark room. All the horrors of the world beset him, unless he is able to remember that there is a mother in the next room, a mother who can be trusted, whose face does not lie. The world cannot be completely evil, if such a mother is living for him. If such an experience of trust were completely missing, the child could see his world only as a dangerous jungle, where everybody is at everybody else's throat.[13]

Thus trust is in dialectic opposition to the horrors of loneliness. The child who has been excluded—for external or internal reasons —from the "dual mode of existence,"[14] from the I-Thou relation with his mother, the child who is lonely and cannot trust, is endangered in his survival—as René Spitz has demonstrated in his work on anaclytic depression.[15] During the last year of her life Frieda Fromm-Reichmann worked on a study of loneliness[16] as a basic feature in the psychopathology of schizophrenia that can be traced back to the breakdown of trust in early interpersonal relations. Ungratified physiological needs such as hunger, thirst, pain, and frustrated sexual desire are distressing—the frustration is subjectively experienced as a partial annihilation—but the distress is lessened by interpersonal relations which promise alleviation of tension; delay of fulfillment can be endured if there is hope and faith. But beliefs and hopes may represent illusions that comfort the frustrated narcissism of a lonely person, left to his own devices. And no amount of mechanical gratification of his isolated needs can substitute for the overall sense of confirmed existence which

13. Melanie Klein calls this potentiality "paranoid position." See Klein, *Envy and Gratitude.*

14. Binswanger, *Grundformen und Erkenntnis menschlichen Daseins.*

15. René Spitz and Katherine M. Wolf, "Anaclytic Depression," in *Psychoanalytic Study of the Child,* vol. 2 (New York: International Universities Press, 1946), pp. 313–42.

16. Frieda Fromm-Reichmann, "Loneliness," *Psychiatry* 22 (1959): 1–15.

arises from a trusting relation and makes the child—and later the adult—at home in a world that surrounds being with the horrors of nonbeing.

Psychoanalytic literature has seldom dealt with the fear of death and annihilation which characteristically torments the imagination of one who is caught in the horror of loneliness. In his essay, "The 'Uncanny,'" Freud gives a description of the dread and anguish of loneliness.[17] In German, the uncanny—*das Unheimliche*—refers literally to the loss of home. The uncanny sense of having lost one's home goes with feelings of emptiness, alienation, depersonalization, doubt about being alive or dead. Freud interprets the yearning for home in the emotion of uncanniness as an incestuous desire to return to the maternal womb. This regressive trend indicates that the person has failed to make the world of the living his home, to find his gratification here and now. If hope—the trust in the rebirth or renewal of maturing relations—has been smothered, and the person returns to the absolute, deadening security of infantile dependency in which the tensions of growth are abolished, his survival is threatened.

Freud's description of this clinging to a deadening security reflects the specific anxiety that Erwin Straus[18] has described as the disgust at decay which pervades the symptomatology of obsessions. Any sign of decay, illness, germs, dirt, excrement, or expression of hostility and destructiveness elicits the anxiety about ego integrity, the uncanny estrangement from the self, and the threat of ultimate annihilation or nonbeing. The mortified narcissism protests against the helpless, powerless state of nonbeing with illusions of grandeur and self-deification. But such illusions are weak compensations, and in the long run they leave the person mercilessly exposed to the despair of loneliness.

Von Witzleben has distinguished between secondary loneliness

---

17. Sigmund Freud, "The 'Uncanny'," in *The Complete Psychological Works of Sigmund Freud*, vol. 17 (London: Hogarth, 1955), pp. 217–56. Anna Freud, in her lecture at the 1953 International Meetings in London, described sensations of essential loneliness in children under the heading of "losing and being lost."

18. Erwin Straus, *On Obsession* (New York: Nervous and Mental Disease Monographs, no. 73, 1948).

caused by the loss of a love object and primary loneliness, the loneliness of the self which is inborn in everyone—the feeling of being alone and helpless in this world. Both experiences of loneliness put the person to a test of endurance.[19]

In the labor of mourning after the loss of a love object, as Freud, Abraham, Melanie Klein,[20] and others have described it, the forsaken person transiently loses his self-esteem and affirmation of life, because the protest against the loss mobilizes unconscious hatred and resentment toward the departed love object. There is no love relation so free of ambivalence that this protest, stemming from possessiveness, is completely missing. Since the bereaved person is still dependent on the love object, even idealizes the image of the departed, he has to turn whatever hatred and resentment there is against himself. This self-hatred threatens the integration of the ego as long as the protest rages against the loss, but the labor of mourning is also a labor of repentance, which widens the boundaries of the ego. The reintegration of the ego, the return of self-confidence, depends on the acceptance of the loss. The self-esteem of the manic-depressive patient is so vulnerable that a painful loss of support cannot be tolerated: in the depression the protest continues to rage; in the manic phase the loss is denied by a flight from the dependency. In the labor of mourning the healthy person's less vulnerable narcissism permits a reintegration on a broader basis, embracing the inevitable pain of frustration and loss without the unrealistic defenses of protest and denial. When the protesting fight against the loss recedes, the ego of the survivor has gained a deeper endurance of painful reality, and his life is enriched by the continuing influence of the departed friend and by the serenity that flows from fortitude in suffering.[21]

Primary or existential loneliness is seldom fully experienced,

19. Henry D. von Witzleben, "On Loneliness," Psychiatry 21 (1958): 37–43.
20. Sigmund Freud, "Mourning and Melancholia," in *Complete Psychological Works,* vol. 14 (London: Hogarth, 1957) pp. 243–59; Karl Abraham, "A Short Study of the Development of the Libido," in *Selected Papers on Psychoanalysis* (New York: Basic Books, 1953), pp. 418–501; Klein, *Envy and Gratitude.*
21. Karl Jaspers, *Philosophie,* vol. 2 (Berlin: Springer, 1932), pp. 221 ff.

since the interdependencies of daily life protect one from recognizing it. Some indication of what such loneliness would be without this protection is provided by experiments by Heron, Bexton, and Hebb at McGill University, and by Lilly at the National Institute of Mental Health.[22] They have produced experimental situations of isolation by reducing external sensory stimuli, thus cutting off the subjects from the ordinary exchange of daily living to a high degree. Such experiments put the subject's integrative powers to a test. After some days of total isolation, the secondary process of reality-oriented thinking is sometimes replaced by the primary process of forming fantastic dreams, hallucinations, and delusions. Lilly has compared these experiences with the autobiographical reports of shipwrecked persons and lonely travelers in polar regions. In one of these reports, hallucinations both of the Savior and of a destroyer indicated the struggle between the wish to live and the wish to die. Some of these reports also show that when a person returns from loneliness to his fellow men he may hesitate to communicate his experience, lest his words betray insanity.

But the regression to the primary process may prove to be a "regression in the service of the ego,"[23] opening deeper resources to the reintegration of the person. Lilly writes, "Most survivors report after several weeks' exposure to isolation a new inner security and a new integration of themselves on a deep and basic level."[24] This new inner security is the experience of trust. By hallucinations and delusions the isolated person seeks to escape from an unbearable present reality. But the hope for survival arising in this predicament allows him to transcend the despair. In this hope and trust the ego can reach a higher level of integration, in which it no longer protests or denies the frustrations of present

22. Woodburn Heron, W. H. Bexton, and Donald O. Hebb, "Cognitive Effects of a Decreased Variation in the Sensory Environment," *American Psychologist* 8 (1953): 366 (abstract); John C. Lilly, "Mental Effects of Reduction of Ordinary Levels of Physical Stimuli on Intact, Healthy Persons," *Psychiatric Research Reports* (American Psychiatric Association, 1956, no. 5), pp. 1–9.

23. Ernst Kris, *Psychoanalytic Explorations in Art* (New York: International Universities Press, 1952).

24. Lilly, p. 4.

loneliness, but is able to endure them for the sake of future salvation. A broader integration might even transcend the horizon of individual existence by the oceanic feeling of being one with the universe. In the practice of meditation the ego seeks such widening of horizons and fortification of its stability by voluntary solitude.

Frieda Fromm-Reichmann, in her posthumous paper "On Loneliness,"[25] has pointed out that every creative activity sets the individual apart from his fellow men and exposes him to the torments of loneliness. When he can, by his labors, keep the sources of his creativity flowing, his self-confidence is maintained even though he may be kept waiting for the recognition of his fellow men. Poetry often gives expression to the suffering of loneliness, the yearning for the healing power of trust, and the temporary transcendence of loneliness in the creative process.

The existentialists, from Kierkegaard to Sartre and Heidegger talk about the horrors of nothingness, of not-being.[26] Sartre and Heidegger appeal to the lonely individual who is "thrown into existence," lost in a mass society, to face bravely his fundamentally lonely, unique, and finite existence; to face death, the awareness of which is so often covered with layers of repression and denial. They and the other existence philosophers appeal to modern man to rise out of the indefiniteness and impersonality of *man. Man* is the impersonal pronoun in German meaning everybody and anybody—a word which, as it is used by the existentialists, implies something similar to Riesman's description of the "other-directed" modern man.[27] The existentialists appeal to the individual who, by processes of mass adaptation, has become leveled to a common denominator of mediocrity, to rise to the authenticity and uniqueness of his "being-in-the-world," to choose to be himself, to take upon himself the freedom and the responsibility of his own deci-

25. Fromm-Reichmann, "Loneliness."

26. Sören Kierkegaard, *The Journals,* ed. and trans. Alexander Dru (New York: Oxford University Press, 1938); Jean-Paul Sartre, *L'Etre et le néant* (Paris: Librarie Gallimard, 1948); Martin Heidegger, *Sein und Zeit* (Halle a.d.S.: Niemeyer, 1935).

27. David Riesman, *The Lonely Crowd* (New Haven: Yale University Press, 1950).

sions, even though they may have tragic consequences. Man's "care" (Heidegger uses the German term *Sorge,* translated by Tillich as "ultimate concern")[28] works out man's destiny within the frame of his limited freedom. By enlarging the awareness of his intentions, man transcends, ever again, the meaninglessness and the powerlessness of his lonely existence. He frees himself from the shackles of a protesting and defensive narcissism; he accepts the limitations of his finite existence and broadens his being-in-the-world to a being-with and caring-for others.

In response to this heroic appeal by the existence-philosophers, psychotherapists may ask: Can a person work out his salvation from the horrors of loneliness all by himself? Many a person who is well integrated in his world is not aware of the problem of loneliness. He is carried by a trust in himself and his world that scarcely reaches the level of consciousness. But the person who is sensitized by constitutional or environmental failures may reach out for help. Martin Buber, like Harry Stack Sullivan,[29] responds to the problem of human loneliness by pointing to the essential relatedness of human beings, which enables them to make their world their home. But this fundamental propensity of man to relate as an I to a Thou, this relation of trust, is constantly endangered by man's dread of loneliness, his fear of risking the tragic in human existence, and his automatic defenses against this threat. But the value of life is enhanced by the risk of its loss for those who trust strongly enough to bridge the abyss of nothingness; and the rediscovery of trust is frequently gained only by wrestling with the anguish of loneliness.

To sum up, the psychoanalyst cannot treat the trust of the therapeutic relation—as it gradually emerges—only as a secondary phenomenon, as a product of sublimation of instincts. The relation of trust, the genuine I-Thou relation, is a primary fact of existence, concerning the individual in his wholeness. The wholeness of being is surrounded by the threats of nonbeing. Frustration of vital needs opens the abyss of despair, the void of nothingness. But the

28. Paul Tillich, *The Courage to Be* (New Haven: Yale University Press, 1952).
29. Buber, *I and Thou;* Sullivan, *The Interpersonal Theory of Psychiatry.*

endurance of frustration, the synthetic ego-strength that bridges the present emptiness with the hope and vision of future fulfillment, grows out of the human ability to find and to maintain relations of trust.

If this ability to trust remains underdeveloped, or if it breaks down under the adversities of fate, the person's life is flooded by disorganizing anxieties. Out of the need for defense against these anxieties—against the horrors of loneliness—his relations to his world freeze into I-It relations. He tries not only to master the material world, but also—compulsively—to manage his interpersonal relations in the service of narcissistic compensations for his loneliness. But neither the highest managerial success nor the approximation to ideals of solitary perfection can gratify the need for interpersonal trust, for the creative process of mutual understanding, which redeems the individual from the rigidities of defense and the anguish of loneliness. Since trust is a basic human need, it can be rediscovered. It opens the way to new alternatives in the process of integration; it turns subjective experience from the despair of nonbeing to the hope of being, to the willingness to accept the limited freedom and responsibility of the individual's unique, authentic existence, his self-realization.

The Goal of Creativity in Psychotherapy

Psychotherapy is, like other therapies, a creative art which applies the findings of biological, psychological and sociological science to reach the goal of mental health. This goal depends on the subjective values and philosophies of patient and therapist. They may or may not arrive at a consensus about these goals, and an outspoken discrepancy of overt or covert goals will, of necessity, hamper a succesful collaboration.

Thomas Szasz has written a book on the *Myth of Mental Illness*.[1] However, we could also talk about the "Myth of Mental Health" as a goal of psychotherapy, since not only the psychotic and the neurotic patient, but also every human being is liable at times to fail, to some degree, in reaching his goals of satisfaction and security in collaboration with his human and nonhuman evironment. Where is the human being who reaches full maturity and mastery of his fate, who in all contingencies rises, with ever renewed force, to reassemble a creative synthesis of his unique identity in harmony with his environment, actualizing the optimal potentialities of his growth and development? And usually when he grossly fails in this attempt, the label of a psychopathological diagnosis is fastened on him. Such a diagnosis is different from the diagnosis of pneumonia or appendicitis. In an organic illness the total personality need not be disturbed, nor the patient's interpersonal relations. Burdened with an organic illness, the patient feels entitled

This article originally appeared as two separate papers, in *The American Journal of Psychoanalysis* (ed. Harold Kelman, M.D.) 24, no. 1: 1–10; and in *New Perspectives in Psychoanalysis* (New York: Grune and Stratton), pp. 267–81. Reprinted by permission.

1. New York: Hoeber-Harper, 1961.

to receive treatment and support from his fellowmen. The mental patient also often reaches out for help, but he is frequently insecure about his claim. He may feel that his integrity is being attacked by his community on which he depends or against which he rebels. He may feel accused as a nonconformist with a more or less disturbed conscience. His guilt feelings may increase the opposition and resentment of the family, the more fiercely the more unstable the family is. When the patient in this struggle loses faith in the potentialities of reconciliation, of reintegration in the groups in which he has sought his security and belonging, he often turns to the psychotherapist, with exalted hopes or with doubt and distrust, leaning on his prestige and authority as a physician and mediator between himself and his community. The aim of perfect mental health, of undisturbed harmony between the patient and his community frequently remains a myth, an unreachable utopia. Yet the psychotherapist can often help the patient to reach a tolerable compromise. To be committed to an absolute ideal of mental or interpersonal harmony can make both therapist and patient ungrateful to the reasonable compromise solutions that can be worked out in the rehabilitation of the patient.

Dr. Rado and Dr. Goldman have distinguished between reconstructive and reparative psychotherapy.[2] Reconstructive therapy or psychoanalysis implies a complete reorientation of the total personality; it is indispensable for optimal training in psychotherapy. The patient who consciously as well as unconsciously accepts the goal of creative reconstruction must not only be willing, but also able to face, all the unconscious anxieties from which each human being automatically recoils. He needs the courage and the flexibility to relax and regress, to let go of his habitual defenses. Kris has called this regression, which is the pre-condition of all creativity, "a regression in the service of the ego."[3] It represents a *reculer pour mieux sauter* (to recede in order to take a higher jump). In reconstructive therapy the patient must ultimately be

2. Sandor Rado and George E. Daniels, *Changing Concepts of Psychoanalytic Medicine* (New York: Grune and Stratton, 1956), pp. 15–30, 89–100, 101–13.

3. Ernst Kris, *Psychoanalytic Explorations in Art* (New York: International University Press, 1952).

abandoned to his own sense of responsibility. There is increasing detachment in the sympathetic attachment of the doctor to the patient; thus the patient feels supported but sufficiently on his own so that he can express even the most contrary, hostile, bitter, disdainful emotions which would destroy all relationships other than a therapeutic one. The creativeness of the psychoanalytic process is tested when all the masks of hypocrisy and accommodating conformity can be dropped. When infantile guilt feelings can be replaced by a true sense of responsibility, then new horizons of understanding and alternative decisions are opened up. The psychoanalyst must be a truly sympathetic listener, tuned in with the most personal, unique needs of the patient, so that he can support the patient through the revelation of the darkest suspicions about others and himself, and through the self-accusations of cowardice and despair which threaten the patient's identity. The therapist must have a creative understanding that sees the light behind the shadows, the saving grace in the desolation and forlorness of human nature, so that the patient can give up the defenses of hypocritical obedience and conformity and regain the authenticity of being true to himself.

Creative reconstruction is characterized by a reevaluation of values. Success does not depend only on the skills and efforts of the therapist, but also on the stamina of the patient, since all change in values arouses deep anxieties in human beings. A patient may only seek support in a transient crisis and not want to get through an anxiety-arousing upheaval. Other patients—either constitutionally or because of early traumatic experiences—may be so deeply damaged that they cannot afford a change in their precariously maintained equilibrium. The psychoanalyst must be able to respect the limits of his art when a patient can, at best, only tolerate a compromise between his inner needs and external reality.

Every patient lives in a reality of his own; there is no standard reality for all. The analyst must enter into the patient's reality with him. In times of political upheaval, the psychotherapeutic goals change rapidly due to external pressures. I experienced drastic examples of such pressures when I worked with private patients during the beginning of the Nazi regime in Berlin. In the course of a morning, I saw a patient who pondered whether he should join the party to save his career and his family. He was followed by a Jewish student who was struggling against great odds to prepare himself for agricultural work and immigration to Israel. The next patient was a social worker who tried to abreact the shock of abuse and humiliation by stormtroopers. She was followed by a communist who doubted whether he could trust me enough to reveal, via his free associations, plans of revolt and destruction which might be incompatible with the neutrality of an analyst.

At that time, I wondered how we could possibly work towards the goals of mental health in an insane society shaken by an upheaval of traditional values. However, as Redlich and Hollingshead have demonstrated, in a relatively stable society, the needs of patients often are at variance in different classes and under different economic conditions.[4] Classical analysis which avoids all parameters may be of insufficient help to a patient who is involved in an unmanageable external situation, for example, a patient who must return from a protective hospital to an emotionally impoverished or unbearably hostile home. The therapist may have to step out of the one-to-one relation and engage in marital therapy or other forms of group therapy to expose a fuller view into the complexities of the patient's maladaptation. Additional management through drug, sleep, or shock therapy may become advisable. Winnicot and Guntrip have indicated that the psychoanalyst must find in each given situation the optimal equilibrium between mothering management and interpretive confrontation.[5]

Reparative psychotherapy that is adapted to a variety of needs in the patient demands a high skill and greater flexibility on the part of the therapist than traditional psychoanalysis. The boundaries between reparative and reconstructive therapy are fluid. What started as reparative therapy may turn into reconstructive

4. E. Redlich and A. B. Hollingshead, *Social Class and Mental Illness* (New York: John Wiley, 1958).

5. D. W. Winnicott, *Collected Papers, Through Pediatrics to Psychoanalysis* (New York: Basic Books, 1953); Harry Guntrip, *Personality Structure and Human Interaction* (London: Hogarth, 1961).

therapy and vice versa. At present, reconstructive therapy or classical psychoanalysis seems to have a higher prestige value than the reparative form of psychotherapy. Freud spoke of "mixing the pure gold of psychoanalysis with the copper of direct suggestion in the future application of our therapy to the masses."[6] But the psychoanalyst may be entrenched in unyielding theories and his need to verify his philosophy may outweigh his ability to adapt to the needs of the patient. Not every analyst is as flexible as Freud; he referred to his theories as a "scaffolding" adaptable to ever-broadening experience.[7] He even called his instinct theory a mythology.[8] The controversies inside and outside the psychoanalytic association bear witness to how difficult it is for all of us to reconcile the need for interpersonal professional solidarity of a shared theoretical orientation, with the need to create individual improvisations in the art of psychotherapy.

It is not enough that the psychotherapist scrutinize his countertransference; he tries to remain aware of his philosophical foundation. He cannot be free from value judgments. In describing the goals of psychotherapy we have to take into consideration the philosophic orientations of the psychotherapists. Freud was a philosopher in spite of himself. He took it for granted that the empirical scientist was philosophically disinterested, as he assumed that he could be neutral to value systems, quoting Th. Visher a German novelist, "Das Moralische versteht sich von selbst" (morality can be taken for granted). Edmund Husserl, a philosopher and contemporary of Freud, suggested in his phenomenology to the scientists that they step back at times from their hypotheses and theories and have a fresh look at the phenomenon they are working at.

Dr. Rado has done just that. He set some of the psychoanalytic hypotheses and theories temporarily aside in order to have a fresh

6. Sigmund Freud, "Wege der Psychoanalytischen Therapie," in *Gesammelte Schriften*, vol. 6 (Leipzig: Internationaler Psychoanalytischer Verlag, 1925), p. 146.

7. Rado and Daniels, p. 18.

8. Sigmund Freud, "Neue Folge der Vorlesungen zur Einführung in die Psychoanalyse," in *Gesammelte Schriften*, 6:249.

look at human emotions and thought processes, and integrations of both, which present themselves as phenomena to inspection and introspection, while instincts or drives, the conceptual building stones of Freud's impressive system, do not lend themselves to direct inspection or introspection. Rado's adaptational psychotherapy has described the phenomenon of psychotherapy as a process of emotional reeducation. In this process the patient accepts the therapist transiently as a parent substitute. As far as he feels unable in a rational way to transform the frustrations of his present situation, he gives vent to his emotions, which impatiently and impulsively crave for magic transformation of the present situation. Since the therapist in the patient's eyes is endowed with the power and prestige of science and medicine, the patient aims at magic transformation though submission to or rebellion against what Rado calls the parentified authority of the therapist. As long as the patient harbors hopeful illusions, he is docile and willing to learn; when he gets discouraged, he is inclined to make the analyst the scapegoat of his frustrated rage. It is the goal of the psychoanalyst to make himself gradually dispensable, as it is the goal of every responsible parent to make his guidance increasingly superfluous so that his growing child learns to work out his own destiny on a self-reliant and aspiring level. In classic psychoanalysis, the therapeutic goal has been formulated as a surmounting of the resistance of transference and countertransference and the acceptance of the directions of the reality principle instead of the passive surrender to the pleasure-pain principle. Transference and countertransference, the repetitive patterns of infantile relations to authority, only interfere with the maturing process as far as self-protective goals are blindly pursued without full consideration of the needs of either the I or the you in the collaborative effort to work out alternative adaptations to reality between doctor and patient. Decisions of these conflicts in psychoanalysis cannot be found by the authoritarian supremacy of the physician, but have to be worked out in the mutuality of respect of both analyst and analysand. There is a danger that the analyst may become a haven of pseudosecurity for the patient through the prestige attributed to the therapist by the infantile needs of the patient.

I would like to illustrate an attempt at reparative psychotherapy which was too short-lived to reach the depth of authentic reconstruction of a deeply damaged personality. We sometimes learn more from a failure than from a success. This treatment experience was more than twenty years ago, yet it stands out in my memory because of what I learned from it. In this case the limitations to therapy lay not only in adverse external circumstances but also in an unfortunate emotional development.

In a hospital setting I treated a thirty-five-year-old German refugee woman who was married to a Russian-Jewish scientist. She was diagnosed as schizophrenic; her main symptom was a destructive rage that made around-the-clock special nursing care necessary. The patient had married shortly before their immigration. She could not have children; her husband was absorbed in scientific research, had become unreachable in his egocentricity, and the patient had lost her devotion to him. They were worlds apart in temperament and interests, and this alienation interfered with the primarily good sexual adjustment. Without goal and direction and having to adapt to a new country, she was overwhelmed by a sense of futility and despair. She had come from a home impoverished in emotions. She did not know her father who had divorced her mother in her infancy. The stepfather was cold and aloof. The mother, conventional and sentimental, was unable to tame her only child's temper tantrums. As a child the patient adopted a veneer of good manners, but in adolescence she broke away from the cold conventionality of her home. In spite of good intelligence, charm and good looks, she was not able to commit herself to extended professional training. A largely negative identity—not to be like her conventional mother—led her into a bohemian milieu where she drifted from one love affair into another, mostly with narcissistic intellectuals for whom she developed a kind of sentimental hero worship. Through identifying with the man's ideals she found sexual gratifications, and her rich gift of empathy permitted vicarious satisfactions in the man's intellectual interests; she was inclined to establish a mimetic type of identification with her lover, but she was unable to commit herself to a relation of mutuality. Whenever she fell out of love, she experienced a loss of identity and a crisis of frustration and rage which brought her to the verge of disintegration. However, the crisis would pass when she fell in love again and identification with a new lover gave her weak ego a new identity. Under the pressures of the political situation, she rather hastily married a man who had been a relative stranger to her. In her middle thirties, facing the challenges of adaptation to a new country and to a man unable to show real understanding, she was thrown into despair by the aimlessness of her existence. She acted out her rage without squarely facing her despair. Her guilt feelings sounded unconvincing; they were the borrowed guilt feelings of a heteronomous authoritarian morality against which she rebelled. In her agitated depression accompanied by hallucinations and delusions, she would have acted out her impulses in a frenzy of assaultiveness and self-destruction had she not been prevented by hospital precautions. In daily interviews the picture changed dramatically; the patient became calm, reasonable, friendly, cooperative. There were no more assaults or fits of self-destruction, no more hallucinations and delusions, but her improvement was not trustworthy. Her rage was only tranquilized. The patient felt supported by my empathy and had fallen in love again. This love for me furnished her with an escape into a borrowed identity, and it soothed her frustration and despair. Her attachment was that of a suffocating dependency; she was improving for my sake. She voiced good intentions of being reconciled with her husband, to endure the inevitable limitations in this relationship, and to work out a better adjustment. The treatment lasted only three to four months and, during my absence, the patient was discharged to her home town on the basis of her spectacular improvement. She was not able to establish a similar attachment to the therapist to whom I referred her, and when the identification with me and the adoption of my goals wore off, she killed herself by throwing herself out of the window. The fact that I had suspected the possibility of such a tragic outcome did not offer any consolation to my distress about it. I had become intimidated by empathizing with the violent rage reactions of the patient, and I learned from this distressing experience that empathy is not enough. My empathy had lured the patient into a soothing positive identification which could not give her sufficient opportunity to work through the rage reactions and overcome her low self-esteem based on a negative identification with the parental authority. My empathy had not been able to convey to the patient a vision of a fuller integration of her potentialities. She had repressed her rage reactions for the sake of her positive identification with me which promised peace and harmony. When this soothing identification wore off, the frustration rage broke through with mortal force. I had not succeeded in strengthening her endurance of frustrations or her ability to visualize the creative goal of a self-actualization by which she could establish an authentic identity and meaningful interpersonal relations. The persisting infantile dependency and defensive identification were the main obstacles in the patient's creative maturing process.

This patient's ego weakness was based on emotional deprivation in early childhood. Though she had reached the level of orgastic genital maturity, emotionally she remained an insecure, impotently rebellious child. She suffered from so great an emotional starvation (which David Levy called "primary affect hunger") that she was willing to sell body and soul for any token of love and security. She fell in love with extremely self-centered male partners so that she was exposed repeatedly to a frustration rage that assumed increasingly destructive proportions. She aimed at magic transformation in psychotherapy and accepted me only as a parental authority. As long as she could harbor hopeful illusions of being passively saved, she was docile and ready to identify with me in a symbiotic surrender that left no room for the development of her own authentic identity. When she felt deserted, she was overwhelmed with frustration rage. Her low self-esteem did not permit a relation of mutuality which would have given her the courage to endure the inevitable frustration of loneliness and self-reliance, and so she yielded completely to despair.

It must be the goal of the psychoanalyst to make himself gradually dispensable just as the goal of every responsible parent is to make himself increasingly superfluous so that his growing child may learn to work out his own destiny on a self-reliant and aspiring level. The creative goal of psychotherapeutic reconstruction demands a long-term dedication so that the symbiotic tendencies of transference and countertransference can be truly outgrown. Transferences are fostered by empathic, symbiotic identifications with authority. Defenses against the existential anxiety of loneliness represent a harbor of pseudosecurity for the patient while he leans on the therapist's presence to satisfy his infantile dependency needs. Only the full relation of the I of the patient and the Thou of the therapist, within the social limitations of the therapeutic situation, permits a maturing process of creative collaboration in which existential anxiety and frustration rage can be fully faced, constructive alternative solutions to present-day conflicts can be found, and the risks and challenges of the uncertain future can be accepted with the enduring courage of self-reliant and aspiring hope and trust.

I have attempted to illustrate by my example the limitations we face when we strive for the goal of creativity. These disappointments can become discouraging for the psychotherapist and he must find in his own philosophy the solidity of endurance which will enable him to accept the frustrations of his daily work. His philosophy may, in more fortunate situations, awaken the resonance of mutual understanding and carry the patient to the goal of creative reconstruction, but the psychotherapist cannot force his own philosophy on the patient.

In trying to clarify the goals of creativity in psychotherapy an orientation in the psychotherapist's philosophy and value systems seems indispensable. The Swiss psychiatrist Ludwig Binswanger, a lifelong friend of Freud, introduced into psychotherapy the phenomenological viewpoint and, later, the *Daseinsanalyse* orientation.[9] Another Swiss psychiatrist, Medard Boss, has further developed the influence of modern philosophy on psychotherapy.[10] Karl Jaspers began as a psychiatrist and became an existential phi-

9. Ludwig Binswanger, "Grundformer und Erkenntnis menschlichen Daseins," in *Basic Forms and Understanding of Human Existence* (Zurich: Niehans, 1953).
10. Medard Boss, *Psychoanalysis and Daseinsanalysis* (New York: Basic Books, 1962).

losopher, but remained rather inaccessible to psychoanalysis.[11] Martin Heidegger and Jean Paul Sartre have become interested in the development of psychoanalysis, and their ideas have penetrated European and American psychotherapy.[12] (They were introduced into American psychotherapy by Rollo May and his collaborators.) American psychotherapists have also become interested in Martin Buber and Max Scheler. All these philosophers show great differences in their approach but they have some trends in common: they all emphasize the intentionality of human behavior in contrast to a mere rational determinism. Intentionality is the precondition of creative reconstruction. The existential philosophers stress the integrative power of will, with a limited freedom to collect the diverse strands of motivations in ever new and unique creations of adaptation. The decisions of will, as far as they are spontaneous responses of the unique individual to a unique now and here situation, are unpredictable. The existential philosophers stress the historicity of the human being that rises above the plane of his biological existence into the awareness of his destiny.

Heidegger, like Dewey and Bergson, revolts against the rational world view of Descartes' *cogito ergo sum.* Heidegger agrees with Bergson that man is *homo faber* before he is *homo sapiens.* Man is thrown into a world with others beyond his willing; in handling, manipulating, understanding, organizing material, tools, opportunities, this world is his own—world and self, subject and object are inseparable. This is expressed in the hyphenated term "being-in-the-world." The psychoanalyst originally was inclined to study the development of the individual in the context of his most intimate relations. The later Freudian and neo-Freudian development of ego psychology has opened broader vistas for the study of the individual in the context of his total cultural environment. In psychopathology, the psychiatrist discovers a simultaneous transfor-

11. Karl Jaspers, "Existenzphilosophie," in *Existentialism from Dostoevsky to Sartre,* ed. Walter Kaufman (New York: Meridian Books, 1956).

12. Martin Heidegger, "Sein und Zeit," trans. John Macquarrie and Edward Robinson, in *Being and Time* (New York: Harper and Row, 1962); Jean Paul Sartre, *L'Etre et le Néant* (Paris: Gallimard, 1948).

mation of the ego and its world. In a depression, the ego and its world are shrunk, while in a manic mood-swing, the ego and its world are overextended; the ego and the world of the schizophrenic are uncannily transformed by alienation, and we find different ego and world transmutations in the hysterical and the obsessional patient.

American psychotherapy was influenced by Dewey's philosophy which conveyed the buoyancy of pragmatism and an assurance of making a better world by sheer force of common sense. American psychotherapy stresses the values of adaptation while the influence of European philosophy, guided by Heidegger's vision of being-in-the-world as a being-to-death, emphasizes the value of authenticity. Jaspers sees in death a "boundary situation" which elicits the basic human mood of dread since the vision of death confronts man with his irrevocable and unutterable loneliness: Man's enduring vision of death marks, as nothing else can, the integrity and independence of his life.

At the time of the First World War, Freud wrote a paper on war and death and described the helplessness of the unprepared, civilized man in the face of the catastrophe of war.[13] He concluded this paper with the advice: "Si vis vitam, para mortem" ("If you want life, prepare for death") in an analogy with the old proverb "Si vis pacem, para bellum" ("If you want peace, prepare for war"). Freud defined the basic human anxiety as separation anxiety, castration anxiety or superego anxiety, biologically determined by the pleasure-pain principle. Heidegger's influence has led psychotherapists to a more basic acknowledgement of anxiety or dread as it was defined by Kierkegaard. Heidegger sees man not as the victim of biological forces but as the active guardian of his existence. In being, he is concerned; he cares for his being. The dread of nonbeing is not only a biological anxiety; man may prefer death to the loss of what he loves, his values, his ideals, or he may survive like a vegetating nonentity when deprived of these goals of integration.

13. Sigmund Freud, *Thoughts for the Times of War and Death*, vol. 14, Standard Edition (London: Hogarth, 1957), p. 273.

The human child is dependent longer than any animal, and the adult, in times of stress and strain, falls back into the dependency of the child. He then loses sight of his far-reaching goal of happiness through love and work. Happiness through love and work which permits an enlightened hedonic control of behavior on the level of self-reliance and aspiration, has been well stated by Rado as being the creative goal of psychotherapy. But work may degenerate into drudgery or slave labor, and love can regress from the level of sympathetic mutuality to that of empathic defusion of ego boundaries and borrowed identity. Under the pressure of unbearable frustrations an overproduction of emergency emotions (fear, rage, guilty fear, and guilty rage) throws the organized behavior patterns of self-reliance and aspiration into the chaos of despair. Since frustrations are inevitable in human existence, it seems to me that an important goal of psychotherapy is to help the patient learn to endure frustration. This implies that he learns to understand and accept his destiny, his very own unique identity with its biological and social limitations. However, in the constant flux of change the analysand may easily become bewildered about his identity.

The topic of identity is taking on a growing role in modern psychoanalytic literature. This interest is reflected in the writings about psychoanalytic ego psychology. The individual is a goal-directed being. A patient who is overwhelmed by the meaninglessness of existence asks: "Who am I?" and "Where am I going?" Thomas French has demonstrated that man's intentions and goals for the future are important facts in the integration of his behavior.[14]

Insight into the past is important for the analysand in order to understand his destiny, how he has arrived at the present stage of his development. Freud's ingenious invention of the method of free association has opened up the past to introspection by the self and to participant observation by the analyst. In an atmosphere of sympathetic understanding the analysand becomes able to drop some of his traditional prejudices and defenses that have barred

14. Thomas French, *The Integration of Behavior*, vol. 3 (Chicago: University of Chicago Press, 1958).

memories, impulses, phantasies, and emotions from an awareness that can be reported and shared in communication. A broadened awareness mobilizes psychic energies that were bottled up and the analysand becomes able to arrive at new conflict solutions and decisions.

However, not all insights into the past lead to foresights and firm intentions that take up the challenge of the future with hope and confidence. At times, many an analysand complains: "I see the chains of cause and effect that have led me into the present impasse, but I still find it impossible to change." He cannot make the change from despair in the past to trust in the future. Freud has postulated that constitutional factors—for example, the untamable character of instincts—are responsible, in some patients, for the interminable state of their analyses. While not denying the importance of hereditary factors in the condition and prognosis of mental illness, it is doubtful that the instinctual endowment as such must make us pessimistic about the prognosis.

When we turn from the study of human behavior to that of animals, as has been done by modern ethology, we encounter a broader concept of instincts and their constructive role in adaptation. Ethology defines instincts as stable, though quite complex, innate behavior patterns that respond to internal and external stimuli in a form adequate to guarantee optimal possibilities of survival not only at the level of the individual but also at that of the species. The following example is taken from an observation by the ethologist, Adolf Portmann.[15] When in a pack of wolves a contest for supremacy breaks out, the battle is fought out until the superior strength of one wolf is established, but this fight does not lead to the destruction of the weaker rival. In a gesture of humility the vanquished wolf exposes his jugular vein to the teeth of the victor, but the victor does not bite. This instinctive behavior pattern guarantees the survival of the individual as well as the solidarity and hierarchy of the group.

Man seems to be in conflict between his trend toward individua-

15. Adolph Portmann, *Animals as Social Beings* (New York: Viking Press, 1961), p. 203.

tion and his need for solidarity with others. In human groups the motivation to eliminate a rival in the hierarchy is not left to an instinctive releaser automatism which dictates whether to kill or exercise mercy. Man uses foresight which mobilizes anxiety or guilt feelings, and he anticipates retaliation or punishment, which counteract and repress the murderous impulse from awareness. But the conflict between impulse and foresight continues undecided in the nonreporting parts of his brain (Freud's unconscious), threatening to return from exile and upset man's equilibrium by an outbreak of uncontrolled rage when his frustrated egocentric impulses overrun his need for group solidarity. Why is man's reasoning power so relatively weak in taming the frustrated impulses? In the introduction to Goethe's *Faust*, Mephistopheles, the devil, bemoans the fate of man before God the Lord: "Man would live a little better, had you not given him the shine of heaven's light. He calls it reason (*Vernunft*) and he uses it only to be more brutish than any brute." Man's instincts are as innocent and free of guilt as the animal's instincts, as long as the needs which guarantee his survival are not frustrated. But man's capacity of foresight, his gift of imagination which anticipates the consequences of his behavior and actions, frequently lead him to overreactions in response to the danger signal of fear or anxiety. The human being is the only animal that is aware of his destiny to die, though he does not keep this knowledge in the focus of his awareness. Yet, in his imagination he may die a thousand deaths, and when this foresight triggers off unmanageable fears, his adaptational behavior may be thrown out of kilter.

Selye and others have described the physiological responses of the human organism to the danger signal of fear.[16] Under stress, man's preparedness for fight or flight mobilizes a whole array of primitive weapons of defense: acceleration of respiration and circulation, evacuation of intestines and bladder, increase of blood sugar and clotting. Man is not as well endowed for flight and fight as many animals; his diencephalic physiology has equipped him rather poorly in his precultural condition to encounter danger.

16. Hans Selye, *The Stress of Life* (New York: McGraw-Hill, 1956).

However, in the course of cultural development man no longer relies mainly on his muscle strength, but on the vast defense systems of civilization that the human cortex has invented and developed. The paleontologist, Père Teilhard de Chardin, has described the trend of evolution as that of integration of ever-increasing complexities.[17] The reliance on these defense systems enriches the potentialities of adaptation but they have become immensely complicated. Dr. Simeons, a British internist who has studied psychosomatic diseases, has described in a book entitled *Man's Presumptuous Brain* the discrepancies between the diencephalic preparedness for danger and the cortical overreactions to the precariousness of human existence which have built up elaborate technical devices of security.[18] These devices can become unmanageable when the organism is flooded by primitive emotions. Men under continuous stress and strain may become victims of psychosomatic ailments. The awareness of danger does not always work to the advantage of man's survival. The drowning man sometimes can be more effectively saved when he is knocked unconscious and no longer fights frantically and inappropriately for his survival. The experience of mortal danger may leave the overreacting individual with a sense of helplessness in the throes of a traumatic neurosis, but it may kindle in others the elation of triumph and renew the zest for living.

Kardiner has described how, in a traumatic neurosis, the ego and its world have changed: the ego has lost the confidence in organization and mastery; its world has become permanently changed into a more dangerous place.[19] Bettelheim's experiences in Nazi concentration camps and Lifton's analysis of brain washing in China in *Thought Reform and the Psychology of Totalism* have demonstrated that there are limits to human endurance of pain and continuous threat to survival under circumstances of depriva-

17. Père Teilhard de Chardin, *The Phenomenon of Man* (New York: Harper Torch Books, 1961).

18. A. T. W. Simeons, *Man's Presumptuous Brain* (New York: Dutton, 1961).

19. A. Kardiner, *The Traumatic Neuroses of War* (New York: Hoeber-Harper, 1941).

tion and isolation.[20] The sturdiest individual may lose his sense of identity and the dignity of personal self-esteem and, therewith, the ability of creative adaptation when, under extreme pressures, he has to submit to physical and mental cruelties. Those individuals who have some prevailing interest, some hope or trust in the future, some goals to which they can remain committed despite frustration, have the best chances to survive and maintain their integrity. Such maintenance of goals provides the optimal strength of defenses as well as a flexibility of adaptation, but overwhelming force and violence of attack on human integrity sets limits to the most stoical endurance. Lilly and others have described various degrees of ego disorganization in states of isolation and sensory deprivation.[21] It seems to me that the disintegrating effect of boredom, monotony, loss of aim and purpose, are important factors in these experiments.

I want to return to the influence of existential philosophy on the goals of creativity in psychotherapy. In Heidegger's terms, the call of conscience is more than the incorporated parental authority —it is man's anticipation of his own possibilities. Man is an historical being, he tries to understand the past and to project his destiny into the future. He grasps the contingencies of his present situation as a challenge to his own power of becoming what he *may* be rather than what he *must* be. This is his limited freedom as well as the source of psychopathology. This basic concern of becoming an authentic self—"To thine own self be true"—is frequently in conflict with values of adaptation which may foster a nonauthentic duplicity not only in the region of psychopathology. The defeat of adaptation frequently occurs in very richly endowed personalities and many so-called normal individuals may lose their authenticity in the struggle for survival. The concern for man's total integration and authenticity is at the mercy of his moods and

20. Bruno Bettelheim, *The Informed Heart* (Illinois: Free Press of Glencoe, 1960); Robert Lifton, *Thought Reform and the Psychology of Totalism, A Study of Brain Washing in China* (New York: Norton, 1961).

21. John C. Lilly, *Mental Effects of Reduction of Ordinary Levels of Physical Stimuli on Intact, Healthy Persons* (American Psychiatric Association, 1956, no. 5), pp. 1–9.

passions of the moment: drowned in forgetfulness, it gets lost and dissipated in self-alienation, lost in the thousand little cares of everyday living, in trivialities, in the restlessness of being busy, distracted by meaningless pleasures, by trading in empty curiosity and gossip or vegetating in boredom. Through self-alienation the human being becomes the other-directed person of Riesman in the indifferent, anonymous crowd that Heidegger calls *man* (the German impersonal pronoun for everybody or anybody), playing the role that society expects him to play, more being lived than living.

Heidegger's concern is not a psychological but an ontological concern. He does not talk about individual man, but about *Dasein*, "being-there," a clearing in the chaos of human experience through the intuitive grasp of being-in-the-world, being with others, caring for one's Dasein and that of others. Heidegger bridges the gap between subjective, emotional experience and objective, mathematical-physical constructs. Other existentialists, such as Jaspers and Sartre who are more interested in individual psychology, relapse into subjectivism. Jaspers professes a philosophical faith in encompassing Being. Sartre expresses a defiant solipsism when he says: "Man is the being who wants to be God, but the idea of God is contradictory and therefore man is a useless passion."[22] Nietzsche's idea of the Superman and his all-encompassing will to power is dictated by a similar defiant individualism. In its extreme forms this overreaching passion may result in the creative achievements of a genius or the chaos of a psychosis.

The psychotherapist who traces the patient's development back to childhood in order to understand the unique destiny of the individual is necessarily guided by a sense of value, the pragmatist's value of adaptation and the existentialist's value of authenticity. The creative integration of both values can only be approximated in a state of maturity, when the individual has acquired the skills, the knowledge and the mastery necessary for optimal survival among equals. The helpless child still depends on the authority of the superior adults; he is directed by ideals and guilt feelings borrowed by empathy, as long as his survival depends on parental

22. Jaspers, p. 417. See also n. 12 above.

gratifications and protection. Parental care can be crippled by excessive anxieties which the child adopts by empathy. Excessive parental anxieties may lead to a misuse of parental authority through punitive domination, exploitation, neglect or overindulgence, thus hampering the maturing process in the child. Punitive domination, neglect, and exploitation tend to produce frustration rage and envy as well as persecutory anxieties in the child, while parental overindulgence fosters self-inflation, filial ingratitude, and/or anxieties of being abandoned in a state of dependency. Due to the failures in parental care, the burden of excessive anxieties and inappropriate defenses can be carried from one generation to another, militating against the maturing process and the individual's creative adaptation to his destiny. The goal of creativity in psychotherapy, the integration of traditional ideals and freely chosen commitments and responsibilities on the level of maturity, can only be reached when the vicious cycle of empathically experienced anxieties can be reduced to a tolerable degree. Among equals able to truly sympathize in mutual respect, there is room for the limited freedom of authenticity and spontaneity in self-actualization as well as for the adaptation through solidarity in interpersonal relations.

Among the existentialist philosophers Martin Buber and Max Scheler have particularly emphasized the interpersonal aspects of human development.[23] Martin Buber has established the contrast of I-Thou relations and I-It relations. Under the stress of fear or dread, interpersonal relations remain arrested at or regress to the level of I-It relations in which man uses force, may even explode in violence, and misuses his fellowmen as a means to his own ends, be it by domination, manipulation or submission. Max Scheler's concepts of empathy and sympathy are necessary tools of psychotherapeutic understanding. But empathy is not enough; it is the outgrowth of infantile symbiotic dependency. The bond of sympathy is more than a tool of psychotherapy—out of the bond of sympathy grows a reverence, a respect for man as man which, in the words

23. Martin Buber, *I and Thou*, trans. Ronald Gregor Smith (New York: Scribner, 1937); Max Scheler, *The Nature of Sympathy*, trans. Peter Heath (New Haven: Yale University Press, 1954).

of Whitehead, "secures liberty of thought and action for the upward adventure of life, the progress from force to persuasion."[24] This reverence discloses the potentialities of creative reconstruction, the goal of psychotherapy.

It is important that the psychotherapist enters into the patient's world by empathy. The world is experienced by everybody in the first place on an emotional level. We see the world bright and shining when we are hopeful and trusting, when the welfare emotions have the upper hand. We see the world gloomy and chaotic when we succumb to emergency emotions, fear, rage, hatred, guilt. Physical sensations of pleasure and pain cannot be shared. My toothache is mine alone. The partner cannot feel it. Physical pain and physical pleasure lock the individual up in the boundaries of his skin. But the participant observer can share the anxieties that accompany pain, the fear of continuation or repetition of pain, the jubilant triumph of relief, the relaxation of satisfaction. The participant observer picks up the patient's emotions by nonverbal communication, mimic expression, gestures, attitudes, somatic signals of pallor or blushing, humidity of eyes and lips, dryness or sweating, sighs and trembling, speed and pitch of voice. The observer may be able to say, "I know exactly how you feel," even before any verbal reporting takes place. H. S. Sullivan told us of a schizophrenic patient who for weeks came to the sessions in a sullen, desperate mood, and Sullivan's dog greeted him each time with an angry bark. One day the dog greeted this patient with a cheerful wagging of the tail and, lo and behold, in this session the patient was in a friendly, cooperative mood.

Empathy represents a kind of contamination, a flowing-over of emotions; Lichtenstein has compared empathy to the imprinting concept of the ethologists.[25] Going back to the beginning of existence, the infant is not born as a self-sufficient individual entity. He depends for his survival on the symbiotic unity with the mother,

24. Alfred North Whitehead, *Adventures in Ideas* (New York: MacMillan, 1933), p. 109.

25. Heinz Lichtenstein, "Identity and Sexuality. A Study of their Interrelationships," *Journal of the American Psychoanalytic Association* 9 (1961): 179–260.

the embeddedness in the family. Margaret Mahler has described this partial continuation of the prenatal symbiosis of mother and infant.[26] This symbiosis becomes pathological when it is overextended; when it is prematurely interrupted, it leads to infantile autism. Even if the infant would receive the necessary calories and mechanical protection from harm, he could not survive without parental concern or tender care by a substitute parent, as Spitz and Bowlby have demonstrated.[27] The concepts of primary narcissism and primary masochism have been dropped by a number of analysts. What Balint calls primary love and Erikson calls primary trust conveys an immediate understanding of the infant's need by empathy, and emotional participation in the mother's trust and hope carries the child through periods of delay in satisfaction, frustration, and pain; at least empathy ameliorates the emergency emotions in such situations of distress.[28]

At first the child learns by emulation and imitation, he learns to master things, toys and tools, his own body by experimentation and identification, before he comprehends his activities. Piaget has described the process by which the child builds up the construction of reality as an alternation between assimilation and accommodation.[29] The child learns the language of the adults automatically, combining imitation with self-expression. He does not learn as the adult learns a foreign language. The adult studies grammar and memorizes the vocabulary. The child takes over any language by wholesale identification. Words charged with meanings and values channelize feelings and thoughts into the powerful currents of traditional authority.

26. Margaret Mahler, "Thoughts about Development and Individuation," *Psychoanalytic Study of the Child* 18 (1963): p. 307.

27. René Spitz with Katherine Wolf, "Autoerotism. Some Empirical Findings and Hypotheses on Three of Its Manifestations in the First Year of Life," *Psychoanalytic Study of the Child* 3 / 4 (1949); John Bowlby, *Grief and Mourning in Infancy and Early Childhood*, vol. 15 (New York: International Universities Press, 1960).

28. Michael Balint, *Primary Love and Psycho-Analytic Technique* (London: Hogarth, 1952); Erik H. Erikson, *Identity and the Life Cycle* (New York: International Universities Press, 1959).

29. Jean Piaget, *The Origins of Intelligence in Children*, trans. Margaret Cook (New York: International Universities Press, 1952).

The symbiotic empathy between the child and his family is from the start not neutral to values. But only welfare emotions—joy, happiness, love, tenderness, gratitude—can be taken over by empathy without conflict; joy is increased by empathic participation. The finale of Beethoven's *9th Symphony* accompanied by Schiller's *Song to Joy* express the all-encompassing human solidarity and fellowship in love and joy.

Emergency emotions triggered off by any danger signal that can be interpreted as a threat to survival may throw both the child and the empathizing mother into a conflict. If there is not the surplus energy of resourcefulness and trust in a mother who can administer comfort to her distressed child, the beneficial cycle of empathy changes into a vicious cycle of mounting fears that neither mother nor child can cope with. The mother may be hampered in her maternal functions by her own psychopathology or by external pressures. She may then transfer her anxieties to the child. Hereditary oversensitivity in the child or prolonged illness may keep the mother in a state of overstrained vigilance. Inconsistency in the mother's care, the unreliability of the so-called "double bind," is detrimental to the security of family solidarity. Fear, the explosive rage of frustration, aims at getting rid of the source of distress by magical means. Denial, indifference, apathy, withdrawal break up the ties of empathic solidarity in despair. The child may reach out for autoerotic or narcissistic comforts, like thumbsucking, masturbation, rocking, or other devices of motoric discharge, but the child's dependency on parental care makes these comforts of loneliness often frantic and compulsive. A precocious intellectual development cannot fill the gaps of insufficiency in empathically shared emotions. The yearning to reestablish the harmony of the original symbiosis produces what Freud called oceanic feelings, particularly in times of loneliness. On the other hand, the child shows increasing pride in establishing his independence and he often fights off his yearning for dependency with protests of defiance, particularly when he defends himself against the reexperience of disappointment, rejection and frustration. Pain dependence appears as a desperate attempt to reestablish the empathic link of being taken care of and comforted at high costs, namely, refusing progress in self-sufficiency. The craving for omnipotence may become a defensive device in the struggle for independent survival, when the faith in the original symbiotic security has suffered severe blows.

I remember a tragic incident of such craving for omnipotence from the time I worked at a children's ward of the psychiatric department in the University of Berlin. A girl between three and four years of age had lost her mother in infancy; her father drifted away; an invalid grandmother was unable to take care of the vivacious, intelligent little girl. She did not appear anxious or depressed, but in her overactivity she was unable to form close attachments to medical or nursing personnel. This child had the habit of rushing to any open window with a jubilant exclamation: "I am a bird, I can fly, I am an angel." She laughed off all warnings and prohibitions. In spite of all precautions taken in a nursing home, the child in an unguarded moment threw herself out of the window and fell to her death. One could not call this accident an intended suicide, which would be very rare in a child. But the stubborn denial of a danger situation which her intelligence was able to grasp seemed to stem from a compensatory claim for magic and omnipotence in a child that had been deprived of tender attachments.

In the growing process of the dependent child, family solidarity and identification on the basis of empathy are more powerful influences than rational instructions. In what Winnicot calls a good enough environment and with the help of reasonably devoted parents, the child feels secure enough to outgrow the symbiotic unity in the process of increasing individuation through assimilation of and accommodation to parental values.[30] Aims are projected into the future, family tradition verbalizes the values of goodness versus badness. The coercion implied in every dependency relation makes the child absolutistic in his adaptive evaluations. What is endorsed by the powerful, gratifying parent appears to be absolutely good; what the parents prohibit appears danger-

---

30. Donald W. Winnicott, *Maturational Processes and the Facilitating Environment* (New York: International Universities Press, 1965), p. 67.

ously bad. Jean Piaget has described the morality of the child before preadolescence as intolerantly perfectionistic, a black and
white morality.[31] As long as the child has not yet learned to endure
frustrations without parental support, he tends to exclude all painful emotions, conflicts and frustrations automatically as far as possible from awareness. For the sake of his security, he idealizes the
parental authority into infallibility. We experience the same process of idealization in psychotherapy when the patient regresses to
infantile patterns of relationship. Even when the parent or therapist is indulgent and tolerant, the dependency of child or patient
makes him appear absolutistic, authoritarian, and intolerant. For
the child and a regressed dependent patient, obedience is the
highest virtue, since obedience facilitates an opportunistic adaptation to the powerful gratifying authority, and rebellion appears
to be bad.

But if the child is consistently frustrated, he is inclined to
blame himself in order to maintain the illusion of the authority's
infallibility. What Anna Freud has called the identification with
the aggressor represents an important step in the development towards individuation.[32] It indicates the necessarily still corruptible
beginnings of a conscience. But when the identification with the
frustrating aggressor takes place too frequently or too early in life,
when the immature child cannot yet endure isolation and independence, when he cannot yet fight with rational means for his
own gratifications, he is more or less overwhelmed by frustrations.
So is the regressed patient who is prematurely discharged before
he has learned again to help himself.

The frustrated child and prematurely discharged patient are
torn by conflict. They still need peace and harmony in relation to
a protective authority, yet they insist against the will of the authority on narcissistic supplies, on receiving passive gratification or at
least elimination of pain and frustration by the authority. This conflict is deepened when the parental or therapeutic authority is also

31. Jean Piaget, *The Moral Judgment of the Child,* trans. Marjorie Gabain
(London: Paul Keegan, 1932).

32. Anna Freud, *Das Ich und die Abwehrmechanismen* (München: Kindler Verlag, 1964), p. 85.

torn by conflicts of ambivalence, by anxieties or guilt feelings, when the parent or the therapist needs the child, or the patient, for vicarious gratification to make up for frustrations in his own life. Under these circumstances the child or the patient is burdened by borrowed guilt feelings and contaminated by adopted anxieties. The identification with an anxious parent (respectively a guilty, desperate therapist who feels defeated in his ambitions) is threatening to the child (respectively to the patient). In the treatment of a psychosis it is either the despair of the patient or the defeatism of the therapist which makes both therapist and patient drift apart, so that their lack of spontaneous rapport is covered over frequently by hypocritical pseudocommunications. The danger of contamination with anxiety and guilt feelings which in extreme cases can deteriorate into a *folie à deux* is heightened by the uncertainty of boundaries or readiness for empathy which make a schizophrenic patient oversensitive and sometimes overdefensive to the influence of the authority. The schizophrenic patient sometimes picks up nuances of smugness, condescension or disgust as defense against anxiety in the therapist that an uninvolved observer or the therapist himself are not aware of. The less the patient is stabilized in his identity, the farther removed he is from self-realization; the more he is threatened in his craving for empathy and symbiotic support, the more he is threatened by annihilation. Thus he vacillates like a child between rebellious overbearing demands for narcissistic supplies and hypocritical submission to authority. Rebellion and submission in psychotherapy interfere with the search for immediate gratifications as well as with trusting postponement of wish-fulfillment or flexible transformation of wishes in the sense of true sublimations.

According to Piaget, we cannot expect true sublimations in early childhood.[33] Due to his long dependency, the young child is necessarily egocentric and opportunistic in his heteronomous morality, a morality determined by parental authority. The child cannot yet detach himself sufficiently from the emotional identification with the parent to endure disappointments alone and to trust

33. Piaget, *Moral Judgment of the Child.*

in the future, standing on his own feet. His insistence on narcissistic supplies is impetuous and impatient; he wants what he wants when he wants it. True sublimations and an autonomous morality, based on the child's own decisions, do not occur, according to Piaget, before the age of nine to twelve years, when the child's strength and intelligence start to match that of the adult. That is the age in which H. S. Sullivan observed "the silent miracle of preadolescence," the first experiences of mutuality and genuine love. The child gradually outgrows the bonds of empathic identification, recognizing that adults are not infallible, that the frustrating parent is identical with the gratifying parent, that there are boundaries between the *I* and the *you* that cannot be overstepped without hurting the self and/or the other one. Likewise in analysis, with the realistic acceptance of ego boundaries, we see a growing respect of the self and the other one, a free encounter of the I and the you in a mutuality which transcends the original empathy, the vicious cycle of contaminating anxieties, and arrives at a true sympathy of fair and creative collaboration. When the child and the patient no longer feel helpless and dependent, they become able to give up the defensive omnipotence which they claimed previously through overbearing narcissistic demands or through manipulation of the presumably all-powerful parental or analytic authority. Gradually the child and the patient accept the responsibility for their own destiny and their limited freedom. In this autonomous morality the child and the patient reach creative solutions in their conflicts between self-love and love of others. No solution stays once and for all, but in each new situation a creative integration becomes possible, unpremeditated and surprisingly opening new horizons of growth.

Due to a lack of progress from heteronomous to autonomous morality or from empathy to sympathy, a persistence of childhood conflicts into adulthood keeps anxieties and guilt feelings in a state of mobilization. They interfere with the erotic playfulness of surplus energies that are not fully available either for direct gratification or for genuine sublimations. Anxiety and guilt feelings dictate defensive identifications that do not originate in the child's autonomous sense of value. The neurotic person bolsters his self-esteem by false ideals, and borrowed guilt feelings force him to continue the ambivalent struggle of dependency on external authority and rebellious protest against fate. Under stress and strain, all human beings tend to regress more or less to a dependency on authority with the claim for protection, or to a defiant and destructive competition with the powers of fate. The residual heteronomous morality interferes with the endurance of inevitable limitations and frustrations, consideration of the partner and fortitude in a realistic pursuit of alternative solutions of conflicts. Preservation of the individual life is not the highest value for the mature personality. The encounter with fate need not lead to a passive, depressive surrender or to impotent protest reactions. In the process of psychoanalytic reeducation the patient may learn to shape his unique individual destiny in tune with his biological and cultural boundaries. Even in view of the ultimate limit of life in death, the ingenuity of Eros can find a meaning in the individual existence. Identification with ego-alien ideals elicits anxieties and guilt feelings which freeze into neurotic patterns of depression or accusation of others. It is the goal of psychoanalysis to transform the futile protest of depression into the sincere labor of mourning and the wasteful neurotic wallowing in self-punishment into an honest insight into individual guilt, a creative uplifting experience of freedom and renewed commitment.

I would like to illustrate some typical neurotic identifications that hampered the natural progress from heteronomous to autonomous morality.

A professor in his middle thirties suffered from a lack of enjoyment in living due to his defensive detachment. He admitted that he had all the goods he could reasonably ask for, an intelligent, good looking wife, who only transiently became exasperated by his detachment, lovely children who also at times were exasperated by their father's detachment.

He was a brilliant teacher and lecturer, but he was satisfied only when he was in full control of a situation. He became disconcerted by any challenge to his uncontested authority and popularity. In his interpersonal relations he showed a high degree of empathy, but his overreactive vigilance was geared to the fearful question, "Are you for me or against me?", and this self consciousness—really unsympathetic to the needs of others—provoked criticism and rejection. When he sensed any resistance or opposition, he was overwhelmed by fear, as if his survival were threatened. He was afraid to lose control in an impotent rage reaction, and he escaped as soon as possible from the situation and his own overreaction into sleep, compulsive eating, or being glued to the television screen.

His father had been a detached scholar, withdrawn in a cloud of silently contained, paranoiac gloom, unapproachable, potentially threatening in his intransigent righteousness. The mother treated the only son with anxious oversolicitude. She waited on him hand and foot, since she saw in him the Messianic hope of making up for all the frustrations of her marital life. Nothing less than perfection was expected from him on the part of both parents, and the son saw in perfection his only salvation from annihilation. He was frozen in his authoritarian attitude, which squelched the freedom of spontaneity.

In this case the progress from heteronomous to autonomous morality was a long and tedious road: The patient had to face in a long series of detached studies of situations how much his false ideals and borrowed guilt feelings led to overreactions and interfered with a spontaneous response to these situations. He was able to throw off the authoritarian viewpoint that the therapist would magically dissolve his detachment, and entered into a collaboration of mutual respect. He recognized with some sense of humor that he was neither so all-powerful as he thought he should be, nor so powerless and fragile, nor so much in need of protection and comfort as he feared to be. His borrowed guilt feelings gradually gave way to a sense of true responsibility and sympathy toward his family and students.

Another illustration of the search for identity in the process of psychoanalysis I found in a woman physician whose childhood had been overshadowed by the helplessness of both parents. The father committed suicide when the patient had recently entered school. The mother concealed the suicide as well as the father's repeated previous depressions from the patient and other relatives. But the patient emotionally shared the family tragedy, the father's desperate moods, the mother's anxious denial, her false pride in maintaining appearances and imposing a hypocritical, conventional morality on the family.

The child was precocious in her emotional empathic participation. She was frustrated in her need for security. This frustration elicited fierce temper tantrums. She learned to repress them, but she hated herself and maintained a precarious self-esteem by mothering the helpless mother. The result of this form of defensive identification was an alienation from her own dependency needs; they appeared ridiculous and humiliating to her, so that the invitation of psychoanalysis to relax and to yield to regression horrified her. She had developed defenses of overcompensating efficiency, almost a superman's efficiency, which could take grim adversities in stride, but the patient could not relax. She had a longing to relax, to be understood and taken care of, but she did not dare to relax, to let go of the defenses of overcompensation, lest she be confronted with the loneliness, the rage and despair of her childhood, when she could not rely upon parental protection. She could not rid herself of her mother's clinging dependency; she hated her and felt guilty about it. Her sensitive empathy had an almost telepathic character, but she could not trust her receptivity, and relied on her defensive, managerial qualities.

She married a schizoid intellectual, who had little to offer emotionally. She had been able to work out only a mothering relation with him, but she could not elicit or accept protection nor gratifications. Her emotional deprivation mobilized frustration rage and depression. An experience of loving mutuality looked extremely desirable, but also forbiddingly dangerous to her.

The anxiety to surrender to her needs had to be relived and transcended in psychoanalysis. This patient tended to turn tables and to make the analyst dependent on her until she permitted the analyst to help her. There is in every patient a repressed nostalgia for the oceanic feeling of trusting harmony, for the original symbiotic unity of mother and infant. This nostalgia is particularly intense in those patients whose security needs in childhood were seriously frustrated. Such a patient reacts to the invitation of analysis to relax and to regress like a burned child that shies away from the fire. The psychoanalyst must have a full empathic understanding of the patient's anxieties and defenses, her intense vulnerabilities. He must respect her ego boundaries that are still fluid, her compensatory attempts of sublimations, the uniqueness of her own destiny. Gradually, this patient—who had missed a basic solidarity in her parental family—regained the trust in human fellowship. Without this trust in fellowship the genital adjustment necessarily remains a relation of one-sided exploitation, and neither man nor woman can confirm their unique identity in a responsible marital relation.

In the case of a woman social worker who lost her mother at the time of her birth, the lack of symbiotic union and early identifications left the growing child in a bewildering insecurity about her identity. After shifting experiences with transient housekeepers, the detached father put the child into a foster home, a social milieu completely different from the paternal home. Occasional unpredictable visits of the idealized father left the child confused and uncommitted. She was in an anxious double-bind, fearful to betray the loyalty toward the father or the foster parents.

As an adult she was unable to establish friendships and erotic relations that had any permanent or deeper meaning. Her best relations were those of sensitive empathy with patients or with colleagues with whom she shared the care for patients. Aside from the empathic sharing of troubles, relationships remained meaningless and mechanical. She herself had a sense of identity only in the role of social worker. When she had to change the place of work she became transiently depersonalized, standing beside herself, watching her functions with a sense of futility until she found herself again rooted in her role as member of the staff in a new agency.

In the beginning of treatment her emotions seemed to be frozen: "I don't know what I feel—tell me what I am supposed to feel." When she for the first time discovered that the therapist mattered to her, she became frightened. She felt depersonalized and stayed in bed, not getting up for her session, unable to excuse herself. But she gradually gained the trust in the therapist and she became able to express her frustration, rage and despair.

The treatment of this patient is still underway. She is gradually regaining a sense of identity, not only as an empathic social worker but as a total personality.

The sketches of these patients' problems illustrate an alienation from themselves due to the identification with the needs of neurotic parents or lack of stable identifications. The inclination of these patients to identify with the analyst, to accept the analyst's values as if they were their own is a serious hurdle of resistance in the process of psychoanalytic reeducation, since the patients seek a new security in exchange for the family security they have lost. But the patient's readiness for empathic participation is also a temptation for the analyst, who gains support from the patient's admiration and emulation. The analyst's need for the patient's identification and loyalty plays an important part in his emotional reaction to the patient, called countertransference. Like an overindulgent parent, the analyst may gain vicarious gratification out of the patient's success and he may share the patient's misery to a degree that he is defeated by the patient's anxieties and guilt feelings. The positive emotional reaction of the analyst that is fed by the patient's positive attachment may change into a negative reaction when the patient in a phase of resistance openly rebels against the loyalty toward the analyst. Such experiences of rebellion and defiance may lead to clarification and greater honesty in the encounter of analyst and analysand. Negative emotional reactions of the therapist can become a more serious obstacle in the process of psychoanalytic reeducation, when the analyst becomes tired and exhausted due to the patient's persisting dependency, or when the patient continues to borrow the analyst's values and ideals or to dwell and harp on the analyst's failures and shortcomings. The analyst feels exploited and manipulated by the patient's malingering tendencies, which tend to squeeze a maximum of indulgence and protection out of him, while the analyst waits for a more independent and responsible collaboration on the part of the patient. Each treatment experience can become a process of reeducation also for the analyst. Modern methods of observation of the psychoanalytic process by tape recording or one-way screen television have given us more insight into the emotional interplay between therapist and patient than self-observation can provide.

Negative therapeutic reactions on the part of the analyst cannot be abolished by a pretense of mirrorlike neutrality. Such negative reactions are always a sign of delayed awareness on the part of the analyst. Conflicts between therapist and patient have been covered over by blind empathy. In dealing with the patient's ego weakness and fluid ego boundaries, the analyst has not been sufficiently aware of the powerful influence of the patient's emotional appeal. For the patient with a weak ego, a short separation, a small disappointment, often looks like a devastating desertion, a prohibition like a threat to the patient's psychological or physical integrity. The psychoanalyst is not always aware how strongly he is pulled into the magnetic field of the patient's anxieties and his defenses against these anxieties. There is no other protection against this danger of contaminating empathy than the training in more subtle self-awareness which has been initiated in the training analysis and supervision and is continued in the self-analysis of the analyst. Through this self-awareness he should reach the optimal balance between attachment and detachment, between empathy and confronting encounter between the patient and himself.

The clarifying elucidation of communications which opens up the spontaneous mutuality of encounter is possible only in an atmosphere relatively cleared of excessive anxieties; at least the analyst should be freer from anxieties than the analysand, so that the patient can gradually gain trust in the therapist's integrity and his respect for the integrity of the patient in this process of reeducation. We cannot expect that the psychoanalyst is always understanding and sympathetic; a transient expression of discouragement or anger may clear the air and prepare the way for better understanding, if the analyst does not insist on his infallibility and admits his failures and shortcomings.

The more isolated the patient is in his narcissistic defensive orientation, the less he can believe in a sincere understanding, relatively free from anxiety, beyond the repetitions of dependence on and defiance of authority. A sincere relation of mutual respect is unpredictable. This unpredictability is uncanny for the patient, who wants security, evasion of conflict and anxiety. He frequently wants to know what is the goal of psychotherapy, while the psychotherapist is not able to predict the outcome with any certainty.

The patients show a variety of behavior, from extreme egocentricity—"I am the patient and the patient's needs have to be considered first"—to extreme self-effacing submission—"You are the doctor and you alone know what is right." The psychoanalysts also show a whole scale of natural inclinations: to stick to the letter of the contract with rigidity or to give in to irrational demands of the patient as determined by a blind, uncontrolled empathy. Conflicts should not be solved by a one-sided dictation by either partner nor by a wiping out of ego boundaries to which either partner may yield without awareness. Instead, conflicts should be solved by the fairness of mutual respect, in a spontaneous encounter in which both partners arrive at a creative integration of their needs. Such a creative integration cannot be predicted by generalizing abstractions or by formulated contracts that cannot include the individual nuances of an I-and-you encounter under the unique circumstances of an unpredictable here-and-now situation.

Psychoanalysis as a science necessarily tries to arrive at the description of typical situations, of repeatable actions and reactions which help us to understand and to control the interpersonal reactions. Psychopathology has collected a large complexity of such repeatable and predictable features. The patient's defensive narcissism reproduces the early conflicts between the child and the more powerful, indulgent, or frustrating authority in which the child may claim unlimited gratification of his possessiveness and/ or the merciless elimination of his rivals. The intransigence and monotony of these infantile demands stem from a deep existential anxiety which prevents the child from outgrowing his dependency and accepting his unique and separate identity. A wholesome solution of these typical conflicts which are repeated in the relationship with the therapist depends on the psychological understanding that makes the various maneuvers of self-defense and evasion of anxiety gradually superfluous.

Liberation through sincere communication is not just a process of rational understanding; the surplus energies of generosity also have to be mobilized. The patient can rediscover trust, not only through the empathy of the analyst, which may get stuck in a *folie à deux* of commiseration, but through his true sympathy that grasps the unique totality of the patient's whole person. This sympathy understands the patient's destiny in the complexity of all his interpersonal relations. This total grasp is no longer the result of rational scientific interpretation alone, though the scientific predictions of psychopathology are very helpful. But the reorientation of the patient is based on an unlearning of repressions, dissociations, automatic shortcut solutions of conflicts in the past and a relearning of surprisingly emerging alternative solutions. These more encompassing solutions consider the needs of the I and the you, the needs of the total personalities. These alternative conflict solutions do not just get rid of troublesome symptoms, but also may transform, by reeducation, liabilities into assets.

The therapist must be an artist in the broadest sense of the word, an artist who sees his partner, the patient, not alone as what he is now, with his repressions, restrictions and adaptational distortions; he visualizes him, too, in his future development in a more encompassing fulfillment of his potentialities. The potentialities of an artist are also alive in every patient, often deeply buried under defensive walls that he uses to protect himself from the anxieties of unsolved conflicts. In the repetition of these conflicts during the psychoanalytic process, the patient's creative potentialities as an artist emerge, as an artist who recreates himself.

In a trusting relation to the therapist, the patient rediscovers the constructive and collective power of hope. The hope of life cannot be separated from the acceptance of inevitable suffering and the expectation of death. In the solidarity of living creatures, the individual life process represents a link in a chain. The patient can sacrifice some of the sterile self-love, of the futile self-defense and the anxiety of annihilation that dies a thousand deaths to the degree as this solidarity, the love of others then becomes meaningful to him. He outgrows his self-centeredness not by the deceitful self-surrender of the malingerer who gives himself up only to gain narcissistic supplies from others. The recovering patient progresses from a heteronomous to an autonomous morality in the acceptance of his destiny, in the fortitude in view of inevitable suffering, in the endurance of anxieties with the trust in resources that transcend past and present conflicts, beyond pleasure and pain in the direction toward a creative integration. The psychoanalyst is able to mobilize creative potentialities of trust if he himself is relatively free from self-centered anxieties, if he is at least honest in facing them, so that he does not use the patient's natural dependency and supernatural expectations of magical cure to reassure himself about his own loneliness and relative powerlessness in meaningless relations. The psychoanalyst may radiate the trust in life and the inexhaustible resourcefulness of Eros that carries the individual beyond his neurotic limitations. It is the goal of psychotherapy to reestablish with the patient the bond of solidarity and mutuality in the sense of Antigone's words: "Not to hate with you, but to love with you am I here."

The Contribution of Pastoral Counseling and Psychotherapy to Mental Health

There was a time in primitive societies when the functions of the priest and the healer were not yet separated, but united in one person. This was a time of prevailing magical thought and action. Nowadays ministers and psychiatrists meet on a more rational basis for the purpose of mutual aid. Under the cultural conditions of mass society the need for understanding of individual emotional conflicts has become increasingly urgent. There are many individuals who do not suffer from illnesses defined by a medical diagnosis; they are suffering from ill-defined unhappiness, loneliness, rootlessness, meaninglessness of living, they may not want to face their religious or spiritual conflicts; they may avoid the church and turn to a psychotherapist for help. Others who still have some emotional attachment to a church and a prejudice against psychiatry may turn with the very same problems to a minister. In the United States this widespread need for help in individual conflicts gives rise to a new professional group of pastoral counselors who in the frame of a church specialize in individual counseling, using the knowledge and the techniques of modern psychotherapy to help their clients. There is a practical common basis for individual pastoral counseling and psychotherapy, this common basis is human understanding.

To be an expert in psychodynamic understanding which includes grasp and management of transference and countertransference is so time- and energy-consuming that it cannot be combined with the duties of a general medical practice or the clergyman's broad obligations towards an extended parish. I want to try

Reprinted by permission from the *British Journal of Medical Psychology* 33 (1960): 269.

to point out the similarities between modern psychotherapy and the new specialty of pastoral counseling that grows out of the need for help in the widespread neurotic misery of our time. Though the professional background of both pastor and psychotherapist is different, their common purpose, the service of the suffering individual, brings them together; they try to reach an understanding that transcends the barriers of communication between the two professional groups. Sociological studies compare the different "untranslatable" terminologies of two symbol systems that attempt to grasp different aspects of reality as well as the different social roles and expectations that characterize minister and client on the one hand and psychotherapist and patient on the other hand. The physician's role is necessarily authoritative when the diagnosis reveals that the patient is unable to take care of himself. When the patient can be helped by surgical, pharmacological or other external intervention, the patient has to follow the physician's orders. But when a relief in the patient's suffering can only be expected from a change in the patient's inner attitude, the doctor-patient relation is no longer authoritative, it becomes a relation of mutual participation. Similarly in pastoral counseling the authoritative role of the minister can become obsolete, for the counselee cannot simply obey the minister's orders to have faith when he doubts and despairs, to love his neighbour when he hates and keeps grudges, to practice devotion when he is full of bitterness. A change in inner attitude, in religious terms a conversion, has to take place and can be reached in a partnership of searching for a new understanding. The pastor needs the diagnostic advice of a physician if there is any doubt whether the patient is able to profit from such a counseling service by active participation or whether he is disabled to such a degree that he cannot actively participate and needs medical care. The minister's counselee as well as the patient in psychotherapy may hold on to the expectation that he can remain passive, to the hope that the minister or the doctor might take the active role of a magic healer or redeemer, but these roles that the helper is expected to play are more an obstacle than a help in the search for understanding of what ails the supplicant and of how he can learn to accept help and help himself.

The verbal frame of reference, be it psychiatric or theological, can also become more an obstacle than a help. The sophisticated patient may have preconceived ideas about his inferiority feelings or some book learning concerning his Oedipus conflict. The counselee of the minister may have deep-seated illusions about unpardonable sin or his own self-justification. Such abstractions are mostly far removed from spontaneous emotional experience and represent a resistance against the process of self-scrutiny which can initiate a change of inner attitude. A debunking of clichés has to take place before both partners arrive at the genuine emotions which dissolve congealed habit patterns and permit new decisions.

I want to look at the similarities in the minister's and the psychotherapist's task from two viewpoints, that of confession and that of conversion. Both concepts belong in the minister's universe of discourse, yet may be also profitably translated into the psychiatrist's frame of reference. A patient or counselee approaches his helper with a need for confession. He does not necessarily talk about his guilt or sin, but considers himself a failure; he does not make use of his potentialities, he does not get enough satisfactions out of his intimate relations, out of his work; he finds himself caught in conflicts in which he cannot arrive at decisions, he is anxious, depressed, antagonizes his partners or feels exploited by them. When an organic illness that needs medical attention has been ruled out, when the patient is able and willing to take some responsibility himself in the healing process he turns to a psychiatrist or a minister to learn to understand about the causes of his suffering and how they can be removed. Shortcut solutions, like exhortation, reassurance, guidance, are frequently not effective, for they offer only transient solace or they represent gifts which the distressed patient cannot yet integrate. They even increase the painful distance between the patient's real being and the ideals he cannot live up to. The psychiatrist as well as the pastoral counselor in our time has arrived at the conviction that a change in inner attitude of the patient or counselee can only take place when he is able to confess not only what he knows about himself, but also what is hidden from his awareness. Since the Freudian discoveries about the unconscious mind we do no longer rely solely on the surface self-presentation of a patient. Every patient or counselee in our time and age has been exposed to so many social pressures that he approaches his helper with distrust. This distrust may be expressed in a readiness to win the helper's approval by hypocritical submission to the expressed or not expressed wishes, suggestions, ideals of the authority; or the patient tests his helper's forbearance by withdrawal, defiance, conscious or unconscious deception. There have always been spiritual leaders and gifted healers who intuitively looked through external appearances to the core of the personality and were also able to communicate their insight to the supplicant. The modern knowledge of psychodynamics has made such insight accessible not only to persons of exceptional inspirational gifts. A trained person can learn to look through the network of lies, self-deceptions, illusions, and rationalizations that separate the suffering individual from the sources of vital energy, and that have made his emotions and other derivatives of his vital impulses partially enigmatic to himself. But the suffering individual has to participate in the investigation. It mostly turns out that his very participation, his engagement in a process of investigation distracts some of the self-tormenting impulses which gnaw at the patient's vitality. In this kind of confessional work both doctor and patient, pastor and counselee have to invest much time and energy. A confession that has become an empty ritual does not reach the depth of individual suffering. The patient or counselee only gradually learns a soul-searching veracity that surmounts conventional communications. He needs time and an atmosphere of calmness, that shuts out the everyday distractions, a nonjudgmental, sympathetic listener to whom he can reveal himself without fear of being forced into conformity or rejected by condemnation. If this confessional self-revelation becomes the goal of a common enterprise in which counselor and counselee, doctor and patient, collaborate, their mutual communications dissolve the private reveries and misleading products of imagination which human beings are inclined to spin in their lonely endeavours to discover the psychological truth about themselves.

In an effective confession we must have a grasp of the psychological phenomena that psychoanalysts have called transference and countertransference. These phenomena of repetition and identification show a clinging to congealed patterns of past relations and to roles which both partners of such an investigation attribute to the other ones and to themselves, roles that mask the original, truthful I and Thou, according to the formulation of Martin Buber, in the here and now of their encounter.[1] The psychological truth cannot be found by logical deductions and abstractions alone. The encounter of the spontaneous I and Thou springs from a trust that can afford to drop the more or less stereotyped masks and roles of defense and to gradually reveal the innermost self of the patient or counselee. But he is only able to respond with cleansing sincerity to a counselor who has purged his own reactions by his self-scrutiny from impulsive or compulsive wishes and fears in his approach to the partner. A human helper is never free from the wish to succeed or the fear of failure but he can learn to tame his impatience, to become aware of his preconceived ideas and prejudices, the egocentricity of his strivings, and to adapt them to the partner's pace and slowly growing understanding so that all interpretations and explanations are concentrated toward the goal to transcend the present conflicts and to regain the wholeness and integrity of the suffering partner.

In religious experience the regaining of wholeness is called conversion. It is a conversion from a life-negating to a life-confirming, integrative attitude. Such a conversion hits a person sometimes with lightning power, as William James has demonstrated in his study *The Varieties of Religious Experience.*[2] The psychotherapist hopes for a similar transformation of his patient, but this is seldom experienced with dramatic suddenness, since the psychoanalyst, particularly the analyst of the classical Freudian school, embarks on a long-term exploration of the individual patient's past. He tries to avoid directions and suggestive influences that impose on the patient the helper's own values, he attempts to liberate gradually step by step the synthetic function of the ego by tracing the

1. Martin Buber, *I and Thou,* trans. Ronald Gregor Smith (New York: Charles Scribner, 1937).
2. New York and London: Longmans Green and Co. 1902.

causes of dissociation back into early childhood. In other schools of psychotherapy attention is more concentrated on the aim of re-adaptation of the patient in the present situation. In order to understand the phenomenon of conversion it may be useful to throw a short glimpse into the causes of disintegration and reintegration in human development.

The dawn of consciousness, the self-consciousness of his separate, unique existence arises gradually out of an unconscious symbiotic unity of the infant with his mother. Consciousness, according to Hegel, is from the start unhappy consciousness.[3] Due to the prolonged dependency of the human infant, the child experiences separation and frustration as painful helplessness and as an alerting threat to his very existence, while the gratified infant sinks back into the happy unconsciousness of sleep. Fortunately, in a trustworthy mother-child relation the transition toward growing independence develops slowly, in this protective dependency the child discovers playfully his growing ego functions. In transient experiences of separation his trusting imagination transcends the frustration and anxieties of the moment and opens the resources of hopeful anticipations. But when the trustworthy relation between parent and child has been broken up by prolonged separation, e.g. due to overwhelming anxieties on the part of the parent, the child is left in hopeless loneliness that threatens his survival, as Margaret Ribble and René Spitz have demonstrated.[4] The child is flooded by chaotic anxieties and if he survives he builds up in his loneliness hardening structures of self-defense against these chaotic anxieties. These defenses curtail the freedom of his development. The defenses of narcissistic isolation intensify the conflict between dependence and independence, between a person's uniqueness and his need for group belonging. The defenses tip the inner equilibrium in the direction of smothering dependency, stupefying gulli-

---

3. G. W. F. Hegel, *The Phenomenology of Mind*, trans. J. B. Baillie (New York: Macmillan, 1949).

4. Margaret Ribble, "The Rights of Infants," in *Psychoanalytic Study of the Child*, vol. 1 (New York: International Universities Press, 1945), pp. 415–16; René Spitz, "Hospitalism: An Inquiry into the Genesis of Psychiatric Conditions in Early Childhood," in ibid., pp. 53–74.

bility and submissive depression or in the direction of precociously sensitive, suspicious alertness to a world of dangers, to the void of nonexistence experienced as estrangement. The defensive preparation for the worst distorts the products of imagination into the hellish projections of anxiety, rage, envy, hatred or scorn. These images of a gloomy forecast elicit in others disgusted withdrawal or angry rejection. A person who grows up in such basic loneliness learns to repress the images of hope and trust in himself as well as in his world. He does not dare to dive into an unknown future, to grow, to experiment, testing the free play of his impulses in an expanding world. He cannot learn from his failures or transcend frustrations in the ever renewed hope and trust in a brighter future. When the lonely, distrustful child grows into adolescence, he misses the regenerative power of erotic experience. His anxieties and defensive cautions keep him in prolonged incestuous bondage. Sexual experience remains meaningless if it is not inspired by trusting love. The anxieties of basic loneliness flood the erotic fantasy life with sadistic and masochistic images and, threatened in his integrity, the discouraged person recoils deeper into this loneliness and does not reach the full life of mature manhood or womanhood.

Such basic loneliness that represses and cripples the potentialities of trust from early childhood on, can lead to extremes of despair and disintegration and to the outbreak of a psychosis. But there is no individual so firmly integrated that his equilibrium could not be shaken by disabling anxieties under severe blows of fate. There are great differences in the individual abilities to endure frustration. The gift of trust may gain strength in transcending the hardships of reality. But the powers of destruction become particularly overwhelming for an individual of highly sensitive endowment who has been deprived of the security and confirmation of his existence, deprived of the consistent tenderness in an harmonious family life. He is frightened by the challenges of life, horrified by death, by the powers of destruction that pervade inhibited, arrested living. Nevertheless, even though a life may be impoverished in constructive experience of trust, we find in the sensitive, neurotic person a longing for the spiritual values, for the potentialities of love and trust that can transcend the conflicts and make life meaningful and whole. The neurotic person is deeply attracted by the charms of beauty, the warming glow of goodness, the dignity of truth. The attachment to the ideals of perfection, to the ultimate values of existence deepens the neurotic suffering under imperfection and inadequacies; he is most vulnerable to the forces of destruction and disintegration which drive the afflicted patient to a helper. His very suffering, panic, depression, and despair bear witness to the indestructible yearning for trust, the repressed, innate longing for peace and serenity. There is a deep remorse about being separated from the actualization of these potentialities. The neurotic person cannot be satisfied with cheap compromises and shallow complacency. He is deeply torn by the conflict of all or none, Kierkegaard's Either-Or, he is torn between an unacceptable reality which for him has become the hell of loneliness and lovelessness and the heavenly gates of redemption. Out of this conflict grows the experience of conversion, the decisive step from the despair of disintegration to the trust in the healing and reconciling power of love. We encounter this experience particularly in the sensitive, emotionally endowed person who is easily carried to extremes by his mood swings. The ecstatic experience of conversion and redemption can become another illusion, a renewed escape from the unbearably painful aspects of existence. The manic-depressive patient is prone to fall into his habitual pattern of escape. But also a more stabilized, less narcissistic person may be lured by self-deception into a state of blissful ecstasy.

Therefore, conversion and confession belong together. A minister as well as a psychotherapist can be helpful to prepare the way for a change of inner attitude—it has not to be a dramatic conversion—to remove the obstacles of conflict, to abolish the network of lies, illusions and self-deceptions by the painful veracity of confession. The encounter with the luminous source of all ultimate values is beyond the reach of human will power, though there is a deep-seated longing to unite all strivings in this one direction. But sincere communication between pastor and counselee, psychotherapist and patient may give rise to a genuine remorse, not only about repressed egocentric and destructive impulses, but also remorse about the repression of potentialities of love and trust that have been crippled or buried. Such genuine remorse is able to hallow human failures and perversions, showing them in the light of redemption, if pastor and counselee, psychotherapist and patient, can reach that down-to-earth, immediate understanding that transforms the I and Thou into a creative We. There is no crime so ugly, no insanity so distorted that the life-confirming potentialities of trust could not be discovered in the most defiant denial of life's values. At the bottom of the most desperately lonely perversion there still glows the hidden yearning for redeeming love, and pastor as well as psychotherapist is able to rekindle this concealed glowing by the sensitivity of his understanding.

PART II

Psychoanalysis and Psychopathology

Narcissism: Benign and Malignant Forms

Freud's concept of narcissism, which he introduced into psycho-analytic theory in 1914, widened horizons, particularly the study of the major psychoses.[1] These Freud differentiated, as the "narcissistic neuroses," from the "transference neuroses"—hysteria, phobia and obsessive-compulsive neurosis—with which Freud and his followers were then more familiar. Later studies in schizophrenia in this country—by, to name only local authorities, Frieda Fromm-Reichmann, Harry Stack Sullivan, Lewis Hill, Otto Will and Harold Searles—demonstrated that the transference of conflicts into the doctor-patient relation is not missing in schizophrenia. Rather, it is intensified, since the existence of the whole personality of the schizophrenic patient is threatened by conflicts that mobilize aggressive impulses to the intensity of destructiveness. Self-love turns into self-hatred, and a benign narcissism—which, with self-interest, aims at preserving the individual existence—turns into the malignant narcissism of self-destruction. Narcissistic defenses, particularly those of a negative malignant kind, offer the greatest resistance to psychoanalytic therapy.

Narcissism was seen originally as an intermediary stage of development between autoerotism and object libido. In the transference neuroses, the aggressive impulses are often masked and mitigated by libidinal impulses. The major psychoses did not lend themselves to treatment and exploration by a private practitioner, since these patients are mostly hospitalized, and a Jewish physi-

Reprinted by permission from *Crosscurrents in Psychiatry and Psychoanalysis*, ed. R. W. Gibson (Philadelphia: J. B. Lippincott, 1967).

1. Sigmund Freud, "On Narcissism: An Introduction," in *Collected Papers* vol. 4 (London: Hogarth, 1952).

cian, like Freud in antisemitic Austria, had no access to leading positions in municipal and academic institutions. Therefore, Freud conducted his studies mostly with neurotic patients and had to fall back on the autobiographical notes of Schreber for a more detailed study of the paranoid form of schizophrenia. Had he seen more psychotic patients, he might have isolated the aggressive from the libidinal drives earlier. Originally, he assumed that the libidinal instincts are opposed to the instincts of self-preservation and lend themselves less to the build-up of human solidarity than the instincts of self-preservation. In his earlier studies, the aggressive instincts were defined as sadomasochistic partial components of the libidinal drives, which are directed against the instincts of self-preservation. After the introduction of narcissism, Freud's instinct theory became centered on the dualism of Eros and Thanatos, libidinal versus aggressive drives. According to his *Beyond the Pleasure Principle*, the preservation of individual as well as communal existence depends on the preponderance of Eros over Thanatos.[2]

When the psychoanalytic ego psychology, on the basis of Sigmund and Anna Freud's writings, was elaborated, a sharper differentiation between primary and secondary narcissism emerged, which marks the transition from the pleasure-pain principle to the reality principle in human development.[3] What had been called the preambivalent phase of libido development[4] became the phase of primary ego autonomy, where the aims of ego and id are still harmoniously intertwined. Margaret Mahler has distinguished a phase of early autism, and a later phase of symbiosis between mother and infant followed by a phase of separation and individu-

2. Sigmund Freud, *Beyond the Pleasure Principle* (London: Hogarth, 1948).

3. Sigmund Freud, *The Ego and the Id* (London: Hogarth, 1929); Anna Freud, *The Ego and the Mechanisms of Defense* (New York: International Universities Press, 1948); Heinz Hartmann, *Essays on Ego Psychology* (New York: International Universities Press, 1964); Erik Erikson, *Childhood and Society* (New York: Norton, 1950); David Rapaport, "The Autonomy of the Ego," *Bulletin of the Menninger Clinic* 15 (1951): 113–23.

4. Karl Abraham, "The First Pregenital Stage of the Libido," in *Selected Papers on Psychoanalysis* (New York: Basic Books, 1953), pp. 248–79.

ation.[5] A prolonged symbiosis or a return to autistic withdrawal interferes with the development of a benign secondary narcissism.

Balint has called the phase of primary narcissism a phase of primary love, although it seems to me an adultomorphic interpretation to call the infant's automatic responses to maternal care expressions of love, just as Melanie Klein's concepts of an early paranoid and depressive position appear to me as adultomorphic interpretations of infantile behavior.[6] It has been suggested that we "drop the primary-secondary narcissism and replace it by the general term narcissism, since actually, we are dealing only with what was called secondary narcissism."[7] I agree that primary narcissism is a physiological stimulus-response rather than a psychological phenomenon. The infant continues to some degree the "embeddedness" in the maternal womb.[8] The infant's helplessness and dependency on maternal care make the boundaries fluid. Against overstimulation, he is protected by the stimulus barrier. He responds to the mother's hope, trust, and loving care with well-being and the unfolding of his potentialities of growth, which imply the promise of trust, hope, and love in his further development.

This symbiosis lasts longer in human beings than in all other animals, which start an earlier independence from parental care. In animals, on the other hand, preservation of the individual and of the species dovetail on the level of instinctive regulations of stimulus and response throughout the life span. Conflicts arise in animals, in life situations and laboratory experiments, but they are solved on a preconscious level, as they remain preconscious in early stages of human development. The ethologists describe such instinctive conflict solutions: When in a pack of wolves a conflict

5. Margaret Mahler, "On Child Psychosis and Schizophrenia: Autistic and Symbiotic Infantile Psychosis," in *Psychoanalytic Study of the Child*, vol. 7 (New York: International Universities Press, 1952), pp. 265–305.

6. Michael Balint, *Primary Love and Psychoanalytic Technique* (London: Hogarth 1952); Melanie Klein, *Contributions to Psychoanalysis* (London: Hogarth, 1946).

7. James Bing, Francis McLaughlin, and Rudolf Marburg, "The Metapsychology of Narcissism," in *Psychoanalytic Study of the Child*, vol. 14 (New York: International Universities Press, 1959).

8. Ernest Schachtel, *Metamorphosis* (New York: Basic Books, 1959).

about supremacy breaks out, the rivals fight till the weaker gives in. He submits his jugular vein by a turn of his head to the teeth of the victor in a gesture of humility, but the victor does not bite. Such instinctive reactions are directed towards the preservation of the individual as well as of the species.

In early human infancy, the cry of distress is not yet a cry of anxiety. The infant is protected by a stimulus barrier even against contamination with the anxieties of the mother. In a highly disturbed mother-infant relation reported in my practice, the nearly psychotic mother was tormented by doubts of her maternal competence. She might drop the baby and break his neck or suffocate him in the feeding process. The infant responded to the flood of agitated stimuli automatically by stopping nursing and bottle-feeding completely, at the age of six weeks. The mother's alarm escalated. Fortunately, the infant had not yet developed object constancy and ego identity. This baby recovered from his hunger strike, which automatically protected him from being flooded by the mother's ambivalent emotions; he recovered by calm and un-conflicted nursing care in a hospital. At a later stage of the child's development at home, with awakening consciousness the maternal anxiety and the child's defenses against it created severe conflicts of ambivalence also in the child.

The human infant, like the animal, is bewildered by contradictory stimuli, but is not yet anxious. Anxiety is an emotional signal. Emotional signals bring instinctual aims closer to awareness. They arouse preconscious reactions and consciousness, which tend to preserve and organize memories of the past and to anticipate future pleasures and pains. Instincts in Freud's definition have sources, objects and aims, but only the sources remain unconscious. Aims and objects become more and more a matter of choice. They are lighted by flashes of emotional signals and, therewith, submitted to transiently conscious or preconscious censoring decisions. These decisions gradually establish the nuclei of ego identity and object constancy. At eight months, the signal of genuine anxiety, the clinging preference for the familiar person, the recoiling from the stranger are observed. When the child begins to say "I," he is no longer part of the mother or the mothering person, but an *I* over against a *you*. The gradually awakening consciousness has beeen called by Hegel an "unhappy consciousness," because consciousness arouses conflicts that call for decisions.[9] The conflicts are between the I and the you, as well as between past and future, being and becoming. The two-year-old child frequently goes through a period of saying "no" to almost everything that the parent proposes. He wants to be himself, to do it himself, leave the past behind; and he clings still to the familiarity of the past, yet reaches out for the uncertain future with a mixture of joyful curiosity and painful anxiety.

The harmony of trust, hope and love experienced in the symbiosis of mother and child remains an aspiration throughout the life span. Emotions signalize the approximation to or the distantiation from this goal. What Rado calls the welfare emotions—hope, joy, happiness, tenderness, love, and gratitude—signalize the approximation to this gratifying goal of harmony.[10] The signals of anxiety, doubt, anger, rage, hatred, shame, and guilt indicate the danger of disharmony and conflict. These emotional signals mobilize the weapons of defense to control the emergency. But often the excess of mobilizing emotions fails to control the emergency; disorganized fight and flight reactions lead to emergency discontrol. They automatically blot out the unbearable aspect of the conflict by repression, distortion and denial, which impair the mastery of emergency.

Freud has denied a drive for perfection in humans.[11] He saw the human being determined by the unconscious energies of his contradictory drives, his constitutional endowment and the contingencies of fate that reality imposes on him. He saw human conflicts arising from the unruly unconscious drives, libido versus self-preservation, narcissism versus object libido, Eros versus Thanatos, and these drives in conflict with reality. It seems to me that conflicts, in animals or the early infant, are more smoothly

9. G. W. F. Hegel, *The Phenomenology of Mind,* trans. J. B. Baillie (New York: Macmillan, 1947).

10. Sandor Rado and George E. Daniels, *Changing Concepts of Psychoanalytic Medicine* (New York: Grune and Stratton, 1956).

11. Freud, *Beyond the Pleasure Principle.*

solved on the unconscious level. The awakening of consciousness creates conflicts, since consciousness demands decisions. According to Sartre, man is condemned to be free in his choices of objects and aims.[12] Once the child has left the unconscious paradise of trusting symbiosis, he is confronted with decisions. He wants to become himself, Sartre's *pour-soi*; he wants to master his destiny in spite of dependencies and contingencies, and he also wants to become what the other one—in the child's case, the parent—wants him to be, Sartre's *pour-autrui*. The child needs, before all, the constancy of being accepted. In his emotional conflicts, he often sacrifices the (for him) inferior value of pleasure-gain or pain-avoidance for the (for him) high value of object constancy and ego identity. But object constancy is not permanent, and ego identity is in a flux of becoming. Once the child has left the comforting symbiosis, he feels forever incomplete. He is only transiently satisfied with what he has received or achieved, and he reaches out for ever new aims and objects. Ives Hendrick has introduced a drive toward mastery, and Robert W. White a drive for efficacy and competence.[13] But mastery, efficacy, competence are goals, not sources of drive energy. In the transition from primary to secondary narcissism, from the pleasure-pain principle to the reality principle, the goals of instinctual drives become increasingly complex and encompassing through the process of sublimation.

According to Heinz Hartmann, the primary autonomous functions of the ego extend into a secondary autonomy by neutralization, deinstinctualization of the libidinal as well as the aggressive drives.[14] Hartmann speaks of desexualization as well as deaggressivization. But the process of sublimation does not imply a quantitative diminution of drive energy. The change of goals is not only inhibiting, it broadens the activation of drive energies in the service of an expanding ego. Expansion takes place on the biologic level by growth and development and on the interpersonal level

12. Jean-Paul Sartre, *L'Etre et le néant* (Paris: Gallimard, 1948).

13. Ives Hendrick, "Instinct and the Ego during Infancy," *Psychoanalytic Quarterly* 11 (1942): 33–58; Robert W. White, *The Abnormal Personality* (New York: Ronald Press, 1947).

14. Hartmann, p. 213 ff.

by increasing object constancy and consolidation of ego identity. Successful sublimations are the basis for a benign narcissism, which never arrives at homeostasis, but in more and more encompassing integrations transcends the here-and-now situation as well as the regressive trend toward autistic or symbiotic withdrawal.

The child that Freud described in *Beyond the Pleasure Principle* who was distressed by his mother's departure, achieved a successful sublimation. He transcended his distress by inventing the play with the thread-reel, which, in the wish for mastery, he could throw away and retrieve, reassuring himself, therewith, that the departed mother could also be retrieved. The child's confidence in the mother's return is reinforced by self-confidence, since he himself can maintain the image of the good mother who returns over against the image of the bad mother who disappears and deserts him. In the phase of differentiation and individuation, which corresponds to the phase of anal erotism, the child learns to distinguish good from evil. In the earlier oral phase, he is still protected by the unconscious stimulus barrier in the fold of primary narcissism or primary love. Now he learns to decide for himself how to preserve what serves him best, how to reject what is dead and bad. He learns to endure frustration, to postpone gratifications; he learns by trial and error and achieves his early sublimations that guarantee his growing independence and a balanced interdependence with others.

The precondition for successful sublimations is the preponderance of Eros over Thanatos in the antagonistic and synergistic play of drive energies. The danger signal of anxiety mobilizes aggressive as well as libidinal energies in the defense of the ego. As long as Eros prevails over Thanatos, an optimal state of defense, which we shall call courage, can be maintained even under the most trying circumstances. The emergency can be controlled when the individual can transcend the danger that he faces squarely and with a heightened sense of integration and competence. Danger may arise from untamed drives that send out emotional signals of alarm, or from an unmanageable reality situation, or from a failure of ego functions.

Freud called this failure of the integrating ego functions *death instinct.* But is it an instinct or a failure of aggressive and libidinal instincts to unite and maintain the goal of life preservation, individual as well as communal life? Death is not the greatest of evils when one can face it with courage, but conscious awareness of danger may intensify anxious emotions to a degree that ego functions fall into disarray. Rado called this disarray "emergency discontrol."[15] Brain damage arouses incapacitating catastrophic panic reactions when it does not wipe out consciousness. The drowning person can more easily be saved when he becomes unconscious than when he fiercely but inappropriately struggles for survival. A person who is overwhelmed by depressive, desperate emotions may consciously decide to end it all and, in Bibring's words, let the ego die;[16] yet at the peak of an emergency, the goal of survival may rise from the preconscious to the conscious and take the lead in restoring the will to live. On the other hand, a less serious suicide attempt may accidentally lead to death due to emotional discontrol in a state of disorganizing panic. Consciousness is not always the best guardian of survival and does not always achieve the most satisfactory conflict solutions, since emotions that reach the preconscious and conscious levels as signals for decision may falsify the assessment of reality. Emotions have the tendency to return to magic wish fulfillment and magic denial of adversity, as we see in the dream. Deep sleep is dreamless and permits the relaxation into unconsciousness. Memories of recent or past conflicts stir up emotions that solve the conflicts with the omnipotent magic of narcissism, but when this magic of omnipotent wishes fails, owing to the severity of conflict, the dreamer awakes in terror, overwhelmed by the emotions of helplessness and powerlessness. Also in waking life, the individual who feels incompetent to make decisions and to solve his conflicts is lured by his emotions into short-circuit, magic solutions of regressive, more or less autistic or symbiotic phantasies. When the omnipotence of these magic solutions fails, the individual can become a victim of emergency emotions of anxiety, rage, despair, most dramatically when

15. Rado and Daniels, p. 95.
16. Edward Bibring, "Das Problem der Depression," *Psyche* 6 (Stuttgart, 1952): 81–101.

he has not enough ego strength to fall back on. This ego strength seems to me the product of a benign secondary narcissism built on successful sublimations. It grows out of mastery of frustrations—adversities that have been endured and transcended in creative conflict solutions; while ego weakness corresponds to a more or less malignant or negative secondary narcissism, which remains dependent on the pleasure-pain principle and the emotional reactions of escape from frustration by repression, distortion and denial.

The negative narcissism is at the core of neurotic and psychotic maladjustments. We find it in those human beings who give in to doubts whether they are able to cope with conflicts, or who have more or less given up faith altogether. They cannot stand the freedom of decisions, and, according to the all-or-none principle of pleasure and pain, they swing from narcissistic omnipotence illusions to illusions of impotence and despair. Constitutional endowment and the past and/or present hardships of fate contribute to the failures of narcissism. The original trust in life deteriorates into a more or less life-negating despair. Rainer Maria Rilke, an oversensitive poet often unable to deal with the frustrations of his existence, transcended his helplessness of negative narcissism in his poetry, which likely saved him from psychotic decompensation. He describes the disposition of malignant or negative narcissism:

> There are people flowering pale like white blossoms
> they die aghast of the cruel world
> and no one sees the horror stricken grimace
> to which the smiling of this tender race
> is distorted in nameless nights.
>
> They are surrendered to hundreds of tormenters,
> Screamed at by every hour's bang
> They err lonely around the hospitals
> And wait anxiously for the day of admission.[17]

17. Rainer Maria Rilke, *Das Stundenbuch Inselverlag* (Leipzig, 1918), pp. 85–86:

Das leben Menschen, weisserbluehte, blasse
und sterben staunend an der schweren Welt

In my practice, I see not a sharp division between benign and malignant narcissism but a continuum from benign narcissism or ego strength, with flexible defenses against disorganizing anxieties, to a malignant narcissism or ego weakness, with the defenses against emergency increasingly breaking down.

A healthy narcissism holds the balance between self-esteem growing out of phase-adequate mastery of dangers, and dependency on auxiliary supplies of parental or other authoritative support. The child becomes increasingly conscious of reality, but what is this reality? Reality in psychoanalytic literature is sometimes understood as the world of science, a system of quantitatively measurable correlations. It is a great help for the growing child to acquire a high level of rational knowledge about the world that he has to live in. But according to Buytendijk, one's world is no system of objective correlations; the scientific reality is a world without elements of quality, of color, sound, touch and taste, a world without meaning, a pure environment.[18] This scientific reality is particularly a world without instincts and emotions. The world that the child learns to master is a world that is already evaluated by parents, teachers, and peers, a conventionally accepted or criticized reality, full of emotional predilections and prejudices, from the scientific point of view full of erroneous, even incorrigible, ideas. The communist grows up in a reality that looks different from that a of a Roman Catholic; the Negro's immediate experience of reality is at variance with that of the white man. Insight into reality is conveyed to the child in the beginning by empathy or emotional participation. The child takes over the predilections and prejudices of his elders, incorporating their standards and values in the form of his ego ideal, their prohibitions in his

---

und keiner sieht die klaffende Grimasse
zu der das Laecheln einer zarten Rasse
in namenlosen Naechten sich enstellt.
Sie sind gegeben unter hundert Quaeler,
und angeschrien von jeder Stunde Schlag,
kreisen sie einsam um die Hospitaeler
und warten angstoll auf den Einlasstag.

18. F. J. J. Buytendijk, *Allgemeine Theorie der menschlichen Haltung und Bewegung* (Berlin: Springer, 1956).

superego. But in the transition from the pleasure-pain principle to the reality principle, the child experiences conflict. He has to make decisions, and decisions demand sacrifices. Is the constancy of interpersonal relations a higher value than the emotional escape from frustration by flight or fight? Parental punishments intensify the child's conflicts, the punishment of abandonment or withdrawal of love intensify his loneliness and helplessness, corporal punishment or castration threats endanger his bodily integrity. But an overprotected, overindulged child reared without setting of limits is also at a serious disadvantage in the development of a benign narcissism. The overprotected child reacts to real or imaginary dangers and frustrations that he has not learned to master step by step, with excessive anxieties, and he develops a mainly defensive narcissism. The overprotected child remains often dependent on narcissistic supplies with disorganized willfulness or discouraged will-lessness, without self-confidence in his own potentials.

Hartmann has distinguished the ego from the self. The ego represents the level of organization that an individual has reached by synthesis of ego functions and the assimilation of a given reality, as well as by the differentiation from those external influences. The ego that has not reached the integration and mastery by sublimations adequate to its age level, whose emotions still automatically respond to pleasure and pain, is a weak ego, responsive but not responsible. The self is the sum of evaluations on which the ego bases its self-esteem in consensus with others or in rebellious dissension. This self-esteem approximates the objective state of ego development in a positive narcissism. The child loves himself not only when he feels loved by his family; in growing independence, he loves himself in spite of rejection by others. But such firmness of self-esteem is hard to reach, because of the power of human interdependence and solidarity. This solidarity is threatened by invidious comparisons, the injustice of fate that metes out unequal frustrations to the young and the old, the males and the females, the rich and the poor. Narcissism is beset by anxieties, doubts, self-consciousness, shame and guilt. A child may feel guilty not only when he displeases his parents, teachers, and friends;

even when he is better endowed and has richer opportunities, he feels exposed to the envy of his parents, his siblings or his peers. A self that he can love unambiguously is forever unreachable; the onward-and-upward thrust of his drives, erotic as well as aggressive, transcends the past and the present; the self is a project into the future. The peace and harmony of the original symbiosis remain a goal that can never be reached. It might be the ultimate goal of Freud's death instinct, but we never reach this goal consciously. We are embedded in the natural rhythm of life and death, waking and sleeping, activity and passivity, satisfaction and frustration. We know that it is dangerous for our survival to refuse the struggle with frustrations. A benign narcissism trancends the blows of frustration by changing the ego or changing the world, as far as possible, in the process of mutual adaptation, by autoplastic or alloplastic transformation. A complete refusal of transformation or transcendence causes death in life, even when a vegetating existence might continue. Thanatos tends to vanquish Eros in a psychosis, whether the ego functions are damaged by organic disease or whether ego development is arrested by evasion of conflicts. Ultimately, the world seems to be destroyed in a catastrophe that wipes out consciousness of a world and a self that have become inseparable. World destruction equals self-destruction in a psychosis. Rejected reality is distorted in hallucinations, illusions, and delusions. Instead of realistic appraisal of the ego, the emotional self-assessment escapes into hypochondriac or self-condemning orgies of frustration rage, or this rage is compensatorily denied in fantasies of grandiosity and omnipotence that set up the false self of a more or less malignant narcissism that denies the defeat of the ego. But as long as there is life, there is hope. The Eros of benign narcissism can rise from defeat. In the repeated revival of original conflicts due to the repetition compulsion, the ego can correct its evasive indecisions and find new alternatives of conflict solution.

The original conflicts that infringe on the development of a benign narcissism arise in intimate interpersonal relations loaded with anxieties. For the sake of pleasing and winning the stronger other one, the weaker ego takes refuge in duplicity, hypocrisy, and pretended conformity. These defenses against interpersonal anxiety become an armor that hampers the spontaneous ego development. The weaker the ego, the greater is the need to be loved, since nothing can so strongly confirm self-confidence as to be loved by another human being. But to be loved is different from the courage of active love, which takes the risk of surrender to the other whom he trusts. In his essay on narcissism, Freud suggests that the ego is weakened by love; the love object is idealized, overvalued, but the ego is supposed to be impoverished, humbled, in the case of unrequited love even humiliated. This passively receiving love is frequently used as a defense against anxiety.

Narcissistic libido does not necessarily impoverish the ego. It is true that there are conflicts between object love and narcissism, between self-preservation and altruism, Sartre's *pour-soi* and *pour-autrui*, the striving to become one's own ideal and the ideal of the beloved. An intimate relation of parent and child, lover and beloved can, under the pressure of anxiety or rage, deteriorate into a master-slave relation. It is true that the commitment to active love implies a risk, the beloved is losable, but a love that transcends anxieties enriches both lovers even in the face of frustrations. The anxious defensive narcissism holds on to life, but the lover is generous through the power of Eros transcending Thanatos. Even in the ultimate loss of life, Eros triumphs in the survivor by the preservation of loving memories; it mitigates the abandoned person's depression. The bereaved partner transcends the blow of destiny to his narcissism. Love transforms depression into grief that accepts inevitable frustration through the labor of mourning.

In the parent-child relation, there is such a discrepancy between the parents' strength, knowledge and competence in comparison to the child's helpless dependency that there is the danger that the loving care of the parent, particularly of the mother, might deteriorate into a sadomasochistic relation of dominance or possession. The mother may exploit or appropriate the child, or she may make herself a slave to the child's whims and wishes. This inequality, which is misused by parental defensive narcissism in a master-slave relation, also creeps into adolescent or adult erotic relations where the narcissistic demands of one or both partners may infringe on their capacity for spontaneous mutuality. The inequality between male and female is a source of latent conflict. Freud thought that the Oedipus conflict is solved by the male's giving up the claim for exclusive possession of the mother for the narcissistic gain of preserving his penis. The girl may give up her narcissistic claims, because she has already been punished by castration, or will be further damaged in her narcissism by cruel penetration. Castration anxiety and penis envy seem to me to be symbolic expressions of a male-female conflict that demands or offers narcissistic sacrifices in order to repress anxieties in the interpersonal relation. Genuine sacrifices must be made and are made by men as well as by women for the sake of the constancy of their mutual relation and their relation to their children. These sacrifices imply the endurance of inevitable frustrations. but they cannot be enforced by threat or punishment. When enforced, these sacrifices deteriorate into sadomasochistic manipulation, into revenge for the frustration rage that makes the other responsible for the hardships of fate, or into surrender to the partner for the sake of exploitation in an unending tooth and claw struggle for supremacy of the defensive narcissism of either partner. Many parent-child relations and husband-wife relations collapse at this impasse if the anxiety-laden conflict between the I and the you has been covered over by foul compromises and has not been faced squarely. The woman, who expects that the husband has to sacrifice his own freedom of development for her narcissistic need to be adored and protected, misses the grace of mutuality as much as the husband, who takes her gifts and services for granted as a tribute to his defensive narcissism. The sexual enjoyment can be a bond of spontaneous mutuality that enriches the benign narcissism of both partners, but the sexual act can also be degraded to a dutiful performance or a form of exploitation that leaves the total personalities empty, bored and unfulfilled, if there is no process of mutual inspiration going on which furthers a transcending development into the future of both. Likewise, the relation of parent and child that does not increase the potentialities of development in both does not contribute to the happiness of either.

Psychoanalysis has to unmask the various self-deceptions and illusions that arise in the pursuit of happiness by emotional alarm signals. Many persons pretend to be happy even if they are not; others complain about unhappiness with the indignant accusations of a typical "injustice collector." Happiness cannot be enforced, it is a gift of grace. A tension will always exist between the present state of development and its aspired transcendence into the future. There is anxiety in all decisions. The yearning for unlimited narcissistic omnipotence that would gratify autistic as well as symbiotic wishes can never be fulfilled. Sacrifices of narcissistic wishes are necessary to transcend inevitable frustrations. Limitations arouse anxieties, which enhance a defensive narcissism that tries to deny the tension and discrepancy between ego and self-image. Man sometimes believes that he is already what he wants to become; conceit, arrogance, boasting, and bragging mask the anxieties of indecision and incompletion. Sartre has expressed this discrepancy in a paradoxical form: Man is not what he is and he is what he is not.[19] In less paradoxical terms this means that man is in a constant flux of becoming. In this process he lets go what he has achieved and received, not to be deprived and to descend to Sartre's nothingness and meaninglessness, but to rise to a higher synthesis of his potentialities. Thus, narcissism cannot settle down in a complacent identity of ego and self. Self-deception, according to Sartre, stems from bad faith. It leads to repressions, dissociations, denial, and other forms of distorting defenses. But it is not the unconscious, anarchic cauldron of instincts that Sartre makes responsible for these defensive distortions. In order to repress, deny, or distort impulses that are unacceptable to oneself or others must pass a censorship, if only fleetingly, in order to be discarded or repressed in view of the danger signal of anxiety. Emotional signals are deceptive because they represent magical solutions of conflicts where frustrations have to be endured and transcended in hard labor. Protesting rage reactions try to remove the source of discomfort by a short-circuiting gesture of elimination or destruction. Egocentric search of pleasure and comfort demands immediate gratification, envy tries to even the score by hook and by crook,

19. Sartre , *L'Etre et le néant.*

vengeful impulses insist on nothing less than a complete defeat of the opponent and his unconditional surrender. Emotions remain tied to the pleasure-pain principle to avoid the pain of conflict, but the rationalist who denies the power of emotions remains under their sway the more he shuts his eyes to them and relies on his rationalizations. Emotions remain self-centered if a defensive narcissism persists and the individual cannot sacrifice part of his self-interest for the sake of the communion with others. The conflict of I and you may lead to tragic guilt when the Oedipus conflict remains unresolved.

The guilt of the Oedipus tragedy stemmed from the parents' anxiety elicited by the oracle that foretold the murder and superseding of the father by the son. Narcissistic anxiety drove the parents of Oedipus to abandon the child, leaving him to a cruel fate of almost certain death. By the complexities of fate, the guilt of the parents is transferred to the descendents. Basically, every parent is destined to be superseded by his descendants. Not only the child's but also the parents' narcissism rebels against destiny. The incestuous motive expresses the persistent regression to parent-child symbiosis; it stifles the process of growing individuation, and it destroys the family solidarity by the murderous impulses of egocentric competition. The classic tragedies of Oedipus and Hamlet demonstrate the conflict between individual self-preservation and family solidarity. Even a guilt that was removed from the hero's intention (Oedipus), the mother's breach of fidelity and the fratricidal murder of the father (in the case of Hamlet)—this all-too human guilt is transferred to the son as a challenge. A sense of guilt that stems from the binding solidarity of men arouses indignation, and it demands from the heir of injustice a decision to be or not to be, a sacrifice, in the case of Oedipus and Hamlet, the acceptance of a tragic destiny.

Sacrifice has frequently been degraded as a form of neurotic masochism in psychoanalytic literature. The very survival of mankind depends on our basic solidarity, which is actualized in the animal by automatic instinct regulation. In man, this solidarity is actualized instinctively in the mother-child symbiosis. But the actualization of solidarity in later life is frequently squelched by prevailing narcissistic interests of the isolated and alienated individual who spends his energies in the conflicts between self-preservation and solidarity, and in failures of defense against the hardships of fate. The Oedipus conflict is of such crucial importance in the development of man because narcissistic self-interest and solidarity come to a clash and demand decisions. Each child inherits his parents' guilt—Freud spoke of borrowed guilt feelings;[20] he inherits their neurotic maladaptations, their disharmonies and human incompletions. The Christians believed in inherited sin and have never been really comforted by the promise of salvation. The Oedipus conflict is a challenge to the child to find a solution for the problem, not only on a rational level of enlightened self-interest, but on the emotional level of a benign narcissism and human solidarity. Man in his existential anxiety has to make conscious decisions between being and nothingness, between his responsibility for personal self-preservation and his loyalty to family and larger units of solidarity. His longing for the peace and harmony of primary narcissism or primary love was in earlier periods of human history gratified by religious experience of unity with God, oceanic harmony, although this peace with God frequently became a sentimental illusion, or was torn up by fanatical persecution of those who did not share the faith. The intellectual of Western culture has, at present, no universal faith that provides security, and human solidarity is still a utopia. Man acts in bad faith when his defensive narcissism in an emotional conflict represses, denies or dissociates his existential anxiety, the danger signal of frustration. He cannot endure the tension between his longing for mastery of fate and divine perfection, on the one hand, and his recognition of his tragic inability to reach this superhuman goal, on the other hand.

Existential philosophy, as well as psychoanalysis, has taken up the cudgels for the individual in his struggle for authenticity, i.e. truth to himself and genuine spontaneity, holding that both are in danger of being lost under the pressure of a mass society whose rational means of technology are far ahead of emotional control. Education is too much directed toward accumulation of tech-

20. Freud, *The Ego and the Id.*

nology, facts, and data. This knowledge, though useful, does not provide the means of emotional control. Psychoanalysis has to stress the responsibility of the individual to revise evasive decisions that have led to lopsided defensive habits. Psychoanalysis cannot abolish tragic sacrifices in the course of responsible decisions. The patient feels frequently irresponsibly determined by the forces of unconscious instincts. When the narcissistic defenses fail, the individual feels doomed to isolation, alienation, disharmony in his intimate relations. Psychoanalysis accepts the challenge to re-awaken the original good faith of the individual by leading him back to the original emotional conflicts in the living experience of transference and countertransference. The emotional conflict between self-preservation and preservation of human solidarity cannot be solved once and for all, but in the encounters of I and You that transcend the split between them, the frustration rage can come into the open and gradually subside. In the psychoanalytic encounter, the patient can learn to forgive himself and his parents, to sacrifice his claim for unconditional love, his grandiose protest against destiny and his enraged craving for magical help; he can give up the masochistic submission to authority for the sake of rewards; and he can outgrow the negative therapeutic reaction of revenge. In psychoanalytic treatment, the genuine I-You relations are gradually crystallized out of the distortions of transference-countertransference maneuvers that are dictated by the narcissistic defenses against emergency emotions of anxiety, rage, hatred, envy and revenge. Neurotic anxieties and psychotic panic are differentiated from deeper existential anxieties, neurotic guilt feelings from existential responsibility. The analyst cannot abolish existential anxiety and guilt, but he can bring repressed conflicts to awareness and strengthen the sense of responsibility. The genuine sacrifice of the distorted goals of a defensive narcissism makes room for a higher level of integration of egosyntonic goals. In the transition from the unconscious innocence of primary autonomy to a preconsciously and consciously controlled benign narcissism, the erotic forces of spontaneous generosity are freed for a new beginning, a new balance between the authenticity of a benign narcissism and a trusting mutuality in interpersonal relations.

The Psychotherapy of the
Affective Psychoses

Manic-depressive psychoses have been approached by psycho-therapists with a certain reluctance. The ambulatory treatment of manic-depressive patients implies a considerable risk of suicide, or of the deleterious effects of acting out. But beyond that, we find a widespread pessimism as to the therapeutic results in their treatment. The pyknic body scheme, the frequency of this psychosis in the same family, the regularity of the cycles, all contribute to the fortification of the assumption that the manic-depressive psychoses are psychotherapeutically inaccessible. Psychodynamically oriented psychiatrists like Sullivan, who showed an inspiring hopefulness and skill in work with schizophrenic patients, were rather hopeless about the manic-depressive.[1] Though the prognosis of a single manic or depressive phase is not bad, the hope of the psychotherapist to change the character basis of the psychosis, and to prevent the recurrence of pathological cycles, is dim. The recommendation of pharmacological, sleep, or shock treatment of manic-depressive patients is more frequent than in any other psychopathological disorder. Karl Abraham, who first applied psychoanalytic techniques to the treatment of circular psychoses, recommended psychoanalytic treatment not in the acute phases of the psychosis, but in the free interval where the patient, according to Abraham, behaves, and is analytically accessible, like an obsessional neurotic.[2] In the psychoanalytic literature, theories about the psychodynam-

Reprinted by permission from *Psychotherapy of the Psychoses,* ed. Arthur Burton, © 1961 by Basic Books, Inc. Publishers, New York.

1. Harry Stack Sullivan, *The Interpersonal Theory of Psychiatry* (New York: Norton, 1953), p. 284.

2. Karl Abraham, *Selected Papers on Psychoanalysis* (New York: Basic Books, 1953).

ics of manic-depressive psychoses prevail over case presentations, and some manic-depressive case histories presented by Helene Deutsch, George Gerö, and Edith Jacobson are partially atypical, since hysteric, obsessional, schizophrenic, and paranoid features complicated the pictures of the treated illnesses.[3] Edward Bibring described the depressive syndrome in various organic as well as psychogenic illnesses, in depersonalization as well as states of boredom, and Bert Lewin has concentrated his investigation on the syndrome of elation.[4] However, the idea that manic-depressive syndromes present a unity has not been dropped by these psychoanalysts. In a Washington study group twelve cases of this psychosis have been studied and certain common character features of them have been elaborated. These criteria, which characterize family background and early life experience of the patients, have been submitted to a statistical comparative study by R. W. Gibson.[5]

In these studies the dynamics of the character structure of the manic-depressive patients have been spelled out in the patterns of their interpersonal relations. The families of these patients occupied an isolated, exceptional role in the community; they were concerned with gaining and maintaining a position of prestige or success and the patients were from childhood on destined to remedy the failures under which the families suffered. The parents were at war with each other. One parent was weak and unable to achieve success, and the more aggressively striving parent, frequently the mother, blamed the partner for the family's plight.

3. Helene Deutsch, "Zur Psychologie der Manisch-depressiven Zustande, insbesondere der chronischen Hypomanie," *Internationale Zeitschrift für Psychoanalyse* 19 (1933); George Gerö, "The Construction of Depression," *International Journal of Psycho-Analysis* 17 (1936): 423–61; Edith Jacobson, "Depression: the Oedipus Complex in the Development of Depressive Mechanisms," *Psychiatric Quarterly* 12 (1943): 541–60.

4. Edward Bibring, "Das Problem der Depression," *Psyche* 6 (Stuttgart, 1952): 81–101; Bert Lewin, *The Psychoanalysis of Elation* (New York: Norton, 1950).

5. Mabel B. Cohen, Grace Baker, Robert A. Cohen, Frieda Fromm-Reichmann, and Edith Weigert, "An Intensive Study of Twelve Cases of Manic-depressive Psychosis," *Psychiatry* 17 (1954): 103–37; Robert W. Gibson, "The Family Background and Early Life Experience of the Manic-depressive Patient," *Psychiatry* 21 (1958): 71–100.

The tensions in the family were often increased by sibling rivalry, and the patient, in a favorite position, was exposed to envy and inclined to undersell himself and to hide his qualifications. The lack of consistent parental authority led to weakness in the consolidation of the patient's ego and superego and made him dependent on the anonymous, vacillating authority of the conventionalities of public opinion. The crucial disturbance of the ego formation could be traced to the early infantile phase of identification with the mother. Due to anxieties in this early closeness, the person of the child and that of the parent are not clearly crystallized; the splitting into a good and bad object, as well as a good and bad subject, maintains the ambivalence so characteristic for the manic-depressive patient.

PHENOMENOLOGY OF THE MANIC-DEPRESSIVE PERSONALITY

I want to continue this study by consolidating the features that the manic-depressive patients that I was able to observe have in common, and compare them with the characteristics that have been elaborated in the former studies.

When we look at the patient between episodes of his illness, we are startled by the change in his external behavior; he vanishes into the background of a given environment with a pseudonymity that reminds one of the mimicry of animals that take on the protective coloring of their surroundings. The patient says what he is expected to say, and he smiles when he is supposed to smile. He takes his clues from his encounters, in superficial imitation obviously intended to please and not to hurt. But this imitation does not give him opportunity to explore what is going on in the other person or in himself. He does not lose time and energy in introspection, since he seems to be preoccupied with the superficial impression he makes on his surroundings. His self-esteem seems to walk on a tightrope and the conventional amiability has to guarantee that he has no enemies, that he does not fall into disgrace. He can play different roles, but this role-playing is geared to applause and it remains unconvincingly artificial. Since it does not reveal the real person, it lacks the subtleties that characterize a person's uniqueness. The manic-depressive patient carries to excess the features of the other-directed individual (Riesman), of the unauthentic "man" in a mass society (Heidegger), who imitates everybody and anybody, is directed by rumor and gossip, by waves of public opinion, without the experience of personal, responsible decisions and direction toward goals of his own.

Nevertheless, the manic-depressive patient remains very vulnerable. His sensitivities are reflected in his changing mood swings, his tendency to be emotionally contaminated, irresistibly weeping with those who are sad and laughing in abandon with the cheering crowd. But the manic-depressive patient is a victim of the emotions which he conceals behind his conventional façade, and which scarcely enter his cognitive sphere, though the patient has a more than average degree of intelligence at his disposal. His emotions and mood swings remain enigmatic to him; they overwhelm him and sweep him off his feet. When the façade of conventional adaptation breaks down under emotional pressure, the patient becomes a captive of a monotonously grinding depression or a runaway, flighty elation. In the manic mood he still hangs on to spurious pride, an illusionary arrogance; in the melancholic episode the self-esteem is lost in a delusion of inferiority. This loss of self-esteem presents a serious danger to survival, for it undermines "the instinct which compels every living thing to cling to life."[6]

THE PSYCHOTIC ATTACK

Freud has compared the outbreak of an acute melancholia to the normal process of mourning. The phenomenology of both processes does show great similarities, with the exception, says Freud, that the disturbance of self-regard is absent in mourning. "In mourning it is the world which has become poor and empty, in melancholia it is the ego itself."[7] The melancholic attack is sometimes preceded by a loss of a beloved person, but at other times it is hard to discover the loss which the patient has suffered.

6. Joseph Smith, "The Metaphor of the Manic-Depressive," *Psychiatry* 23 (1960): 375–83.

7. Sigmund Freud, "Mourning and Melancholia," in *The Complete Psychological Works of Sigmund Freud*, vol. 14 (London: Hogarth, 1957), pp. 243–58, 249.

One patient became depressed just when he had reached the summit of success, a highly responsible and independent position, but he had no superiors from whom he could secure advice and guidance; he was left to his own devices, and was exposed to demands, criticisms, and envy. He felt deeply unsure whether he could live up to the expectations of others. He suddenly felt isolated and became depressed.

Another patient became depressed at the time when he became engaged to be married. As long as he strove toward this goal he was elated, carried by hopes and images of future fulfillment. He struggled tirelessly to conquer the doubts of his beloved woman and the resistance of her parents. But when he had reached his goal, his hopes suddenly collapsed and he became beset by doubts: Could he live up to the realistic commitment? Was his love strong enough to endure the monotony and tribulations of daily adjustment? He suddenly became aware of flaws and shortcomings in his previously idealized partner. Would not disappointments, fault-finding, resentment, and hatred creep up and mar the image of perfect marital bliss by which his former drive had been carried?

The ego of the depressed patient is impoverished by the loss of hope. But not only is the ego impoverished, his world becomes poor and empty too; it appears dark and colorless, tedious and estranged when the light of hope and trust in love is extinguished. The contours of his scene of living become the walls of a prison. The closeness to the partner becomes suffocating while he clings to her. The windows into the future are closed by blinds. The patient and his world are both impoverished. What Heidegger calls "being-in-the-world" becomes meaningless. The contrast becomes particularly poignant when the depressive mood has been preceded by ecstatic hopes and ideal expectations which carried the stamp of illusionary wish fulfillment. The all-embracing hope for perfect bliss changes into the bleak despair of nothingness. Entering into a depression is like entering into Dante's Inferno, "Lasciate ogni speranga voi ch'entrate." The proverbial saying "While there is life, there is hope" could be turned around for the melancholic patient:"While there is hope, there is life."

The vital functions of the melancholic patient are deeply disturbed, since he has no hope. His appetite is low; there is no taste in his food; less frequently he gorges his food as if he could fill an inner emptiness. He does not sleep, or his sleep is fitful, unrefreshing, as if the fear of annihilation kept him alerted and when he awakens from a restless sleep he faces another day of hopelessness. He struggles through the agitations of despair and may find some relief in evening hours from sheer exhaustion. The agitation and anxieties indicate agitation against the tragedy of his fate. In a retarded depression he succumbs to mute despair. The agitated patient's self-expression is reduced to monotonous whining and wailing, resembling the crying of a deserted child. But the tragedy is that the cry for help remains frustrated; the comfort that is offered does not bring relief and may even increase the despair. The patient clings to the doctor or the nurse, follows him or her around with a sticky insistence on being relieved, but there is no comfort in the tender touch either.

The melancholic patient, unlike the paranoid patient, seldom accuses his helper, and mostly accuses himself of his hopeless condition. Freud has pointed out that the self-accusations of the melancholic patient are insincere and imply a more or less veiled blame of the object by whom the patient feels deserted.[8] The patient's anger, rage, hatred, resentment, and vindictiveness that have been repressed return out of repression, and torture not only the patient, who is sensitive to these painful emotions but also his immediate environment, which cannot offer any relief. The insistence on being frustrated is interpreted as a turning of the patient's hostilities against himself and as an attempt at expiation of guilt. Edward Bibring has warned against applying this formula automatically to the understanding of the depressed patient's predicament.[9]

I see an even closer similarity between the depressed patient and the mourning person. In his bereavement the mourner is deprived of hope. He has not so much to eradicate his memories of the past—these memories may become in the long run a blessing—but he has to shift the goal of his hopes for the future and that is a painful

8. Ibid.
9. Bibring, "Das Problem der Depression."

process. There is no love relation so free from possessiveness and ambivalence that the loss of the beloved partner would not leave the bereaved person with a bleak look into the future, with some resentment against the desertion, and some indignant protest against fate. As to the past, the bereaved person is mortified that the passed love relation has not been deeper or more fulfilling. The higher the ideals of blissful union, the deeper is the pang of remorse. For the bereaved person cannot turn his accusations against the lost partner who is now more than ever idealized—*de mortuis nil nisi bene.*

The labor of mourning is therefore also a work of repentance, implying the wish for a deeper capacity for love and dedication. It is not only the sober acceptance of reality—that the dead person is definitely lost—which lifts the mourner gradually out of his state of painful bereavement. Neither is it the magical belief of expiating his guilt by suffering that liberates him from his grief. When the mourner gradually gives up his bid for omnipotence and his raging against fate, it is the awakening of hope and trust in his creative ability to love and dedicate himself which rises out of the humiliating, yet clarifying and cleansing, experience of mourning and repentance. In the labor of mourning a sublimation takes place, a resignation as to immediate gratification and a shift of hope toward new, sometimes more removed goals. When the bereaved person outgrows the selfishness of his egocentric clinging possessiveness, his attachment to the memory of the departed as well as to the world that is still left to him may rise to a level of less demanding and more promising spiritual integration.

The melancholic patient is seriously handicapped in the labor of mourning as well as in the work of repentance. He has been so much infatuated with the image of his goodness, his perfection, and with the power of being successful that he is entrenched in a position of all-or-nothing-demands identical with his ideals. There is no distance between him and his ideals, as there is no distance between him and the object of his personal attachment. He has lived in illusions about his realistic limitations. His hopes were directed toward an unreachable goal, as if it were immediately reachable, and his striving lacked a realistic humility. If a person is intoxicated by the ideal to be Caesar or nihil, he may find him-self sooner or later in the abyss of the nihil, the despair of nothing-ness. His hopes lose their meaning, but he is not yet capable of going through the process of renunciation and reorientation which would give his hopes new directions.

Thomas French has pointed out how important the goal-direc-tion of hope is for the integration of the total personality.[10] Hope provides the experience of subjective freedom of choice, since the libidinal and aggressive instinctual energies are collected and converge toward a goal that has the ego's confirmation. There-with the erotic drives are in the lead over the aggressive drives. In the despair of melancholia this directive, organizing function of hope is lost, the complete disorganization of a psychosis threatens, or the patient is compulsively driven into suicide, since life has lost its positive values for him. But the pains of melancholia can become the birth pains of renewal, liberating the potentialities. Immediate gratifications are relinquished in the labor of mourning. In this very renunciation, a redirection toward new goals prepares the reintegration of the personality. Every creative process of sub-limation is initiated by some labor of mourning.

Another pathological way out of the depression is the flight into a manic state of defense which represents a caricature of hope, a distortion of trust into gullibility, an illusory self-definition in which the patient loses the distance from his ideals. There remains sufficient residues of doubt to interfere with the patient's sense of security. He changes the images of his aspired identity, his plans, his foresights, so rapidly and so abruptly that the observer is alarmed by the process of accelerated movement, of disregard for boundaries and interpersonal considerations. The patient is fleeing from his anxiety of disintegration; he puts little trust in his hopes, his aggressive impulses win out over the impulses of Eros, a diffusion of instinctual impulses explodes the collectedness and goal-directedness of the personality. His interpersonal contacts be-come attenuated, spurious, and transient, directed only toward a momentary exploitation of ego support by outsiders. Mourning

10. Thomas M. French, *The Integration of Behavior*, vol. 1 (Chicago: Univer-sity of Chicago Press, 1952).

and remorse are more or less completely repressed. In the transition from a depression to the sudden activation and expansion of a manic attack the danger of suicide is most intense; the prison walls break down, but as yet there is no trust in a hopeful rebirth of a widened and fortified personality.

CHILDHOOD HISTORY

The outstanding features of a lack of hope and trust lead us back into the childhood history although the outbreak of a typical manic-depressive psychosis does not occur until after puberty. Psychoanalytic literature has stressed the oral phase of libido development and the accompanying incorporative tendencies which may determine the development of a later affective psychosis. Melanie Klein has described the "depressive position," the struggle of the infant to accept the good and the bad mother as a total person, incorporating enough of the good mother to endure the frustrations of the bad one.[11] René Spitz and Margaret Ribble have described the anaclitic depression.[12] The loss of the mother's tender care in the period of oral, nutritive dependency leads at first to an agitated, anxious protest, then to a waning of vitality that, without the return of the mothering relation, leads to death. We may see in the anaclitic depression a precursor of later melancholia, but there are many stages of possible recuperation and solidification between this early deprivation and the outbreak of an illness in adulthood.

The oral deprivation is certainly an important factor in the history of manic-depressives, but it has perhaps been overemphasized in psychoanalytic literature. Bowlby, under the influence of ethological literature, has pointed to other primary factors in the infant's tie to the mother, the crying, the clinging, the responsive smiling, and the following. And distortions of these primary func-

11. Melanie Klein, *Contributions to Psychoanalysis* (London: Hogarth, 1950), p. 291.
12. René Spitz, "Anaclitic Depression," in *Psychoanalytic Study of the Child*, vol. 2 (New York: International Universities Press, 1946); Margaret Ribble, *The Rights of Infants* (New York: Columbia University Press, 1943).

tions appear in the melancholic attacks—the crying, clinging, and following—while the smiling seems completely extinguished.[13]

The predisposition for a manic-depressive illness is influenced by the total parent-infant relation in all its emotional aspects and their further development in childhood. Therese Benedek describes the total "depressive constellation" in childhood.[14] She distinguishes three types of mother-child relations. The first, which gives the child the most secure preparation for life, is that of the discerning, responsive mother who trusts her own instinctive motherliness as well as the growing potentialities and self-sufficiency in the child; she lets him use his imagination and allows him playfully to experiment with new discoveries without exposing him to unnecessarily discouraging frustrations.

The second relation is loaded with frustration, anger, and rejection. The mother either did not welcome the child in the first place, or she trusts him and her motherliness so little that she misinterprets his cries for help or his clinging, as signs of her own failures. She throws her hands up in angry despair and the child finds himself forsaken, rejected, and he reacts to his mother's anger with defiant withdrawal, anger, or hatred. When the child survives the frustrations of this constellation, he may develop a distrustful toughness, a determination not to be fooled, and to shift for himself. He seemingly resigns himself to frustration, convinced that he has a bad parent, but his brittle self-sufficiency may break down under stress and strain, if no trustworthy experiences come to his rescue later.

The third type of relation, according to Benedek, represents the depressive constellation: it is that of the anxious, oversolicitious and over-protective mother who does not trust her child's growing abilities, nor her own adequate response; she remains at the beck and call of his wishes, and she tries to protect him anxiously against inevitable frustrations, she keeps him captivated in the primary symbiotic unity which should be gradually superseded

13. J. Bowlby, "The Nature of the Child's Tie to His Mother," *International Journal of Psycho-Analysis* 39 (1958): 1–24.

14. Therese Benedek, "Toward the Biology of the Depressive Constellation," *Journal of the American Psychoanalytic Association* 3 (1956): 389–427.

by a mutual encounter between an *I* and a *you* as two unities gradually becoming independent.

In the depressive constellation there is a lack of trust—that basic trust which Erikson called the matrix of all wholesome development.[15] This basic trust provides for the future of the growing child the unshakable security that he is not alone; that there is hope also in times of frustration; that somebody is there to understand and meet his needs. The concept of basic trust describes the mutual responsiveness and gratification between mother and infant better than the concept of primary narcissism which makes of the dependent infant a self-centered tyrant. But when the basic trust is defective, we observe the development of a secondary, defensive narcissism growing out of the anxiously disturbed mother-infant relation. In the depressive constellation the original symbiosis fails in due time to be replaced by an encounter of an *I* and a *you* who define their needs to each other, experience pleasure and pain, joy, and angry protest, yet arrive ever again at the harmony of mutual understanding and gratification. In the depressive constellation the symbiotic identification persists. The anxious, overprotective mother clings to the child. She is not able to hope wholeheartedly for his growing independence and she worries and clings to him for solace as he clings to her. The child is seduced to exploit her solicitous submission to his unlimited wishes for his defensive narcissism, yet he feels insecure about the lack of defined boundaries in his field of action. The mother feels guilty for any frustration to which the child has to be exposed and the child shares the mother's anxiety, grief, and despair first on the preverbal level where the wordless emotional contamination becomes a powerful, overwhelming experience.

Later the child becomes the parent's confidant on the level of verbal communication, when the symbiotic identification still partially persists. The emotional contamination outweighs the rational understanding; the child cannot digest the communications and is swept off his feet by the parent's worrisome complaints or stunned by the adult's self-defeat. The child's imagination is overstimu-

15. Erik Erikson, *Childhood and Society* (New York: Norton, 1950).

lated by the waves of intense contaminating emotions. He cannot yet sufficiently distinguish between imagination and reality, and the progress from the primary to the secondary process of thinking is delayed. The child remains more an onlooker than an actor. When his own wishes and impulses urge him to act, to defiantly declare his independence, to protest against the imposition of social rules and regulations, like cleanliness, sphincter control, and later forms of disciplined behavior, he encounters parental distress: "How can you do this to me!" The child's aggressiveness is unacceptable to the parent, for it disrupts the symbiotic identification violently and the child shrinks away from his explosions of anger and rage. He does not learn to tame them in experimental play and fighting encounters that settle the differences between the *I* and the *you* in reasonable and creative integration. The persistent identification does not permit a clear definition of boundaries between the *I* and the *you*. The child's aggressiveness appears uncanny and dangerous to him and becomes even more intimidating when it explodes in temper tantrums and uncontrollable scenes of mutual aggravation and spiraling exasperation.

Since the child is handicapped in changing his world to suit his wishes by techniques of alloplastic action, he withdraws more and more into the world of autoplastic imagination. The aggression that is not channelized into the skills of self-defense and self-assertion builds up air castles of victorious grandiosity. These omnipotential fantasies of a secondary narcissism are further nourished by a position of favoritism in relation to one or the other parent who seeks his or her vicarious gratification in close identification with this child; the symbiotic identification may shift from mother and child to a similarly close identification between father and child. The parent plans the child's future from his egocentric point of view. A daughter has to be trained for the artistic career that the mother missed because of her marriage. A son has to make up for the disappointments his father suffered when he had to sacrifice an academic career to make a living for an economically hard pressed family. A child has to replace a deceased sibling, and to live up to idealization that glorifies the image of the dead child in the eyes of the parents.

Sullivan has impressively described the havoc created in a child's development by the contamination of parental anxieties.[16] Freud has mentioned "borrowed guilt feelings" in the childhood history of melancholic patients.[17] We frequently find depressions and pathologic mourning processes in the family to which the patient has been exposed in his childhood. Heredity may be an important factor contributing to the development of a later affective psychosis. But in addition, the favorite child of a depressed parent is exposed to contamination by intense anxieties, depressive and desperate emotions which stunt his development. Some sketchy examples may illustrate this thesis.

A child who was born soon after her father's suicide had to share the mother's nagging guilt feelings and despondency from the early days of her existence. She lacked the zest for living and maintained a persistent pessimism, a chronically depressive outlook on her chances of survival. Where the depressed parent in his own despondency leans heavily on his favorite child as a redeemer and savior, the child is seduced to believe in his omnipotent, messianic role, but on the other hand he finds himself again and again impotent to stave off the parental despair. The child's vital need for admiration and emulation of a vitally strong parent is frustrated. He dreams of heroic and demonic roles, but he cannot try them out and fit them to his real size because his aggressive impulses elicit the weak parent's worried wailings. When he tries to shake off the dependency and overidentification with the depressed parent, such acts because of shame and defiance engender new guilt feelings and insecurities about his identity.

A manic-depressive patient spent the first six years of his life alone with a depressed mother while the father tried to build up a new economic existence in a far-removed country. When mother and son joined the father in a completely strange environment, the son was bewildered about his identity. He became ashamed of his mother and yet guilty for deserting her in her depressions. He did not want to be a sissy and shifted his clinging dependency to

16. Sullivan, *The Interpersonal Theory of Psychiatry.*
17. Sigmund Freud, "Das Ich und das Es," in *Gesammelte Schriften,* vol. 2 (Leipzig Internationaler Psychoanalytischer Verlag, 1925), p. 395 n.

his contemporaries outside the family. He now imitated the big boys in his environment. His rage exploded in minor delinquencies; his explosive aggressiveness was unskilled, fumbling, and enigmatic to him and others. In adolescence he became a joiner restlessly preoccupied with failure and success. He was compelled to prove his magic power in a constant gamble with the risks of fate. He could not relax in his pursuit of dazzling success, for he had never given up the omnipotent position in early childhood. His bravado was unconvincing because it remained intensely vulnerable to failure. When a person of prestige did not greet him, when his schedule was not filled with appointments, when his appeal for popularity fell flat, he sank into a feeling of worthlessness and complete defeat. As an adult he was still clinging to the compensatory pseudosecurity of his bid for omnipotence. He was late wherever he went, as if he could magically overcome the barriers of time and space and gain pretentious prestige from keeping people waiting for him. Whenever he could afford it, he let his temper fly in boisterous anger, as if his noisy indignation would have a magic power over his fellow men. But an accumulation of failures threw him into the nothingness of melancholic despair.

A woman patient had as a teenager succeeded by her managerial talents to separate the parents who were embroiled in a sadomasochistic interdependence. This separation saved her father from alcoholism and her mother from a depression. The daughter sank into a depression when her heroic efforts became dispensable and the parents could again take care of themselves. She felt hopeless since she now missed the justification for her existence and ruminated in an agitated depression about the meaninglessness of life, insisting stubbornly that only a convincing supernatural knowledge about man's fate after death could give her peace. Hidden in her impetuous, obsessive ruminations lay the nostalgic longing for basic trust and hope for a new lease on life.

The disturbed emotional development of the patient who sooner or later becomes the victim of an affective psychosis precludes ever reaching the level of the Oedipus conflict. The prolonged symbiotic identification with a weak, possessive, and exploitative parent has provided the patient with a position of favoritism and ill-defined ego boundaries, so that his self-esteem vacillates between over- and underestimation of his real potentialities. In his arrogant imagination he considers himself at times the victor in the family battle centered around the Oedipus conflict. Parental over-indulgence and overprotection have not confronted his impetuous bid for omnipotence with realistic limitations and necessary renunciations. He has missed a strong parent whom he could admire and emulate; his compassion for a helpless, weak parent turns sooner or later into impotent rebellion, shame, and contempt; and his borrowed guilt feelings, the residues of persisting identifications with the parent, elicit self-doubt and self-contempt. Libidinal and aggressive impulses have remained partially diffused. These impulses remain untamed and unskilled, explosive, and poorly controlled. There is a nostalgic yearning for basic trust, but his hopes reach only fleeting products of his imagination. There is no consolidated *I* able to encounter a *you* and to respect the mutual boundaries. The weakness of the ego elicits a constant defensive selfish concern and need for narcissistic supplies. If a partner does not lend himself as a means of support, there is not enough trust to prevent the anxiety of annihilation. The lack of ego consolidation corresponds to a lack of definition of the superego. Freud called the superego the heir of the Oedipus conflict; but when the Oedipus conflict remains unsolved the superego is more a super-id, deeply anchored in the archaic desires for emotional omnipotent mastery, but buffeted by the waves of approval and disapproval by external authority without a rudder of his own. Instead of the rationally consolidated superego we find a multiplicity of ego ideals, images of absolute perfection and grandiosity. The ideal of being the parents' redeemer is one of the most exalted ideals, but its realization is doomed to failure.

ADULTHOOD

Erikson has masterfully described the identity crises of a religious genius who suffered from manic and depressive mood swings in

Young Man Luther.[18] The lack of ego cohesion makes for a prolonged adolescence; the young person needs a moratorium from
society to find himself and the goal toward which he is striving.
The dependence on conventionality and external approval is only
a protective shield hiding the deep insecurity in the young person's
self-realization. He has a great versatility in imitation and role-
playing, he vacillates between active and passive, masculine and
feminine roles, his fantasy may roam like that of Kierkegaard
through the vast realm of historical and mythological ancestry to
find a suitable image for identification and emulation. Far beyond
biological adolescence the modern manic-depressive patient visualizes himself in most contradictory roles, e.g. as successful capi-
talist and businessman on the one hand, and as a socialistic pacifist
on the other hand. The manic-depressive woman patient visualizes
her future as that of a dedicated wife and mother and, at other
times, as that of an ambitious career woman. Introjected into the
ego is the image of the defeated, despondent parent from whom
he has not dared to emancipate himself in healthy aggressiveness. He has not gone through the resignation of the Oedipus conflict and has not accepted the boundaries of his ego. The projection
of fantastic omnipotent ego ideals militates against the introjected despondency. The shifting ego ideals carry the hope for
perfection and redemption. If his hope collapses the ego is left in a
state of hopeless, helpless impotence. The nostalgic yearning for
the original symbiotic closeness to the parent is reflected in the
religious wish to lose himself in an all-embracing cause, in an all-
consuming passion that threatens to devour the ego; but the very
threat of annihilation is so loaded with anxieties that the patient
clings to self-confirming supplies from the outside and submits
to conventional behavior patterns to secure his survival. But in the
midst of success the fear of defeat creeps up on him in enigmatic
mood swings. A passage in Kierkegaard describes this abrupt
alteration of mood: "I have just returned from a party of which
I was the life and soul; wit poured from my lips, everyone laughed
and admired me—but I went away—and the dash should be as

18. Erik Erikson, *Young Man Luther* (New York: Norton, 1958).

long as the Earth's orbit——————and wanted to shoot my-self."[19]

Under the biological pressure of instincts and the social pressure for cultural adaptation the individual strives for self-realization, or authentic selfhood, which transcends the limits of his biological and social functions in the vision of an integrated self-image projected into the future. This self-image has a supreme value for the human being because it gives meaning to individual existence. The existential philosophers, with the exception of Sartre, who considers human existence as meaningless and absurd, have pointed out that the individual by his capacity of self-awareness struggles to maintain his authentic selfhood and his spiritual uniqueness, even to the point of sacrifice of his own life in defense against internal and external pressures. In the manic-depressive patient this spiritual uniqueness and vision of authentic selfhood is tragically threatened by the nostalgic yearning for the archaic symbiotic union of the self with the other, the defective use of aggressiveness for self-assertion and self-definition, and the leaning on conventional adaptation for the sake of social confirmation that has to make up for incomplete self-definition. The ill-defined ego boundaries or lack of cohesiveness of the ego are reflected in "phenomena of depersonalization in which the individual is aware of his body without being aware that it is his."[20] Phenomena of depersonalization, of self-alienation, are very frightening experiences; they are accompanied by a subjective feeling of loss of freedom and self-determination. Milder forms of self-alienation are boredom and a feeling of inner emptiness.

Side by side with the compulsive submission to conventionality we find in the manic-depressive patient symptoms of rebellion, a search for freedom from the chains of unauthentic conventionality. There are a number of artists among the manic-depressives who struggle for self-expression. Ernst Kris has described the artist's

---

19. Søren Kierkegaard, *The Journals*, ed. and trans. A. Dru (New York: Oxford University Press, 1938).

20. Henry Elkin, "On the Origin of the Self," *Psychoanalysis and Psychoanalytic Review* 45 (1958–59): 61.

regression in the service of the ego.[21] As long as the artist is creative he is relatively free from depressions; in sterile episodes he often sinks back into self-contempt and despair. Like Kierkegaard, the artist tries to free himself from the "sickness unto death," from the paradox of desperately wanting to be himself and desperately not wanting to be himself; the artist creates himself and simultaneously loses himself, in a creation that encompasses his world and recreates the archaic symbiotic unity between the self and the other.

The search for selfhood enters into a critical phase when the manic-depressive patient is confronted with an experience of love. Insofar as the manic-depressive patient is tied by the chains of conventionality, the erotic experience remains superficially determined by the dependence on success or failure. The erotic conquest provides a triumph, a powerful confirmation which silences the doubts about his worth. The sexual competence is not necessarily weakened by the inability to solve the Oedipus conflict in childhood. Among the patients that I have treated there were persons who demonstrated a considerable prowess in sexual performance but an excessive anxiety in view of any commitment. The manic-depressive patient is frequently intensely attracted by a person on whom he projects the fantasy-image of goodness and perfection, and the attachment seems to promise complete bliss and happiness. But a commitment awakens his anxiety, the anxiety of inner disintegration due to the awakening of his repressed aggressive-destructive impulses which might destroy the love object and/or himself. We frequently find a tendency towards Don Juanism in the manic-depressive patient; he escapes from one love object to another with the ever-renewed illusory hope that a new love relation might bring redemption from the evil within him. The sexual prowess does not suffice to convince the manic-depressive of his goodness and wholeness. "Where the persecution-anxiety for the ego is in the ascendant, a full and stable identification with

21. Ernst Kris, *Psychoanalytic Explorations in Art* (New York: International Universities Press, 1952).

another object, in the sense of looking at it and understanding it as it really is, and a full capacity for love, are not possible."[22] Since the cohesion of the I is not established, the patient is not able to experience the full, real You; the projections of his wishes and fantasies stand between the *I* and the *you*. An intense yearning arises for full identification, for the oceanic feeling of perfect union, the bliss of the primordial symbiosis, but the demonic images of anxiety to be possessed, exploited, annihilated or to possess, exploit, annihilate the other drive him into flight. A classical example of such a flight is Kierkegaard's engagement to Regina Olsen: as soon as he committed himself, he became aware of the death of his love and after a year of torturous conflicts and ruminations he dissolved the engagement. He experienced a deep despair; the words that Dostoevski put in the mouth of the Staretz Sossima describe the state of mind that Kierkegaard went through: "What is hell? I think it is the pain that one is no more able to love."[23]

The marital relations of manic-depressive patients are burdened with severe tensions of ambivalence. The manic-depressive patient frequently has the illusion of being a good lover, since his hostilities have been repressed since early childhood days and he may take his need to depend on the partner, or to make the partner depend upon him, as an expression of his ability for warmth and affection. But there is a lack of distance, of respect for the boundaries of the *I* and the *you* which acts as a constant irritant infringement on the partners' need for self-assertion. The enthusiasm that wipes out the boundaries and fills the partners with momentary joy and bliss wears off in daily frictions when a consensus or a balance of interests cannot be reached. The manic-depressive patient expects not only himself but also the partner to live up to standards of perfection. Any departure from the ideal of a perfect union gives rise to the specter of ambivalence which is insufficiently neutralized in the fusion of identification. The manic-de-

22. Klein, *Contributions to Psychoanalysis*, p. 291.

23. Fëdor Dostoevski, *Die Brüder Karamasoff* (Munich: Piper Verlag, 1916), 1:651.

pressive patient is, as I have described before, intensely vulnerable to disappointment and even minimal slights or indications of the possibility of desertion; these give rise to feelings of resentment and hostility to which the manic-depressive is sensitive. The divergences cannot be argued out in free communication since mobilized hatred cannot be endured. Withdrawal intensifies the inner conflict, "the shadow of the deserted object falls on the subject,"[24] and the manic-depressive is tormented by self-reproaches which may initiate the sliding into depression.

I have mentioned before the lack of sincerity in melancholic self-reproaches. Genuine repentance and true humility would imply an acknowledgment of resentment, envy, and hatred, of all those negative emotions which are mobilized by the closeness of the I and the you. Such acknowledgment would broaden the boundaries of the I, not in the sense of boundless ecstasy but in the sense of a more realistic definition of his self which permits also an acceptance of the you in a loving respect for the boundaries. The marital relation of the manic-depressive patient rarely leads to such resigned awareness of the limiting defensive selfishness and to an experience of a genuine encounter of the I and the you. The intimate relation of the manic-depressive patient returns in most cases to that of ambivalent dependency, to denial of competition, castration anxiety and penis envy, to denial of inner loneliness, since the tragic human uniqueness and loneliness remains unbearable for him. A more or less superficial peace can be maintained; since the patient is an excellent manipulator, he manages a tolerable adjustment, using the partner as a provider of narcissistic supplies and generously providing for the partner. He masters the interpersonal situation by domination or submission, and in this using and being used, exploiting and being exploited, there may be enough instinctual gratification, mutual companionship, and tender care transmitted to keep the marital relations mutually satisfying and pacified. But serious conflicts which might lead to a deeper awareness of the I and the you are avoided.

The extroverted manic-depressive frequently turns to the out-

24. Freud, "Mourning and Melancholia."

side for confirmation of his worth, driven by the gnawing doubts of his inferiority feelings and by his anxieties about being deserted. He pursues a gambler's race for success; he gambles for prestige, for wealth, for popularity, but he gambles always for more than he needs. His friendships are characterized by buddy-buddy familiarity; but familiarity breeds contempt, and negative emotions are unbearable. Ruthless opportunism also does not fit into the high standards of the manic-depressive and yet a certain degree of opportunism is necessary for the pursuit of success. Failure mobilizes anxieties and thus the manic-depressive maintains a high speed in his daily activities, a speed that does not permit relaxation or a patient dedication to a task that does not provide quick results. The restlessness of external activities deprives friendship and family life of depth and intensity, and sooner or later the patient loses the hope and the courage of continuing the struggle for escape from his anxieties.

Further crises of his sense of identity arise at the turning point of biological development after the birth of a child. The upheaval in the instinctual and emotional equilibrium at the time of delivery threatens the person who is disposed to develop an affective psychosis. A new horizon opens up and self-doubts crop up as to whether the young mother can meet the challenge. Also, an unstable father might become oppressed at the sight of new responsibilities. The unresolved identification of the young mother with her own mother reproduces an opportunity to reestablish a similar identification with the newborn child. There is the same lack of trust in the patient's mothering abilities and in the adequate response to the infant's vital needs; instead she compensates by oversolicitude and overprotection for the hateful riddance reactions that may painfully break into conscious awareness and cause guilt feelings, self-blame, and self-defeat or flight into manic self-expansion and vagueness. But the post partum affective psychosis has largely a favorable prognosis and an equilibrium may be soon reestablished—which does not exclude the possibility that the tradition of symbiotic identification may be carried over into the next generation.

The time of involution is another critical period in which the patient has to change his ego ideals and redefine his identity. This change implies restriction of goals, limitations of expansive ambitions, loss of partners and friends, separation from children who are now living their own lives, all of which requires renunciation and a turning inward of hopes, for which the extroverted manic-depressive personality is ill prepared. His dependence on success and external applause suffers painful defeats. His hopes shrink when he cannot transform his needs for immediate gratifications into investments in sublimated interests. The narcissistic loss of physical beauty and body strength elicit protest in form of hypochondriacal preoccupation. The reduction of opportunities for expansion produces unrealistic worries about the impending doom of impoverishment. Lack of hope and trust, and limitations in the ability for serious dedication make the reintegration of the manic-depressive personality in the involutional period particularly strenuous. If his being-in-the-world loses its meaning, he may succumb to psychotic despair or suicidal defeat.

PSYCHOTHERAPY

The treatment of an affective psychosis confronts the psychotherapist with paradoxical difficulties. The patient urgently demands help and yet he desperately refuses it. Freud thought that schizophrenia and the manic-depressive psychosis, the narcissistic neuroses, in contrast to the transference neuroses, were not suitable for psychoanalytic therapy. Modifications of classical psychoanalytic techniques are certainly necessary; but it has been found that the functional psychoses too develop intense transference phenomena during treatment. The psychotherapist may be able gradually to melt the armor of distrustful withdrawal and seemingly resigned hopelessness in his long and arduous work with the schizophrenic patient. But the manic-depressive patient is frequently carried away by spurious hopes and gullibility. He demands narcissistic supplies and ego support, but he is easily discouraged when his desires for magical help cannot be met with a quick successful relief.

It is therefore necessary that the psychotherapist does not offer false promises and cheap comfort, but examines the emotional situation thoroughly and fathoms the depth of the depression and the dangers of manic escape. It is inevitable for the therapist to enter into close contact with the patient's relatives when the patient suffers from a manic-depressive illness. He explains to the patient that this contact is a precondition for treatment and does not violate the patient's confidential communications. The illness is frequently enigmatic to his relatives and the patient's despondency puts a heavy burden on their shoulders. This burden can, to a certain degree, be eased by the psychological understanding that the therapist can provide. And this understanding also diminishes the patient's guilt feelings in relation to his family. The therapist explains to the patient as well as to the family that the patient is in a process of mourning; the loss he has suffered may not be so obvious but can be gradually discovered. It can also be made understandable that the patient cannot yet accept the loss and that he is like a mourning person who rages inwardly against fate. And since the patient is related to whomever or whatever he has lost by a tenaciously close, possessive identification, he also partially lost himself, his sense of identity; he is a kind of penitent and though his self-accusations are fantastic, sometimes outrageously unrealistic, it is no use trying to talk him out of them. Deeper investigations will gradually put them into a more realistic perspective.

Since the manic-depressive patient is in a crisis of lost identity, he needs a moratorium, protection against self-damage or suicide; he is transiently unable to take care of his self-preservation and, if the family is not able to provide the protection of a moratorium, suitable hospital care has to be provided. It is important that the therapist convey to the patient the fact that his extremely painful emotions are not useless; that they represent a self-healing process comparable to the fever of a contaminated organism. Even though the patient cannot as yet consciously participate in his therapy, the process of mourning and penitence goes on in his unconscious mind, and he will gradually learn to participate. The serene, firm security of the therapist calms the anxious agitation of the patient and his relatives.

If external security measures cannot be provided, the therapist, the patient, and his family take a considerable risk. The therapist may ask the patient to call on him at any time of day or night, when the compulsion to damage or kill himself becomes overwhelming. If the patient is already able to establish some positive attachment to the therapist, this attachment is in itself the best safety that can be offered. But the therapist's readiness to be at the patient's disposal at any emergency call can seduce the patient to test his power when his attachment to the therapist is highly ambivalent, and the therapist may become contaminated by his patient's anxieties. A similar unfortunate involvement may result from the dispensation of sedatives, tranquilizers, or electroshock treatment. It is preferable that the relation between the patient and his psychotherapist be kept free from all nonpsychotherapeutic measures and that these be delegated to a cooperating administrator. If the patient is in a very desperate condition, around-the-clock nursing service has to be established.

In a manic episode the patient is no less in need of a protective moratorium to regain his sense of identity. He may gradually learn to see that his overactivity and restlessness represent a flight from very painful emotions and that it is to his advantage to face and endure the pains of an inner rebirth. Some modern obstetricians recommend that the pains of delivery not be avoided, so that the patient can rally all her energies to join in the natural process. I mentioned before that it is the tragedy of the manic-depressive that he is not able to mourn or to repent sincerely. In melancholia he flees into an orgy of self-torture unconsciously aimed at a magic expiation of guilt feelings; in the manic state he escapes into extroverted distraction from the inward battle and into illusions of expansion.

It is true that the manic-depressive defenses are directed against insight, but that does not mean that the patient lacks the ability of introspection. He can be gradually won over to an attitude of meditation, for an exploratory look into himself, when the therapist conveys to him his conviction that there is a meaning in the process of his illness and that his spastic defenses against the pains only increase them and postpone the solution. Where therapist and patient can settle down for a lengthy exploration into the unconscious causes of the illness, as well as into the unconscious aims of the inner process, this very endeavor kindles some light of hope; and I have pointed out before the organizing and integrating power of hope. It is an uphill struggle because of the patient's flighty defense of extroversion. He cannot be forced to stick to the job, and only the trust in the therapist's serious dedication can prevent the patient's rebellious escape.

It is important to sort out the fantastic guilt feelings and the patient's realistic failure, his lack of authenticity. The patient, due to a persistent archaic relation of identification, suffers from borrowed guilt feelings. He has protested against this identification with a depressed and clinging parent; he may now hate and despise him and deny the identification that unconsciously persists. It is painful to discover how similar he is to his object of contempt. Only a deepened understanding of the parent's tragedy may free the patient from his prejudices, his black-or-white morality, the all-or-none ambivalence in the relation of identification. Forgiveness due to deepened understanding of the object of identification enables him to accept himself too.

The patient's guilt feelings are not so much linked up with his erotic, incestuous wishes. In psychoanalytic terms, the libidinal development of the manic-depressive patient has not reached the level of the Oedipus conflict. Eros is the integrating force of life. The creative experience of love is the great healing agent and it remains healing even in the process of mourning in which the possession of the love object has to be relinquished. The patient feels guilty about his sexual intentions due to the admixture of pregenital possessiveness and exploitativeness that tends to devour or to be devoured, to cling and be captivated. The addiction of identification deprives the partners of their freedom and mobilizes the counterforces of aggression and destruction, rage, resentment, and hatred. The manic-depressive patient is afraid of love, because his freedom is threatened by any commitment—a commitment to an individual as well as to an ideal. Not having reached ego cohesion and a consolidated superego he pursues his ego ideals with the same all-or-none possessiveness as his love objects and loses distance from them. When he loses the faith that he can appropriate his ideal in complete identification he faces the horror of nothingness. The manic-depressive patient is afraid of his self-assertive aggression and of his unskilled destructive impulses. Their positive meaning has to be reinterpreted to the patient as stemming from his healthy fight for freedom and constructive self-love. The tragic tension in human existence between being and not-being, death and rebirth, the tension between yearning for union and the need for uniqueness, can be transcended when the individual ceases to cling to the pseudosecurity of symbiotic identification or does not escape into an isolating, defensive narcissism. The manic-depressive patient shies away from this human tragedy; but it is a relief when he can understand that his fight, the upsurge of rage and hatred, is not a perversity, a pathological absurdity, but an accentuation of the human condition itself.

In the self-cure to which Kierkegaard submitted his melancholia he illustrates the process of mourning and renunciation by the Biblical legend of Abraham willing to sacrifice his only and beloved son Isaac. Kierkegaard suffered himself from the possessive over-identification with a melancholic father. In Kierkegaard's interpretation of the Biblical story, Abraham achieves in his most personal, not socially sanctioned, understanding of the will of God the "infinite movement of renunciation," the leap into nothingness, because his sacrifice extinguishes his rational hopes for the future, but in achieving this renunciation he reaches a higher level of love *sub specie aeternitatis.* In the infinite movement of faith the son is given back to him, not as a reward for obedience, not in a life after death, but here and now in a new, more meaningful relation that opens the deep sources of trust. The *credo quia absurdum,* the "leap into faith," represents more than a resigned mourning about the hardships of a rationally interpreted reality. The new hope in living springs from the basic trust through which man does not only passively submit to fate, but embraces destiny in a new dedication which unites him with the ground of existence.[25]

25. Søren Kierkegaard, *Furcht und Zittern* (Jena: Eugen Diederichs Verlag, 1923). It is significant that Kierkegaard chose the legend of Abraham and Isaac to illustrate the double movement of resignation and renewal of faith in the human process of mourning and repentance. The transfer of guilt from father to son gave

The manic-depressive patient in psychotherapy does not have to go through the labor of mourning alone. He goes through the phases of repetition together with the therapist. The transference represents repetition and resistance against change and transformation. In the psychoanalytic treatment of neurosis the development of a transference neurosis is encouraged; it is the core of the treatment, for the transference neurosis recapitulates the emotional development under the observation of a relatively intact ego able to relax in free associations and assisted by the interpretations of the analyst. Conversely, the manic-depressive patient has a less intact ego. He is mostly too anxious to relax in free associations. He has too little distance from himself and from the participant observer to engage in much observing and he is anxious to identify himself with the therapist and anxious to escape from close identification. There is little of the object relation that allows a full encounter of an I and a you. The patient projects the images of positive and negative identification on the therapist; he sees in him a savior, a magic helper, a demon, or a useless bystander. The psychotherapist therefore cannot passively wait for the development of a transference neurosis and he cannot hide in an unreachable neutrality. He has to be there with his personality fully present, asking pertinent questions to elucidate the patient's past and present situation. He tries to penetrate the patient's armor of conventionality. He does not avoid the question "guilty–not guilty" about which the patient ruminates monotonously, but he questions the competence of the court of justice before which the patient argues this question. The patient's court of justice is a sick conscience, sickened by the precocious assumption of an omnipotent parental role in childhood. The therapist accompanies the patient through the painful process of reevaluation of values. But the

rise in the Christian dogmatic development to the concept of "original or hereditary sin" and the concept of expiation of sin through the son's sacrifice (crucifixion). The Jewish Covenant between God and man, which originated in the legend of Isaac's sacrifice, introduced the rite of circumcision, the symbol of submission of sexual desire and of human selfish desire in general to the broader aspects of procreation. The spirit of procreation in the literal and sublimated sense gives the repentant mourner hopes and meaningful goals to live for, after he has given up the narrow self-seeking goals in the labor of mourning and repentance.

therapist is not the judge, nor does he stem the patient's repressed rage of accusations against whomever or whatever the patient has lost. He understands his rage against fate, but he does not lose time in sentimental sympathy; he demonstrates the repetition in the patient's significant relations and the repetition that takes place here and now in the relation to the therapist, the lack of distance, the exalted expectations which cannot stand the test of reality, and his horror of desertion from which he recoils. He also shows the patient how he provokes this desertion again and again.

There is some degree of identification taking place in every transference, particularly in that of a deeply regressed melancholic patient; he uses the therapist transiently as a "parasitic superego." But the psychotherapist of a depressed patient does not foster this transference; he interprets the transference, wherever it shows up, he works toward the goal of making himself superfluous, encouraging the patient to use his own judgment, to find his own values, and to recognize where his narcissistic defenses, his overweening arrogance, hidden behind hypocritical humility, make him truly guilty. This arrogance reveals itself blatantly in manic episodes. The therapist does not become impatient with the patient's repeated relapses into infantilism and clinging dependency; the child in man is after all his most promising asset. The patient has to run backwards to gather momentum for a better leap. What Kierkegaard called the "leap into faith" frees the individual from the addiction to security and opens the potentialities of a self-transcending, creative encounter. The patient's trust in himself can only be gained through a better understanding of himself, of his struggle for freedom and authenticity. This trust in himself goes hand in hand with a trust in mutuality: an acceptance of the boundaries of the *I* and the *you,* and an ability to grant each other the freedom of spontaneity.

The working through of the transference represents a long struggle, until the manic-depressive patient rediscovers the sources of basic trust. The psychotherapist should have all the qualities of an unanxious, responsive mother who gives her child as much protection as he needs and enough freedom to experiment and develop his potentialities. That implies that the psychotherapist should be able to trust his patient's trend toward recovery. This trust is put to a hard test. The patient's tendency to give up, to let himself die, his escape from facing his loss, his true guilt, his horror of desertion sometimes elicit the countertransference of discouragement in the therapist. When the therapist becomes discouraged, there is no use denying it for the sensitive patient will feel it. The therapist is exposed to a barrage of contaminating anxieties. This holds particularly true for states of involutional melancholia, when the patient has lost the hope for a meaningful future. When the therapist accepts the responsibilities of treating a manic-depressive patient, he asks himself whether he is able to accept the risks of the work. If his self-esteem is dependent on proving his therapeutic success, he had better refuse the job and save the patient from a repetition of his desolate experience of being deserted. He himself must have had a good insight into the despair which surrounds a human existence with the horror of nothingness. But he should also be removed from the fashionable wallowing in false, masochistic despair which has become a defensive habit among the generation of beatniks and "angry young men" who avoid the real despair in the atomic age in literary productions of gloom. Since the manic-depressive patient is the victim of self-deception and illusions in his interpersonal relations, the psychotherapist should be able to encounter him with simple, straightforward honesty. He has to watch the pulse of his countertransference, being alerted to the tendency to become identified with the patient, or defensive against his clinging dependency.

Some psychotherapists have recommended provoking the depressed patient into outbreaks of anger and rage to stave off the dangers of self-punishment by which the patient turns the rage against himself.[26] Outbreaks of rage may become inevitable and the therapist, being human, cannot help at times being provoked into anger himself. Such clashes are not fatal, they may even clear the air. But an artificial provocation does not seem necessary to me, because it interferes with the immediate honesty of the emotional exchange. When an explosion of anger occurs, it is only useful

26. Sandor Rado, "Psychosomatics of Depression from the Etiological Point of View," *Psychosomatic Medicine* 13 (1951): 51–55.

if the therapist keeps his head sufficiently above water to explore and interpret the emotional exchange thoroughly from the angle of both transference and countertransference.

The psychoanalyst should on the whole remain receptive, listening, and observing with wide-open attention, not with the narrowly focused attention of a policeman who is on the trigger to jump at the next danger signal. The patient's own narrow, defensive attention is contagious; he is alerted and tends to alert the partner to his own forecasts of gloom. The analyst's hovering, wide-open attention does not recoil from facing and discussing all potential dangers that the patient's imagination brings up with horror. These dangers touch on murderous impulses, death, annihilation, all forms of nonbeing which the patient tries desperately to avoid. The calmness, even a mild sense of humor, with which the therapist meditates with the patient about these tragic aspects of living help also to widen the passive attention of the patient and shift his active energies from emotional protests and upheavals to a more practical rational scrutiny of the evil which he fears to encounter and tries to deny. But the calmness of the therapist has to be genuine, otherwise it carries no conviction. Since emulation plays an important role in the treatment of the manic-depressive patient, it is desirable that the therapist be free from defensive egocentricity and from prejudice against the heightened egocentricity in the patient. The therapist meets the patient's intense need for close symbiotic identification with generous detachment. It becomes clear in the treatment that maintaining distance and perspective allows an encounter that is free from ambivalence, from exaggerated hopes and fears, and provides the emotionally overstimulated patient with a clear, fresh air to breathe—an atmosphere in which there is a good chance to find himself, his own identity. It is important that the therapist is free to express his own identity in which there is a harmonious collaboration of active and passive, masculine and feminine potentialities, but this harmony cannot be preached. It is enough that the patient be exposed to the nonverbal self-expression of the therapist's personality. The most important factors of the therapeutic process cannot be put into the rational terms of a teachable technique, for they depend on the total personality of the therapist, on his ability to understand clearly the patient's total personality, on his realistic visualization of the patient's past as well as his future and his capacity to discover the patient's repressed resources that open up a new hopeful meaning of his existence.

Conditions of Organized and Regressive Responses to Danger

Before we enter into the description of group reactions to danger, let us first consider the effect of danger on the individual. Danger elicits anxiety or panic in an individual. On the one hand, this anxiety may mobilize libidinal energies and physiological resources which transcend anxiety; i.e. neutralize the destructive results of anxiety in the constructive pursuit of the goal: mastery of danger. In this case we observe organized growth and realistic expansion of the ego. On the other hand, danger may elicit an amount of panic which leads to a defusion of instincts. The magic principle (Rado) takes over, and the destructive impulses get the upper hand. The result is a disorganized regression which leaves the danger unmastered and the ego shrinking. Between these extreme responses to danger we have all the shades of fusion or defusion of instincts, partial organization, partial disorganization, depending upon the relation of favorable and unfavorable constitutional and environmental factors.

We can observe the effects of leadership in relation to danger in the "two-group" of parent and child, which is a group of exceptional character. The baby is on the point of learning to walk. He is in danger of losing his equilibrium in the yet unfamiliar situation. In the trial-and-error phase of experimentation he falls, bumps his head against a chair. There is not only pain; there is the confrontation with the uncanny unknown, which presents a danger and produces anxiety. The baby recoils from the undefined danger of reality by disorganized muscle action, screaming and

Reprinted by permission from *Psychoanalysis and the Social Sciences*, eds. W. Muensterberger and S. Axelrod, vol. 4 (New York: International Universities Press, 1955).

kicking. He regresses to the familiar security in mother's arms, from the reality principle to the pleasure-pain principle. Mother is the leader in this emergency. She empathizes with the baby's anxiety. The empathy may reach various degrees. In extreme cases the mother is so fully identified with the anxious child that she is herself flooded by anxiety. Regressing with the child, her leadership abilities disintegrate. In this case her anxiety puts a damper on the child's adventurous spirit and on his curiosity to discover the unknown. In other cases the mother's anxiety produces defensive compulsion: the danger has to be mastered here and now. Her own ambitious defense against anxiety denies the child's anxiety and therewith increases it. Or the mother may partially identify with the baby's need to get rid of the danger by magic; she playfully punishes the devil of a nasty chair that has hurt the baby, comforting the child by a sense of pseudomastery and triumph. A realistically triumphant expansion is only reached when the child learns to maintain his equilibrium in the mastery of a new function.

Whatever mother does to help the child in this learning process, important for the outcome is the fact that the mother not fully identify with the child's anxiety, but more with the child's growing potentialities; mother and child need a relation of mutual trust, in which the child can identify with the mother as stable leader. Mother's libidinal relation to the child optimally is more than a passive, pleasurable or painful closeness to the child; integrated in this closeness is the realistic assessment of the child's present assets and liabilities and a realistic appreciation of the danger that has to be met.

If the mother is too immature for such libidinal relation of concern and respect for the child, if the mother, in an emergency, regresses to the child's sadomasochistic level, inconsistently buffeted by waves of pleasure and pain, vacillating between overprotection and overambition with coercion, the child cannot help but develop a hostile dependency on her at the expense of his own expanding autonomy. Partially, the child withdraws his libido from the broadening conquest of reality and specializes more or less in manipulating the mother, the magic helper. Success for the overdependent child does not mean in the first line learning, expanding by mastery of real dangers, but forcing the mother into the service of avoiding danger. She is supposed to react according to the pleasure-pain principle. She is good if she gives pleasure and avoids pain and anxiety; she is bad if she does not. She is all or nothing, God or the devil, from the child's narcissistic point of view, and the child's libidinal energy remains largely concentrated on transforming the bad mother into the good mother by hook and by crook. We can see in the mother-child relation a "two-group" with successful or unsuccessful leadership. If we interpret success not as the clinging to the pleasure-pain principle, but as the progress in adaptation to the reality principle, we seldom find all successful or all unsuccessful leadership in danger, but mostly any shade between these extremes.

Leaving the mother-child relation, let us turn to a danger situation in a larger adult group: a shortage of food threatens a crowd massed in alarm before a food store. Waves of panic sweep over the crowd. Disorganization results; potentially everybody is at everybody's throat. Then a leader arises who manages to elicit the libidinal response of trust, since he calmly and realistically assesses the emergency and swings into organizing action. He finds out how much food there is available compared to the amount of demands, he lines the crowd up in orderly files, gives everybody his place and his function. He does not promise unlimited fulfillment of demands, but everybody is going to have his proportionate share. The panic subsides and makes room for a sense of limited but realistic security.

In the same danger situation another leader may arise who identifies with the panic of the crowd to a degree that the aroused emotions offer an opportunity to satisfy his defensive greed for power. He is not so much interested in the realistic needs and the realistic emergency situation, but in a passionate shortcut solution according to the pleasure-pain principle. Intuitively he offers a shortcut solution which appeals to the crowd where panic has produced flight from reality and regression. The opportunistic leader swings himself into the role of a superman, understanding by empathy that panicky people demand an all-gratifying God more than a man to solve the problem. He promises illusionary security and gratification. Such illusionary promises produce suggestibility and automatic submission and obedience. The leader acquires a power which is not safeguarded by reasonable scrutiny; it is the all-or-none power of passion, which uses reason only for more or less flimsy rationalizations. In order to fortify his power against the unreliability of his followers, the leader has to open outlets for the hostilities resulting from the panic. A devil has to be invented who presumably has caused the frustration. The leader suggests ransacking the foodstore of the "dirty Jew" or the capitalistic hoarder.

In the first case we have a group in progressive organization; the members of the group identify with a leader who tends to master the danger on the level of mature libido development and realistic creativeness. In the second case the leader identifies with the group on a regressive, sadomasochistic level; the group is in danger of deteriorating into a disorganized mass; they are at the mercy of extreme emotions, screaming hallelujah or crucify. They can only be held together by force or falsification of reality.

In this paper, we try to find what psychoanalysis has to contribute to the theme of leader-group relation in danger. It would be impossible to review the great amount of contributions that psychologists and sociologists have made to this topic. I only want to mention some ideas of the Swiss psychiatrist, Ludwig Binswanger.[1] The European history of the last decades has given much food for his socio-psychological interests. Binswanger has stressed the polarity between ego autonomy and we-participation. In the organization of a group each individual gives up part of his autonomy, part of his freedom to investigate reality and therewith to arrive at his own decisions. He partially surrenders this autonomy to the group, to the we, of which he is a part. This is part of the process of division of labor in group formation. As the member of a group the ego partially replaces his own knowledge of reality by appropriation of a knowledge which is not immediately, by his own senses, accessible to him. He takes over the knowledge or the in-

1. See his *Grundformen und Erkenntnis Menschlichen Daseins* (Zurich: Max Niehans Verlag, 1953).

terpretations of reality suggested by a leader. But since such appropriated knowledge does not stem from his own observations and scrutiny, it becomes his property only on the basis of the group member's suggestibility. Such knowledge by means of suggestion and suggestibility is no longer flexible; it becomes rigid, unchangeable.

In a group of scientists it may be possible to maintain a high degree of scrutinizing ego autonomy of the majority of members. But in a group centered around art, politics, or religion—even in the field of psychology we are far from safe—emotionality outweighs reasoning and responsible scrutiny. Knowledge is partly replaced by suggestion and suggestion may become a dogma, which produces submission or rebellion in the group of followers. Insofar as the loss of ego autonomy increases in a group member, a regression takes place to the sadomasochistic level of libido organization, and the ego is partially estranged from reality to the degree that the ego loses its autonomy. This loss of ego autonomy and simultaneous reality estrangement is greatest in infantile, primitive men, or among people who under the acute pressure of danger and anxiety regress to a more primitive level of libido organization. Only on the level of genital maturity, in the experience of love, there is no loss of ego autonomy. We can even observe in the experience of love a creative broadening of personality, an increased sense of responsibility and a widening of reality horizons.

When, therefore, a group member can respect and love his leader, identify with the values for which the leader stands, his partial surrender remains voluntary, and ego autonomy, sense of responsibility, and free decision remain relatively unimpaired. The stability of group formation depends on the degree of unimpaired ego autonomy of its members. The greater the loss of ego autonomy and the corresponding estrangement from reality, the greater is the danger of group dissociation, though fanatical surrender and dogmatic adherence frequently give the impression of a very closely knit unity.

2. Sigmund Freud, *Complete Psychological Works* (London: Hogarth), 18:67–134.

But the very fact that force and falsehood have to be used, iron discipline and militarization, proves that the totalitarian togetherness and we-participation is endangered principally. The we-participation on the basis of emotional suggestibility may at any time elicit extreme emotions, like ecstasy or panic. If such extreme emotions sweep over a group, the group ties break, everybody is isolated in extreme ecstasy or extreme panic. Loss of autonomy and sadomasochistic regression run parallel. Loss of autonomy increases suggestibility. Fear which is realistically mindful of a danger situation and therefore prepares the organism by increased mobilization of energies to meet the danger deteriorates into vague anxiety of the uncanny, the unknown. The individual who trades his ego autonomy for suggestible surrender to a leader may be less fearful, that means mindful, of danger, but he becomes more anxious, since he leaves the task of mastery of reality to the leadership. He becomes less able to control his fears and his trust by his reasoning power and responsible autonomous decisions.

An anxious group gravitates toward a demagogic or dictatorial leader. The more the group members are estranged from reality testing by extreme anxiety, the more they demand impossible satisfaction and fantastic securities from the leader. He has to be god-like to reassure their anxieties. Here a vicious cycle is established. The regression of the group may elicit regression in the leader. He may respond to their masochistic surrender with a sadistic and therefore unrealistic, inhuman form of mastery. He may no longer be able to wrestle patiently with the emergency; he has to produce salvation at a frenzied speed, by force or even violence, in order to fulfill illusionary promises. Since the danger of group dissociation in panic hangs over his head and threatens to curtail the power of his influence and domination, he may be forced into more false promises, estrangement from reality, more rigidity of discipline and dogmatism to squelch the threatening rebellion that smoulders underneath the veneer of docile suggestibility of his followers. The demagogic leader is as much at the mercy of his followers as they are blindly dependent on him. Their dependence is extremely undependable. Any rumor that runs like wildfire through an anxious crowd can overthrow the regime of a dictatorial leader, since his followers in their regressive state are unstable, buffeted by the waves of pleasure and pain as far as they are estranged from reality.

Only a leader who is himself a well-integrated person can resist the temptations of power. He sets the mastery of reality and reasonable satisfactions and securities of his followers first; he uses power only as a means in the service of those primary purposes. Under such conditions the leader has optimal potentialities to master a dangerous reality situation, if he remains aware not only of the external, but also of the internal dangers in himself and his group. Only such a leader can elicit the devotion and respect of his followers that preserve an optimal degree of ego autonomy in them. Therefore he can count on their thoughtful, not only their emotional, collaboration.

A Contribution to the
Theory of Schizophrenia

If psychoanalysis and psychiatry find themselves at variance owing to the difference of outlook with which they approach identical
material, it is nonetheless a fact that opportunities for mutual understanding occur in plenty precisely in the field of schizophrenic
theory, where they are in a position to bring about or at any rate to
stimulate an advance in both these sciences. It is obvious that the
psychiatrist concentrates his attention more on the ego aspect of
schizophrenic phenomena, whereas the psychoanalyst lays greater
stress on their id aspect. As Freud has pointed out, it is precisely
by investigating paranoia and dementia praecox that we are bound
to increase our insight into the psychology of the ego. I propose
on this occasion to consider schizophrenic phenomena in one of
their ego aspects: I refer to psychomotor manifestations, which
occupy a specially prominent position in the catatonic forms of
dementia praecox.

The path to an understanding between psychoanalysis and psychiatry has perhaps been made smoother by the presence of a
tendency in psychoanalytic research to do away with the antithesis
which seemed once so firmly established between the "psychical"
and the "somatic," a point which has been elaborated by Felix
Deutsch.[1] Schilder requires us to apply in the investigation of
schizophrenia the "principle of a double approach," the treatment
upon equal terms of psyche and soma.[2] The schizophrenic process

Reprinted from the *International Journal of Psychoanalysis* 17 (1936): 190–201.

1. See "Biologie und Psychologie der Krankheitsgenese," *Internationale Zeitschrift für Psychoanalyse* 19 (1933): 132.

2. Paul Schilder, *Entwurf zu einer Psychiatrie auf Psychoanalytischer Grundlage*,
Internationale Psychoanalytische Bibliothek 17 (Leipzig: Internationaler Psychoanalytischer Verlag, 1925).

is so complex a phenomenon that it is open to us to consider it alike from a psychological and from a physico-chemical standpoint, from the angle of the endocrinal and vegetative processes and from that of neural regulation. But if the very profusion of these possibilities is not to be allowed to obscure the fact that the entire personality falls a victim to the pathological process, the psychoanalyst must deem it a prime necessity to orientate himself with regard to the schizophrenic's libidinal economy, related as it is to both psyche and soma. The psychiatrist, however, fails to appreciate the important part played by researches into the libido in arriving at an understanding of the total personality. Since Freud's pioneer work, the study of libidinal economy has afforded us not only glimpses into the id but also understanding of the structure of the ego.[3] Consideration of schizophrenia in its id aspect will often vouchsafe to the analyst versed in the interpretation of dreams surprisingly deep and rapid perceptions. Thus as far back as 1909 Jung was able to demonstrate the correspondences between the complexes in hysteria and in schizophrenia. But from his starting point it was hard to differentiate the two illnesses. He assumed that the complex in schizophrenia besides its psychological effects brought into being a hypothetical toxin responsible for the "enormous tendency to automatization and fixation . . . in other words the enduring nature of the operation of the complexes" in dementia praecox.[4] Other authors too have pointed out the resemblance of an acute schizophrenic condition to a toxically induced psychosis, to the clinical pictures presented by states of delirium arising from fever or other causes. Behringer has compared the condition found in schizophrenia with mescal intoxication.[5] It may be difficult to arrive at a differential diagnosis between dementia praecox and an alcoholically induced hallucinosis.

However, the consistent development of the libido theory in the hands of Freud and Abraham has enabled us to dispense with

3. See "On Narcissism: An Introduction," in *Collected Papers*, vol. 4 (London: Hogarth, 1952).

4. C. G. Jung, *Über die Psychologie der Dementia praecox* (Halle: Marhold, 1907), chap. 5.

5. Karl Behringer, *Der Mescalinrausch, seine Geschichte und seine Entstehung*, Monographie der *Neurologie und Psychiatrie* (Berlin: Springer 1927).

Jung's hypothetical toxin. Abraham conceived the regression to autoerotism and the loss of object cathexes and sublimations of the libido as constituting "the psychosexual differences between hysteria and dementia praecox."[6] Freud, in the Schreber analysis, depicted paranoia as essentially a regression to narcissism. As a result of the new concept of a narcissistic libido, the mysterious toxin postulated by Jung as a hypothetical element in the etiology of dementia praecox was revealed as dammed-up ego libido, although Jung has never recognized this development of Freud's libido theory.

It is illuminating when one considers that the damming-up of ego libido brings about much greater toxic effects than does the damming-up of object libido which occurs in the actual and transference neuroses; for in the latter the workings of the subject's fantasy take up his thwarted and introverted object libido and act as a safety valve which protects his ego. Where the course of development is a psychotic one, the ego is unable to withstand the impact of the dammed-up ego libido. In hypochondriacal conditions and states of depersonalization, far-reaching alterations are observable in the ego. In paranoia there is a break-down in the functions of the ego, and this is still more the case in other forms of schizophrenia. Freud has defined the ego as an organ of mediation between the id and the external world. The turning away of the libido from the external world, often felt subjectively as the end of the world, has as its counterpart an impairment of function and disintegration of the ego.

Among the psychiatrists too, we frequently find the failure of the "synthetic functions" of the ego mentioned in a descriptive sense as an essential factor in dementia praecox: Wernicke speaks of a disintegration of the individuality, insufficiency of the real personality; Gross, of a disintegration of consciousness; Vogd, of a restriction of consciousness; Janet, of *abaissement du niveau mental;* Minkowski, of *la perte du contact vital;* Berze, of an insufficiency of psychical activity, and hypotonia of consciousness. These

6. Karl Abraham, "Die psychosexuellen Differenzen der Hysterie und der Dementia Praecox," *Zentralblatt für Nervenheilkunde und Psychiatrie* 19 (1908): 521–33.

psychiatrists find in an insufficiency of the actual, present-day, conscious personality, which should comprise in a single integral entity the whole of the realized potentialities of the individual, the basic disturbance (toxically or constitutionally determined) that underlies schizophrenia.

Psychiatry is here by no means so far removed from psychoanalysis. Freud, however, regards the ego's ability to perform its synthetic function as dependent on the state of the libidinal equilibrium. A free interchange of ego and object libido secures the integrity of the ego as a correctly functioning organized whole. In the light of this conception the ego appears to be constantly in the process of "becoming," continually being built up afresh, with the aid of desexualized libido, out of the realized potentialities of the individual. The integral nature of the ego is experienced subjectively as freedom, its dependence on the id as compulsion.

The repressive processes of hysteria and the isolation mechanisms of the obsessional neurosis also produce rents and cleavages in the ego; the transference neurotic's ego has only imperfectly achieved the task of mastering reality. But the loss of reality and derangement of the ego present in the psychotic are more radical, no longer subject to recall; for the lost object-world is replaced autoplastically.[7] The second stage in the illness, one which corresponds to the return of the repressed in the neuroses, develops in the psychoses as a grandiose attempt at reparation, at constructing this lost world afresh, with the help of projective mechanisms, hallucinations, and delusional systems which, as Freud has shown in the Schreber analysis, in their noisy manifestations attract more attention than the essential pathological features, which are those connected with the withdrawal of libido. This attempt at recovery which we find in the psychoses, with its mechanisms of projection, is especially characteristic of paranoia and the paranoid forms of schizophrenia which, in comparison with the hebephrenic and catatonic forms, reveal a relative capacity for resistance on the part of the ego and which, again unlike hebephrenia and catatonia, mostly break out at a more advanced age, when the ego has had

7. Cf. Freud's account of this process in "The Loss of Reality in Neurosis and Psychosis" (1924), in *Collected Papers*, vol. 2.

time to become more stable. The synthetic forces of the ego are once more apparent in the systematization which the delusion undergoes. This is seen especially clearly in the history of Schreber's illness which led to a comparatively favorable remission. The powerful tensions existing in a strongly marked individuality confronted with a narcissistically fixated instinctual life are reconciled by means of a religious delusion and are assimilated into the total personality at the cost of a few contradictions and absurdities. A regression to narcissism which, compared with autoerotism represents a certain concentration of libidinal forces, makes it possible to give a more favorable prognosis for the restoration of the ego than a regression to autoerotic strivings whose lack of coordination reproduces the disintegration of the schizophrenic ego. To complicate the picture still more, the real symptoms of the morbid process are, as in the case of paranoid conditions, combined with manifestations of a still existent normality or neurosis and with attempts at recovery. These complications place considerable difficulties in the way of approaching schizophrenia in its ego aspect.

I shall now turn to the essential theme of this paper, namely the far-reaching disturbances to which the ego falls a victim in catatonia, but I should first like to add that there is no reason to infer from what I have said above that we are dealing in catatonia with a chaotic medley of organ-libidinal strivings which have taken the place of a coherent ego organization; even in catatonia a certain tendency to unification can be observed. When the laws of logical thinking are abandoned in cases of serious ego disorder the modalities of the primary process take their place. We must expect to find a similar regressive transformation in the psychomotor conditions of catatonia. In the final phases of a catatonic illness which has reached a stage of terminal dementia, it very frequently happens that the ego assumes a monotonously cramped, unchanging posture. I am reminded of a patient who year in year out used to rock a wooden doll in her arms as a substitute for her dead child. An ego thus impaired shows in comparison with a healthy ego a grandiose simplification in its outward appearance. But this uniformity bears the same relation to the organization of a healthy ego as a despotic system, obliged to suppress every incompatible striving, does to a more elastic one which allows conflicting tendencies to balance one another out. Should the ego fail in its synthetic function, its striving after completeness, other regulating principles must take its place. There exists in the psyche, as in all living substance, an inherent tendency to organization; when the higher principles of integration have been abolished, those of a more lowly order are called upon the scene. Jelliffe deserves the credit for having brought Head's concept of "vigilance" into line with psychoanalytic enquiry.[8] On the basis of a vital vigilance (or state of tension) in the central nervous system, purposive reactions of adaptation to external stimuli are found to occur even in decerebrate animals. The regulations of the conscious system transmitted by the cerebrum are replaced by automatic regulating mechanisms from deeper and phylogenetically earlier centers which possess the capacity to ecphorize ontogenetic and phylogenetic engrams. The automatic acts are conditioned by mnemonic schemes, patterns and internal attitudes. These primitive mechanisms exercise a far more rigid control than the ego, a fact which may well cause astonishment when we reflect that it is of the essence of the ego that it should perform an inhibiting function, so that one might have expected a removal of inhibition when that function failed. I should here like to borrow an example from the field of neurology. We know that heightened reflexes and an increased state of tension of the voluntary musculature will follow on elimination of the cortico-pyramidal pathways. This is due to the circumstance that one of the functions of the cerebrum is to inhibit and damp down the excitations streaming to the executive organs from deeper pallidostriatal centers, which are more strongly influenced by affective factors. We may well draw a comparison between the inhibiting functions of the cerebrum and those of the ego. The elimination of the inhibiting functions of the cerebrum does not remove the inhibition of volitional movement (the interplay of synergistic and antagonistic movements whose harmonious cooperation gives rise to muscular action), but the excess of excitations pouring into the spastically innervated muscular system

8. Smith Ely Jelliffe, "Vigilance, the Motor Pattern and Inner Meaning of Some Schizophrenics' Behavior," *Psychoanalytic Review* 17 (1930): 305–30.

leads in fact to paresis. The failure of the inhibiting functions of the ego in psychosis leads to like results; the schizophrenic is anything but an instinctual creature with his inhibitions removed, although at times some external stimulus, often of minimal importance, may provoke a violent eruption of instinct, akin to the mass-reflex of the hypertonic subject. The schizophrenic has on the whole a severely inhibited and restricted personality. My only reason for interpolating this comparison from neurology has been to provide an analogy which may be of assistance in understanding the effect of the failure of the ego's inhibiting functions upon psychomotor conditions.

The psychiatrist Zutt summarizes the primitive mechanisms underlying schizophrenic motor conditions in the concept of an "internal attitude"; they confront the ego as automatisms freed from its control.[9] In the psychology of the normal individual also, ego and automatism stand in contrast to each other. Whenever it is a question of learning some skilled accomplishment, the ego acts as arbiter for all the impulses and inhibitions which together make up the aggregate of the movement. A conscious act of attention, accompanied as it may be by anxiety signals, is not favorable to the smooth carrying-out of this aggregate of movement. For the sake of "rationalizing and economizing motor conditions" (to use Homburger's phrase) the ego's volition is confined to initiating the carrying-out of the movement which has been learnt, after which it hands over the direction of this to deeper regulating centers. The activity which has thus become automatic is regulated by sensory currents each one of which need no longer reach consciousness. Topographically the regulation of these automatisms is to be assigned to the preconscious. The automatisms of schizophrenia, on the other hand, are incapable of becoming conscious. Consequently the catatonic subject regards the automatisms which hold sway over him with a helpless sense of strangeness. "My movements are made for me" are words we often hear from the lips of catatonic patients. In his portrayal of the catatonic attack Nunberg says in the same way that the censorship over conscious-

9. Jürg Zutt, "Die Innere Haltung," *Monatsschrift für Psychiatrie und Neurologie* 73 (1929): 52.

ness which is localized in the preconscious loses control over motility.[10] The intensified self-scrutiny of the catatonic subject is a product of the involution of this censorship.

Tausk sees in the increased attention paid to the subject's own mutually antagonistic motor impulses an inhibiting influence upon the motor functions, which in extreme cases leads to stupor.[11] So far as one's capacity for empathy permits, one divines in catatonic stupor the presence of an enormous affective overcharge, an intense tension of libidinal and destructive forces which, however, are held in check by inhibiting impulses called into operation by anxiety of an equal intensity. The depth of regression is matched by a corresponding intensity of defusion of libidinal and destructive instinctual tendencies which in their mutual interaction demand a great expenditure of inhibiting energies. The conscious ego which is able to consider and decide between impulse and inhibition is replaced by a stabilized balance of forces, an automatism foreign to the ego, which blocks the paths to motility.

Another catatonic attitude difficult to grasp by empathy is that of automatic obedience with echolalic and echopractic manifestations. It is hard to understand how the catatonic subject can passively submit to being forced into the most fantastically strange attitudes, apparently without emotion, and without claiming the right to determine them himself. We are very sensitive in our reactions if ever our physical attitude is criticized from without or altered by interference from without, for a person's individual attitude is strongly cathected with narcissistic libido. The attitude of automatic obedience admits of an explanation in the light of the "state of fascination in infants" postulated by Bernfeld.[12] The state of fascination in infants according to Bernfeld represents the identificatory assimilation of an undeveloped ego to external objects in a prenarcissistic stage at which object relationship and identification have not yet become differentiated. Automatic obedience

10. Herman Nunberg, "Ueber den Katatonischen Anfall," *Internationale Zeitschrift für Psychoanalyse* 6 (1920): 25–49.

11. Victor Tausk, "Über die Entstehung des 'Beeinflussungsapparates' in der Schizophrenie," *Internationale Zeitschrift für Psychoanalyse* 5 (1919).

12. Siegfried Bernfeld, Über Faszination," *Imago* 14 (1928).

represents a regression of the ego to a prenarcissistic stage of un-formed ego boundaries such as this, in which the capacity for discovering and mastering objects does not yet exist. The absence of this capacity results in an attitude of motor indifference; a heightening of attention aims at keeping hold of the object inter-nally, reproducing its movements exactly (on echolalic or echo-practic lines). This identificatory assimiliation to the object is an early form of true identification and represents an alteration of the ego in the service of the id, only that ego and id are here as yet imperfectly differentiated. Accordingly automatic obedience would represent a compromise (fixated as an internal attitude) be-tween instinctual gratification and inhibition at the level of an ego in an advanced state of regression. Bernfeld directs attention to the feelings of helpless anxiety which result from the impotence of the infant's ego, its inability to obtain mastery over objects. This helpless anxiety is also met with habitually in schizophrenic states of fascination. It forms the basis for the development of the cata-tonic subject's delusions of being influenced, his feelings of strangeness towards his own body, his feelings (arising by way of identification) that changes are taking place in him, and finally his similar feelings with paranoid mechanisms, feelings that he is the victim of suggestive, hypnotic and electrical influences, feel-ings of having thoughts imposed on him and withdrawn and other feelings the successive course of whose development has been described in such detail by Tausk.[13] The projection of the ego represented as a genital constitutes an attempt at recovery by get-ting rid once more of the pathogenic narcissistic libido which has been conjured up by the anxious helplessness of the ego in its state of regression.

A direct contrast to the automatic obedience of catalepsy is pro-vided by the catatonic attitude of negativism which, with the help of muscular rigidity and opisthotonos, forms a mechanism for blocking out the frustrating and unattainable object-world and is comparable to an infant's fits of defiance. Automatic obedience

13. Tausk, "Über die Entstehung des 'Beeinflussungsapparates' in der Schizo-phrenie."

and negativism are both reactions to the ego's helplessness, results of a deep regression of the ego to prenarcissistic phases of development. Either attitude is capable of passing directly over into the other. The alternation between the *flexibilitas cerea* of the skeletal musculature characteristic of automatic obedience and the muscular rigidity of negativism finds a counterpart in the atonic and spastic innervations of the intestinal musculature during the anal phase; these are the expression of attitudes of defiance and obedience—attitudes which may be regarded as early forms of an ego in process of consolidation.

The catatonic attitudes in question are clearly seen to be dependent upon affects. The disturbance of affect in schizophrenia comes about through the automatized schizophrenic attitudes becoming rigid—Jung speaks of the agglutination of complexes—so that they preserve only that affect which corresponds to the particular attitude prevailing at the time, thus rendering the schizophrenic personality incapable of being moved by current affective experiences. The increased adhesiveness of the narcissistic libido becomes evident in a tendency to perseveration, to stereotype and rhythmicize the automatic attitudes, characteristic also of the play manifestations of childhood.

Stupor, automatic obedience, and negativism are attitudes most often accompanied by intense feelings of pain and consequently fail to achieve any real satisfaction for the narcissistic libido. But there are periods in the development of the schizophrenic process when this lack of narcissistic gratification is overcompensated in delusions of grandeur. These narcissistically satisfying attitudes remind one of the impersonations which are a feature of children's play; one has only to think of the little boy who tried to portray his father with a hat and stick, or of any child imitating a horse or train by means of rhythmical movements. Freud shows how a child in his second year overcomes the loss of an object by resorting to an activity which repeats the trauma in play.[14] The impersonations at which the child plays defend him against the disappointments of

14. "Beyond the Pleasure Principle," in *The Complete Psychological Works of Sigmund Freud*, vol. 18 (London: Hogarth, 1955), pp. 14–16.

his object-world and enable him to hold firmly to his fantasies of omnipotence with the help of magic gestures which belong to one of Ferenczi's stages in the development of the sense of reality.[15] The play of the growing child gives expression to mechanisms of *partial* identification; he becomes increasingly conscious of the phantastic "as if" character of his games. The impersonations of the hysteric, the pathological liar and the impostor, in which they act out their infantile instinctual wishes or need for punishment, possess likewise the character of *partial* identifications. In the case of the schizophrenic on the other hand, we find that *complete* identifications absorb his libido (which has regressed to narcissism) and provide his megalomanic wishes with a hallucinatory gratification. A complete identification of this sort is an internal attitude in Zutt's sense; it determines the impersonation attitudes of the schizophrenic personality and takes the place of the ego (which has regressed) in controlling the approaches to motility. For example a catatonic subject experiences himself as a saint; his gestures involuntarily assume the character of prayers and blessings, his speech is affected and sanctimonious. Those parts of his personality which do not coincide with his ego ideal of saintliness are projected into the external world whence they descend upon him disguised as the voices of temptation. Schilder assumes the existence of a multitude of ideal egos which are liable to be reanimated in the course of any regression of ego libido. If we hold that the ego arises out of identifications, we shall see in schizophrenia a disintegration of the ego. The identifications composing the ego each in turn seize control of the libido.

A patient of Zutt's, in whom a short-lived attack of catatonia was succeeded by a favorable remission, expressed her own experience of an internal attitude as it appeared in retrospect in the following words: "The healthy mind is in ruins; its owner takes the stage disguised in some form or shape in which he then vegetates. This puppet may imagine himself to be Napoleon or a porter; in any case it preserves some sort of physical existence. But the personality openly cracks in the process. One gives the will its way, the protec-

15. See Zutt, "Die Innere Haltung."

tive arrangements come into action. 'Clown' is quite a useful general term; he can be as tragic a figure as King Lear and as comic as a fool without having to change his mask. It is his good fortune if one fine day he realizes that his everyday clothes are hanging ready for him and if energy remains for the quite conscious, increased effort of will required to put them on again."

Allied to the concept of an internal attitude is that of a "motor disposition," as we find it applied by Schattenbrund, the neurologist, in a work to which Jelliffe again has called our attention.[16] By selective stimulation of the pallidostriatal system Schattenbrund produced, besides the amyostatic symptom-complex, certain motor dispositions which in their stagnancy are characteristic of Parkinsonism. The motor dispositions are regulated by the motor organization localized in the hypothalamus. There are varieties of motor dispositions which can be traced back in their typical forms to our animal forebears. According to Uexküll (referring to Darwin), the motor dispositions of beasts of prey fall into three groups: apprehensive movements of flight from an enemy, states of angry, watching preparedness on sighting prey, and alluring dance-like movements directed to sexual objects.[17] The stagnancy and independence of such motor dispositions do not develop only in Parkinsonism. The internal attitude which takes over the control from the ego in schizophrenia may succeed in dominating the clinical picture by means of specific motor dispositions in those cases in which psychomotor conditions have an especially large share in the illness.

I should like finally to give two short examples which illustrate this.

In a corner of a ward for difficult cases we see a twenty-year-old patient squatting motionless, her chin resting on her knees and the bed-clothes drawn up over her nose so that all that remains visible are the half-closed eyes and puckered brows, and above, two perpendicular lines creasing her forehead: the watching attitude of a beast of prey. At irregular intervals she springs up suddenly from

16. Jelliffe, "Vigilance."
17. J. von Uexküll, *Theoretical Biology* (London: Routledge and Kegan, 1926).

this watching position, and quick as lightning precipitates herself upon a nurse, who awakens echoes of a mother transference in her, and whom she tries to throttle. Another scene: a patient, also twenty years old, without any training in gymnastics or dancing, glides in dancing steps across the floor of the ward; with inimitable grace, in ever faster and more furious rhythms, she lets her night-gown fall from her shoulders, waves it like a veil to accompany her dance or winds it like a turban round her head; her steps are full of surprising ideas; she seems to be indifferent to her surroundings, only a sweet seductive smile is addressed to an invisible spectator.

We shall have no difficulty in recognizing in these patients the internal attitudes or motor dispositions described by Darwin and Uexküll as states of angry, watching preparedness and alluring dance-like movements, as they are manifested in the beasts of prey. It would be idle to discuss whether it is here a primary lesion in the hypothalamus which gives rise to the disordered condition of the motor organization or whether fixation to certain libido positions produces this stagnancy of motor dispositions which, as we have stated, had already assumed typical forms in our prehistoric ancestors and are especially qualified therefore as primitive mechanisms, to take over control from an ego which has abdicated. It may be that the two conceptions correspond to the anatomical and to the functional aspects respectively of one and the same problem.

Typical clinical pictures such as these may well suggest to one that these attitudes which so surprisingly shatter the framework of the personality as it existed originally are determined by certain typical primary prototypes, conjured into existence by the downfall of the ego. It would be worthwhile pursuing this idea further.

If I have given what is essentially a one-sided account of schizophrenic attitudes, proceeding from a psychomotor (ego) standpoint, it is because I wished on the one hand to forge a link between the sciences of psychoanalysis and psychiatry and on the other to give an impulsion to the analysis of character which forms so great a part of analysis as it is practised today. The "illogicalities, eccentricities and follies," which we encounter in the analysis of characterological attitudes, stand in a relation to the psychoses similar to that of the perversions to the neuroses.[18] In schizoid neurotics we discover resistances in the form of automatic attitudes which represent a compromise between instinctual gratification and inhibition and curtail the ego's jurisdiction to a considerable extent. The power of these automatisms must be broken by analysis so that the ego may develop effectively in free communication with the id.

18. Freud, "Neurosis and Psychosis" (1924), in *Collected Papers*, 2:254.

The Subjective Experience of Identity and its Psychopathology

The concept of identity appears in modern psychoanalytic literature[1] as a descriptive term designating a subjective experience that reflects the success of the "synthetic function of the ego," a psychodynamic term introduced by Nunberg.[2] The synthetic function integrates the dependencies of the ego on the instinctual impulses of the id, the exigencies of reality, and the demands of the superego, the internalized authority. Before the dawn of self-consciousness the synthetic function of the ego works automatically, the infant fits into his world as the animal during his life span is directed by the instinctive reactions to his environment. But the human child out of his original symbiosis, still embedded in the security of the family develops the freedom of consciousness. Consciousness is always selective, it is consciousness of something, intentionally directed toward an object of pleasure. But the pleasurable is not only the soothingly familiar that alleviates the tensions of need and induces sleep. As Jean Piaget and Ernest Schachtel (whose cogent, excellent book helped me to organize my thoughts) have pointed out, consciousness is from the start also directed toward exciting new stimuli.[3] The child is eager to discover the world and new ego functions. Consciousness mobilizes activity,

Reprinted by permission from *Comprehensive Psychiatry*, vol. 1, no. 1 (New York: Grune and Stratton, 1960).

1. See Erik Erikson, "The Problem of Ego Identity," *Journal of the American Psychoanalytic Association* 4 (1956): 56–121; Allen Wheelis, *The Quest for Identity* (New York: Norton, 1958).

2. Herman Nunberg, "The Synthetic Function of the Ego," *International Journal of Psycho-Analysis* 2 (1931): 123–40.

3. Jean Piaget, *The Origins of Intelligence in Children*, trans. Margaret Cook (New York: International Universities Press, 1952); Ernest Schachtel, *Metamorphosis* (New York: Basic Books, 1959).

it is open to the world and to the future. The child first discovers the continuity of the *you,* the trustworthiness of a mother who returns after each failure to gratify. The experience of continuity in the care of the *you* leads to the discovery of the *I.* The child speaks of himself in the first person usually in the third year, in some cases already in the second year. Before this time the child cannot well be called good or bad, his aggressive expansive action, biting, kicking, tearing, and screaming cannot yet have a destructive motivation as long as the wholeness of the *you* and the *I* are not yet discovered.

The earliest subjective experience of identity is still rooted in the symbiotic union and the child's first outlook on the world is autocentric in this embeddedness, as Schachtel has put it, but the developing ego functions, distance perceptions, skills of motility, verbal communication, and the beginnings of abstract thinking shift the emphasis from autocentricity to allocentricity. The child is eager to encounter the *allon,* the other, the new, the unfamiliar. The insecurity of identity "who am I; where are the boundaries of I and you?" marks the overreaching demands of the Oedipus conflict with doubts in masculine and feminine identity reflected in castration anxieties and penis envy. Introjections and projections keep the boundaries of identity fluid. The superego, according to Freud, the heir of the Oedipus conflict, combines two main trends: (1) archaic introjections, dictated by anxiety-arousing prohibitions and regressive clinging to the symbiotic union. Particularly in an anxious family atmosphere this superego trend may lead the child to shrink into a protective mimicry and may hamper his growth potential by rigidity. (2) In the atmosphere of trust the progressive trend of the ego ideal or superego expands the child's horizon of consciousness by the encounter with new possibilities of identification which set limits in tune with his growing potentialities of ego mastery.

Immersed in the study of the manifold chains of causality which we trace back to the wellsprings of unconsciousness, we psychoanalysts sometimes lose sight of the wonder of consciousness. Daily man awakens from sleep, from the regressive diffusion of identity in his dreams, where he appears in various roles, in fragmented scenes of the past, the present and the future. Is it not a miracle that he awakens in one piece with the sense of continuity in his uniqueness, encountering the now and here as a wholeness, though his awakened sense perceptions give him only fragmentary surface aspects of the world into which he is thrown? The wholeness of his identity and the wholeness of his world belong together, they are not static, but in a flux of change.

The achievement of a continuous identity open to the world and to the future results from a creative process on the level of preconsciousness where, according to Kubie, the shuffling and sampling of perceptions and thoughts, memories of the past and imaginations of the future converge to a unity under the guidance of affects, which crystallize into values shared with others.[4] When a person lives in harmony with himself and his world, his subjective sense of identity scarcely emerges from preconsciousness, but when he doubts his own value and the value of his world, a painful self-consciousness arises. He follows his behavior and activities as if detached from himself with disapproval and apologies, which indicate the lost sense of wholeness. In the crisis of identity in adolescence (Erikson) the creative process of ego identity is put to a hard test when the young person leaves the embeddedness in his family, searching new pathways for his potentialities, new opportunities for work and pleasure in exacting competition, reconciling them with the need for a secondary embeddedness in the hierarchy of job positions, new allegiances and family ties. The enormous labor of integration that reconciles the introjects of the past with broadening present experience and imaginative anticipations of the future on the preconscious level is mostly taken for granted when it is successful. But an emotional crisis may indicate the failure of synthesis. A loss of identity with symptoms of depersonalization and derealization emerges painfully into consciousness.

A few quotations from an interview with a young schizophrenic patient may illustrate the subjective experience of lost identity.

4. Lawrence Kubie, *Neurotic Distortion of the Creative Process* (Lawrence: University of Kansas Press, 1958).

A 25-year-old student of chemistry, very well endowed and praised for scholastic performances, yet without self-confidence, stood in his childhood between a violent alcoholic father and a doting mother whom he had to protect against the father's physical assaults. From early days, I assume, he had to repress the impulses of murderous rage. Near his 20th year he broke down on the shooting range in military training and this experience may have triggered off the danger of derepression. He described the onset of his illness with his own words: "It was terrifically frightening. It was as if I was being abandoned, lost all friends and everything. It was as if everything was closing in all of a sudden and then I removed myself from it. I practically forced them to put me in the hospital, because I could not go home." What preoccupied him in this recorded interview was the sense of time. "I can't get time straightened out. It seems to me, there is no such thing as a yesterday or a tomorrow or a future. Time is like climbing upstairs, literally—and that you reach a certain point and then you fall down. It is all confused. One day I live one experience and then it seems that I go way back to an early point in my life. I suppose, physically I am here, but I don't have a feeling that this is today and that there will be a tomorrow. It is as though when I think of time that I revolve around. I am not moving forward, it seems.—There is a great discontinuity between my mind and my body. My body is some sort of thing, it has not any practical purpose. I can't get it into my head that there are things and people. They appear like cardboard cutouts. I feel, they are going around in the same confusion I am in. I look at the patients as being little people and the attendants as being terrifically large in comparison to the patients. I did not even know that I was taller than my mother until the other day, and yet actually I have always had the feeling that I was looking up at her.—I can tell you facts all day. You can ask me anything you want to know and I can tell you the right answer, but I can't feel it. When you ask me who am I and what significance have I, then I don't know, because I can't feel any such thing as being a person, a human being.

Motions don't seem to have any significance. One object is farther away, I can tell that, than another. I can't seem to feel that it has any depth. There is nothing which I do that has any significance. I guess, I should not use the word I. There is no such thing as a distinct person—I—as being one separate individual. When I go out with a group of men, then I do not exist. I am a part of them. Even now I see people and I think that makes me part of them, I listen to them, I become like that, too."

What in this excerpt characterizes the lucid description of lost identity is the loss of what Schachtel calls "activity affect"[5] which followed an unbearable panic: "and then I just removed myself from it." With this removal the preconscious labor of integration seems to have stopped, a meaningless existence is rattling on. The patient feels that his inner growing has come to a stop, there is no future, astronomic time floats by, the patient cannot find his place in space and time, subjective experience of time and space is unstructured. His world is altered in the same sense as his own personality, people are cardboard cutouts in confusion. Schreber spoke of "furtively fabricated little men."[6] There are no boundaries between him and others, he feels like a passive victim. Movements are automatic, aimless, the patient is deprived of the experience of living his own life. Loss of identity and loss of reality, described by some schizophrenics as world catastrophe, belong together.

Harold Searles in his excellent paper on "Anxiety Concerning Change" has described the slow recovery of the sense of identity in schizophrenic patients under psychoanalytic treatment.[7] The emotional experience of mutuality rediscovers the integrating power of trust and transcends the anxiety about the unpredictability of change. Psychoanalytic treatment grew out of the cathartic method with the aim of shaking up repressed emotions and therewith initiating reintegration. Freud amplified this method by

5. Schachtel, *Metamorphosis.*
6. Sigmund Freud, "The Case of Schreber," in *The Complete Psychological Works of Sigmund Freud,* vol. 12 (London: Hogarth, 1955), pp. 3–82.
7. Harold Searles, "Anxiety Concerning Change," paper given at the Winter Meeting of the American Psychoanalytic Association, New York City, 1959.

the elucidation of resistance and transference, but genuine emotional experience, the precondition of true insight, remained the cornerstone of the curative process. The patient whom I quoted before complained that a loss of feeling accompanied his sense of lost identity, while his cognitive functions remained intact. I want to devote the second part of my paper to the discussion of emotions in relation to the subjective experience of identity.

Every strong emotional experience, particularly a sudden emotional upheaval due to an external event that breaks through the stimulus barrier or a sudden derepression threatens the individual with a loss of identity and a collapse of his reality structure. The emotional upheaval elicits dissociating anxieties, but also the spontaneous reconstructive labor of trust. We are paying more attention to the anxiety effect of emotions than to the reconstructive side of affect. In everyday language we speak of emotions that sweep a person off his feet, he loses control, is beside himself, or goes to pieces. Strong emotions have a pathological connotation. The heroes of Homer raved and roared in the grip of emotions. But in modern Western culture man tries to hide his emotions shamefacedly. He puts on a conventional front. But self-control, particularly when dictated by an unbending, archaic superego can become a compulsive habit, lead to self-deception and estrangement from the self under the pressure of emotions.

Jean-Paul Sartre asserts that emotion is an attempt to transform the world by magic when it becomes too difficult to cope with in a rational way.[8] Similarly pessimistic is T. S. Eliot when he says: "Human kind cannot bear very much reality."[9] In Freud's early theories he gives a signal function to emotions that elicit the discharge of tensions.[10] Reconstruction in the face of dissociating discharge is the outcome of a taming, controlling, and restricting countercathectic process imposed by the ego on the instinct-en-

8. Jean-Paul Sartre, *Existential Psychoanalysis* (New York, 1933), *L'Imagination* (Paris, 1948).

9. T. S. Eliot, as quoted by Angus Dun, "Caught in a Hurricane," *Washington Post*, 15 November, 1959.

10. Sigmund Freud, "Three Essays on Sexuality," in *The Complete Psychological Works*, vol. 7 (1953), pp. 125–244.

gendered affects that upset the homeostasis. Sullivan emphasized the regressive search for security that tames emotional behavior.[11] In Freud's latest instinct theory the tendency towards homeostasis and subjective security is attributed to the death instinct, but Eros is not seen by Freud only as a disturbing, confusing force, it is also the integrative power of construction and reconstruction.[12] Eros implies the strength of trust which gives the lead to the ego functions in the striving for what Hendrick calls the "instinct to master."[13]

Let us look at some descriptive impressions of emotional behavior in relation to the experience of identity.[14] A sudden experience of danger has a startling effect. Fear shakes man loose from the familiar sense of identity and his habitual grasp of the reality scene. As long as the cause of fear can be faced, trust or what Schachtel calls the "activity affect" mobilizes unusual physiological and psychological energies, respiration and circulation are accelerated, alertness quickens reactions, ingenious ideas of rescue crowd into consciousness and inspire rapid decisions that are pursued with clarity and concentration. In face of the unknown and unknowable, the trusting attitude inspires awe which is different from passive, blind submission to fate. But when fear opens up into anxiety, when man passively succumbs to danger, when he in Bibring's words "lets the ego die,"[15] he detaches himself from the realistic encounter with danger by repression or denial. He shuts his eyes to reality and leaves the field of vision to autocentric or autoplastic imagination that protests and transforms magically the unbearable reality in the sense of illusional security, preoedipal dependency or embeddedness. The mobilized emotions are wasted

11. Harry Stack Sullivan, *Conceptions of Modern Psychiatry* (New York: Norton, 1953).

12. Sigmund Freud, "Beyond the Pleasure Principle," in *The Complete Psychological Works*, vol. 18 (1955), pp. 3–64.

13. Ives Hendrick, "The Discussion of the 'Instinct to Master'. A letter to the editors," *Psychoanalytic Quarterly* 12 (1943): 561–65.

14. Jürg Zutt, "Vom aesthetischen im Unterschied zum affektiven Erlebnisbereich," *Wiener Zeitschrift für Nervenheilkunde* 10 (1955): 163.

15. Edward Bibring, "Das Problem der Depression," *Psyche* 6 (Stuttgart, 1952): 81–101.

in aimless agitation. Future loses its meaning when the now and here is no longer encountered. In a given danger situation there will always be a mixture of alloplastic fears and autoplastic anxieties depending on the gravity of danger and the stamina of ego strength.

Hatred that does not take the risk of encountering the adversary deteriorates into smoldering resentment. Rage repressed by anxiety leads to a shrinking of identity and falsification of reality. In autocentric imagination hostility grows into fantastic proportions. The typically angry young man may become addicted to the magic power of explosive rage reactions. He maintains a negative identity in continuous protest against his reality scene. This habit of hating engenders self-hatred that paralyzes the forces of active transformation. But the enemy can be encountered, rage can be channelized into communication by words and actions appropriate to the now and here. The air can be cleared of falsifying products of an autocentric imagination. The adversaries can arrive at liberating decisions and a strengthening redefinition of their differences of identity.

The emotional upheaval of grief at the loss of a beloved partner may deteriorate into passive resistance and wasteful protest reactions against fate in a depression. The imagination holds on to the status quo in autocentric withdrawal. Addicted to the magic power of self-torment the ego shrinks into impoverishment, the world becomes bleak, time seems to slow down, future loses its meaning. But the encounter with bereavement also mobilizes an active emotional response. The labor of mourning gradually arrives at an acceptance of painful reality and creative transfiguration of identity. The bereaved person need not dismiss the beloved partner in bitterness or bury him in hateful identification. The departed can remain present to the mind. The awareness of his personality may even grow into a deeper understanding and inspire the growth potential in the bereaved person.

The emotional experience of guilt or failure also mobilizes two trends of emotional response. A passive wallowing in guilt feelings holds on to the self-image of success, of righteousness by magic atonement gestures of self-justification that distort identity and

196

reality. On the other hand the experience of guilt or failure that can be faced squarely initiates the active labor of genuine regret which opens up sobering insight, acceptance of realistic limitations, and reorganization of identity with new alternatives of development.

Even a sudden joyful experience of success or triumph shakes the subjective sense of identity by its newness. The ego feels lifted to unknown heights. Unlimited horizons of hopeful possibilities arouse a kind of vertigo, when the ego passively yields to the accelerated pace of autocentric imagination. The ego is swept off its feet by a flight of ideas and a turmoil of overstimulation. There is anxiety in this passive response to a joyful experience. The bright magic transformation of identity and reality may suddenly collapse, if there were not the growth potential represented in the spontaneous trusting labor of adaptation which patiently, step by step, restructures the sense of identity and the image of reality on the basis of the new challenge.

In the same sense we might look at the passive intoxication and infatuation of a new love experience which can lead to a runaway ego inflation due to autocentric imagination. A strawfire that is fed onesidedly by narcissistic supplies burns out quickly. Anxieties smother the potentialities of mutual erotic adaptation. On the other hand the creative labor of love in the spontaneous mutuality of allocentric orientation gradually broadens the horizon and deepens the sense of identity in both partners.

Every emotional upheaval elicits a mixture of active and passive responses. The passive response leads to a withdrawal from the challenge of reality into the realm of autocentric imagination, falsifying reality in the sense of magic transformation, most outspokenly in hallucinations and delusions, or falsifying identity by passive surrender or illusional ego inflation. But the active response remains in close contact with reality in the labor of mutual adaptation.

These sketchy examples show the fluid boundaries between pathological and so-called normal emotional behavior. The time factor seems to be an important element. The young schizophrenic whom I quoted marveled about the discrepancy between subjective and objective time. Particularly in view of the sudden onslaught of an emotional crisis man needs a moratorium, as Erikson has put it. He needs time for the labor of mourning, for the labor of remorse, for the readaptation of identity and reality, for the shift from autocentric to allocentric imagination. One could speculate why the problem of identity concerns us so much in our time. It concerns not only the psychiatric patient who is particularly inflexible or helplessly volatile in the face of change—there is a general insecurity about identity in our time. Existentialist philosophers have pointed out the loss of authenticity of man thrown into a mass society. The German sociologist Max Scheler wrote: "We are in approximately ten thousand years of history the first generation in which man has become completely and without residue problematic to himself, in not knowing any more what he is, at the same time, however, knowing that he does not know it."[16]

It is possible that the pace of technical progress and the complexity of living have become too rapid for man's potentialities of emotional adaptation. There is not enough time for meditation and reorientation. Psychoanalysis is timeless, it takes the patient partially out of the flux of time. It represents a therapy of working through conflicts particularly needed in our time. For the lonely, uprooted patient it offers in the participant observer an opportunity to regain the allocentricity, the flexibility in the experience of identity, the openness to the world and the future in a constant flux of transfiguration. Every emotional crisis elicits a double movement in response to the challenge. The passive autocentric movement could be compared to a withdrawal into a circle, the center of which is the identity with the ego of the past. Autocentric imagination dictated by anxieties holds on to the illusion of magic transformation within the unchanging circumference of a static reality horizon. The circular movement in this static arrangement must lead to stagnation, boredom, and ultimately to a loss of identity. The active allocentric reaction to emotional experience permits a change of the reality horizon similar to the movement of a

16. Max Scheler, *Philosophische Weltanshauung* (Munich, Bern: Lehnen Verlag, 1954), p. 62.

double focused elliptical structure; the ego in one focus and the *allon,* the other, in the second focus are moved by the dynamic tension between closeness and distance, commitment and freedom. In psychoanalytic treatment the therapist enters into the neighbor focus, attracted and repelled by positive and negative transference. The other one, the therapist, is simultaneously a stimulus and a threat to the patient, he gradually dissolves the magic images of his autocentrically oriented transference. The analyst can appear as the personification of the powers of evil which the patient tries to exclude from his circular system, stretching the inner distance to the breaking point. He can become for the patient the dangerous seducer or the vindictive competitor, the punishing authority or the possessive mother. But when the patient focuses his attention long enough on the other one, the therapist, he discovers that there is no impulse either in his partner or in himself which is so completely destructive, no wish so onesidedly egocentric that they could not be redeemed and enter into a broader ego integration by a deepening understanding. The acceptance of the self and the other opens the wider range of interpersonal relations. Every emotional crisis in the treatment shakes the patient's and frequently also the therapist's subjective experience of identity. There grows the awareness of the *you* and the *I;* the *I* can be discovered most saliently through the awareness of the you in a dynamic encounter. The *I* takes the risk of a transient loss of identity in every step that transcends its previous boundaries, but the endurance of the anxieties mobilized by the risks opens the potentialities of creative transfiguration.

PART III

Theoretical and Technical Problems in Psychoanalysis

Dissent in the Early History
of Psychoanalysis

It is doubtful if sufficient time has elapsed since the experiences of early psychoanalysis for us to understand the development of psychoanalytic orthodoxy in its struggle with dissenting psychotherapeutic schools. These experiences were dramatic and passionate. I remember the impact of dissenting opinions on conventions, excited discussions, adherents of Jung attacking the orthodox Freudians, the pupils of Adler fighting the pupils of Freud, and the poor candidate in training in the midst of it, torn between his loyalty for his training analyst and rebellion against him.

The psychoanalyst knows that he is not working in the vacuum of pure science. Even the most objective branches of science are influenced in their development not only by economic and cultural conditions, but also by personal, psychological motives of dogmatic adherence to influential predecessors or rebelliousness against whatever happens to be currently dominant. The very interest that leads the analyst into his special field of science, the interest in the emotional entanglement of human relations, exposes him particularly to emotional turmoil in others as well as in himself. I think it cannot be denied that, despite thorough-going personal analysis, an intense struggle of opinions, love and hatred, adherence and rebellion, play lively parts in the development of psychoanalysis.

Freud's discoveries were the most courageous and revolutionary in the science of his age. He frankly altered his own theories—for example the instinct theory—in accordance with his growing in-

Reprinted by permission from *Psychiatry: Journal for the Study of Interpersonal Processes* 5 (1942): 349–59. Copyright 1942 by the William Alanson White Psychiatric Foundation, Inc.

sights. And yet this revolutionary movement, in the early stages of its development, was accused of being an orthodoxy that fenced the gains of Freud's insights in a hard, inaccessible terminology. It would have been much more fair on the part of the dissenting opponents to designate the original Freudian formulations as classical, since the term of orthodoxy implies the reproach of rigid narrowness. But there was an element of defiant seclusion in the group spirit of the first adherents of Freud. Freud did not mind challenging his contemporaries. He audaciously challenged the prudery of the bourgeois society of the Victorian age. He accepted their resentments and outrageous hostilities as natural consequences with calmness and a good sense of humor. However, the relations to his closest followers were pervaded by a strained loyalty on the one hand, and bitter resentments in the event of dissenting opinions on the other hand. It is understandable that men who expose themselves to the hostility of the world want a security of agreement in the circle of their closest friends. The apostasy of Jung, Adler, Rank, and Stekel provoked bitter resentments in the orthodox group of Freud's followers. The majority of the younger members of the group shut their eyes and ears to the dissenting doctrines in order not to become confused, or disturbed in their loyalty.

Nevertheless, the different psychotherapeutic doctrines of the age somehow belong together. There are bridges between dissenting personal viewpoints. Sometimes the jargon of one school can be translated into the terminology of another. A part of the difficulty is in the field of semantics. Historic analysis of the diverging energies, all invested in these various attempts to liberate the psychoneurotic person, may in the long run lead to a reintegration of psychotherapy. It may still be too early for such a reconciliation. The experiences of different analysts in their personal relations with different patients and the theories that crystallize therefrom are certain to clash before they can grow together into a new entity.

Every historic review will recognize the absolute leadership of Freud in the field of psychotherapy because of his pioneering creativity and his comprehensive revolutionizing ideas. But no one is justified in settling into a protective personal devotion to this leadership. The creativity of a leading authority obliges his followers to a creativity of research in terms of their own experience.

The original contributions made to psychoanalysis by Harry Stack Sullivan and Karen Horney are well known. Since their work is familiar, I shall limit my study to those pupils of Freud who dissented at an earlier stage of psychoanalytic development. Their theories are less known to the younger psychiatrists. The student feels confused by deviating terminologies and differing viewpoints. All seem to be on the defensive against these outsiders and know much more about their shortcomings than about their positive contributions. What I would like to show is that one can be a serious follower of Freud and yet appreciate and profit from experiences and theories of those who dissent from his authority. I shall here restrict myself to the study of Adler's and Jung's psychotherapy.

In 1911 Alfred Adler withdrew from the editorial staff of the International Periodical of Medical Psychoanalysis. At that time the pupils of Freud were deeply impressed by Freud's discoveries of the unconscious. Every follower of Freud was preoccupied with learning and understanding the language of the unconscious in dreams, parapraxes and symptoms. This overwhelming new insight necessarily first pushed the questions of ego psychology into the background. This mood of prevailing interest in the unconscious was smilingly admitted in a joke that I heard in the Berlin Psychoanalytic Society: "An airship is of course primarily a penis symbol, but you can also cross the ocean with it."

At the time of Adler's dissent his prevailing interest in the aspects of the neurotic character from the ego's point of view was interpreted as a flight from the unconscious. By turning away from the frightening aspects of instinctual power to the studies of ego psychology Adler escaped from the indignant prudish resistance of the public. His work was much more accessible to general understanding and easily won public acceptance. Freud suspected that Adler was driven by the motives of the rebellious son who tries to overthrow the father's authority and to minimize the master's discoveries. In his *History of the Psychoanalytic Movement* (1914) Freud quoted Adler as saying: "Do you think it is such a great pleasure for me to stay all my life in your shadow?"[1] But even if such motives played an instigating role, they do not minimize the value of Adler's contributions to ego psychology.

In 1914 Freud still believed that psychoanalysis could explain nothing but neurotic symptoms, not the total personality. He considered it as pretension on the part of Adler that he tried to explain behavior and character in the same way as neurotic and psychotic diseases. The later development of Freud's conceptions has justified Adler to a certain degree. To the orthodox analyst also the need to supplement symptom analysis with character analysis became more and more evident. But Freud stressed the instinctual part of neurotic character problems in biological terms—the transformations of pregenital and genital drives. He did not see any justification for Adler's formulations of neurotic conflicts in the language of an ego psychology which stressed the ego's need for adjustment to reality with a certain one-sidedness.

In the problem of reality adjustment Adler attributed much more importance to the aggressive than to the sexual instinct.[2] He started with studies of "organ inferiority" and descriptions of all those compensating mechanisms by which a personality restricted by physical shortcomings tries to balance his values in the struggle for existence. Physical shortcomings as well as other frustrations—such as the experiences of the pampered or the hated child—establish an insecurity, a feeling of inferiority, that determines the plan of living in the neurotic character. This plan or "directive line" of the neurotic tries to overcome this insecurity by incessantly intense aggression at the expense of his social feelings and his sense for coöperation.

1. Sigmund Freud, "Zur Geschichte der psychoanalytischen Bewegung," in *Gesammelte Schriften,* vol. 4 (Leipzig: Internationaler Psychoanalytischer Verlag, 1924), p. 461.

2. Alfred Adler, "Individual Psychology," in *Psychologies of 1930,* ed. Carl Murchison (Worcester, Mass.: Clark University Press, 1930), pp. 395–405. A table of Adler's publications is to be found on p. 404.

Adler was not interested in the causes of a neurosis, but in its purposes. He followed the neurotic character in his struggle with his environment, in his attempts to assert himself at the expense of others despite neurotic shortcomings, or even with their help. This spiteful, parasitic self-assertion introduces typical tendencies into the life of the neurotic: the distortion of adult relations into parent-child relations with the features of obedience and defiance, the greedy demand to be loved, no matter how he behaves, the reckless ambition to excel in comparison with others, the incapacity to take defeat, dominating and possessive tendencies, guilt feelings and self-punishment in order to gain reconciliation without active contributions to a relationship. All these character features are purposed to reestablish the threatened security of the neurotic, to compensate or overcompensate for his unbearable feeling of inferiority. In the same way, Adler interpreted every symptom as a weapon of parasitic self-assertion; anxiety has the unconscious purpose of enforcing attention, it is a cry for help.

Freud had not overlooked this self-assertive aspect of neurotic symptomatology, he described it under the title of ego resistance, more specifically labeled as the secondary gain of illness. Originally Freud had the idea that anxiety was the result of instinctual energies being dammed up behind a wall of repression. His later interpretation of anxiety as a warning signal to the endangered ego is much more close to Adler's conception.

While Freud was absorbed by the exploration of the disturbed instinct economy and the unconscious roots of the neurosis, Adler more and more neglected the difference between conscious and unconscious mental activity. He considered the repression into the unconscious as another weapon of distorted self-assertion. By such an escape the neurotic evades the main tasks of adjustment to society, vocation and love. Although this one-sided interest in the surface of neurotic problems seems rather flat, something may be gained from Adler's detailed descriptions of the actual reality relations of the neurotic. In practical work one has primarily to meet the resistances of the patients and to start from the surface, as Freud recommended.

Adler offered rich material describing how the neurotic person wrestles in intense self-assertion with the specific demands of culture. In this capitalistic, masculine, and competitive culture—with efficiency and exploitation of the weaker by the stronger—the intense self-assertion of a neurotic person leads to the typical reaction which Adler called "the masculine protest." He illustrated this masculine protest in men, as well as in women, frequently even more emphasized in women, since cultural and economic disadvantages evoke greater insecurity in them. The psychological phenomenon that Adler labeled as masculine protest is related to the notion of penis envy in Freud's terminology. The choice of the terms "penis envy" and "castration fear" indicates Freud's conviction, that the child experiences the anatomical difference as a sign of feminine inferiority without regard for cultural prejudices. Adler understood castration fear as the fear of losing the superiority that under the conditions of the culture are gained by masculine efficiency and successful self-assertion.

Out of his one-sided interest in compensating superiority strivings Adler saw the libidinal demands of his neurotic patient in the service of his need for prestige. The complaints about sexual dissatisfaction, the various deviations of sexual behavior are a symbolic expression for the neurotic person's feelings of inferiority. The difficulties and obstacles in sexual satisfaction grow out of a self-assertive, competitive refusal of real companionship. The neurotic man, and the neurotic woman, misuse their assets as sexual partners to dominate and to exploit their love object in a child-like, possessive way. Reckless conquest—Don Juan type—or, in a more indirect way, feminine or even masochistic submission tries to enslave the love object by sexual fascination. In Adler's interpretation the Oedipus conflict is no longer a tragic conflict of contradictory instinctual drives, but the typical pattern of competition in the family life of this culture.

Adler "cured" his patients by making them understand the errors of their plan of life. These errors are rooted in egocentric strivings for superiority which are not sufficiently checked by the social sense of cooperation. In his efforts to cure the patient by understanding Adler experienced the transference, the relation of the patient to his therapist, as a resistant struggle for power.

The patient fights the therapist's influence, tries to defeat the curing process in order to establish his superiority over the physician. Even when he seeks the doctor's love by conforming obedience, he tries to defeat the purpose of the cure by the submissive form of masculine protest.

Adler called his theory and method of treatment "Individual Psychology." He showed the person in his struggle with the cultural conditions of society, which may be sometimes overlooked by the Freudian analyst. Adler pointed out self-defenses in disguised behavior patterns that respond to the specific demands of a competitive culture. But Individual Psychology takes society's part against the person. Individual Psychology needs as supplement a cultural psychology such as Erich Fromm has given in *Escape from Freedom*.[3] Adler confounded the society of this culture with the ideal human society. He did not recognize the limitations and pathology of a culture that at times forces neurotic or psychotic rebellion on people. It is true, the psychotherapist has not to reform the world, he has to help the person make a bearable adjustment. But in order to reconcile a person with his culture, he has to understand both sides. Adler did not sincerely sympathize with the neurotic rebellion of a person who as a child of this culture did not find the conditions suitable for the productive development of his instinctual energies. Crippled in his instinctual expression this person needs a transitional neurotic rebellion for his liberation. In this painful transition only a psychotherapy free from conventional morality can lead to a better creative adjustment.

Adler's terminology remains on the level of the conventional morality of this culture. To him a good adjustment to society is at the top of a scale of values and maladjustment at the opposite end. Individual Psychology talks about the neurotic person's egocentricity, self-inflation, vanity, pretentious domineering greed, ambitions and aggressions, and lack of courage in these terms of general morality, so that the patient like a naughty child feels that he alone is in the wrong. It is much less painful to be confronted with

3. Erich Fromm, *Escape from Freedom* (New York: Farrar and Rinehart, 1941).

deeply unconscious instinctual needs than to recognize in one's personality character-distorting self-defenses, incompatible with the code of conventional morality. The biological terms of Freud's character analysis—penis envy, castrative tendencies, oral, urethral, and anal desires—are neutral towards moral values, they take the sting of offended moral vanity out of his interpretations.

On the other hand, the plain English of Adler's terms may sometimes strike home more effectively than Freud's biological terms. Sometimes it may be more important to dwell on the level of actuality than to dig back into childhood memories. The patient may refuse actual change, because he clings to childhood resentments and does not want to face actual problems.

By the adherence to conventional morality Individual Psychology has conquered the field of pedagogy. But the pedagogic success implies the danger that the patient tries to correct himself in a rational way, in order to conform with his therapist's moral standards. In this case he does not wait for a dynamic liberation of his misdirected instinctual energies and a spontaneous new orientation of instinct economy from the sources of the unconscious.

Freud claimed that Adler did not mention love in his writings, only hatred in all the various forms of the masculine protest. Neither do Freudian analysts talk much about positive transference in their practical work. They work, for the most part, on the negative side, trying to liberate hatred and resentments, in order to free the way for unhampered capacity to love. I even feel that, in some respects, Adler talked too much about love, about fair comradeship, about social feelings and cooperation. He preached the necessity of overcoming the masculine protest and alleged that he, for his part, had outgrown it to a high degree. I feel that in psychotherapy love should not be preached. The preaching of love makes each one feel incompetent and guilty. Nevertheless, love should be experienced in the understanding relation of the therapist and the patient.

A comparison of the two early apostate pupils of Freud shows that, whereas Adler was motivated by socialistic ideals, Jung— the descendant of a Swiss minister—was influenced by a religious background. Adler stressed the rational approach to the problem of psychoneurosis, while Jung, deeply impressed by the irrational powers of the unconscious, regards them with almost religious reverence. His approach to psychoneurosis is more intuitive, anticipating the revelation of the unconscious as an artist foresees the completion of his work. Adler's more rational approach implies a degree of intellectual activity, amounting almost to a masculine protest against the revelation of the unconscious, independent from willpower. Freud esteemed Jung even less than Adler. Now and then he scoffed at those mystics, who worship the irrational powers of the unconscious like a new religion. Such remarks imply a repudiation of Jung and his group.

I do not want to dwell on Jung's descriptive contributions, his definition of introverted and extroverted types and further psychological classifications. I wish to point out Jung's personal contributions to psychotherapy and to understand his development, which is partly in agreement with and partly in contradiction to Freud.

Jung certainly outgrew the narrowness of his traditionally religious background, but the problem of religious bondage and creative liberation have kept him fascinated his life long. He studied the myths, cults, legends, and religions of various races and times. He was particularly attracted by the passivity of Eastern religions and philosophy, which he welcomed as a relaxation from the tense overactivity of a Western masculine culture. More recently he delved into the mysticism of medieval alchemy. Everywhere in his worldwide studies he rediscovered the ingenious discovery of Freud, the universal symbolism of the unconscious.

I once witnessed an interview in which Jung talked about the enormous labor of his anthropological studies and expressed with deep bitterness the lack of recognition that his work found with Freud. I felt in him the tragic love-hatred relation of the Christian pupil to the Jewish master, not yet free from racial prejudice. There was an impressive contrast of personality. The reserved severity and law-abiding strictness of Freud adhered almost dogmatically to science, even though his keen genius overthrew many a dogma of his ancestors. Jung is a more artistic personality, charming and beaming in his vitality, vague and whimsical in his formulations, in comparison to the classical clarity of Freud's style. Jung is more affectively free, he appeals more to the emotions of the public, while Freud's almost suspicious intellect was sharpened by the aggravating experiences of racial antagonism. Freud relied only upon the response of rational insight. Jung, the less original thinker, was more spoiled by the applause of the public. His appearance in public evoked a tide of positive transference. To many of his patients and pupils he became the prophet of a new religion, a priest-physician who met the strong need for adherence. He refused with disgust when the Nazis tried to make him the hero of a racial psychotherapy. Yet he is more emotionally bound to the traditions of blood and soil than his revolutionary master.

The first points of disagreement between Freud and Jung arose on the ground of psychoanalytic theory. Freud and Jung, both wrestling with the problem of schizophrenia, came to different formulations of the instinct theory. Freud considered it necessary to build his libido theory on a biological basis, even though he recognized that biology cannot yet furnish any exact, scientific definition of libido. Freud's libido theory, in its different changes, implied always a dualistic interpretation of instinctual energies, although in reality observation one admittedly sees only fusions of the dualistic instincts. In 1912 Jung developed a monistic conception of libido in his *Transformation and Symbols of Libido*.[4] In his conception, libido is a monistic vital energy of ambivalent character, creative as well as destructive. If the weakened ego fails to assimilate this vital energy, its unconscious forms of expression tend to split the personality into pairs of conflicting contrasts. This split is most definitely marked in schizophrenia.

Jung rejected the biological basis for his libido theory. He buttressed it on the hypothetical interpretation of prehistoric devel-

---

4. Carl Jung, *Wandlungen und Symbole der Libido* (Leipzig and Vienna: Franz Deuticke, 1912). The further publications on which this study is based include Carl Jung, *Die Beziehungen Zwischen dem Ich und dem Unbewussten* (Darmstadt: Otto Reichl Verlag, 1928); Carl Jung, *Seelenprobleme der Gegenwart* (Zurich: Rascher und Cie, 1931); Richard Wilhelm and Carl Jung, *Das Geheimnis der Goldenen Blüte* (Zurich and Leipzig: Rascher Verlag, 1939).

opment. In this process of development Jung sees a constant in-flux of libido transformed and organized into the service of human self-assertion and self-preservation. The symbol is the agent of transformation. Jung illustrates this libido transformation in his hypothesis concerning the invention of fire, of the plow or other progressive cultural gains. According to Jung, the production of fire by drilling wood or the plowing of the soil grew out of a playful symbolic imitation of the coitus rhythm. The symbolic repetition of the pleasure-seeking activity led to a desexualization of libido. The results prove to be essential for reality mastery and human self-assertion. Thus Jung tries to show how the progress of cultural development desexualizes and converts libidinal energy into the service of creative self-preservation and by doing so liberates a person from dependency on protective parents and ancestor habits. The process of sublimation transforms primarily the incestuous libido. This progress, in the sense of human self-assertion, breaks down more or less in schizophrenia. According to Jung's theory the neurotic only suffers from restrictions in the field of direct pleasure-seeking libidinal energies with secondary effects on his self-assertion. In schizophrenia the sublimation of libidinal energy breaks down and this regression threatens the self assertion in a much deeper sense. The function of reality mastery is replaced by introverted archaic fantasies.

Freud and Ferenczi have attacked this historical libido theory of Jung.[5] Ferenczi pointed out that Jung built up his anthropological hypotheses by application of knowledge acquired in the analysis of the person in this time and culture. He is therefore, not justified in using these same anthropological hypotheses to explain the libido economy of modern people. In the light of current anthropological studies, both Freud's and Jung's anthropological theories may also be considered as speculative. Freud was more reserved, he only used psychoanalytical insight for anthropological speculations. Jung used his anthropological hypotheses to interpret the psychology of modern man.

5. Sigmund Freud, "Zur Einführung des Narzissmus" in *Gesammelte Schriften*, vol. 6 (1925), 162–64; Sandor Ferenczi, "Kritik der Jungschen Wanderlungen und Symbole der Libido," *Bausteine zur Psychoanalyse* 1 (1927): 243–68.

Between the goals of direct libido satisfaction and the gains of libido transformation in the sense of self-assertion and reality mastery, there lies the field of human fantasy. In fantasy production the abundance of nontransformed libido seeks an outlet of symbolic expression in myths, cults, legends, folklore, religious and artistic creation. Jung called this field of human fantasy with its repetitive patterns of symbolic expression the "collective unconscious." He distinguishes in his analytic work two layers of unconsciousness, the personal unconscious containing personal repressed memories and the collective unconscious containing phylogenetic memories, the symbolic forms of typical emotional conflicts. I personally cannot follow Jung in this distinction. To my understanding, the personal conflicts and repressions are rooted in unconscious instinctual dispositions that each person has in common with the whole of mankind. Cultural patterns and personal history shape the personal conflicts. Practically, Jung's collective viewpoint may lead to hasty generalizations. Jung seems to fall back on typical explanations before he has exhausted the possibilities of personal analysis.

Jung has populated this collective unconscious with a series of mythological figures, demons, or halfgods. Their names characterize the imaginative, artistic attitude of the inventor, but confuse the noninitiated student of Jung's psychology. Jung believed that emotional conflicts lost their liveliness in the terms of scientific language. Therefore, he introduced mythological figures—archetypes—who represent the repetitive patterns of symbolic expression for typical emotional relations and conflicts.

According to Jung archetypes of the father and mother relation outgrow the forms of personal dependency and become immersed in general religious forms of bondage. The typical conflicts of such superpersonal bondage are expressed in various motives of mythology and religion, the motive of incest, of rebirth and others. Jung no longer considers the Oedipus complex as the problem of sex attraction and prohibition that a person experiences in relation to his actual parents. Jung sees in the Oedipus complex the symbolic expression for the typical conflict between dependent and independent tendencies in the relation of the younger to the older generation. This conception found the enthusiastic approval of all those who were opposed to Freud's so-called pansexualism.

In the life of the adult, dependency on the protective older generation is mostly transferred into the relation with the sex partner. The eternally unattainable beloved woman is, according to Jung, the archetype of *anima* for the man. The inaccessible prince charming is the archetype of *animus* for the woman. These archetypes burden the real personal relation to the sex partner with the typical features of archaic bondage. The freedom of personal development is overshadowed by the typical conflicts of ambivalent dependency. Married life is often ruined by the specters of animus and anima.

Jung conceives the process of cultural development as a slowly growing progress of individuation that liberates the person from the ties of the collective unconscious. The ritualistic forms of living in primitive cultures represent a state of close mutual identification among the members of one tribe which does not yet allow much individual distinction or display of personal freedom. In this state of mutual identification the person becomes immersed in the tribal patterns of the collective unconscious. Jung calls this state of mutual identification, with the French anthropologist Lévy-Brühl, *participation mystique*. The process of liberation from the ties of the collective unconscious does not succeed without delay and regression. Even the freedom of Western civilization has not prevented repressions, restrictions and character distortions. Particularly the family relations of modern man are still deeply immersed in mutual identifications and experiences of mystic participation and strongly resist personal liberation. Failure of individuation leads to relapses into atavistic forms of family dependency or religious bondage. Similarly to Reik, Jung considers the neurosis of modern man with its obsessional rituals, with its dramatization of symbols and its backwards directed dependencies as private forms of religion.

Family dependency and private religious bondage interfere with a person's adjustment to adult group life. In primitive cultures the initiation rite enacts a step of the transition from family adherence to adult group adjustment. In this culture, which opens the way to a higher degree of personal freedom, psychotherapy has to take the role of the initiation rite in cases of obvious failure of adjustment.

Jung does not esteem the well-adjusted personality of this culture so highly as Adler. From his viewpoint the so-called well-adjusted personality may lead a rather masklike existence. Under this mask the person may live in a disturbed relation to his real self, trying to satisfy the expectations of his milieu. He tries to live up to conventional standards of what he is supposed to be as a member of the family, of his club, of his class: an authoritative father or a loving housewife, a self-sacrificing nurse, a fearless soldier, a brilliant student, an efficient, yet amiable businessman. Jung calls this masklike ideal *persona* and points out that this persona frequently does not permit enough room for the development of the real self. The center of the real self is not so much in conscious intentions of adjustment, but in the unconscious instinctual sources of the personality. Jung's conception of persona is related to Freud's notion of *superego*. The superego however, is a heritage of the Oedipus conflict, a remnant of the dependency on each one of the personal parents. The persona implies the dependency on behaviour patterns of the actual cultural setting a person lives in.

According to Jung's description this conventional pattern of reality adjustment may break down under the pressure of vital energies that have not found expression in this narrow frame. Excluded from the integrating activity of consciousness, the archetypes dominate the person. Thus, an efficient, successful businessman breaks down and turns into a complaining, whining, helpless creature like the caricature of a woman. According to Jung, after the breakdown of his *persona,* the patient is overwhelmed by the archetype of his anima. Freud would say, he is overwhelmed by the castration fear linked with his infantile instinctual drives. Similarly, a woman who, according to Freud, is haunted by her penis envy, is in Jung's language possessed by the animus, a series of masculine ideals, that, unobtainable to her desires for satisfactory object relation, become images of a caricature-like identification with these men. The biological terms of *castration fear* and *penis envy* on the one hand, the mythological terms of anima and animus on the other hand express the problem of the neurotic to find a reconciliation with his own sex role or to find a satisfactory object relation to the other sex.

Jung leaves no doubt that the breakdown of the frame of adjustment represents a serious danger. The impact with the archetypes of the collective unconscious may lead to an irreparable psychotic disaster if the ego is not capable of assimilating the overwhelming dream world. The process of assimilation is accompanied by intense suffering and to complete it demands the whole courage of the patient. Jung describes the types of resistance that threaten to stall the process of broadening consciousness. One type of personality reacts with depression; he cannot reconcile the subterranean powers of a revolting unconscious with the protecting ideals of his conventional morality. Another type welcomes this revolution with triumphant defiance and hypomanic self-inflation, avoiding a deeper integration by superficial intellectual acceptance of unconscious potentialities.

But Jung does not consider the emotional crisis of a neurosis only as an evil. He sees a drive for self-completion at work. The breakdown which broadens the personality frame implies the start of readjustment; a creative healing process opens new channels of energy. Jung compares the process of reintegration to a religious conversion or to the experience of artistic creation. In psychotherapeutic work Jung therefore does not stress rational interpretation so much as he stimulates his patients to express their emotions in dreams, fantasies, drawings, paintings or other artistic performances. He does not want art of any socially accepted value, but personal self-expression as archaic as possible, a sort of experimentation with the patient's own unconscious potentialities. Jung's interpreting cooperation does not claim any scientific cogency, he fantasizes with his patient. He judges his interpreting contributions only according to their efficiency to keep the creative current in his patient alive. Jung does not look so much into the past to find the causes of his patient's development. Like Adler he is more concerned about the patient's final tendencies. But he does not stress with Adler's one-sidedness the neurotic long-ing for power to compensate the infantile insecurity. He stresses the creative potentialities of the unconscious and anticipates the synthesis that broadens the personality and transfers the center of gravity from a one-sided rational consciousness into the deeper layers of creative emotions. Jung does not expect his patients to turn out to be artists. He intends to give his patient the chance to develop his spontaneity, finding an unbarred access to the sources of the unconscious.

The anticipation of the synthesis in his patient separates Jung from the uncompromising analytic attitude of Freud. Freud insists that the psychoanalyst must refrain from proclaiming any philo-sophical viewpoint in his work, he should not be concerned about the goal to which his work will lead. He should point out the un-conscious instinctual drives, for example, concealed destructive tendencies, and this awareness will awaken in the patient com-pensatory powers of the life instinct.

In the darkness of a psychoneurotic crisis every patient asks for the goal, for personal guidance. According to the degree of ego insecurity of the patient each analyst practically finds some com-promise between an extremely analytic and a so-called synthetic attitude. No analyst can completely conceal the values he is striv-ing for. But an overemphasized intention to alleviate the patient's anxiety makes him more dependent and fearful and does not give enough space to the spontaneous integration process. I feel, in the treatment of psychotics, Jung's more supporting method of therapy may furnish some useful suggestions.

In agreement with Freud, Jung considers the transference as a factor of main importance in the curing process. Here again Jung is inclined to dwell on the superpersonal aspect of this relation. The analysand does not only repeat in the transference relation the features of personal experiences with his parents, he projects into this relation his yearnings for an all-gratifying god who will compensate for all the incompetences of personal parents. On the other hand the patient attributes to his analyst the role of the per-secuting devil insofar as his demands for omnipotent satisfaction are frustrated. Jung discovers this religious function in the most rational atheist or agnostic among his patients. If the analysis leads him to a certain depth, the neurotic patient—even more the psychotic—will work out the archaic mythological patterns of religious dependency in his transference relation.

Jung warns his pupils and patients against imitating any traditional religious symbolism as an outlet for instinctual energies. Adherence to a conventionally accepted religion satisfies the sentimentality of the person, but adds another bondage that smothers his creative potentialities.

The psychotherapist has to withstand his patient's seductive appeal to accept the role of the all-gratifying god and savior and yet to give him sufficient sympathy, human understanding and love, so that he dares to verbalize or find other creative expressions for his religious needs. No human being, only an omnipotent and all-loving god could fulfill the patient's religious needs for perfect protection, for perfect instinct gratification all in one. Jung observes, that when the patient's transference fantasies grow into mythological grandeur, the personal relation of each patient to his therapist slowly shrinks into reality boundaries. A separation of boundless fantasy and limited reality relation takes place. In a creative analytic process libido is sublimated and transformed into the service of self-assertion. Creating godlike images, the patient recognizes the infantile passion of his religious demands and slowly outgrows them. He loses in the transference relation his need to be dependent on a god outside of himself. The boundaries of his ego consolidate in the proudest and most humble of all religious relations, the dependency on a fellow human being whose limitations he learns to respect.

Jung's conception of the analytic process as a creative religious function makes the transference neurosis look like an artificial psychosis with fantasies of grandiosity and destructive boundless greed, except that the maintenance of insight guarantees a favorable prognosis. The analytic process looks like the dangerous way through a psychotic purgatory.

The way is not only dangerous for the patient, it is also dangerous for the therapist. The patient's appeal to the therapist's godlikeness implies the temptation to respond with all-embracing

219

gratification. Many a patient seems to be cured by the gift of positive countertransference. The therapist may become intoxicated by what Jung calls the *mana,* that is, the magic power of the profession. More particularly, the therapist who experiences his psychotherapeutic capacity as an artistic gift, whose intuition transgresses the limits of personality, is in danger of getting into a state of self-inflation about his godlike therapeutic omnipotence. Consequently he suffers from the setback of guilt feelings that arise from presumptuous responsibilities. I cannot judge how far Jung himself avoids this main danger of countertransference. At least he frankly puts his finger on this problem and does not withdraw into the protection of scientific aloofness.

Jung admits that not each of his patients goes the way of a breakdown and complete new orientation of the personality. His impression is that different types of patients come to him, to Freud, and to Adler. Two-thirds of Jung's patients are beyond middle age. Freud did not give an optimistic prognosis to the analysis of older patients. They cannot feel encouraged to start a Freudian analysis. Younger patients with typical difficulties of sexual adjustment will expect more help from a Freudian analysis. Patients with more superficial difficulties in their social adjustment may prefer the Adlerian approach. Jung's patients have frequently been successful in their various adjustments, but are often haunted by dissatisfactions in their philosophical, political, or religious activities. Their life has lost meaning, they hope to restore it, with the help of Jung, by liberation of creative self-expression.

I have given here only the rough outlines of what characterizes these two psychotherapists who early dissented from classical Freudian psychoanalysis. Both of these apostates felt the need to reformulate some of Freud's findings in a nonbiological language, considering the sexual expression for tendencies in human relationship frequently as a symbolic formulation. Both stressed the necessities of cultural adjustment in the psychoneurotic process, feeling that Freud's emphasis of instinctual mechanisms neglects to a certain degree the part of actual cultural demands to which the neurotic has found only a distorted form of adjustment.

Both Adler and Jung have built on Freud's discoveries stressing a one-sided aspect of his findings. Adler dwelt on the ego side of human conflicts, neglecting their libidinal part. Jung neglects the part of the rational ego. In his presentation the human adjustment grows as a mystical sublimation process out of instinctual drives. The vital tension between irrational and rational activities is abolished.

The separation of Adler and Jung from Freud was partly motivated by personal competition. Personal resentments deepened the contrasts. But Freud's anger against his dissenting pupils can also be understood on its objective basis. Freud found the dynamic complexities of his psychological insights simplified and distorted by the one-sidedness of Adler's and Jung's presentations.

Understanding the rational as well as the emotional part of this struggle of opinions one may feel enriched by Adler's and Jung's contributions to psychoanalysis, although there may be disagreement with them on many points. Why should psychiatrists maintain walls of separation between psychotherapeutic schools, when they could profit from common discussion? Freud welcomed Groddeck, a very original psychotherapist, in the psychoanalytic association. At this opportunity he stated that Groddeck's recognition of the dynamic factors of transference and resistance in his work guaranteed sufficient common ground for cooperation. Conceptions like orthodoxy and apostasis fit into a religious movement, not into a field of scientific research. Secret religious propensities enter not only into the transference relation but also into the adherence and opposition to psychoanalysis in general. The psychiatrist is not exempted from fighting for creative liberation from religious bondage in his own professional work.

The Importance of Flexibility in Psychoanalytic Technique

Psychoanalytic science has grown out of an art: Freud's art of investigating and treating psychoneurotic patients. The scientific discoveries of the dynamic unconscious, of the steps of human libido development, of repression, regression, transference, repetion compulsion, etc., have in turn influenced the art of psychoanalytic practice. Psychoanalytic practitioners, the artists in this profession, remain the pioneering vanguard of psychoanalytic science. The scientists follow them, consolidating their intuitive discoveries and conquests. Such a vanguard has to be flexible and mobile, not to get frozen in what Freud called the "pseudoexactness of modern psychiatry."[1]

The technique of psychoanalytic art is built on a set of rules or suggestions for practical procedures which cannot in the least cover the almost infinite variety of therapeutic situations arising in analysis, which Freud compared with the complex constellations of a chess game. Freud, in his papers on technique, as well as Ella Sharpe, Fenichel, Glover, Strachey, and other early authors who wrote on technique, has stressed the need for flexibility for various reasons:

1. Freud emphasized that his technical suggestions were suited to his individuality and that another personality might be led to a different attitude toward the patient and the therapeutic task. This remark shows Freud's respect for differences in technical style. The unconscious of the analyst is a receiving organ. His

Reprinted by permission from *The Journal of the American Psychoanalytic Association* 2 (Oct. 1954): 703–10.

1. Sigmund Freud, "Zur Technik," in *Gesammelte Schriften*, vol. 6 (Leipzig: Internationaler Psychoanalytischer Verlag, 1925), p. 67.

countertransference, lifted into consciousness, becomes an important source of information in the analytic process. Any rigidity, any automatization of attitude or procedure can become a defense against intuitive insight and block the passage from the unconscious to the conscious processes of the analyst. It is therefore important that the spontaneity of the psychoanalyst not be muffled by the rigidity of his technique.

2. In 1918 Freud said: "Different forms of illness which we treat cannot be handled with the same form of technique." The treatment of hysteria differs from that of a phobia or that of an obsessional neurosis. Since that time analytic treatment has spread out beyond the field of the typical neuroses. Nowadays it is even sometimes difficult to pick typical psychoneuroses for teaching and training purposes since there are more atypical character neuroses seeking treatment. Psychoanalytic treatment has come to encompass children, adolescents, persons in the advanced age group, character neuroses with difficulties of adjustment in marriage, family, or work relations, psychosomatic diseases, psychopathic conditions, and borderline cases. The functional psychoses or narcissistic neuroses have been tackled, proving Freud's original thesis that loss of reality and corresponding shrinkage of the ego are only quantitatively not qualitatively different in psychoses and neuroses. A great differentiation of technique became necessary to do justice to the variations of therapeutic needs of all these patients newly admitted to psychoanalytic treatment.

3. A third source of change in technique stems from the very development of psychoanalytic science during the lifetime of Freud and thereafter. For instance, the change in the concept of anxiety has provided us with a new searchlight not only into libidinal repressions but also into inhibitions and distortions of aggression and their influence on the pregenital as well as Oedipal stages of libido development. Our new insight into the structure of psychoses has enriched our knowledge about the early development in neuroses. The narcissistic withdrawal into fantastic grandiosity and magic manipulations which seemed originally inaccessible to transference interpretations has entered into the orbit of psychoanalytic treatment. A much more detailed knowledge of the ego

and its defenses has intensified our resistance analysis and more and more prevented a premature, intellectualized communication of unconscious contents, before the resistances have been "melted in the fire of transference." In navigating between what Fenichel called the "Scylla and Charybdis of psychoanalytic technique"— the resistance of acting out and that of intellectualization—we find that the resistance of intellectualization has increased with the growing popularity of psychoanalysis.[2] Sophisticated patients use technical terms without emotional participation. We have increasingly to insist that the patient express himself in plain English, which is closer to his emotions.

The rapid growth of psychoanalysis and its popularization contain other dangers. Freud has predicted that the spreading of psychoanalytic therapy would lead to the gold of analysis being alloyed with the copper of a psychotherapy working with suggestion and reeducation. We find it difficult to draw the line between psychoanalysis and psychotherapy. For instance, the modification of the patient's superego, a precondition for further change, is accomplished by the personal influence of the analyst as "auxiliary superego" in early stages of analysis. This is a form of reeducation. The borderline between nondirective interpretation and directive reeducation is fluid. We have become more aware of the elements of reality estrangement and ego shrinkage in character neuroses, and realize that these infantile elements need reeducation as well as analysis, just as children need this combination, according to Anna Freud.[3] In the infantile arrested ego there are gaps of alienation from reality loaded with anxiety.

The pillars in the edifice of psychoanalytic technique are the elucidation of resistance and transference. In recent papers by Gitelson, Whittacker, Paula Heiman, Annie Reich, Buxbaum, Mabel Cohen, and others there is a growing emphasis on the importance of lifting countertransference into the consciousness of the analyst, not for communication to the patient, but in order to

2. Otto Fenichel, "Problems of Psychoanalytic Technique," trans. David Brunswick, *The Psychoanalytic Quarterly* (1941), pp. 6, 41.

3. Anna Freud, *The Technique of Child Analysis* (New York: Nervous and Mental Diseases Publication Company, 1928), pp. 42–59.

improve and refine the standards of the work.[4] The most thorough analytic elucidation of resistance, transference, and countertransference is the essential criterion of value in the psychoanalytic work. Granted, it is not easy to assess the management of resistance, transference, and countertransference in the intricacies of another analyst's therapeutic activities. If, instead of the study of microscopic findings in the analytic workshop, we use the macroscopic criterion of adherence to certain rules, our judgment might easily be misled, since adherence to rules can be the expression of an unanalytic rigidity. I agree with what Fenichel said about technical rules:

> The observance of a prescribed ceremonial produces a magical impression and may be misinterpreted by the patient in this sense. We know . . . that we can and must be elastic in the application of all technical rules. Everything is permissible, if only one knows why. Not external measures, but the management of resistance and transference is the criterion whether a procedure is analysis or not.[5]

Let us look more closely at some of the rules on which psychoanalytic technique is based. The fundamental rule of free associations represents an ideal of spontaneous freedom, conducive to the revelation of the unconscious. But this ideal is only approximated in advanced stages of successful analysis. The manifold individual deviations from the fundamental rule are grist to the analytic mill. Analysis lives on resistance. The ways in which each patient circumvents the basic rule, by halting, silence, rambling, obscurities, deliver important information about individual resistances and instinct derivatives. The basic rule cannot be en-

---

4. Maxwell Gitelson, "Emotional Position of the Analyst in the Psychoanalytic Situation," *International Journal of Psychoanalysis* 33 (1952): 1–10; Carl Whittacker, Warkentin, N. Johnson, Stanislaus Szureck, "The Psychotherapeutic Impasse," *American Journal of Orthopsychiatry* 20 (1950): 641–47; Paula Heiman, "On Counter-Transference," *International Journal of Psychoanalysis* 31 (1950): 81–84; Annie Reich, "On Counter-Transference," ibid. 32 (1951): 25–31; Edith Buxbaum, "Technique of Terminating Analysis," Ibid. 31 (1950): 184–90; Mabel Cohen, "Countertransference and Anxiety, *Psychiatry* 15 (1952): 231–43.

5. Fenichel, "Problems of Psychoanalytic Technique," p. 23–24.

forced. The rule about "no major decisions" also has to be handled with flexibility, otherwise patients who are inclined to act out would discontinue prematurely, or a patient who is well enough progressed to make such decision might hide his ability to take responsibilities behind the defense of literal obedience to the rule.

The rule about the reclining position has, according to Freud, historical reasons (development of analysis out of hypnosis). The position of the analyst out of sight of the analysand was a convenience personally agreeable to Freud. It has the disadvantage that the analyst cannot observe the facial expression of the analysand. If this rule is used with flexibility, the patient being permitted to change his position, he may reveal therewith defenses or impulsive derivatives. In any case, it is important to analyze the magic implications of this and other rules, which the patient accepts as conventionalities in submission or rebellion.

Since Alexander and his collaborators have introduced their well-known experiments in "psychoanalytic therapy,"[6] the rule about frequency of analytic interviews has particularly stirred up clouds of distrust and alienation among analysts—a reaction which seems to me contrary to the spirit of psychoanalysis and the intimacy of mutual understanding. Freud saw his patients six times weekly; lighter cases and more progressed patients were seen three times weekly. This arrangement was obviously adjusted to the Central European working week, which did not include the long weekend of the Anglo-Saxon British and Americans. The "Monday crust" that Freud described in those patients whom he saw six times weekly is often a phenomenon of resistance, a reaction formation against frustrated dependency needs. Similar resistances cannot, and need not, be avoided. They may throw dependency, separation anxieties, reactions of grief or rage into relief which might go undiscovered or be delayed in their access to insight when an instituted frequency rule has become a habit on which the patient relies automatically. The spirit of the rule that analysis has to be carried out in abstinence, specifically in abstinence of

6. Franz Alexander et al., *Psychoanalytic Therapy* (New York: Ronald Press, 1946).

infantile satisfactions, may be violated by a rigidly maintained frequency rule. A patient with a weak ego and rarefied reality relations may develop an addiction to analysis which can form a defensive armor, harder to pierce than the Monday crust of the typical psychoneurotic.

It is obvious that the development of transference needs a steadfast continuity in the relation between analyst and analysand. But the rhythm of this continuity varies from patient to patient and in different phases of analysis. In severe panic states even daily interviews are not sufficient to maintain a continuity of relation. Hospitalization may become necessary and distribution of transference over a continuously available rotating hospital staff occurs. The degree of free-floating anxieties which are no longer or not yet crystallized in defenses is a means of determining the optimal frequency of psychoanalytic hours at a certain period of analysis. If anxieties and therewith libido cannot be sufficiently mobilized, the most religious maintenance of daily interviews does not break through the defensive armor and a classical form of analysis cannot yet be established. For instance, a very withdrawn, schizoid obsessional character felt so threatened by the closeness of daily interviews that he increased his defenses of indifference and boredom which made him more unreachable.

A certain differentiation in frequency often seems useful in a character neurosis with pregenital fixations. I think here of a type of schizoid patient who nowadays frequently seeks treatment, who does not so much suffer from acute symptoms due to actualized conflict but from emotional immaturity, partial withdrawal from reality and vague anxieties about a possible psychotic break. Such a patient has often a good intellectual grasp of his difficulties, describing them in analytical terms but without living through their emotional impact. When this patient talks rather glibly about his castration anxieties, his fears of incorporating or being swallowed up, this does not indicate an untamable id strength that floods the ego with unconscious material, but an estranged aloofness from inner as well as outer reality which splits the weak ego into a rather cynical observer and a more or less unstable actor. In the schizoid patient the observer keeps the upper hand. This split in the schizoid patient is very different from the therapeutic split in the acutely regressed neurotic patient described by Sterba which is most helpful when the patient had partially reached the genital level before. As long as the pregenital fixations prevail due to early arrest of libidinal development, the split remains untherapeutic, the power of integration is poor, the sublimations are unstable and the patient is inclined to fill his inner emptiness by making out of analysis a pseudoreligion and to establish an addicted transference. The ambivalence of this transference is neutralized in dependency ingeniously disguised, since the schizoid patient is attracted to and deadly afraid of this dependency. Such a patient said to me after a long period of daily interviews: "I do not dare to work wholeheartedly outside of analysis, since I feel compelled to remain completely absorbed in analysis." In this case, in which I was consulted, a change from five to three weekly hours was suggested and the masochistic transference became accessible to analysis. The patient recognized that he had tried to achieve a magical cure by absorption in analysis. His work inhibition decreased while he dared more to experiment on the outside.

We have found it useful to spread the analysis of a schizoid patient out over a longer period of time in which the transference, and particularly the pregenital character of transference, remains exposed to analysis. The analyst is at the patient's disposal for intensified treatment whenever an emergency or unusual stress occurs. But the maturing process needs time and gradual increase of realistic experiences so that the patient can catch up with the gaps in his libidinal development. He needs to test out his gains from the protected analytic experience in his less protected extraanalytic relations. When the analyst succeeds in eliciting trust in the patient on the basis of an aim-inhibited libidinal attachment, the split in the schizoid patient becomes truly therapeutic, his integration becomes more stabilized, his sublimations spread out. The intuition and the tact of the analyst discover whenever the patient becomes more accessible, his defenses yield, and free-floating anxieties can be analyzed.

At the other end of the scale we meet the cycloid patient whose instability is manifested in mood swings and a tendency to act out.

He may petulantly insist on daily interviews which he is compelled largely to waste by monotonous complaints, throwing the responsibility for the treatment in the lap of the analyst in whom he sees mainly the magic helper. This demonstrative dependency does not yet establish a profitable working relationship. In the system of defenses of the cycloid patient the erotization of anxiety stands out and may mislead the analyst. Only to the degree that these defenses can be melted do anxiety and libido become available for the analytic work. A change of frequency sometimes brings frustration and infantile conflicts into focus, which the patient covered by petulance or pacified with daily interviews. A patient of this kind told me after a reduction of hours: "For the first time I have understood my dependency needs on you not with my head but with my heart." Simultaneously a dream brought a lost memory of a terrifying desertion experience in the third year of her childhood, a tonsillectomy in which the parents failed her. The anxiety was relived in full force.

I have mentioned the schizoid and the cycloid types of patient. Mostly we are confronted with mixed types, as we meet various degrees of mixture between hysteric and obsessional symptomatology. A differentiation of frequency seems to me particularly to be recommended in chronic cases, character neuroses, where factors of arrested development outweigh the incidents of acute regressions. A neurosis with acute symptomatology, I think, needs daily, or near to daily, interviews as long as the pressure of actualized conflicts mobilizes anxieties. But when the patient has reached a higher degree of integration and self-sufficiency, he is highly encouraged by a reduction of sessions which acknowledges his progress. Once he has developed, besides the transference, a reliable realistic relation to the analyst, he can maintain the continuity of the work over even longer interruptions.

I have pointed out this variety of possibilities in order to warn against an inflexible ruling in matters of frequency. We have recently observed in the pediatric discipline a change from a rigidly instituted feeding schedule according to the clock to a demand schedule which arranges the frequency of feedings according to the needs of the infant. This change helps to establish a better rapport between mother and infant. It replaces the letter of the law by the spirit of mutual understanding. With the growing development of psychoanalysis we become able to learn from our pediatric colleagues to adapt ourselves better to the needs of our patients. I do not mean merely the consciously expressed needs, since these may at times be pathologically overheated demands which distort the deeper repressed real needs. We are of course interested in maintaining the regularity of our schedule. But when in addition to the natural tendency toward automatization of habits we press the institutionalization of a frequency rule—four weekly hours are analysis, three hours are not—then we regress from the spirit of psychoanalysis to a legalized form of it.

It is true, more inconvenience is implied when in matters of frequency we try to observe the needs of the patients in different phases of their analysis. But all technical rules, far from being unessential, are important observation points for manifestations of resistance, transference as well as countertransference. If we do not take an instituted frequency rule for granted, we have to come to terms with a possible unconscious aversion to seeing the patient more frequently, or with an unobserved hesitation to offer him more independence. Such investigation of our countertransference gives us an opportunity to become conscious of those factors in our own psychology which make us deviate from the benevolent neutrality which is the most effective attitude toward the patient and the therapeutic task. The factors of narcissistic counterresistance can be sorted out. After that, the countertransference reactions inform us about the patient's unconscious needs in a given situation. Glover called this daily self-scrutiny, which is of course not communicated to the patient, "the toilet of the analyst."[7]

We can improve our technique when we use the analytic microscope in the mutual assessment of our work, when we dare to expose not only transference but also countertransference resistances in our analytic reports to each other. It is evident that detailed and intimate reports are only possible in smaller groups, for instance in a mutual consultation service such as Oberndorf has recom-

7. Edward Glover, "Lectures on Technique in Psychoanalysis," *International Journal of Psychoanalysis* 8 (1927): 504–20.

mended in protracted, stagnating analyses. Such a more intimate exchange will make a streamlined ruling for mass consumption superfluous. It will strengthen the autonomy and spontaneity in our group work, while fixation of rules is a danger for a science that has set liberation from compulsion as an essential goal.

Let me sum up: The progress of psychoanalytic art and science depends to a high degree on the flexibility of psychoanalytic technique. In order to maintain our alertness to the essential analytic tasks of elucidating and dissolving resistance, transference and countertransference, we must avoid the dangers of habit formation, magic ceremonials, submission, or rebellion in relation to rigid rules which do not correspond to the genuine needs of the patients. Deepened self-scrutiny of countertransference and intensified collaboration of psychoanalysts in mutual exchange will remove resistances of distrust and compulsion and maintain the freedom of spontaneous growth and creative development of psychoanalytic technique.

Doctor – Patient Relationship in Therapy

The doctor–patient relation is built on trust. The physician's trust in the patient's own tendency toward recovery is an important factor in the process of cure. The psychotherapist depends on a trusting collaboration with his patients. The patients who suffer from psychoneuroses and functional psychoses are essentially disturbed in their ability to trust others or themselves. In daily practice we meet a variety of different doctor-patient relations in which distrust, genuine trust, and all kinds of false hopes and fantastic expectations are intermingled in varying degrees.

But only trust can reveal what the patient unwittingly conceals from himself.

Progress in ego psychology inside and outside of classical analysis has increasingly concentrated attention on anxiety. The central position of anxiety in the psychodynamic theories of Horney, Sullivan, and Rado is well known.[1] Anxiety has become a more central concern in classical psychoanalysis, since Freud had redefined anxiety as a cause and not as an effect of the repression of impulses.

The psychoanalytic concept of transference is well known. Transferences demonstrate the typical forms of distrust which have to be dissolved so that insight can reach the patient and the neurotic pattern can be reversed.

In psychoanalytic literature, the countertransferences have

Reprinted by permission from *The American Journal of Psychoanalysis* (ed. Harold Kelman, M.D.) 15, no. 1 (1955): 10–13.

1. See K. Horney, *Neurosis and Human Growth* (New York: Norton, 1950); H. S. Sullivan, *The Interpersonal Theory of Psychiatry* (New York: Norton, 1953); Sandor Rado, *On the Psychoanalytic Exploration of Fear and Other Emotions, Transactions of the New York Academy of Sciences*, Series 11, 14, 7 (1952), pp. 280–83.

mostly been treated as private handicaps of the psychoanalyst, residuals of his own uncompleted analysis. I would like to emphasize that countertransferences are largely codetermined by the patient's concealed excessive anxieties which tend to elicit typical defensive responses in the therapist. The patient unwittingly urges the therapist into the role of the originally harmful significant partner, since he proves thereby the necessity to maintain his habitual defenses. Due to his passive position, the therapist senses a strong tug to yield to the patient's urging, and thus to enter into an unconscious conspiracy with him. But just as the transference gives valuable information, so the therapist can learn much from the countertransference propensities which impede the development of a liberating therapeutic relation.

I should like to relate some typical transference-countertransference defenses to anxiety which emerge from the individual varieties of psychopathology that frequently intermingle and overlap. I think here of the fundamental anxieties of loneliness, powerlessness and vulnerability which threaten human existence and become unbearable to neurotics and even more to psychotics. Philosophical existentialism, from Kierkegaard to Heidegger and Sartre, has stimulated the phenomenological study of anxiety.[2] Authors like Horney, Rollo May, Masserman, Frieda Fromm-Reichmann[3] have dealt with existential anxieties and have studied the psychoneurotic defenses against them.

A typical defense against the anxious experience of loneliness is the denial of distance, demonstrated particularly in hysterical symptoms and character features. In his transference reactions the patient is determined by the fear of desertion to comply and sub-

2. See S. Kierkegaard, "Furcht und Zittern," "Der Begriff der Angst," in *Gesammelte Werke* (Jena: Eugen Diederichs Verlag, 1923); M. Heidegger, *Sein und Zeit* (Frankfurt/Main: Vittorio Klostermann Verlag, 1927); Heidegger, *Ueber den Humanismus* (Frankfurt/Main: Vittorio Klostermann, 1949); Jean-Paul Sartre, *L'Etre et le néant* (Paris: Gallimard, 1943).

3. See Horney, *Neurosis and Human Growth*; R. May, *The Meaning of Anxiety* (New York: Ronald Press, 1950); J. H. Masserman, "Faith and Delusion in Psychotherapy," *American Journal of Psychiatry* 110, no. 5 : 324–33; Frieda Fromm-Reichmann, *Principles of Intensive Psychotherapy* (Chicago: The University of Chicago Press, 1950).

mit, to deny differentiation, or, even more, any antagonism; he tries to establish closeness, even at the cost of losing his own integrity. He tries to please the analyst by good intellectual understanding, conforming to the therapist's terminology and theories; he makes progress in the sense of a so-called transference cure. The patient may display great skill in manipulating the therapist to fulfill his needs for parasitic dependency. This seemingly so positive transference is quite hypocritical. It expects rewards. In the patient's background, aggression and competition frequently have been strongly prohibited. The patient does not dare to stand up for himself, to experience distance, differentiation and healthy independence. In cases of greater ego weakness the depressive features are emphasized. The patient complains, is sorry for himself, plays strongly on the analyst's sympathy, clinging to him as if he alone were salvation. But this credulity is far removed from genuine trust. The patient does not really cooperate, he belittles his assets in order to keep the therapist in his service. He may even be unconsciously compelled to undergo any amount of suffering in order not to be confronted with separation and loneliness. In this way the therapist cannot become a real person to the patient. He remains a tool, a means to an egocentric end, fundamentally untrustworthy. The patient drifts nearer to the danger of loneliness he has tried so urgently to avoid.

The countertransference reaction to this pattern of defense against loneliness can mislead the therapist in two opposite directions. He senses the patient's seduction to enter into a conspiracy of overidentification: he might feel tempted to fulfill the patient's defensive claims, or he might feel flattered at being so indispensable. Since in the beginning of the psychoanalytic movement those hysteric patients escaping from the danger of loneliness presented themselves most readily to the new method of treatment, the early technical rules were devised to protect the therapist from the pitfalls of countertransference. Placement of his seat behind the patient, for example, proved very practical. Parsimony in interpretations is indicated as long as the patient can hear them only as approval or disapproval. On the other hand, the typical anxiety in relation to the patient who refuses distance, the fear of being engulfed by the demanding, dependent patient, has driven some therapists to lean over backward, in the direction of a stiff, unspontaneous, forbidding inaccessibility. In particular, the patient who threatens suicide can make the therapist quite insecure. By worrisome sympathy he may enhance the patient's guilt feelings, or in embittered annoyance he may recoil and confront the patient too abruptly with his fundamental loneliness.

The typical defense against powerlessness is the illusion of being in power and control, which is elaborated in the obsessional neuroses. The other fellow's needs are experienced as threats, since the patient feels safe only in solitary, exclusive control. Exchange with others is highly ritualized. Monotonous repetition safeguards against surprise and unfamiliar experiences. The frequently excellent reasoning power of the patient is used not for the clarification of interpersonal situations, but for the one-sided purpose of ego-dominance. The patient who thus defends himself against powerlessness has experienced in his formative years overwhelming impotence in relation to merciless forces, anxiety-ridden exploitation, harsh discipline, or unforgiving punishments. In such impotent childhood experiences the powerless patient has built up a view of the world as a merciless jungle. You cannot soften by admitting the yearning for tenderness, affection, and understanding. In order to be safe you need power, but not the power of broadening horizons, of participation. The powers of the outside world have to be subjugated, instead of developed and directed. If the anxiety of powerlessness is intense enough, the response to external influences is not only stubborn nonacceptance, but violent counterattack. In anticipation of merciless retaliation the full violence cannot be expressed and corrected by catharsis. Due to concentration of aggressive energies for defensive purposes only, suspicions are intensified and may reach the level of paranoic isolation.

The countertransference reaction to the defense of the patient who is particularly afraid of his own powerlessness may, again, prevent the full cooperation of the therapist and patient in two ways. The poorly disguised hostility and violence of the patient may arouse the therapist's anxieties; he may avoid the hurdle of exposing himself by appeasing the patient, letting him get away too long with his pretense of omnipotence, without being contradicted at the right time and place. Or the therapist may not be able to resist being drawn into argumentative competition. He may feel so intensely antagonized by the patient's presumptuous claims that he confronts him with his antisocial destructive impulses before the patient has gained sufficient trust in a benevolent fellowship to hear interpretations as anything but moralistic condemnations. The therapist needs patience and endurance to withstand the patient's testing attacks. When his suspicions can be displayed, the patient will be able to experience their actual absurdity. The therapist thereby gives the patient the opportunity to relive the anxieties of childhood with him, without withdrawing into rationalistic superiority. In this way the patient can transcend these anxieties in fellowship with the therapist and discover the integrative function of trust, which extends from the experience with the analyst to reality at large.

The most restrictive and paralyzing defenses result from anxiety over individual vulnerability, which is frequently reinforced by fears of loneliness and powerlessness. The defenses of withdrawal and detachment are intensely isolating since the individual senses mortal dangers hidden in persons as well as in things. The human being is the only animal who knows that his destiny is death. The warning signal of anxiety is useful only to the degree that the individual proceeds from the pleasure principle to the reality principle, defending himself rationally against danger by flight or fight. Existential anxieties remain more or less unsurmountable to the mentally handicapped immature individual. Nobody and nothing can be trusted. Warning fantasies of castration and rape, humiliation and mutilation accompany and smother the outgoing impulses toward interpersonal intimacy. When the other fellow can no longer be used, either for parasitic dependency or for exploitative domination, because the patient is mortally afraid of being hurt, he frequently withdraws into the unrealistic atmosphere of private illusions; but the defensive illusions of invulnerability, perfection and self-sufficiency are so contradictory to realistic experience that they tend toward a break with reality.

Yet there is for the patient in these illusions a liberating trend away from conventional values, a trend to free himself from the smothering influences which originally made him withdraw. These highly vulnerable patients seem frequently inaccessible to psychotherapy; they elicit the countertransference of discouragement, particularly when their panic reaches psychotic proportions. But the aloofness of a schizoid patient who is well defended can also have a forbidding influence on the therapist. His assistance seems unwanted. He feels impotent to break through the shell of evasive vagueness, of a noncommunicative language of private meanings and symbolism. The countertransference of the analyst implies the temptation of overidentification and overindulgence, but such overcloseness is particularly threatening to the patient who has been hurt by possessiveness and lack of distance in previous relations. Besides, the analyst cannot live up to the promise of continuous closeness and the patient recoils, even more frightened, when the traumatic inconsistency of former relations is repeated in the therapeutic setting.

The patient needs understanding that permits distance, respects the difference between therapist and patient, acknowledges the tragedy of the patient's fear of annihilation and is able to share these panicky experiences without being engulfed by them. Such attitude of the therapist maintains genuine hope and may gradually convince the patient that he need not deny his anxieties but can learn to face them and transcend them in a creative experience which establishes in him the beginning of trust.

Such a beginning of trust can be a turning point in analysis. It changes the patient's direction from despair to hope, from suspicion to confidence. This change in the psychoanalytic drama is always the result of long, tedious working through of the obstacles of repetition and resistance. The therapist's understanding has to make the beginning. He must become aware of the repetitive compulsion by which the patient unconsciously tends to reinforce his own, as well as the doctor's, habitual defenses, and urges the therapist into the role of a harmful partner of the past. If the therapist recognizes this harmful function, he will be able to interpret the transference distortions to the patient. He can then accompany him through threatening anxieties, accepting the challenge which is able to elicit creative reactions instead of the restrictive, habitual defenses.

When both patient and therapist expose themselves to the excessive anxieties hidden behind the defenses, they gain a deeper comradeship. Like soldiers who have shared the experience of a battle, they are drawn together by mutual respect, on a realistic basis. Passing through the danger zone of excessive anxiety makes both therapist and patient more humble. Neither of them has to live up to the standards of a superman's perfection. In other words, the cruelties of an infantile superego become mitigated. This does not mean that ideals and values are abandoned. They are experienced as goals in a realistic distance. Striving in human comradeship, although not providing any absolute security, elicits the courage to transcend the anxieties of loneliness, powerlessness, and vulnerability.

Countertransference and Self-Analysis
of the Psychoanalyst

In recent papers on countertransference by Maxwell Gitelson, Paula Heimann, Margaret Little, Annie Reich, Leo Berman, Winnicott, Mabel Cohen, Macalpine, Fliess, and others, the gain in insight into the patient's unconscious through elucidation of the countertransference has been emphasized.[1] These papers stress the similarities rather than the differences between transference and countertransference. In accordance with Freud's definition of transference Leo Berman has defined countertransference as "the analyst's reactions to the patient as though the patient were an important figure in the analyst's past life." This definition stresses the regressive and projective character of countertransference. Countertransference, like transference, has positive and negative aspects. We know that not all aspects of transference are adverse to therapeutic progress. Positive transference is an important ally in the struggle between repression and therapeutic derepression. "In so far as his [the patient's] transference," said Freud, "bears the positive sign, it clothes the physician with authority, transforms

Reprinted by permission from *The International Journal of Psycho-Analysis* 35 (1954), pt. 2.

1. Maxwell Gitelson, "The Emotional Position of the Analyst in the Psychoanalytic Situation," *International Journal of Psycho-Analysis* 33 (1952): 1–10; Paula Heimann, "On Counter-Transference," ibid. 31 (1950): 81–84; Margaret Little, "Counter-Transference and the Patient's Response to It," ibid. 32 (1951): 32–40; Annie Reich, "On Counter-Transference," ibid. 32 (1951): 25–31; Leo Berman, "Counter-Transference and Attitudes of the Analyst in the Therapeutic Process," *Psychiatry* 12 (1949); D. W. Winnicott, "Hate in the Counter-Transference," *International Journal of Psycho-Analysis* 30 (1949): 69–74; Mabel Cohen, "Counter-Transference and Anxiety," *Psychiatry* 15 (1952): 501–39; Ida Macalpine, "The Development of the Transference," *Psychoanalytic Quarterly* 19 (1950); no. 4, 501–37; Robert Fliess, "Counter-Transference and Counter-Identification," *Journal of the American Psychoanalytical Association* 1 (1953): 268–84.

itself into faith in his findings and in his views. Without this kind of transference, or with a negative one, the physician and his arguments would never be listened to. Faith repeats the history of its own origin; it is a derivative of love and at first it needed no arguments. Not until later does it admit them so far as to take them into critical consideration, if they have been offered by someone who is loved."[2]

While the analysand is free to display his transference, it is widely considered the duty of the analyst to keep out of the regressive movements, to prove resistant to countertransference. As Ida Macalpine has put it, "he [the analyst] remains neutral, aloof, a spectator, and is never a co-actor."[3] Even though I agree with Dr. Macalpine that the analyst tries to keep away from manipulative role-playing, which is the tool of the hypnotist, it implies the danger of self-deception to assume that such absolute resistance to countertransference can ever be attainable. Besides, countertransference has not only a negative effect, adverse to therapeutic progress. The counterpart of the therapeutically valuable positive transference of the patient is the analyst's benevolent neutrality, his dedication, his ever-deepening understanding of the patient, and the faith in the patient's potentialities for recovery. This positive countertransference has its roots in the identification with a benevolent parent, largely freed from the conflicts of ambivalence, and resulting in successful sublimation. The patient's resistance, however, his withdrawal, doubts, obscurities, attacks, or insults put the analyst's benevolent neutrality to a hard test. But while the patient is exposed to the storms of emotional upheaval on an uncharted sea, the analyst is guided by the experiences of his training analysis and his psychoanalytic knowledge. He is less exposed to surprising projections upon the patient from his own past. He is alerted to his inclinations to deviate from the ideal of benevolent neutrality, to misuse the patient for reliving his own conflicts, for which the patient is not responsible.

2. Sigmund Freud, "Vorlesungen zur Ein führung der Psychoanalyse," Gesammelte Werke, vol. 7, p. 463.
3. Macalpine, p. 19.

But training analysis and psychoanalytic knowledge are not static factors. Training analysis is interminable and psychoanalytic knowledge is ever expanding. Therefore there always remains a certain tension between the ideal of positive countertransference and its realization in daily professional performances, a tension which at times elicits anxieties or defenses against anxieties in the analyst. The supervisor observes such anxieties in his supervisee when he is confronted with a hurdle of not understanding the patient. If such anxiety passes by unobserved or unclarified, it incapacitates the analyst further in his understanding. Let me give a simple example. A supervisee asked me for an emergency appointment. The mother of a promising young analytic patient had broken into an analytic hour and insisted on interruption of the work. The trainee had to excuse himself and had left the session overwhelmed by distress and confusion. This confusion lifted when I asked him whether he was not enraged about the interference with a work in which he had invested so much hope and pride. He had been unable to recognize his anxiety and rage reaction, because he was blinded by a taboo: The analyst must not have countertransference reactions. After the analyst had understood his anxiety and rage reaction and its ramifications he was fully able to understand his patient's conflict and anxiety and could act accordingly.

In order to deepen the understanding of the patient the analyst cannot always remain free from anxieties, nor can he afford to stay completely outside the regressive movements of his patients. There is the danger that he might use a pretense of psychoanalytic aloofness as a defence against the anxiety of not understanding and separation from the patient. Such anxiety may also be covered by overactive interpretations or undue passivity, in which the analyst may wander off into private preoccupation or drowsiness. Anxiety interferes with the freely hovering attention and makes the analyst recoil from accompanying the patient into the painful conflicts of regression. The uninhibited understanding of the patient is facilitated by the dynamism of introjection which, according to Fenichel, leads to partial identification and is closely related to empathy—*Einfühlung*—the intuitive grasp of the real mental states of another person. While transferences of the patient are primarily characterized by projections, the analyst's countertransferences are to a higher degree determined by introjections.[4]

Federn has taught that identifications in later life rest on an expansion of ego boundaries, mental and bodily, so that they include the other person within themselves. "The same phenomenon also occurs in every object relation or interest in an object, but then in only a transitory manner at the ego boundary that exists at that time."[5] Fliess considers "transient trial identifications" an important part of countertransference. The analyst's ability to expand his ego boundaries is a precondition for his work. He encompasses not only the patient's conscious reports, he also receives information from the nonverbal, unconscious parts of the patient's personality. The analyst's empathy puts him into the patient's shoes, enables him to read between the lines, to take his clues not only from the patient's verbal communications, but also from the intonation of his voice, changes in breathing, his facial expression, gestures, automatic movements that are taken in on the preconscious level. In addition, the analyst experiences emotional responses, unwittingly elicited by the patient. If the analyst were to dismiss his own angry, indignant, enraged, resentful, sympathetic, or tender reactions without further private scrutiny, he would miss important information.

In order to evaluate the information gained from empathy the analyst must be aware of the danger of subjectivity involved in processes of identification. Object representations included within the ego boundary or resulting from the expansion of the ego boundary over the object are endangered by pathologically invested narcissism which falsifies reality. Federn's differentiation between healthy and pathological narcissism seems to me very helpful. "The purer are our object representations, the more our thinking becomes objective and free from subjectivity and the

4. Otto Fenichel, "Die Identifizierung," *Internationale Zeitschrift für Psychoanalyse* 12 (1926).

5. Paul Federn, "Healthy and Pathological Narcissism," in *Ego Psychology and the Psychoses* (New York: Basic Books, 1952), p. 356.

dominance of the ego."[6] There is a constant vacillation between subjectivity and objectivity in the attitude of the analyst. Robert Waelder has pointed out the dialectic structure of psychoanalysis.[7] In the relation of the analyst to the patient there exists a polarity between participation and observation, transference and real relationship; the latter coincides with what I have already referred to as the ideal positive countertransference. The pendulum of the analyst's libido investment must be able to swing freely from participation to observation, from attachment to detachment. The objectivity of self-scrutiny is as necessary as the observation of the patient in order to correct the falsifications of reality implied in the process of identification. But I consider it inappropriate to communicate countertransference discoveries directly to the patient, unless the analysand has arrived at a terminal phase.[8] During the course of analysis the communication of countertransference can easily degenerate into an undisciplined discharge reaction. Lack of discipline is not spontaneity. It is important to keep the emotions aroused by the patient's transference in suspense, and to use the mobilized energies for reflection, investigation, and analysis of both patient and analyst.

In order to evaluate the usefulness of his countertransference reactions the analyst must be alert to the danger signal of minimal anxieties which indicate obstructions in both phases of the pendulum swing between identification and objectivity.

(1) Identification is impeded by any form of prejudice on the part of the analyst. Prejudice and empathy are absolutely incompatible. Differences of cultural background can be and have been transcended by understanding, but not the barriers of prejudice that serve as rigid defences against anxieties. The analyst can very well be established in his group loyalties and value systems. But the fanatic adherents of any creed are hampered by their prejudice

6. Ibid., p. 364.
7. Robert Waelder, "The Problem of the Genesis of Psychological Conflicts in Earliest Infancy," *International Journal of Psycho-Analysis* 18 (1937).
8. See below, the following chapter, "Contribution to the Problem of Terminating Psychoanalyses."

and are, at least unconsciously, prone to convert. Also, the conventionally adjusted person may be handicapped when he takes it for granted that his value system is generally accepted and represents "reality." An agnostic analyst who takes his agnosticism for granted cannot well empathize with a devout believer, and vice versa.

We assume that the training analysis succeeds in liberating the analyst from ingrained prejudice. But each new patient may represent a new challenge; certain aspects of the patient's pathology may confront the analyst with anxieties elicited by the unknown. It appears desirable that the young analyst during his training be exposed to a rich variety of types of patient and forms of illness. The psychogenic illnesses, neuroses as well as psychoses, psychosomatic illnesses, and character disorders are not sharply separated from each other. We learn from the treatment of psychoses what we can apply in the treatment of neuroses, and vice versa. It has been proved by Federn, Fromm-Reichmann, and many other analysts that the difficulty in treatment of the narcissistic neuroses does not lie in the lack of transference.[9] The transference is more vehement and less manageable than in neurosis. Obstacles in the treatment of psychoses arise rather in the limitations of countertransference. It is more difficult to identify with the psychotic, to accompany him on the regressive descent into the panic, despair, and loneliness of a psychosis. The analyst has to assess his stamina of endurance. He may become inflicted by the patient's deep discouragement and lose the vision of and the faith in the patient's potentialities for recovery. In the great number of borderline cases that nowadays apply for private psychoanalytic treatment the question frequently arises: Is the doubt in the patient's curability a realistic assessment or a prejudice of the analyst, a defense against the anxieties mobilized by the patient's despair?

By his own prejudice the analyst may unwittingly reinforce the patient's prejudice against his own pathology which militates against modification and integration of unacceptable trends in his

9. Federn, "Healthy and Pathological Narcissism"; Frieda Fromm-Reichmann, "Some Aspects of Psychoanalytic Psychotherapy," in *Psychotherapy with Schizophrenics, A Symposium* (New York: International Universities Press, 1952).

personality. Freud has stressed the task of the analyst to create an atmosphere of tolerance in which the patient can look at his illness as a dignified adversary. As long as the patient despises his pathology, he is compelled to continue repression or other defenses which delay integration.[10]

A trial period of analysis can help to decide whether doctor and patient can profitably work with each other. An initial aversion against the patient's pathology may later yield to a challenging interest. For instance, the tolerance of an analyst was put to a hard test when his analysand reported how he mistreated a helpless child; the analyst felt frustrated and enraged, inclined to reject the patient. But since the analyst was able to keep his emotional response in suspense and to use the mobilized energies in a search for understanding, the compulsive behaviour of the patient became elucidated and modifiable.

Sometimes a prejudicial discouragement creeps into the analyst's attitude outside of his awareness. A student in training presented the recordings of his sessions with a slowly moving patient. The trainee's voice sounded stereotyped, mildly irritated, preaching, not in content but in tone. His colleagues stimulated his self-scrutiny and he discovered that his stereotyped attitude masked his anxiety and rage about the patient's negative therapeutic reaction. After having been able to admit his negative countertransference to himself and the group he was in a better position to tackle the patient's resistances spontaneously and effectively. Defensive rigidity of the analyst's ego boundaries walls him off against the patient; he can be helpful only to the degree that he can broaden his ego boundaries to encompass the patient and his pathology.

(2) The countertransference of the analyst becomes an impediment not only when his ego boundaries are loaded with counter-resistance. An overflexibility of the analyst's ego boundaries may also set a limit to the therapeutic effectiveness. A supervisor is sometimes baffled by reports of a supervisee who is overidentified

10. Sigmund Freud, "Zur Technik," in *Gesammelte Schriften*, vol. 6 (Leipzig: Internationaler Psychoanalytischer Verlag, 1925), p. 115; "Further Recommendations on Technique, Remembering and Repeating," in *The Case of Schreber: Papers on Technique and Other Works*, vol. 12 (London: Hogarth, 1958), p. 152.

to such a degree with his patient that the supervisor does not know where the analysand ends and where the analyst begins. In such a treatment situation, there is usually a good emotional rapport. The analysand is gratified by his analyst's understanding, yet treatment makes no further progress. Closer scrutiny reveals a partiality that sanctions the patient's infantile demands. The analyst has taken the patient's side in his controversy against the parents or members of his recent family. This has been necessary since the patient has become ill owing to insoluble conflicts carried from the past into the present. The parents have given him an inadequate preparation for life and he has to get rid of an accumulation of resentments, and even vindictiveness, which first had to be made conscious with the help of the analyst's permissive understanding. But the patient may get stuck in this phase. He repeats his accusations against the past and cannot make peace with the present which represents largely a repetition of the past. At this juncture it is important that the analyst stimulate increased reality testing which goes hand in hand with reinforced cathexis of ego boundaries. It implies the confrontation with the inevitable frustrations rooted in the Oedipus conflict. If there exists an archaic identification of the analyst with the patient on the pregenital level, if the analyst cannot freely swing from identification to differentiation, he may reinforce the patient's resistance to working through the Oedipus conflict. Like an overindulgent parent who vicariously enjoys his child's grandiosity and fails to set limits to his demands for omnipotence, the overempathic analyst may not be able to confront the patient with the dose of frustration which the patient can handle at a given time without recoiling into regression. If the analyst becomes overanxious about the patient's destructive tendencies, his identification with him loses its transient character and becomes instituted as a means of withdrawal from challenging anxieties in the analytic situation. An unconscious conspiracy between analyst and analysand takes place which limits the therapeutic progress. The patient may feel close to the analyst, transiently relieved from loneliness and despair. The analyst is an ally against the world, but the world remains unbearable. Such unconscious conspiracy can lead in extreme cases to a *folie à deux*.

Analysis fails to mobilize the anxieties of frustration and the libidinal energies to surmount them.

A young analyst came to a supervisor with heavy self-reproaches because he had fallen in love with a woman patient. Closer scrutiny revealed that he had not fallen in love, but had failed to rise from identification with a seductive, anxious patient to a more sincere object relation. Becoming conscious of his anxieties which prevented him from disagreeing with the impetuous patient, he became able to interpret her seductive manipulations and to overcome her resistance.

Summary: The ideal positive countertransference, the maintenance of benevolent neutrality depends on the alertness to the swings of countertransference. The action of interpretation, its appropriate depth and timing is based on empathy, an optimal flexibility of ego boundaries, which becomes disturbed by the analyst's anxieties. In each countertransference experience new territory can be discovered. New facets in the patient's personality may touch off unknown boundaries in the analyst's ego. The confrontation with the unknown arouses anxieties not only in the patient, but in the analyst also, although he is fortified by professional knowledge and experience. A new experience may even arouse transient withdrawal and estrangement, before it can become an integrated insight. It is important that the analyst admit such anxieties to himself. The young analyst frequently feels that he should not have any countertransference reactions, that he should be a mirror, unswerving in his neutrality, detached like a surgeon. He is ashamed of his anxieties, he would like to be relaxed and spontaneous. It is true that the analyst becomes useless to the patient when his own anxieties exceed those of the patient. But the patient, in phases of negative transference, goes all out to arouse the analyst's anxiety and to defeat him therewith. He may be very intuitive in spotting the weaknesses in the analyst's armor. If the analyst becomes preoccupied with mending his own fences he loses sight of the essential job of understanding the transference-countertransference situation and he impairs the patient's trust. It is understandable that the young analyst particularly is at times tempted to deny his anxieties to himself and to pretend a false equanimity. But such inner division and conflict decrease the analyst's ego strength. It is important that the supervisory analyst stimulate the self-analysis of the analyst. The pretense of courage is just as detrimental to the development of genuine courage as hypocritical dedication is in precluding the growth of real devotion. The analyst must expect anxieties, whenever his benevolent neutrality is challenged by limitations of trial identification or by overextension of introjection. In supervision as well as in my own experience I have found the most visible progress made when the analyst can become conscious of a formerly unconscious counter-transference reaction.

Contribution to the Problem
of Terminating Psychoanalyses

Is there a definitive end to a psychoanalysis? This question was raised in 1937 by Freud, as it had been ten years earlier by Ferenczi.[1] We know that the unconscious is timeless. All attempts to force the analytic experience into the boundaries of time interfere with the optimum of relaxation that favors the process of self-revelation by means of free associations. Ferenczi postulated that treatment has better prospects of quicker results, the more "endless" time there is at our disposal. In his later years Ferenczi disapproved setting a date of termination to accelerate analysis as he had become dissatisfied with the results: "As long as the patient wants to come, he belongs in analysis." On the other hand, Ferenczi admitted that some patients misuse this timelessness.

The psychoanalyst has a double function. He is not only the advocate of the repressed or dissociated instinctual impulses; he is also the representative of reality who tries to reeducate the patient to an optimal reintegration in reality. In his own mind he forms and reformulates in a flexible learning process an estimate of how the patient may function after the termination of the analysis with his instinctual resources largely restored. Whenever analyis does not end by default for rational or irrational reasons— and there are many which do—the analyst has the responsibility of clarifying in his own mind the goals and indications for terminating analysis, not with the intention of forcing his convictions on

Reprinted by permission from *The Psychoanalytic Quarterly* 21 (1952): 465–80.

1. Sigmund Freud, "Analysis Terminable and Interminable," *International Journal of Psycho-Analysis* 18 (1937): 373–405; Sandor Ferenczi, "Das Problem der Beendigung der Analysen," *Internationale Zeitschrift für Psychoanalyse* 14 (1928): 1–10.

the patient, but with the hope of arriving gradually at a mutual agreement about this aim.

Since the patient frequently enters psychoanalysis with the wish to rid himself of disturbing symptoms, it would be natural for both analyst and analysand to judge the disappearance of symptoms as the indication for terminating treatment. However, symptoms often disappear rather early in analysis, in response to a positive transference, without deeper changes in the structure of the character. Symptoms may reappear in phases of negative transference or, even after profound changes of character, they may be remobilized to prevent the ultimate separation from the analyst.

Freud doubts whether even a deep character analysis can always prevent the return of neurotic symptoms under the pressure of frustrating life circumstances. Psychoanalysis cannot immunize a patient in every case against future hardships which may mobilize old or new conflicts, since analysis can only deal with actual conflicts which have emotional urgency now and here. Freud considered analysis, therefore, as potentially interminable. Wellknown is his recommendation of a psychoanalytic refresher every five years for psychoanalysts on whom the fate of so many patients depends and who are exposed by the nature of their work to more than the usual stresses and strains.

Continuation of or return to analysis can only be profitable if the analysand feels disturbed, if he suffers from symptoms, anxieties, some degree of discontent, or from a sense of unfulfilled potentialities. The fact that he may disturb others who wish him to change is seldom a sufficient incentive to further analysis, unless such disturbance reactivates his own.

If termination of analysis has to be decided not upon disappearance of symptoms but upon the depth of characterological change, we must fall back on the ideal of mental health, the value of maturity, the standards of adaptation to reality. These concepts are rather vague and ill-defined. In a neurotically confused culture such standards are far from uniform. The concept of "adjustment to reality" particularly can be interpreted in almost as many varieties as the theological concept of "being at peace with God." There is not even agreement about the value of mental health. An outstanding theologian told a group of psychoanalysts that he wished some broadening neurotic experience for some of the "normal" representatives of our culture. I have heard Zilboorg, among others, express doubt about the value of a smooth adaptation without conflict to our neurotic cultural environment. Least of all does the complacency of being "normal" befit the analyst who should understand firsthand what his suffering patient is talking about. It is, of course, mandatory that his own neurotic suffering no longer interfere with his work. But a static, emotional equilibrium, more or less opportunistically oriented toward conformity with general standards, is not a vital response to neurotic suffering. The psychoanalyst needs a dynamic equilibrium which allows him to accompany the patient into the hell of anxieties, tensions, and conflicts without undue reservations of self-protection, and to recover anew his inner balance each hour, each day.

In spite of all the uncertainties that attend evaluation of the termination of analyses, I am in accord with Ferenczi's conviction that psychoanalysis is not an interminable process; that it has its natural end even though, like Ferenczi, I cannot count many completed analyses in a practice of some twenty years. I believe that the end of an analysis can be determined only by the analyst and the analysand. Standards have to be carefully adapted to individual needs; rules and regulations, particularly in terms of time and frequency, can easily become crippling impositions.

Psychoanalysts have, however, a very refined instrument, in the observation of the transference and the countertransference, for measuring the end phase of analysis. We know that the resistances of transference disappear toward the end of a successful analysis and that a greater spontaneity between analyst and analysand is established.

The spontaneity of the analysand is only possible if he no longer feels compelled to please, to placate, to test, or to provoke the analyst. Ferenczi asserted that free association in an ideal sense is possible only toward the end of analysis. As long as the analyst has still the function of an "auxiliary superego," each renunciation of an instinctual striving, each acceptance of displeasure or pain by the patient will be necessarily accompanied by a sense of untruthfulness or hypocrisy; the patient's morality is still opportunistic, not genuine. Whenever the analysand is able to be completely candid and spontaneous the resolution of the transference and the termination of analysis are approaching.

There are plausible reasons why in the last phase it is especially difficult to achieve and maintain analytic frankness. The termination of analysis is an experience of loss which mobilizes all the resistances in the transference (and in the countertransference too), for a final struggle. Termination of analysis can be compared to a difficult landing maneuver in which a whole crew of libidinal and destructive forces are on deck and in action. Every step forward in the patient's real life—as well as in his analysis in which he catches up with his incomplete development—implies a painful loss: the desires and gratifications of yesterday have to die that today can be fully lived. That holds true from weaning through all the learning processes of the growing ego. Graduation from analysis is a seriously painful loss which calls forth the labor of mourning. In all neurotic patterns, the patient has habitually avoided this labor.

Recently Adelaide Johnson described the terminal conflict of analysis as fully reliving the Oedipus conflict in which the quest for the genitally gratifying parent is poignantly expressed and the intense grief, anxiety, and wrath of its definitive loss are fully reactivated.[2] Such a terminal reliving of the Oedipus conflict in the transference is important because therewith residual unconscious pregenital wishes and fears have become remobilized and deprived of their disguises as aim-inhibited genital strivings. Unless the patient dares to be exposed to such an ultimate frustration he may cling to the tacit permission that his relation to the analyst will remain his refuge from the hardships of a reality that is too competitive or too frustrating for him. By attuning his libidinal cravings to an aim-inhibited, tender attachment to the analyst as an idealized parent, he can circumvent the conflicts of genital temptation and frustration.

2. Adelaide Johnson, "Some Heterosexual Transference and Countertransference Phenomena in Late Analysis of the Oedipus Complex." Unpublished paper delivered at the meeting of the Washington Psychoanalytic Society, 10 March 1951.

Toward such an analytically disingenuous compromise in the transference—which makes analysis truly interminable—gravitate particularly those patients whose egos were weakened by pregenital conflicts; those who had never in childhood fully reached the level of the Oedipus conflict. They may have found in the analyst the first understanding, permissive person, one who could not be provoked or antagonized by temper tantrums or stubborn withholding. The analyst has thus alleviated feelings of guilt about pregenital transgressions. Even this dissolution of infantile guilt which has strengthened the patient's ego does not always permit him to dare go further in his striving for natural and unconstrained independence. Gratitude toward the analyst sometimes reinforces the resistance of a tender, dependent transference which keeps the genital and hostile potentialities of the transference in fusion and abeyance.

Freud described the most typical forms of resistance against termination of analysis as first, the neurotic man who does not dare fully to face competition with other men because of the threat of castration anxiety; second, the incurably neurotic woman who will not relinquish her infantile claim for a penis. Both types cling to a narcissistic claim for bisexual omnipotence and an all-gratifying mother at the expense of a mature integration of the ego.

A patient may discover in analysis the malevolence of the "bad," the depriving mother of infancy and early childhood, and may hate and reproach her without fearing uncanny retaliation from her magic omnipotence; but he can take such daring steps only from the protected harbor of analysis, using the analyst as the magically "good" mother. He may still unconsciously expect the analyst who helped him to surmount the magic malevolence of the early mother to continue to protect him against the hardships of reality for which unconsciously the demonic mother has been held responsible.

It is an analytic commonplace that treatment has to be carried out in an atmosphere of abstinence as well as tolerance; that infantile claims must be permitted to appear in the transference but not gratified so that the negative transference can be worked through. Narcissistic claims, however, appeared to be unanalyzable in the early days of psychoanalysis. Only recent progress in analysis of the ego and analytic experiments in the treatment of psychoses give us hope that we may learn to resolve these narcissistic resistances which interfere with a true completion of analysis.

In the terminal phase of each analysis, facing the separation from the analyst, the patient becomes more aware of his narcissistic fixations, his unconscious adherence to an eschatological hope for an all-gratifying mother, a particularly tenacious resistance of the "all or nothing" type which defies disillusionment. The maternal type of analyst, particularly, who has been most helpful in rebuilding a poorly integrated ego frequently meets such resistance to the dissolution of the transference. The unconscious expectation of the patient is that the analyst should remain forever the supporter who guarantees a parasitic security.

This unconscious expectation, sometimes concealed by protestations of pseudoindependence, is reflected in a belief, widespread also among psychiatrists: "If only the mother had been truly loving, the neurotic or psychotic tragedy would not have occurred"; or, "A permissive, harmonious family would have safeguarded the psychological health of the child." There is, of course, much truth in such popular belief, but it is an oversimplification. It does not take into account such concepts as Freud's *Triebstärke*—the constitutional intensity of instincts. This consideration may make us more modest and more realistic in our expectations concerning parents and psychoanalysts. Popular beliefs tend to overburden parents and psychoanalysts with superhuman responsibilities, producing more intimidation than encouragement. A patient may cling to this belief in the "good mother" as the rationalization against a realistic dissolution of a tender transference; against the final loss of and separation from the analyst; against the acceptance of the loss or the hate of the early mother.

Winnicott postulates that even the most loving mother cannot help but unconsciously in some measure hate her newborn infant because of the amount of pain, frustration, self-sacrifice, and threat that are—besides the rich gratifications—implied in its delivery and the care of the infant and the young child. The harmonious, permissive family, says Winnicott, often creates an unrealistically sentimental atmosphere which is intolerant of direct instinctual gratification, and of hate in response to frustration. By this very intolerance the integration of the child's ego is impeded. The child learns the compromise of pseudoresignation, partial repression of instinctual needs, of paying for peace and harmony by partially persisting dependent fixations.[3] Freud says, "the attitudes of love and hate cannot be said to characterize the relation of instincts to their objects, but are reserved for the relations of the ego as a whole to objects."[4] Winnicott characterizes the earliest relation of the infant to the mother, who is not yet a differentiated object, as "ruthless love." Only when the ego is more integrated can the child be said to hate; only when the frustrating pain of hate can be endured does the more fully integrated individual learn to love.

Psychoanalysis does not always succeed in tracing infantile instinctual needs to their secret reservations and compromises; in winning them back for the patient's free disposal so that he can strive for direct gratifications, as well as for ideals of sublimation, with a good conscience. The failure to retrace and mobilize infantile instinctual needs is not only due to the patient's narcissistic resistances. There may be fear of the psychotic chaos which threatens to break loose if an infantile all-or-none relationship, the "ruthless love" of the infant, is remobilized. Not only the patient but the psychoanalyst himself may automatically shy away from the intimate closeness in which such infantile emotional attachments can only be relived. Such closeness is both alluring and threatening. It implies potential temptation and frustration for both analyst and analysand: temptation because in the goal-inhibited tender closeness of psychoanalytic intimacy the infantile longing for union can be secretly gratified; frustration because this tenderness dissociates the genital component of the attachment, the guilt about its overreaching intentions, and the hatred resulting from frustration. The analyst may tacitly allow the patient to

3. D. W. Winnicott, "Hate in the Countertransference," *International Journal of Psycho-Analysis* 30 (1949): 69–71.

4. Sigmund Freud, "Instincts and Their Vicissitudes," *Collected Papers*, vol. 4 (London: Hogarth, 1952), pp. 60–83.

use analysis as a sanctuary, a refuge. Analytic intimacy becomes a compensation for childhood frustrations. At last the patient has found the substitute parent who seems fully to understand him, and in the countertransference the analyst may vicariously enjoy a protective permissiveness that he could never experience in relation to his own parents.

Such an unconscious conspiracy between analyst and analysand represents resistance plus counterresistance against the progress of analysis. Sooner or later, the patient, if his ego is strong enough, will rebel against the sentimentality of such overprotection and overindulgence and break away in protest, or the analyst will become impatient of a stagnating analysis. Annie Reich has given a series of examples of such pathological countertransferences which call for further analysis of the analyst, if self-scrutiny cannot resolve the counterresistance.[5]

In discussing termination of psychoanalysis both Annie Reich and Edith Buxbaum have stressed the possibility of either misjudging or delaying the resolution of the transference because of the countertransference.[6] The patient may be discharged prematurely because of narcissistic, ambitious needs of the analyst, or discharge may be delayed when the analyst clings to the satisfaction derived from the patient's dependency.

I cannot agree with a definition of countertransference which emphasizes only its negative character. It is true, as long as countertransference remains unconscious, that it may function as a hindrance to the analytic process. But, since we assume the analyst's continuous self-analysis during his work, I would like to suggest a definition of countertransference which acknowledges the valuable insight that we gain from it.[7] Countertransference is the counterpart of transference. Transference has been recently redefined by Nunberg as a projection as well as a tendency to establish

5. Annie Reich, "On Countertransference," *International Journal of Psycho-Analysis* 32 (1951): 25–31.

6. Reich, "On the Termination of Analysis," ibid. 31 (1950): 179–83; Edith Buxbaum, "Technique of Terminating Analysis," ibid. 31 (1950): 184–90.

7. Maxwell Gitelson, "The Emotional Position of the Analyst in the Psychoanalytic Situation," ibid. 33 (1952): 1–10; Paula Heinmann, "On Countertransference," ibid. 31 (1950): 81–84.

identity of old and new perceptions. In "certain depths of analysis it is difficult to discern between identification and projection." The patient "is very deeply immersed in his unconscious id; . . . transference is like Janus, two-faced, with one face turned to the past, the other to the present."[8]

Countertransference has also this twofold aspect. The analyst in his work integrates two functions: first, empathic identification with the patient (by projection and introjection the unconscious of the analyst responds to the unconscious of the patient and to the images of his past); second, reeducation for reality (the analyst swings back to detachment and current reality). It seems to be in accordance with Nunberg's concept of transference to define countertransference as *empathic identification with the analysand.* Identification is a more primitive form of relation than the object libidinal relation on the level of genital maturity. In identification the boundaries of the ego are more fluid. On the basis of this empathic rapport, countertransference furnishes valuable direct information about the patient's unconscious. The fluidity of the ego boundaries, however, implies the danger of unrealistic aberrations, particularly if the analyst wanders off from the images of the patient's past into fantasies of his own. It is therefore important that the analyst swing from identification to a differentiating and detached object relationship. Margaret Little has pointed out that transference—originally estimated only as an element of interference—has become a useful tool of analysis. She adds, "If we can make the right use of countertransference, may we not find that we have yet another valuable, if not indispensable tool?"[9]

Throughout analysis it is important to observe correctly the microscopic pendulum swings of the emotional galvanometer to which I would like to compare empathic countertransference. Far from being a nuisance it is the most refined instrument for determining the progress of analysis. Ferenczi has taught us that the dissolution of transference, apparent in the uninhibited truthfulness and spontaneity of the analysand, indicates the approach to

8. Herman Nunberg, "Transference of Reality," ibid. 32 (1951): 1–9.

9. Margaret Little, "Countertransference and the Patient's Response to It," ibid. 32 (1951): 32–40.

the termination of analysis. I would like to supplement this with the statement that the resolution of the countertransference permits the analyst to be emotionally freer and spontaneous with the patient, and this is an additional indication of the approaching end of an analysis.

In earlier phases of analysis the emotional freedom of the analyst is restricted by the analyst's obligation to remain neutral, neither prohibitive nor indulgent, any deviation playing into the patient's infantile strivings. Since it is at times difficult to maintain objectivity, the analyst cautiously curbs his spontaneous responses and frequently remains silent whenever the communication of an intuitive insight would be premature and therefore inaccessible to the patient. The patient might, moreover, accept such insight intellectually and reinforce his emotional defenses. During the course of analysis the tact of the analyst, his empathic identification—the function of his sensitive countertransference—is an indispensable guide. It spares the patient's sensitivities as far as unnecessary pain can be avoided; it determines the timing and the depth of interpretations; it offers whatever the analyst sees as the tentative truth, and in such doses that the patient can absorb it at the time. Ideally, tact and truth, identification and objectivity are well integrated in the analyst's work. Wherever tact and truth are in conflict, the primary obligation of the analyst is to remain the objective representative of reality by not misleading the patient into indulgence by identification. On the other hand, interpretations should not strike the patient unprepared.

The tact of the analyst is directed by microscopic countertransference swings in response to the patient's transference which, though automatic and preconscious, are accessible to the self-observation of the analyst who knows, as Ella Sharpe has put it, his personal sources of error, his inclination toward sadistic or masochistic deviations. When the analyst observes that he can be unrestrained with the patient, when he no longer weighs his words to maintain a cautious objectivity, this empathic countertransference as well as the transference of the patient is in a process of resolution. The analyst is able to treat the analysand on terms of equality; he is no longer needed as an auxiliary superego, an unrealistic deity in the clouds of detached neutrality. These are signs that the patient's labor of mourning for infantile attachments nears completion. The patient steps from an enslaving and crippling pseudoresignation to a liberating acceptance of reality which terminates analysis.

Annie Reich has noted that the problem of terminating analyses is aggravated by the fact that "the analyst was hardly ever a real person: he became the recipient of the patient's fantasies. The lack of reality around the analyst makes it impossible to see him with his foibles and weaknesses as an ordinary human being."[10] The analysand in training to become a psychoanalyst is in this respect better off than the average patient who leaves his analyst definitely. The training analysand still has the opportunity of meeting the analyst in their common work. Therewith the analyst comes down to earth and the analysand corrects his illusions. He is able to complete the unachieved labor of mourning for unresolved infantile attachments after termination of analysis.[11]

But why should this work of mourning be postponed until after analysis? The lack of realism and spontaneity in the analytic situation, as Annie Reich describes it, counteracts the resolution of transference and countertransference. Only when strict observance of objectivity and detachment on the part of the analyst can be loosened will the patient really feel that he is on his own and is accepted as an equal. This is not possible in those cases where analysis for external or internal reasons cannot reach completion. But whenever the end phase of analysis can be reached it seems important to me that the analyst be more spontaneous, a real human being, whatever vulnerabilities may be revealed in spontaneous, emotional responses. The analyst need not resort to artifices to dispel the patient's illusions about the analyst's perfection: nature prevents trees from growing into the sky, and analysts from attaining perfection.

The patient's achievement of a feeling of equality with the analyst does not occur without resistances. Particularly those patients

10. Reich, "On Countertransference."

11. Marion Milner, "A Note on the Ending of an Analysis," *International Journal of Psycho-Analysis* 31 (1950): 191–93.

who had little opportunity to compete with equals, or those who habitually competed in the reverse fashion by pseudoresignation or masochistic submission, resist the acceptance of equality and the impending loss of the analyst's authority to be defied or obeyed. When termination of analysis is contemplated these patients frequently respond with a recrudescence of symptoms. Such relapses are sometimes accompanied by the unconscious aim: "I cannot let the analyst have the triumph of curing me." This is what is called the negative therapeutic reaction.

This danger was accentuated in the terminal phase of the analysis of a woman who had secretly competed intensely with an emotionally infantile mother. The rebellious and seductive father had obviously preferred the daughter to his wife. But the longing for reconciliation with the mother had frequently interfered with the daughter's success in life. The mother could neither hate nor be hated. She had endured the estrangement from her husband with the sentimental righteousness of an innocent child who had God on her side. The patient could only win her over by pseudoresignation, by denying her own intelligence and her emotional and sexual needs. "If mother only knew," had been the secret anxiety of her life.

Though the patient's cruel superego had become much more tolerant and the ego strengthened by working through the Oedipus conflict, a plan for terminating the analysis threw her into regression with a return of symptoms. It became obvious that she competed with me by self-defeat. The intensity and impetuosity of the patient's emotions in this regression had a different effect on my countertransference from the earlier phases in which I had reacted to her narcissistic vulnerability with cautious neutrality. I no longer felt compelled to maintain complete objectivity. The patient's mother had not been able to tolerate her own or her daughter's hate. It seemed important, and not only theoretically, to puncture the illusion that honest expression of negative emotions destroys a relationship. The narcissistic withdrawal into sentimental pseudoresignation had to be attacked. I not only interpreted the purpose of the regression—to defeat me by defeating herself—but showed frank disappointment and anger about this destructive form of competition. I admitted that I was provoked and worried, that I was afraid I might lose the competitive battle, and that she might leave with partial intellectual insight and a negative therapeutic reaction. My anxiety and anger was each time of short duration, and I resumed the analytic work with increased insight. I never lost my goodwill toward the patient and my belief that we could work through the terminal resistances. If I had remained disturbed or angry it might have been damaging to a patient who was already so prejudiced against her own hatred which barricaded the access to her yearning for reconciliation.

Naturally the countertransference needed the same detailed interpretation as the clarification of the transference. Additional self-analysis, which exceeds the direct analyst-analysand relation, is not appropriate in the doctor's office especially if the patient at times would like to turn the tables.

The spontaneous expression and interpretation of my countertransference had first a shocking, then a liberating effect. The shock was due to the disillusionment: the psychoanalyst is not perfect. The need for the perfection of the analyst was inevitably strong in a patient who had been exposed to a more than usual number of imperfections in her father and to the pretense of perfection in a mother who did not dare to hate and love.

The frank avowal of my reactions had the liberating, beneficial effect of a mutative interpretation for several reasons.[12] First, the patient experienced it as a sign of trust that I dared to express my emotions to her; that I no longer maintained the rigid self-discipline by which her mother had made her feel guilty and inferior. Alexander has noted instances in which it is important that the analyst react differently from the parent when habitual conflicts are repeated in transference.[13] The patient sensed that her trust in analytic authority had features of infantile trust in magic, transcendent power. Against this infantile trust of oral greed and dependency arose the anal protest of defiance which had made her

12. James Strachey, "The Nature of the Therapeutic Action of Psychoanalysis," ibid. 15 (1934): 127–59.
13. Franz Alexander, "Analysis of the Therapeutic Factors in Psychoanalytic Treatment," *The Psychoanalytic Quarterly* 19 (1950): 482–500.

afraid of passivity and her own femininity. The patient became aware that she was longing for a more mature form of trust. Second, venting the emotions of countertransference gave the patient the courage to come out herself with some intensely destructive impulses which had been kept in repression by a magic system of expiating self-punishment. Beyond this painful discovery loomed the possibilities of real reconciliation. Third, competition lost the desperately tragic aspect which had pushed her into the narcissistic defense of pseudoresignation as if she did not care to succeed. With the discussion of terminating analysis, this form of competition entered into the transference as the threat of a potential negative therapeutic reaction. Afraid that she was too strong, too intense, too violent for me—as she had found her mother too aloof, too weak, too scared with a problem child—as long as she assigned to me the role of the detached parent whom she could please or placate by the magic of pseudoresignation—sincere resignation could not yet be integrated into her personality. She could still cling to claims of infantile omnipotence. My anxiety and anger showed that I really cared, was eager to succeed with her; but my quick recovery from such disturbance indicated that I could not be made desperate by defeat; that I could accept it if necessary and go on trying to succeed with her.

At the termination of analysis, both analysand and analyst experience sadness and relief. Beyond all suspicions, accusations, threats of revenge, envy, and jealousy which made the child originally feel hopelessly bad, there returns from repression genuine affection, gratitude, and tolerance, not only toward the analyst whose countertransference was sometimes painful and not always useful, but toward the parents who can also be regarded with greater tolerance and forgiveness. They, too, have been victims of neurotic tragedy. The patient who has sometimes complained, "What is the use of changing if my parents do not change, my husband or my wife does not change," not infrequently discovers with surprise that the benefits of his own changes have favorably influenced his environment. One step removed from the analytic process, the parent or spouse has participated in the experience of insight and its liberating effects.

I am convinced that the truth of psychoanalysis has to be experienced; it cannot be indoctrinated. Indoctrination and unscientific battles are a sign of unresolved transference and countertransference.

Special Problems in Connection with
Termination of Training Analyses

I would like to start with two quotations from Freud to Ferenczi in the fall of 1909, recently reported by Balint. They are probably some of the earliest remarks on training analysis. "Eitingon is here, goes twice weekly on a walk with me after supper and there he lets himself be analyzed," and "Eitingon who has picked me up twice weekly for an evening walk on which he lets himself be analyzed, comes Friday for a last time and then goes to Berlin for a year." Early training analyses, according to Balint, were short and informal. When the dynamics of the unconscious and of transference were demonstrated to the trainee, his further training was left to his personal ingenuity. In a later generation of European psychoanalysts, Balint reports, there was a frequent need for additional analysis after completed official training. This was mostly carried out privately and secretly in order to spare the prestige of the analyst.[1]

I do not want to go deeper into the history of training analysis, Balint and Ekstein have reported this history very aptly.[2] They have shown that training analysis and its termination has been and is full of unsolved problems. The differences and similarities between training and therapeutic analysis have been frequently discussed. Anna Freud has pointed out the similarity between

Reprinted by permission from *The Journal of the American Psychoanalytic Association* 3 (Oct. 1955): 630–40.

1. Michael Balint, "Analytische Ausbildung und Lehranalyse," *Psyche* 7 (Stuttgart, 1954): 698–99.

2. Ibid.; Rudolf Eckstein, "On Current Trends in Psychoanalytic Training," in *Explorations in Psychoanalysis*, ed. Robert Mitchell Lindner (New York: Julian Press, 1953).

training and child analysis.[3] In child analysis modifications of classical technique were found to be unavoidable. Modifications in the technique of training analysis have been discussed by Alexander, Grotjahn, and others.[4] Even those psychoanalysts who prefer no modifications of classical technique are fully aware that the reality situation in which training analysis takes place is different from that of a therapeutic analysis.

The training analyst is not cloaked in complete anonymity. Both training analyst and analysand belong to a group of teachers and students. Even when both strictly avoid social contacts during analysis, sources of collateral information may influence the transference-countertransference situation. Further, termination of a training analysis does not represent a definite separation, since analyst and analysand continue to live and work in the same professional group and for the same or similar goals. Though the termination of training analysis may be completely separated from examination and graduation and the analyst even deprived of any official influence on the trainee's career, the analysand still counts on his analyst's advocacy or fears its loss. Due to these hopes and fears the analysand frequently looks forward to the termination of analysis as a symbol of personal and group acceptance. The exclusion of the training analyst from official influence on the analysand's career indicates some doubt in the analyst's objectivity, i.e. his mastery of countertransference.

Therapeutic analyses are frequently terminated when the patient is freed from symptoms. Many training analyses are motivated by the trainee's therapeutic needs. The termination of such analyses is largely dependent on changes in the analysand which make his psychoneurotic symptoms superfluous. However, since psychoanalysis in this country has gained so much public recogni-

3. Anna Freud, "Probleme der Lehranalyse," in *Max Eitingon. In Memoriam* (Jerusalem: Israel Psycho-Analytic Society, 1950), pp. 80–94.

4. Franz Alexander, "Psychoanalytic Training in the Past, in the Present, and in the Future," address to the Association of Candidates of the Chicago Institute for Psychoanalysis, 26 October 1951; Martin Grotjahn, "Present Trends in Psychoanalytic Training," in *Twenty Years of Psychoanalysis* ed. Franz Gabriel Alexander (New York: Norton, 1950), pp. 80–91.

tion and prestige, there is an increasing number of applicants for training analysis who are not motivated by personal suffering; some of them are even, at first sight, rather unfamiliar with mental suffering. They are motivated by research interests, by professional aspirations to reach an optimum of psychiatric efficiency, as well as by individual needs for security and recognition. The training analysis, in these cases, is more educational than therapeutic. The motive of liberation from suffering is replaced by the goal of increase in ego strength and mastery of reality. Thus, a training analysis is for the most part an asymptomatic character analysis. If the defenses of the analysand function smoothly he may tend to intellectualize and accept analytic knowledge as indoctrination. It is therefore important that training analysis does not take place in an ivory tower but in lively expanding institutes. Various interpersonal aspects bring forth anxieties as well as typical defenses, and for the majority of the trainees the analysis is what it should be—an intense emotional experience. It implies the challenge to differentiate the realistic factors of the training situation from the crosscurrents of transferences and countertransferences.

By its nature an educational analysis is interminable.[5] Termination cannot be defined in terms of accumulated knowledge. But the emotional relation between analyst and analysand tends to develop ultimately toward an optimum of frankness, directness and mutual trust, which allows both partners in the process to arrive at a consensus concerning the termination of analysis. Shadows of doubt, dissatisfaction and insecurity that becloud this consensus stem in the main from transference resistances, but countertransference distortions can also impair the optimal development toward a consensus. Errors about the termination of analysis are mostly due to an acting out of transference, but sometimes also to an acted-out countertransference.

According to Ferenczi, the dissolution of transference—apparent in the uninhibited truthfulness and spontaneity of the analysand

5. Sigmund Freud, "Analysis Terminable and Interminable," *International Journal of Psycho-Analysis* 18 (1937): 373–405.

—indicates the termination of analysis.[6] This dissolution of transference is a process in which the unconscious sexual and hostile factors of transference become conscious and the sublimated positive transference gains therewith in strength.[7] This process of dissolution of transference resistance is accompanied by a firmer integration of the patient's personality and by a greater frankness and clarity in the free associations. Simultaneously the potential countertransference reactions of the empathic analyst subside, he feels freer from anxieties and more spontaneous. In a previous paper I have used the dissolution of the countertransference potential as a supplementary indication for the termination of analysis.[8] Ekstein criticizes "the introduction of moral issues where technical considerations are in order." I do not think that we can avoid using moral terms to describe the goal of training analysis. Training institutes rightly insist that a person entrusted with the responsibility of analyzing patients have reached a degree of integrity and truthfulness which allows a steady, alert self-analysis. Self-deception on the other hand is characteristic for a blind acting out of unconscious impulses. Ferenczi said: "Our analyses show with full certainty that in a phase of transition from original amorality to acquired morality each instinctual renunciation and each acceptance of displeasure is still accompanied by a sense of dishonesty, i.e., of hypocrisy." Ferenczi was the first to insist that a training analysis must go deeper in the reeducation of the unconscious than a therapeutic analysis.

In a paper on "Countertransference in the Training Analyst" Therese Benedek has pointed out that not only transference but also countertransference phenomena are reinforced by the situation of the training analysis.[9] Since the analyst has gone through a

6. Sandor Ferenczi, "Das Problem der Beendigung der Analysen," *International Zeitschrift für Psychoanalyse* 14 (1928): 1–10.

7. Heinrich Racker, "Notes on the Theory of Transference," *Psychoanalytic Quarterly* 23 (1954): 78–86.

8. See above, the preceding chapter, "Contribution to the Problem of Terminating Psychoanalyses."

9. Therese Benedek, "Countertransference in the Training Analyst," *Bulletin of the Menninger Clinic* 18 (1954): 12–16.

similar experience in his own training analysis, his empathy with the analysand is refined in spite of personality differences; his own transference propensities are touched off when he accompanies the trainee through his anxieties and conflicts with authority. Impulsive communication of countertransference propensities implies the danger of acting out. The acting out of the analysand is, at times, inevitable; the acting out of the analyst has to be avoided. When the analyst subjects his own countertransference stirrings to as careful an analytic study as the transference manifestations of the analysand, the training analysis becomes a "research work," as Balint suggested—research in which "the candidate with the help of the analyst gathers experience about the deeper layers of his soul, and the analyst with the help of the candidate finds out about the potentialities and limitations of his own understanding and his technique." What happens in analysis, according to Balint, "is not alone determined by the associations and transferences of the patient, nor alone by the interpretations of the analyst, but by a mutual influence of both." It seems to me therefore worthwhile to consider the transference-countertransference situation in a training analysis as a total picture. The optimal elucidation of this total picture of analyst-analysand relation gives us an indication of the termination of analysis in operational terms. The fact that sometimes frictions or even hostilities arise in psychoanalytic societies on the basis of personal or ideological differences indicates frequently unsolved transference and countertransference conflicts; ideological differences would otherwise be taken as a stimulus for further research.

The professional group to which both analyst and analysand belong has similarities with the family structure. The representatives of the older and younger generation strive for high professional standards, there is sibling rivalry between the contemporaries of both groups, realistically intensified by the bottleneck due to the shortage in training personnel. Typical anxieties of the Oedipus complex are stirred up in the analysand, and what one could call a Laius or Jocasta complex in the analyst. These are experienced in a variety of individual forms. In the mind of the training analysand the anxious question arises, "Will I ever achieve the knowledge, the skill, the security of the older colleague?" The training analyst may at times be preoccupied with corresponding fears or compensatory wishes, "Will the student outgrow me, find out my inadequacies? Will he let me succeed in living up to the standards of Freud, of my own training analyst, and to the expectations of the contemporary professional group?"

The analysand is encouraged to set aside the defenses of conventional behavior, to give full expression to the necessarily threatening aspects of destructive competition, penis envy and castration anxieties, to reveal residual childhood patterns of distrustful, defiant, pregenital isolation. The trainee is permitted the catharsis of self-expression, but not the analyst. He is committed to maintain his benevolent neutrality and his emotional equilibrium even when the analysand in his acting out tries hard to overthrow it, to test the analyst out by rebellious accusations or by self-righteous argumentation, for the analysand readily hears interpretations as recriminations. If the wrongs of the past weigh heavily on him he tries to prove that the analyst does not let him succeed, demands too much from him, he may even for his own unconscious vindication feel compelled to defeat the analyst by an explosive termination of analysis.

The sophisticated training analysand may be inclined to suspect his needs for tenderness and affection as danger signals of incestuous or homosexual involvement, and this unconscious anxiety may harden his unconscious narcissistic defenses. Though the analyst is obliged not to give vent to his reactions of frustration under the stress and strain of such a training analysis, the intuitive analysand may sense them, if the analyst does not study carefully the countertransference potentialities that are stirred up. The analyst may feel that his reputation is threatened if he does not succeed. He may feel rejected, especially if the analysand's acting out spills over into the professional community and leads to aggravated complaints on the part of colleagues. He may feel tempted to overidentify with the patient, evade his rebellion with long-suffering forbearance and miss the right timing of painful but useful interpretations. If the analyst is not aware of his anxieties, if his equanimity becomes forced instead of spontaneous, his patience may suddenly break in a surprise reaction and he may wield—untimely—the powerful weapon of nonacceptance. In some situations a change of analyst at the proper moment may clarify the transference-countertransference involvement to the satisfaction of both analyst and analysand. Kemper, in his paper on countertransference at the London convention, 1953, has differentiated between useful and not-useful countertransference reactions and he has attributed part of the not-useful countertransference to "protest reactions" against the abstention from immediate self-expression imposed on the analyst during his work. In a lengthy analysis the analyst can become worn out by the control of such "protest reaction," and a change of analyst may be indicated in such cases.[10]

Only when the full transference-countertransference situation can be elucidated, when the narcissistic defenses on both sides yield to the working through of underlying anxieties about mutual nonacceptance, when acting out has subsided, do analyst and analysand arrive at a convincing agreement about termination of analysis. In some instances analyst and analysand come to the consensus that psychoanalytic practice is not the appropriate field for the analysand. I need not say that it is a difficult task to arrive at a consensus and that we do not always succeed. But after the analysand has come to full expression and reasonable correction of his ambivalence, the dissolution of transference and countertransference resistance is experienced with marked relief. Energies that had been tied up in mutually incompatible defenses are free for more spontaneous self-expression on the part of the analysand and productive collaboration of both in mutual trust.

There is sometimes more insecurity about the termination of a training analysis in which the transferrence emotions are shielded from full expression, in which the atmosphere remains more intellectual and the revelation of the unconscious is retarded by the typical defenses of compliance and submission. Acceptance by the analyst and secondarily by the institute becomes a goal more important than the process of self-revelation. Free associations are

10. Werner Kemper, "Die Gegenübertragung," *Psyche* 7 (1954): 593–626.

unfree in so far as they are directed by the unconscious wish to bribe the analyst, to conform to his expectations. The analysand is driven unconsciously to manipulate the analyst into the role of the gratifying, protective parent, the magic helper. A trainee not only emulates the analyst in his style of work, he incorporates his philosophy, he intuitively reads the analyst's mind, listening to his interpretations as if they were compelling orders of an auxiliary superego. He follows the automatic pattern of earlier adjustment to authority. The analysand assumes that the analyst wants him to be more aggressive or less conventional, more ambitious or more affectionate, and he adjusts to these assumed superego commands by unconsciously pretending the desired behavior. The subtle unconscious hypocrisy of such adaptation, the "as if" performances of the analysand which bring to mind my previous quotation from Ferenczi, interfere with the autonomy of the superego and the growth of ego strength. Therefore, the defensive compliance may sooner or later turn into scornful rebellion if the analyst does not succeed in time in seeing through the analysand's unconscious maneuvers.

The training analyst is aided in his understanding of the psychoanalytic situation by observing his countertransference reactions, e.g. his boredom at the unspontaneous conformity of the analysand. He is alerted to the possibility that he may derive narcissistic gratification from the compliant student as a parent may unconsciously use a convenient child for the gratification of narcissistic needs. The observations of supervisors, seminar leaders and other students can be quite helpful in breaking up the complacency of a stagnating training analysis. An interruption of the training analysis can stimulate separation anxieties and throw a dependency pattern into relief. Or the rising difficulties of the student-analyst in his own practice may help him to shed the reservations of conformity and to render his own analytic work more alive, more spontaneous, more creative.

The end of a training analysis is characterized by symptoms of mourning. Trainees have reported very vivid Oedipal dreams after termination. The analysand, in terminating, does not only lose the projection screen for his unconscious imagos. He experiences a real loss, as one trainee has put it in departing: "I have never had and never will have a relation in which I can be so unreservedly frank as in this analysis."

This sketchy illustration of the rebellious and compliant type of trainee does not do justice to the enormous variety of individual problems in training analysis which prevent or retard a satisfactory termination. Rebellion and compliance point to their sources in early childhood, to what Melanie Klein's school calls the paranoid and depressive position.[11] There are paranoid features in rebellion, depressive features in compliance. Balint explains the growing length of training analyses by the increasing endeavor to activate the negative transference and to bring destructive pregenital impulses with concomitant dependency into focus, that represent the paranoid and depressive potentialities of a normal person. Balint challenges here Freud's doubts about activating inactive unconscious conflicts in analysis, these doubts being expressed in "Analysis Terminable and Interminable." Balint assumes that the introjection of the idealized training analyst prevents the activation of hostility, while simultaneously hostilities have been drained off into antagonisms against adversaries of psychoanalysis or representatives of different ideologies. The idealization of the training analyst is a most serious handicap for the termination of a training analysis.

Termination is indicated when the analysand dares to relinquish a dependent identification for a mutually respectful differentiation, when the anxieties about loss, about incorporation or being incorporated, anxieties reflected in an unrealistic concern about success and failure, can be transcended. Anxieties keep the partners in analysis at arm's length, shielded by unconscious defenses. The consensual validation of the end of analysis gains conviction when the self-deceptions and mutual deceptions of unconscious transference and countertransference have become elucidated as narcissistic residues that prevent analyst and analysand from meeting each other fully, meeting each other's genuine needs, as defined by their team work. Not only the analysand needs

11. Melanie Klein, Paula Heimann, Susan Isaacs, and Joan Riviere, *Developments in Psycho-Analysis* (London: Hogarth, 1952).

the analyst's acceptance, the analyst needs the analysand's genuine acceptance as well. As long as the need is seen only one-sided, as long as the analysand strives unconsciously for acceptance by opportunistic conformity, so long will analyst and analysand be in danger of using each other as a means for an unconscious, narcissistic end. A consensus relatively free from transference and countertransference deceptions can be reached only when both collaborate freely toward goals and values that are not superhuman, but human, in full awareness of the distance from the realization of these values in both analyst and analysand. Analytic investigation reduces anxieties and guilt about the distance from these values and decreases defensive pretences and prejudices. The commitment to psychoanalytic truthfulness—i.e. the broadening of consciousness—provides a common ground for fruitful collaboration. It keeps the team of analyst and analysand alert to narcissistic falsifications. The common psychoanalytic understanding elicits a spirit of genuine humility. Psychoanalysis is a process for approximating truth, a process to arrive at higher levels of maturity and integrity. We are all striving for these values, and yet insecurities about the evaluation of training analyses show that more has to be done for the analytic definition of these values. The assumption that psychoanalysis could or should be a science free of values delays such definition.

The optimal collaboration between analyst and analysand is made possible by a gradual liberation from repressed hostilities and redistribution of libido, a shift from narcissistic, defensive libido to a more discriminating object libido. Anxieties which separate analyst and analysand, as well as wasteful defenses, have to be worked through and transcended, because anxieties and habitual defenses concentrate the individual's libido on his own imaginary safety, his distrustful isolation. The decrease of the level of anxiety manifests itself in greater spontaneity and creativity of the analysand's productions. But the analyst also feels freer. During the course of analytic work he could not remain untouched by his analysand's anxieties. He responded empathically and his own defenses became mobilized, even though his self-analysis, his past experiences, guarded his objectivity. At the end of the work the growing spontaneity of the analysand frees the analyst from cautions and anxieties in his countertransference. The optimal collaboration between analyst and analysand in what Balint calls "research analysis" permits both to arrive at a consensus about its termination which can also be communicated to the training committee. It seems important to me that we not only *name* training analysis "research analysis," but that we accept the spirit of research.

The termination of a training analysis is not a matter of accredited hours and frequencies, although we need this external frame, but we must be on guard that the external frame in a growing organization be not used as pseudoscientific compulsion which expresses distrust. The termination of a training analysis is essentially a matter of trust, mutual trust as well as the trust that the trainee will thereafter be able to carry on his self-analysis, the fullest possible exploration of his transference and countertransference propensities. Trust is as far removed from gullibility as from suspicion. The word "trust" stems from the same root as the word "truth." The psychoanalytic understanding of human personality is a way of approximating the ideal of truth; truth not only in the sense of understanding the past determinant chains of cause and effect, but also in the sense of realistic predictions of future development. At the ended of a training analysis there should be a realistic trust in the trainee's future development. Trust in psychodynamic terms characterizes a relation of post-ambivalent libido investment, relatively free from unconscious anxieties and hostilities of transference and countertransference. Trust grants an optimal freedom for spontaneous and creative development, as well as for productive collaboration.

If, with Balint, we come to regard the training analysis as our research instrument, not in name, but in spirit, we will succeed better in eliminating the prejudicial elements of reward and punishment which complicate the transference-countertransference situation. A research analysis emphasizes the common goal of both analyst and analysand, to strive for the ideals of scientific truth as well as for freedom from unconscious anxieties and conflicts. The training analyst should not remain the superego of the

274

analysand. His advantage is only that of greater experience. If the training analyst would consider himself the perfect representative of professional standards and ideals he would be in danger of becoming a victim of narcissistic falsification and of hampering his own creative development. The channels for experimentation and reform must remain open. A return to personal analysis, e.g. under conditions of stress is no disgrace, but deepens psychoanalytic research. I join Balint in his final recommendation to all training institutions: *Semper reformari debet.*

Psychoanalysis as Therapy

The broadening of the clientele of patients who turn to psychiatrists for help increases the urgency to decide who among these patients need psychoanalytic treatment, and who among them can stand a psychoanalytic treatment of classical style. Intensive psychoanalytic treatment is not needed in cases of acute adaptational conflicts due to external challenges that cannot yet be mastered by a patient. In such cases some change in the environment, some increase of self-understanding or goal-directed psychotherapy can reestablish satisfactory adapation. On the other hand, classical psychoanalytic treatment frequently cannot be endured without considerable modifications by psychotic, prepsychotic, or postpsychotic patients or borderline patients whose ego structure is either overly rigid or extremely fluid, so that the therapist cannot expect the patient to live up to standards of adaptation which are suitable for a patient of a more flexible endowment. The psychotherapist must be familiar with the social structure of the world his patient has to adapt to, and its values and means of communication. Frequently patients are hampered by pathologic dependency on family members who have to be won over for an understanding collaboration.

The Columbia University Psychoanalytic Clinic has pointed out that it is a difficult diagnostic and prognostic decision whether reparative psychotherapy or reconstructive psychoanalysis of classical style can and should be recommended for a patient.[1] Roy

Reprinted by permission from *Psychoanalysis and Human Values,* ed. Jules H. Masserman (New York: Grune and Stratton, 1960), pp. 244–49.

1. Sandor Rado, "Adaptational Psychodynamics, a Basic Science," in *Changing Concepts of Psychoanalytic Medicine,* ed. Sandor Rado and George E. Daniels (New York: Grune and Stratton, 1956).

Grinker goes so far to say: "One has to be a relatively healthy neurotic to be analyzed without modifications and deviations."[2] This should be a decision on the basis of the patient's needs and potentialities. Practical considerations of the patient's financial resources enter into this decision, and the preference of classical psychoanalysts to apply exclusively the difficult technique they are trained for does not always correspond to the broad needs of a widening clientele of patients, as Redlich and Hollingshead have pointed out.[3] The problem of excessive anxieties that prevent the processes of integration is the focal point of therapeutic interest which different schools of psychotherapy have in common, in spite of great differences in their approaches.

When we take a bird's eye view of the model of classical psychoanalytic technique applied to suitable patients, we may raise the question: How does the individual patient find the reconstruction of his wholeness in the complexities of this world with the help of this one-to-one therapeutic relationship? The classical technique offers the patient what Erikson called a moratorium in his conflicts[4] by the recommendation of relaxed self-expression in free association, dreams, and other products of the primary process, by the suggestion to postpone major decisions, by the unprohibitive, understanding attitude of the analyst and the application of the rule of abstinence. The patient, for one hour of his day, enters a cloistered existence which exposes his fundamental egocentric loneliness, when the mask of a hypocritical adjustment and the false peace drop away that the neurotic patient has tried to establish by repression of needs and a compulsive conformity to the mores of his environment.

The rule of abstinence has been called "controlled frustration" by Karl Menninger.[5] Gratification pulls two persons together. In

2. Roy Grinker, "A Philosophical Appraisal of Psychoanalysis," in *Science and Psychoanalysis*, vol. 1, ed. J. H. Masserman (New York: Grune and Stratton, 1958).

3. Frederick Redlich and August Hollingshead, *Social Class and Mental Illness* (New York: John Wiley and Sons, 1958).

4. Erik Erikson, "Problem of Ego Identity," *Journal of the American Psychoanalytic Association* 4 (1958): 56.

5. Karl Menninger, *Theory of Psychoanalytic Technique* (New York: Basic Books, 1958).

the joy of shared gratification they find both their existences confirmed. Insurmountable frustration and despair separates human beings and threatens existence with annihilation. The threat of annihilation cannot be endured without the ego strength, the freedom to hope and trust in future reunion and renewed gratification. Out of loneliness and anguish can arise a new inner security and a new integration on a deep and basic level. The patient's innate hope and trust gives psychoanalysis a chance. Freud has pointed out that the patient is first touched by trust (*Glaube*) which is the child of love before he can gain rational understanding and insight.[6] But due to man's basic loneliness and egocentricity the images of his hope and trust have the tendency to deteriorate into illusions which split pleasure from pain, good from bad experiences. He is inclined to exploit his interpersonal relations for the maintenance of an illusionary security which eliminates the painful aspects of reality. The psychoanalytic process is therefore one of progressive disillusionment, gradually revealing the patient's basic loneliness. Frieda Fromm-Reichmann, in a posthumous paper "Loneliness," has focused our attention on the overt or covert experience of basic loneliness in human psychopathology.[7] The rule of abstinence or controlled frustration in psychoanalysis cannot expose the basic loneliness of the patient directly, since the experience of loneliness mobilizes the excessive anxieties of nonbeing or annihilation, resistances expressed in anxious agitation or angry protest, and the complexity of habitual defenses. The patient escapes into the regressive development of a transference neurosis. This transference neurosis gives important information about the patient's personal development; the analyst is forced into a parental role which brings the struggle of dependence versus independence gradually to full awareness. In the struggle between dependence and independence we see the longing for gratifying harmony and symbiotic unity as well as the fear of loss of identity and authenticity, or being engulfed by parental protection and crushed by authoritative directions. The transference neurosis implies the

6. Sigmund Freud, "Die Übertragung," *Gesammelte Schriften*, vol. 7 (Leipzig, Vienna, and Zurich: Internationaler Psychoanalytischer Verlag, 1924), p. 463.

7. Frieda Fromm-Reichmann, "Loneliness," *Psychiatry* 22 (1959): 1–15.

danger that the patient whose ego weakness shuns the anguished loneliness of progressive independence remains arrested in ambivalent, more or less rebellious submission to the analyst's authority, particularly when the analyst has a stake in this authority position himself.

Simultaneously with the growing interest in psychoanalytic ego psychology we find an increasing study of all aspects of countertransference which, if brought to the analyst's awareness, prevent him from falling automatically into the parental roles, or from becoming emotionally contaminated with the patient's anxieties and identified with his defenses. The low soft voice of reason is not enough to turn the patient's regressive clinging to the past into a daring, confident progression towards an unknown future, though it is a powerful adjuvant to disentangle phenomena of transference and countertransference from the spontaneous potentialities of a meaningful, trustworthy therapeutic relation. Interpretations represent gratifications of the need for understanding and meaning. But they may at times represent shortcut solutions on the level of verbal, intellectual communication. The rule of abstinence commits the analyst to avoid such shortcut solutions and compromises of mutual gratification that sidestep the experience of basic loneliness in the patient. The merely intellectual agreement often does not prevent the analysand from using the analyst as a comfort in his loneliness, as an object of possessive and exploitative passions, as a means to alleviate guilt feelings, as an ally in a campaign of revenge and defiance, for the discharge of envy, hatred, and rage or a compensatory display of contemptuous conceit. The analyst, in order to be useful to the patient, has to accompany the patient in this regression to the level of emotional experience, permit himself not only to empathize, but to expose himself, sympathetically and compassionately, to the emotional contagion which implies the danger that he be tempted to commiserate, to be antagonized, to retaliate, to be swept off his feet by anxiety and despair, or to regain his homeostatic equilibrium by reproachful or contemptuous withdrawal. The analyst learns from his own inner emotional response, and if he does not lose himself in discharge reactions this awareness of his emotional response broadens his understanding of the patient. Intense emotional outbursts on the part of the patient tend to wipe out the boundaries of the *I* and the *you,* elicit confusion of identity and increase anguish and helplessness. The patient may be thrown back into the autistic loneliness of what Melanie Klein called the "paranoid position,"[8] in which he can see the analyst only as threatening enemy, or into the depressive position in which he seeks reconciliation at any cost, by self-surrender. The analyst's cool and firm sympathy may be able to endure and to transcend this dangerous involvement, he sympathizes with the patient's rage of frustration and basic loneliness when he is able to live through this predicament himself without compulsive need for success or excessive anxiety about failure. He interprets the destructive aspect of the patient's emotional involvement but visualizes also the patient's repressed potentialities, his constructive yearning for liberation that is hidden in his narcissistic and sadomasochistic defenses and his longing for a reconciliation without loss of self-respect. Here the analyst is no longer only a scientist who reconstructs the past on principles of psychological determinism. He sees the ego of the patient not as a closed system, but with potentialities open to the world with a broader range of freedom in decisions. Freud told the analyst to work like a sculptor removing the encrusting material to free the original Gestalt of the patient.[9] The Gestalt of the patient's potentialities and his realistic limitations rise more and more clearly into awareness. Beyond the clouds of transference and countertransference both visualize the outlines of a meaningful therapeutic relation in the spirit of trust that the differences and separateness of the *I* and the *you* can exist side by side without condemning either of them to the frustrating rage of loneliness.

I have avoided the technical terms in this thumbnail sketch of the model of psychoanalytic technique. The verbal terms of these concepts set up a distance between the doctor and the patient, to whom the doctor has to talk in common sense terms. The analyst not only uses conceptual verbal tools, but is a tool himself, and to

8. Melanie Klein, *Envy and Gratitude* (New York: Basic Books, 1957).
9. Freud, "Über Psychotherapie," in *Gesammelte Schriften,* vol. 6 (1925), p. 15.

make himself a better tool, he learns to tame or sublimate his emotional responses and to put them into the service of the patient. The neutrality of the analyst remains artificial as long as he tries anxiously to accept the patient and to silence the voices of nonacceptance. He needs more than a knowledge of psychodynamics; he needs a wisdom that transcends ambivalence, that sees acceptance and nonacceptance, love and hate, construction and destruction together, trusting in the basic wholeness of the individual patient. This trust runs the risk of failure, because the processes of growth and integration are unpredictable. The wisdom of trust creates the atmosphere of genuine sympathy in which doctor and patient endure and transcend the hardships and frustrations of the analytic process together. This can become a corrective emotional experience for the patient. The analyst's sympathy in reliving with the patient the lonely miseries of his past, and his genuine trust in the patient's potentialities for the future are not the outgrowth of an authoritative relation; they establish an honest comradeship in this battle for liberation from the tyranny of repressed and untamed anxieties and are frequently able to turn the patient's despair and loneliness into hope and trust in his spontaneous interaction with his fellow men.

Doctor and patient may have a choice whether to embark on a reparative analysis aiming at readaptation and social recovery or at a deeper reconstructive analysis leading to a self-realization of the patient in his uniqueness. But it is not always predictable what depths of experience can be reached in the living through of the tensions between loneliness and communion in the analytic relation.

PART IV

Ethology, Mythology, and Existential Philosophy

Human Ego Functions in the
Light of Animal Behavior

It is the intention of this paper to explore whether the modern study of animal behavior, which is called ethology, might not throw some light on human development as it is studied in psychoanalysis. The observer of animal behavior uses a different frame of reference from the psychoanalyst, but there are bridges of mutual understanding, as, for instance, Masserman in this country, and Bally and Lincke in Switzerland have demonstrated.[1] In this paper I can make only a limited contribution to the building of such bridges, although I hope to stimulate further thought along these lines.

Animal behavior seems to a very high degree determined by innate patterns, similar to those which appear in the behavior of the human infant during the first year of his life. Adult human behavior is much more flexible and adaptable. While the animal responds automatically to a stimulus in a given situation, adult man responds to the total situation; he is able to perceive the gestalt of the total situation and has the freedom to evaluate the significance of each stimulus within this situation.

This freedom to evaluate exposes man to conflicts which may interfere with the integration of action. The animal's range of varia-

Reprinted by permission from *Psychiatry: Journal for the Study of Interpersonal Processes* 19 (Nov. 1956): 325–32. Copyright 1956 by the William Alanson White Psychiatric Foundation, Inc.

1. Jules H. Masserman, *Behavior and Neurosis* (Chicago: University of Chicago Press, 1943); Gustav Bally, *Vom Ursprung und von den Granzen der Freiheit* (Basel: Benno Schwabe, 1945); Harold Lincke, "Bemerkungen zur Triebpsychologie der Ersatzbefriedigung und Sublimierung," *Psyche* 7 (Stuttgart, 1953): 501–20; Lincke, "Ueber Angstlust und infantile Sexualitaet," *Psyche* 8 (Stuttgart, 1954): 427–49.

tion in action, dependent on automatic responses to stimuli, is much more limited; yet the animal, too, develops neurotic symptoms in a conflict situation. Experiments with animals such as those of Koehler, Masserman, and others, have shown that neurotic conflicts can be produced artificially.[2] Even under natural living conditions the complex instinctual behavior of animals is not free from aberrations which are similar to human conflict symptomatology.

But there is no way of knowing what the animal experiences in a conflict situation unless one interprets his behavior by empathy. The ethologist, unlike the psychologist, cannot rely on subjective, introspective reports; he relies on observation of behavior and analyzes it by studying its causes as well as its results. The results indicate, in teleological interpretation, the directedness toward goals.

Instincts do not present themselves as data of observation, for observation shows only behavior patterns which integrate a series of needs, highly ritualized according to a strictly hierarchical principle of organization. The concept of instinct is, however, a useful working hypothesis. It should be noted that the ethologist's concept of instinct differs from the concept of instinct or drive in psychoanalytic terms, and that the ethologic concept of instinct tries to avoid psychological interpretation. In the following discussion, I shall describe the ethologic concept of instinct and certain related concepts without necessarily identifying myself with them.

The ethologist Tinbergen has tentatively defined instinct as "a hierarchically organized nervous mechanism which is susceptible to certain priming, releasing, and directing impulses of internal as well as of external origin, and which responds to these impulses by coordinated movements that contribute to the maintenance of the individual and the species." The survival of the individual is guaranteed by feeding behavior, sleep, and flight from external dangers such as animals of prey. But fighting for territory or for a sexual partner, courting and mating behavior, and care of the offspring are also directed toward the survival of the species. Tinber-

2. Wolfgang Koehler, *Intelligenzpruefungen an Menschenaffen* (Berlin: Springer, 1921); Masserman, *Behavior and Neurosis.*

gen and other ethologists have described a plurality of instincts that can replace each other so that, fundamentally, the ethologic concept of instinct could be called monistic. Animal behavior is highly integrated, and it can be described in a series of motor patterns which characterize the consecutive periods of the animal's development. Observing, for example, a fish—the male stickleback—Tinbergen finds the following stages of instinctual activity: (1) fighting for territory, and the threatening of rivals from carefully guarded positions; (2) nest building, including digging, testing of material, drilling, and other movements; (3) courting, which is characterized by a complex zigzag dance constituting the ceremonial introduction of the female into the nest; (4) insemination, followed by complex motor patterns of care for the eggs, and, after they are hatched, gathering and fanning movements that provide oxygen for the offspring. Each consecutive level of instinctual behavior is characterized by motor patterns which result in action that extinguishes need.[3]

According to a theory developed by Beach and elaborated by Tinbergen, each predetermined motor pattern is blocked up to the time when the charge of a "central excitational mechanism," receptive to hormone influences, sensory stimuli, and innate motivation, makes the activation of the motor pattern possible. If, at such a time, the appropriate external stimuli are available, an "innate releasing mechanism" removes the block from the instinctual centers. The dispatch of impulses, released in full force to the neural circuits of consummatory acts, eventually extinguishes the tensions of need. An instinctual conflict may arise when a strong excitation cannot be discharged, perhaps because two activated instinctual needs are in competition with each other, or because the external situation does not suffice to trigger off the appropriate consummatory act. In such a conflict, displacement actions have been observed which have some similarities to human neurotic symptoms.[4]

3. Nikolaas Tinbergen, *The Study of Instinct* (Oxford: Clarenden Press, 1951) p. 112 and passim.

4. F. A. Beach, "Analysis of Factors Involved in the Arousal, Maintenance, and Manifestation of Sexual Excitement in Male Animals," *Psychosomatic Medicine* 4 (1942): 173–98.

From the wealth of observations I shall mention only a few examples of this. For instance, the male stickleback, whose behavior Tinbergen has described in detail, fights his male rivals when they intrude into his own territory, but seeks to escape when he meets a competitor on foreign territory which belongs to an adversary. When the stickleback meets a rival at the borderline of his territory—a situation which can be experimentally created by introducing a dummy—he is in conflict between contradictory stimuli, one eliciting the fight reaction and one eliciting the flight reaction. His conflict behavior is not dissimilar to that of the human being in a state of indecision. The stickleback, in his dilemma, neither tries to escape nor fights, but starts to dig frantically—behavior which, under normal circumstances, represents the beginning of nest building. In the phase of competitive fighting for territory this digging is premature; set off by the conflict situation, it represents a discharge phenomenon, an "irrelevant movement" without a goal. Similarly, in the stage of courting behavior, if the stickleback is rejected by the female, he turns to the irrelevant movement of fanning, which belongs to the later phase of providing oxygen for the offspring.

Such futile activities have been observed in various species of animals. One of the earliest observers of these activities, Makkink, called them *Uebersprungbewegung* (sparking-over movements), while Masserman speaks of "substitutive symbolic activation."[5] Most ethologists have adopted the term "displacement actions." These displacement actions serve as a safety valve of discharge. Yet as far as the survival value for the individual or for the species is concerned, displacement actions can become as useless as neurotic symptoms in human beings. It is true, however, that in some instances they gain secondary usefulness—for example, as warning signals.

The ethologist Hediger and others have observed an increased frequency of displacement actions in animals living under unusual conditions—for instance, in isolation, captivity, or various degrees

5. G. F. Makkink, "An Attempt at an Ethogram of the European Avocet (Recurvirostra Avosetta L.) with Ethological and Psychological Remarks," *Ardea* 25 (1936): 1–60; Masserman, *Behavior and Neurosis*.

of domestication. The exposure to strange environmental stimuli which do not fit with instinctual habit patterns elicits futile searching movements which can mount to disorganizing panic. But many animals can be calmed by human intervention if this is carried out with empathy and psychological understanding. Particularly those animals used to hierarchically ordered group life are quite ready to have the leadership of their own kind replaced by man's firm and understanding guidance. Yet distortions of instinctual behavior patterns are inevitable in captivity. The sexual behavior of wild animals is highly ritualized; the customs vary from species to species in a series of behavior patterns which range from promiscuity to lifelong monogamy. In captivity, these patterns become more diffuse; for instance, the cycles of heat in female animals are spread out, and sexual precocity, homosexuality, and "hypersexuality," as the ethologists term it, are frequently observed. Hediger assumes that the irregularities of sexual behavior of animals in captivity can be understood as displacement activities. These displacement activities in turn are due to the surplus charge of instinctual centers and the lack of opportunity for discharge of those nervous energies which are primed for activities of subinstincts preparatory to consummatory acts, such as the searching and hunting for food, the conquest of territory, courtship rituals in search of a sexual partner, or threatening maneuvers against rivals. In other words, animals in captivity are largely cut off from these preparatory activities of sub-instincts which consume many of the energies of wild animals in their natural habitat, and precocious sexual activities displace the missing preparatory actions and distort the normal course of integrated instinctual behavior. These displacement activities are frequently accompanied by signs of anxiety and show similarities to human neurotic behavior.[6]

While the ethologic concept of displacement action deals with distortions on the level of consummatory acts, ethologic theory has introduced another concept which explains the integration of instinctual behavior on the higher level of preparation for action—the concept of "appetitive behavior" (*Appetenzverhalten*). The

6. H. Hediger, *Wildtiere in Gefangenschaft* (Basel: Benno Schwabe, 1942).

central excitational mechanism remains blocked when appropriate external stimuli are absent; but in a partial, tentative release, neural and muscular energies are engaged in a random search for external stimuli, the so-called appetitive behavior.[7] In contradistinction to the consummatory acts which run their strictly predetermined course, appetitive behavior is variable and plastic, and may find new stimuli and new chances for integrated actions. The random search of appetitive behavior can be observed in the human infant —as in other mammals—at times when he is ready for the behavior pattern of nursing. At first, there is a release of energy in the random search for external stimuli: a nipple, a finger, or other objects can start the sucking pattern. But this is only a partial release of energy; if all the energies were spent in this agitated search, the hungry infant would be exhausted by a chaos of futile movements. Only when the appropriate nutritional fluid is offered are the full energies released; and the infant's movements then become concentrated and channelized into the smooth performance of the consummatory act of sucking. In the course of development, the integration of sensory stimuli and responsive motor patterns becomes automatized and serves instinctual gratification as well as the purpose of self-preservation. In the further maturing process new instinctual needs arise, and behavior patterns develop from the onset of appetitive search to the integrated achievements of consummatory acts.

Some examples may illustrate the contrast of appetitive behavior and consummatory acts in animals. In Koehler's well-known experiments with the chimpanzee, he hung bananas too high for the animal to reach. When the chimpanzee turned away from the unobtainable object, he became engaged in random play activities with nearby bamboo sticks. In the course of playing with the sticks he discovered that they fitted into each other and thus formed a pole with which he could reach the bananas: the aimless play of appetitive behavior had led to a useful discovery.

Another experiment by Koehler shows the usefulness of appeti-

7. See, for instance, W. Craig "Appetites and Aversion as Constituents of Instincts," *Biological Bulletin* 34 (1918): 91–107; Karl Lorenz, "Ueber den Begriff der Instinkthandlung," *Folio Biotheoretica* (1937), no. 2, pp. 17–50.

tive behavior in contrast to the rigidity of consummatory acts. A dog was placed in a cage, the back door of which was open. A piece of meat was then put in front of the cage, outside the bars. As long as the meat was in direct proximity to the bars of his cage, the dog's appetite remained fierce, blind, and frustrated; but as soon as the meat was moved farther away, he became less tense, his behavior more relaxed and playful. Appetitive behavior permitted a searching roaming around; the dog found the back door and a detour way to gratification.[8]

In this context, Lorenz's experiments with birds provide important clues. He observed that young birds who experienced gratification of their hunger by feedings from the parent or foster parent became engaged in playful pecking activities in preparation for independent self-feeding. If the feeding parent relinquished the young bird prematurely, the tension of frustration would become overwhelming and the playful pecking activities would be blocked. An overstimulating continuous presence of the feeding parent, however, had an equally paralyzing effect on the searching functions of appetitive behavior. An optimal state of reduced tension was most conducive to those playful experiments of the young bird which led to the adult behavior of self-feeding.[9]

Let me now turn from animal to man and examine how far these ethological observations and concepts can be applied to human behavior and its interpretation. Man's childhood is relatively longer than that of any animal. In this period of protected preparation and experimentation the human child is engaged in innumerable variations of appetitive behavior, shaped by imitation and habits. Aberrations of these into displacement actions is possible in many ways. The appetitive behavior manifests itself mainly in play activities which are either progressive or regressive in character. Regressive play—such as thumb-sucking, rocking, and stroking—has, primarily, a soothing effect. On the other hand, children anticipate gratifications in their play activities even when the organism is not

8. Koehler, *Intelligenzpruefungen.*
9. Karl Lorenz, "Der Kumpan in der Umwelt des Vogels," *Journal für Ornothologie* 83 (1935): 137–213.

yet ready for the consummation of these activities. The child plays with dolls and pets; his playful curiosity explores the body and its functions, particularly the genital organs. Stimuli that entail prohibition and danger seem to intensify the search of appetitive behavior, giving rise to steep climactic excitement.[10] Children as well as adults are attracted by dangerous games: they become engrossed in mystery stories; they enjoy the thrill of the roller coaster and the challenge of fate in gambling and fighting. All these playful activities can, in ethological terms, be understood as expressions of human appetitive behavior. They contribute to growth and development in the direction of what the ethologist calls "integrated behavior."

Every step forward in the conquest of self and reality implies the potential danger of a transient disturbance of homeostasis in established behavior patterns. And with this disturbance may come a surplus charge of central excitation which floods the organism with agitation until the appetitive behavior succeeds in its search for new stimuli and new functions. Even if one does not postulate with Hendrick a separate instinct of mastery,[11] one must acknowledge that successfully integrated behavior is directed toward the goal of mastery and accompanied by feelings of euphoria, of trust in self and in reality. The experience of mastery frees the person from the tension of needs and anxieties. It is attained by immediate instinctual gratification—which always implies the satisfaction of ego interests—as well as by those successful displacement actions which the psychiatrist calls sublimations. The learning of a new function is initiated with some anxiety and agitation, as one can observe in the sucking infant who searches for his mother's nipple before he succeeds in the consummatory act. The novice in skating or violin playing suffers for a while under chaotic trial-and-error movements, until the technique is mastered, until the impulses, uncontested by defensive counterimpulses, flow into an elegant

10. This observation has been made by Phyllis Greenacre, "Problems of Infantile Neurosis—a Discussion," in *Psychoanalytic Study of the Child*, vol. 9 (New York: International Universities Press 1954), pp. 18–24.

11. Ives Hendrick, "Work and the Pleasure Principle," *Psychoanalytic Quarterly* 12 (1943): 311–29.

performance which increases self-confidence. A masterful performance—like an integrated behavior pattern—concentrates all energies in the direction of a chosen goal; it extinguishes the tension of
need and anxiety.

But let me turn to displacement actions that fail. Already in
1905, Freud described what the modern ethologist would call displacement actions: The development of sexual excitement in situations of stress and strain, in situations of intense physical and
intellectual exertion, or in states of painful affect such as anxiety,
horror, or dread.[12] This kind of excitement does not lead to an
integrated action in the service of gratification and self-interest;
rather, it leaves the person in a state of frustration and tension. In
his earlier writings Freud had pointed out the physiological
similarities between anxiety and sexual excitement, and he had interpreted anxiety as the result of frustrated libido. Later he emphasized the function of anxiety as a danger signal of the ego, introducing inhibition, repression, and other forms of dissociation in
defense of the organism against the internal dangers of instinctual
drives.[13]

But before an ego develops that can perceive danger signals and
experience anxiety, libidinal and self-preserving interests are automatically integrated in the behavior patterns of the infant, in much
the same way as in the animal. In the light of the theories of integration of instinctual behavior patterns in animals, the question
arises whether instinctual drives as such are menacing to the person—as Freud has postulated—or whether anxiety arises from failure to integrate instinctual behavior patterns at a given stage of
maturation, when the search of appetitive behavior does not arrive
at the satisfaction of consummatory acts. The mobilization of anxiety, with the intensification of neural and muscular energies, as
described by Cannon, braces the organism in its search for new
outlets and in its preparation for appropriate consummatory acts.

12. Sigmund Freud, "Three Essays on the Theory of Sexuality," in *The Complete Psychological Works of Sigmund Freud,* vol. 7 (London: Hogarth, 1953),
pp. 123–245.
13. Sigmund Freud, *The Problem of Anxiety* (New York: Norton, 1936).

a high degree of unmanageable anxiety decreases the probability of mastering achievements.[14]

In a recent paper, Schachtel has pointed out that the developmental progress from the pleasure principle to the reality principle depends on the ability to concentrate energies toward a goal. Under excessive tension of need and anxiety, sensory and motor patterns disintegrate. For example, in a conflict between fight and flight, the thought processes, the function of which consists in testing reality, become vague and diffuse and interfere with the achievement of mastery.[15]

The Swiss psychoanalyst Bally and the Swiss biologist Lincke have—under the influence of modern ethology—interpreted infantile sexuality in man as a manifestation of appetitive behavior. This appetitive behavior of the human child is expressed in exploratory curiosity and experimental play, and is particularly intensified between three and six years of age.[16] In contradistinction to wild animals, the human child grows up under highly domesticated living conditions, and he remains dependent on the protection of his elders much longer. Precocity of sexuality and "hypersexuality" appear more frequently in animals in captivity, while the energies of appetitive behavior of animals in their natural habitat are engaged in instinctual behavior patterns that serve the preparation of independent gratification of needs. Since such independence develops rather late in the human child, the automatic inhibitions imposed on a central excitational mechanism—speaking in ethological terms—have the function of protecting the child from exhausting his energies in trial-and-error movements and a random search for stimuli. There is a wealth of displacement activities which serve as safety valves in situations of overcharge. The domesticated living conditions of the closely knit human family or the ritualized functions of institutional life frequently confront the child with inappropriate stimulation, lack of stimuli, overprohibi-

14. Walter B. Cannon, Bodily Changes in Pain, Hunger, Fear and Rage, 2d ed. (New York: Appleton, 1929).

15. Ernest G. Schachtel, "The Development of Focal Attention and the Emergence of Reality," Psychiatry 17 (1954): 309–24.

16. Bally, Vom Ursprung; Lincke, "Bemerkungen zur Triebpsychologie"; Lincke, "Ueber Angstlust."

tive influences, overstimulation, or inappropriately timed stimuli; all of these may prevent the smooth integration of instinctual needs on the successive oral, anal, phallic, and genital levels of maturation. Hormone disturbances or innate precocity or retardation in the development of sensory and motor patterns belonging to each phase of maturation contribute further to an overlapping of phases and an intensification of displacement actions. If one assumes that the central excitational mechanism is overcharged, the displacement actions may not suffice for discharge, and the failure to integrate may manifest itself in futile agitation and sexual excitement.

When the human child outgrows the animal stage of automatically integrated behavior patterns, he acquires a wealth of tools for the gratification of needs and the pursuit of self-preserving interests—tools that distinguish him from the animal. These tools are consciousness—which acquires increasing continuity in recall and foresight—symbolization, and verbalization, all of which enter into the service of interpersonal communication and the testing function of organized thought processes. With these tools the human child gains a freedom in his appetitive searching behavior which no animal can ever attain. This freedom opens up seemingly unlimited horizons to human aspirations toward omniscience and omnipotence, as Bally has shown in his yet untranslated book.[17] These unlimited horizons become the playground of human fantasy, from which arise the manifold achievements of creative spontaneity, resourcefulness, and everexpanding inventiveness. While the animal is closely tied to predetermined patterns of behavior which leave but little room for variation in his searching activities, man's appetitive behavior roams freely and mobilizes energies which may ultimately change the face of the earth and man's own destiny. This human appetitive behavior is subjectively experienced as freedom—freedom to evaluate the stimuli of one's total situation. This freedom implies the potentiality of failure of integration, which gives rise to anxiety and to neurotic and psychotic development if the limitations of individual and social adaptation are overstepped.

17. Bally, *Vom Ursprung.*

In the presentation of the Schreber case, Freud showed how psychotic symptomatology arises out of the decay of sublimations.[18] In the terms of the ethologist, sublimations could be called displacement actions which successfully reconcile the hierarchy of libidinal and ego interests with the level of maturation and external reality. The libidinal interests are tamed into tenderness, devotion, and respect. The overreaching fantasies of an unleashed secondary narcissism are channelized into rational thought processes which accept the boundaries of reality. Man feels degraded by voracious addiction to oral greed, by ruthless grasping after power and possessions. Sexual relations become meaningless when tenderness and respect are absent.

Disintegration—according to the ethologists I have mentioned— is the result of failing inhibitions. According to their instinct theory, the release of central excitation is automatically blocked until circumstances make consummatory acts possible. In Freud's dualistic instinct theory, disintegration is due to a defusion of instincts. In the development of his theories, the concept of an instinct of self-preservation represents a fusion of narcissistic libido and aggression. Ultimate destruction of life can be visualized by the analyst as the result of defused aggression or failing integration. The automatic inhibitions which prevent boundless—that is, destructive—release of instinctual energies in the animal and in the infant are, in adult man, largely replaced by consciousness, the discriminating, selecting, channelizing, and limiting functions of the ego.[19] Man is the only animal that knows about his destiny to die, his potential to kill. He is not always able to prevent the destructive results of passion, but his foresight of destruction functions as inhibition.

Consciousness of his freedom makes the primary, narcissistic innocence of the animal and the infant forever inaccessible to adult man. His consciousness separates him from the mystic union

18. Sigmund Freud, "Psycho-Analytical Notes upon an Autobiographical Account of a Case of Paranoia (Dementia Paranoides)," in Collected Papers, vol. 3 (London: Hogarth, 1925), pp. 385–470.

19. See, in this connection, Heinz Hartmann, Ernst Kris, and Rudolf M. Loewenstein, "Comments on the Formation of Psychic Structure," in Psychoanalytic Study of the Child 2 (1947): 11–37.

with nature, and his experience of freedom is linked with the sense of responsibility and guilt. Freedom constitutes a threat to him because it implies the danger of disintegration, experienced as anxiety. Man frequently projects his fear of disintegration onto the animal; thus the word *panic* stems from Pan, the Greek god in animal shape. Prometheus—who challenges fate and wrestles with the gods—symbolizes the tragedy of boundless human freedom. The Greeks called this overreaching freedom *hubris*. From the manic ecstasies of narcissistic aggrandizement man is thrust into the abyss of animalic despondency. Shaken in his identity by Dionysiac abandon, he yearns for the rational moderation of Apollonic dignity. But this dignity is genuine only if it is not cut off from the instinctual roots, if it is free in the mastery of instinctual needs—that is, free from the shackles of greed and excessive anxieties and distorting defenses against these anxieties. The freedom of human appetitive behavior implies the freedom to accept the limitations of community life and the unalterable boundaries of nature which guarantee his limited self-preservation. In this acceptance of reality man finds his place in nature and in the human community, which he is in danger of losing in his overreaching *hubris*. With this acceptance he responds to the melody of life like an instrument tuned to the harmonies of nature.

The testing ground for the human ability to integrate needs is the fundamental experience of the Oedipus complex. Here the child encounters the temptation to overstep the boundaries. In Sophocles' tragedy, Oedipus is presented as the hero who is carried away by his *hubris*, the overreaching challenge of fate. The child, at the age of the Oedipus complex—because of the precocity of his germinal glands and his domesticated living conditions—is confronted with the potential temptation to abandon himself to his overreaching secondary narcissism and to the slavery of frustration tied to prohibited desires. Constitutionally or environmentally conditioned impairment of those automatic inhibitions which, according to the ethologist, regulate the innate releasing mechanism may intensify and perpetuate the Oedipus conflict in such a way as to become a lifelong shackle of neurotic behavior patterns. Tenderness, which implies respect for the real needs of the other, helps the child to transcend the Oedipus conflict. If the tenderness needs are thwarted, the tensions of need and anxiety become excessive and bind the child to the object of the hatred and resentment which have resulted from frustration. Gratification of tenderness and exploratory curiosity relax the tension and open the way for displacement actions which have the character of true sublimations and grow into consolidating ego functions and reliable suppressions. The internalized images of parents—to the extent that they can be respected and loved—set flexible limits to the free search of appetitive behavior.

Psychoanalytic treatment is based on the idea that human beings have the freedom to change, even though their behavior is to a certain degree compelled by predetermined patterns. The lever of the therapeutic change is transference, which is closely related to the concept of displacement. Transference, with the help of free association, loosens the bondage of futile excitements and destructive displacement actions which fail to integrate needs. The experience of transference, detached from consummatory action—that is, acting out—reopens the search of appetitive behavior and redirects consciousness toward new alternatives and better integration. The achievements of these alternatives and of a higher degree of integration are experienced by man as the ever-renewed miracle of his creativity.

The Cult and Mythology of the Magna Mater from the Standpoint of Psychoanalysis

Psychoanalysis in its principal contribution to culture, the shedding of light into the irrational darkness of the depths of the soul, must necessarily ever and again come into contact with the problems of man's religious creations. Freud and—among his followers—Reik see above all else in religion and morals the efforts of mankind to form society, in the way of which stand the asocial human instincts, among which the sexual instincts are a particularly dangerous foe. "The sexual urge is incapable of uniting men as does the need for self-preservation."[1]

In neurosis and psychosis also there is the conflict between the demands of society and the instinctual desires of the individual. The psychoanalyst therefore sees many parallels between the psychoneuroses and religion, between "dogma and ideas of compulsion."[2] In neurosis and psychosis the individual cannot bring his instinctual wishes and the demands of society into accord. In the course of a long psychic illness, we observe the "return of the inhibited material," testifying to the greater strength of the instinctual demands, defying inhibition. In similar manner, the psychoanalyst sees in the secular process of religions the insolubility of these deep human conflicts, Kierkegaard's "sickness unto death"— designated by the modern theologian Karl Barth as the hopelessly lost condition of mankind. The impossibility of solving the conflict between the individual and society drives man to the other ex-

Reprinted by permission from *Psychiatry: Journal for the Study of Interpersonal Processes* 1 (1938): 347–78. Copyright 1938 by the William Alanson White Psychiatric Foundation, Inc.

1. Sigmund Freud, "Totem und Tabu," in *Gesammelte Schriften,* vol. 10 (Leipzig: Internationaler Psychoanalytischer Verlag, 1934), p. 91.

2. Theodor Reik, "Dogma und Zwangsidee," *Imago* 13 (1927): 247–382.

treme, to the cosmic representative of society, before whom he is like a helpless child.

In most historical religions, religious experience is in the form of the child-parent relation, and the typical conflicts found in the family recur in religious form. Jones expressed this thought in his lecture on the psychology of religion in the following words: "The religious life is a dramatisation projected into the cosmos of the fears and desires arising from the child-parent relation."[3] The psychoanalytical train of thought stimulated by Freud's *Totem and Taboo* centers chiefly about the typical father-son conflict. The filial opposition arising from the son's sexual jealousy, falls powerlessly in guilt before the father. In myths manifesting the contrast of father and son divinities, we see this conflict portrayed.[4] In history we meet the sanguinary struggles between the followers of the "own god and the alien god." Reik and Fromm have shown that not even Christianity, the source of the doctrine of the unity of father and son, could overcome this deeply human conflict, that in the very dogmatic strife as to the essential unity and equality of father and son, this conflict breaks out anew with bitter stubbornness, the field of action being shifted to tiny details, to an iota. Reik emphasizes the individual ambivalence of man in his relation to his father; Fromm, the shifting of this ambivalence to the opposition between the ruling classes and the ruled.[5]

As we follow the tragic signs of the father-son conflict in the history of religions, the question arises whether in the forms of religion with the mother-son relation in the foreground, the peace and satisfaction attained outweigh the stubborn tendency to discord and to guilt. Freud left this question open: "What place the great mother divinity should be accorded in this development, I cannot say."[6]

3. Ernest Jones, "The Psychology of Religion," *British Journal of Medical Psychology* 6 (1926): 264–69.

4. Otto Rank, *Der Mythos von der Geburt des Helden* (Leipzig and Vienna: Franz Deuticke, 1922).

5. Theodor Reik, *Der eigene und der fremde Gott* (Leipzig: Internationaler Psychoanalytischer Verlag, 1923); Erich Fromm, "Die Enwicklung der Christusdogmas," *Imago* 16 (1930): 305–73.

6. Freud, "Totem und Tabu," p. 180.

Schjelderup found in the analysis of religious individuals that "the mother theme plays a role as important or more so than the father theme for the religious attitude."[7] Jones points out how Christianity strives to appease the need of humanity to worship a maternal divinity in the form of the Virgin Mary.[8] Storfer has dedicated a psychoanalytical study to this subject.[9] Jones describes the tendency to eliminate mother worship from the Christian religion because of the intensification of the father-son conflict resulting therefrom, which increases the sense of guilt and thereby the tendency of believers to self-castration and femininity, as demonstrated in celibacy and in the special clothing of priests. Jones makes clear that in the Christian doctrine of the trinity, the maternal divinity is concealed beneath the concept of the Holy Ghost. The phallic creative power of the Holy Ghost appears to be inseparably connected with the maternal divinity of earlier religions.

In view of the material brought by Jones as to the role of the maternal deity in religion, we must expect an intensification of the tendency to discord in religions with manifest mother worship, for to the fear of the mother arising from the intolerable rivalry with the mighty father, is added all the fear of earliest childhood arising from the necessity of the child's progressive separation from the mother. As a matter of fact, other psychoanalytical works on the mother theme in religions, in particular Daly's work on Hindu mythology and the castration complex and that on the essence of the Oedipus complex, give us no more hopeful picture of human conquest of the mother-son conflict.[10] From Hindu mythology, a flood of uncontrollable fear streams out to us, fear with the en-

7. Harald and Kristian Schjelderup, *Ueber drei Haupttypen der religiösen: Erlebnisformen und ihre psychologische Grundlage* (Berlin and Leipzig: Walter de Gruyter, 1932) p. 107.

8. Ernest Jones, *Essays on Applied Psychoanalysis* (London: International Psycho-analytical Press, 1923). See in particular "The Madonna's Conception through the Ear," and "A Psycho-analytic Study of the Holy Ghost."

9. A. J. Storfer, *Marias jungfräuliche Mutterschaft* (Berlin: Hermann Barsdorf, 1914).

10. C. D. Daly, "Hindu-Mythologie und Kastrationskomplex" [The mythology and castration complex of the Hindus], trans. P. Mendelson, *Imago* 13 (1927): 148–98; Daly, "Der Kern des Odipuskomplexes," *Internationale Zeitschrift für Psychoanalyse* 21 (1935): 165–88.

dangering of the penis as its chief content. This is fear of the maternal divinity, who inspires terror like the Medusa. We find the same prominence of the castration theme in the sagas and myths of the matriarchal Trobriander tribe in Melanesia as reported by Malinowski.[11] The deep ambivalence in the relation of the sexes manifested in this fear is due to the menstruation taboo, according to Daly, to the taboo of the woman just at the time of greatest sexual excitement. Without wishing to cast any doubt on the weight of this argument, I should like to ask whether matriarchal forms of society do not develop typical conflicts characterised by the castration theme. Do these not strive for solution in the acting out of cults and in the production of myths, and do they not stamp religious development with typical features persisting in changed forms of society, due to the special persistence of religious tradition?

In order to answer this question, I have studied the cult and myths of the Great Mother of Asia Minor. I shall indeed cite related forms of religion for purposes of comparison, but my chief object of study will be the details of the Phrygian-Roman Magna Mater religion—psychoanalytical experience has taught that even the abstruse details of any product of the human unconscious, the dream and the symptom, as well as the myth, are of great value for the work of interpretation. The description of the ritual of the cult precedes that of the myths. Even if these myths are later products of creative fantasy, secondary to the rites of the cult and invented to explain them, they have a value for analytical interpretation similar to the subsequent associations of the dreamer for the interpretation of his dream.[12] In the interpretation of cult and myth, I shall endeavour to explain psychoanalytical terms in order to be understood by the nonanalytical reader, as well as the analytical.

---

11. Bronislaw Malinowski, *Das Geschlechtsleben der Wilden in Nord-West Melanesien* (Leipzig: Grethlein, 1931). For the English translation see *The Sexual Life of Savages in Northwestern Melanesia* (New York: Liveright, 1929).

12. William Robertson Smith, *Lectures on the Religion of the Semites* (New York: Appleton, 1899).

In Asia Minor, traces of a matriarchal society have lingered especially long, although the bearers of these traditions have changed frequently, due to the invasion of various races. Herodotus writes of matrilinear inheritance among the Lycians in Southern Asia Minor. The Greek sagas of the Amazons point to Asia Minor, too, the home of the Great Mother, known under the names of Cybele, Cybebe, Mâ, Ammas, Agdistis, Artemis of Ephesus, and magna deum mater.[13] Her cult spread far and wide in the Roman Empire, awakening as it did half-forgotten memories of related maternal deities. In other lands, we frequently find maternal deities united in a triad with a father and a son deity—in Egypt, Isis, Osiris and Horus; in Sidon, Astarte, Baal and Esmum; in Babylon, Baalat, El'Kronos and Adonis; in Carthage, Tanit, Ball-Hammam and Esmum.[14] In Asia Minor, on the contrary, the Great Mother supplanted all other gods with the exception of her "Paredros" Attis, who united features of son and lover. Zeus, the son of the Mycene mother of the gods, Rhea, not only kills his father Kronos, but also drives his mother far into the background, due to alterations in mythology brought by the later Greek culture.[15] Attis, however, remains merely the companion of Cybele, never named nor worshipped without her. It is not until much later, in the union with the Persian Mithras, the sol invictus of the end of antiquity, that Attis acquires masculine authority, and the eunuch becomes a lord of procreation; in his union with Zeus Hypistos, he becomes the paternal lord of heaven.[16]

13. Eduard Meyer, *Geschichte des Altertums* (Stuttgart and Berlin: J. G. Cotta, 1907), pp. 562–63.

14. Wolf Wilhelm Friedrich Baudissin, *Adonis und Esmun* (Leipzig: J. C. Hinrichs, 1911), p. 15.

15. Meyer, p. 645.

16. Henri Graillot, *Le Cult de Cybèle, mère des dieux à Rome et dans l'empire romain* (Paris: Fontemoing, 1912). This work represents the main source of these and the following remarks. Other sources are: Hugo Hepding, "Attis, seine Mythen und sein Kult," in *Religionsgeschichtliche Versuche und Vorarbeiten* (Giessen: Wünsch und Dieterich, 1903); Franz Cumont, *Die orientalischen Religionen im*

The Indogermanic Phrygians, who, about 1200 B.C. wandered from Thrace to Asia Minor, are especially connected with the worship of Cybele, but the inexplicable name Cybele points to times before the Phrygian immigration. Cybele is almost identical with Rhea or Gaia of the Mycene culture and is closely related to the Greek Demeter and the Thracian Kotyto. On the other hand, she has many characteristics of the semitic Mother of the Gods Atergatis, Ishtar, Astarte, and of the Syrian Dea, the Cypric Aphrodite, and the Egyptian Isis. The syncretism of the Roman Empire almost completely obliterated the distinctions between these individual deities.

The character of the Asiatic Mother of the Gods has strange and awful features, as has the god Kali of the Hindus, described by Daly.[17] Freud has demonstrated in the feeling of strangeness an inhibited feeling of familiarity.[18] In the image which her worshippers have made of the Great Mother, we find both characteristics, that of familiarity and that of strangeness, the "fascinans" and the "tremendum," as the religious psychologist Rudolf Otto has called the opposing currents of feeling in religious experience.[19]

Sharply contrasting emotions are aroused by this goddess of mountain peaks and caves of the earth, of procreation and birth, and none the less, of death and destruction, sending the horrors of war. She protects burial places, the dead return to her. From her lap spring trees, plants and springs, but also stupefying vapours. She is the mother of dreams and prophesies, it is she who robs men of their sanity, who sends the dizzy rapture of orgasm. She alone can heal the mad, she alone can forgive sin. The Great Mother is the founder and protectress of cities; she wears a crown of city walls (mater turrita), but she destroys these same walls herself in

---

römischen Heidentum, 3d ed. rev. (Berlin: Burkhardt-Brandenburg, 1903); Sir James George Frazer, *The Golden Bough,* 12 vols. (London: Macmillan, 1927), in particular pt. 5, vols. 1 and 2, "Adonis, Attis, Osiris."

17. Daly, "Hindu-Mythologie und Kastrationskomplex."

18. Sigmund Freud, "Das Unheimliche," in *Gesammelte Schriften,* vol. 10 (Leipzig: Internationaler Psychoanalytischer Verlag, 1934), p. 394.

19. Rudolf Otto, *Das Heilige* (Breslau: Trewendt und Gramer, 1922). For the English translation see *The Idea of the Holy,* trans. John Wilfred Harvey (London: Oxford University Press, 1923).

the frenzy of love. She coaxes the lions and snakes from their hiding places and charms them. Apollonius describes the Great Mother in the following terms: "A wealth of fruits fell from the trees, the earth brought forth flowers before her feet, the wild animals forsook their lairs and came to her wagging their tails in friendliness, bountiful streams of water sprang from the desert peaks of Dindymon."[20] When the stormy winds of spring sough in the mountain forests, the goddess rides through the land in her lion-drawn chariot, with a wild host of corybants, a crowd of phallic spirits.

The mother of all things seems to be both man and woman; she begets the very phallic spirits who fructify her in turn.[21] The phallic symbol, the black meteoric stone, is one of the oldest tokens of the Mother of the Gods. In her service, the phallic dactyles of the mounts of Ida mine the ore in the deeps of the earth like the giants and pygmies of Northern fairy tales.[22]

Originally the Mother of Earth is confined to one small locality, as can be seen from the numerous local epithets, usually derived from the mountains dedicated to her, as: Dindymene, Idaea, Berecynthia, Sipylene, Pessinuntia. On Pessinus, in the homeland of the Cybele-Attis cult, a theocratic priestly state sprang up about the world-famous shrine of the deity, which persisted into Roman times, though never attempting to spread its power by conquest. Then it fell, a prey to internal intrigues. The form of society which originated about the worship of the deity remained strictly local, it did not possess the thirst for conquest of peoples whose principal object of worship is a father-god. Bachofen,[23] however, has pointed out that there are numerous traces of maternal worship persisting as a deep chitinous layer in the Greek and Roman religions founded

20. Apollonius Rhodius, *Argonautica* (Leipzig: Teubuer, 1928), book 1. For the English translation see *The Argonautica,* trans. Robert C. Seaton (New York: Macmillan, 1912).

21. Albrecht Dieterich, *Mutter Erde, ein Versuch über Völksreligion* (Leipzig and Berlin: B. G. Teubner, 1925), p. 83.

22. Meyer, *Geschichte des Altertums,* p. 647.

23. Johann Jakob Bachofen, *Urreligion und Antike Symbole,* ed. C. A. Bernoulli, 3 vols. (Leipzig: Philipp Reclam, 1926) and *Mutterrecht und Urreligion* (Leipzig: Kroner, 1927).

on paternal authority. Dieterich, in *Mutter Erde*,[24] has described the religious reality of this deep layer. These occidental religions were very ambivalent to the Great Mother of the Orient. The Athenians had a metroon, a temple of Meter, from the fifth century on, but the cult of Attis was despised up to the fall of Greek culture.

The Romans, who raised the rights of the father, the patria potestas, to the limits of absolutism, only returned to the ancient Asiatic maternal deity at a time of greatest need, in the Second Punic War, when Hannibal was on Italian soil. They then transported the idol of the Great Mother, the meteoric stone, in sacred procession according to the directions of the oracle to the Roman Palatine. Along with political consideration for the Attalides of Pergamon, and the wish to place a rival strong in tradition in opposition to the Carthaginian mother goddess, the virgo caelestis, the necessity of giving the lower classes a comfortress, discouraged as they were by war and bad harvests, seems to have driven the Romans to this step.

The cult of the magna mater, however, remains for a time a stranger in Rome. It was forbidden for a Roman citizen to enter the Phrygian priesthood, which was present in Rome with the goddess.

In the further course of the spread of the magna mater religion in the Roman Empire, the "weary and heavy-laden" were especially attracted to this cult. After great suffering, after castration in the service of the goddess, they were promised deliverance and ascension into heaven. Women, slaves, and freedmen were the most devout proselytes of this maternal worship. According to the fragments of Diodorus's works extant, the great slave rebellion of the year 134 B.C. in Sicily was instigated by the fanatic prophesies of the disciples of the magna mater.[25] Maternus attempted the assassination of the Emperor Commodius under concealment of the carnival at the Phrygian Easter celebration in Rome. The formation of the Workers' Guilds, the Dendrophores and the Cannophores, which were under the protection of the Great Mother, was forbid-

24. Dieterich, *Mutter Erde*.
25. Diodorus, Book 24, fragments 2 and 5. Cited in Graillot, *Le Cult de Cybèle*.

den in the Oriental provinces, because Rome feared the rise of political parties among these lower classes.

When the paternal power of the emperor rose to insufferable pitch, the rulers, in fear of the wrath of the populace, furthered the cult of the Great Mother. This cult was fused in great measure with that of the Egyptian Isis and the Cappodocian Mâ introduced by Sulla. "The nearer the power of the emperors approached to an absolute monarchy, the more it relied on the Oriental priesthoods for support."[26]

The magna mater became the patron goddess of the Julians. Claudius opened the cult to Roman citizens as well. Julian Apostata was initiated into various mysteries, including that of Cybele; he wrote a textbook on her cult. The Syrian Emperor Heliogabal, who identified himself with the Great Mother, is said to have sacrificed his manhood to her. In the orientalized Rome of the second and third century A.D., contempt for the eunuch priests and their masochistic cult disappeared, contempt which in former times had been expressed in the derisive proverb: "A Phrygian is all the better for a beating." Toward the end of the power of the Empire, there was a day set aside each year when the Roman aristocracy begged in the service of the Great Mother.

If we follow the development of the magna mater religion through the centuries, we come everywhere upon the deep ambivalence which lent the image of this deity the characteristics of "fascinans" and "tremendum," even in ancient times. For the rulers, proud in the consciousness of being the national representatives of the world empire, the Great Mother of the Orient meant a familiar attraction and a strange danger. In the great spiritual disorder of the late Roman Empire, it gave those deprived of home and rights the comfort of a religion of their own.

Christianity came to power due to tenable repressions which it acquired from the masculine and national ethos of Jewry, but it took over a strong anonymous inheritance from the magna mater religion, nor has the longing for the Great Mother been brought to silence in Christianity. The young church in the beginning felt her-

26. Cumont, *Die orientalischen Religionen* p. 35.

self to be a woman, the bride of Christ, and this allegory was celebrated with the richness of images of the Song of Solomon. In the fourth century, Christians began to worship the Virgin Mother Mary, in place of the Virgin Church.[27] Julian Apostata in his time, titled Cybele the Virgin Mother, "Parthenos." No deep religious change was necessary for the Mother of Christ to be worshipped as "Nea Cybele." In Italy, she remains the "Gran Madre."

THE PHRYGIAN-ROMAN CULT

What did the cult of the Great Mother mean to her individual worshipper? Here, there was a development from the crude, barbaric natural religion, with its very ancient traditions, to a differentiated religion of mystery, which was able to compete successfully with young Christianity, appealing as they both did to the "weary and heavy-laden." In studying this development, we ought to be able to see the old nature religion in the sublime richness of form of the mystery religion.

The Phrygian cult[28] of Cybele and Attis, as taken over by the Romans, began on March 15 with the feast of the Cannophores, the bearers of rushes, which was commemorative of the birth and putting away of the son god Attis.[29] According to one version of the myth, the child Attis was found by the goddess set out in the bulrushes.[30] From this feast day on, the believers prepare themselves with fasting and religious ceremonies for the death of the young god. On the day of Attis' death, March 22, the day of the Dendrophores, a spruce tree, wound with bindings and bedecked with flowers like a corpse was carried into the temple of the magna mater, and there mourned with loud wailing. This custom reminds one of similar traditions described by Mannhardt in *Baumkultus*

27. F. C. Coneybeare, "Die jungfräuliche Kirche und die jungfräuliche Mutter," *Archiv für Religionswissenschaft* 8 (1905): 373–83 and 9 (1906): 73–86.

28. See footnote 16 above for sources of the description of this cult; see also the group of articles entitled "Gallos" in the Pauly-Wissowas *Realencyklopädie der Altertumswissenschaft* 8:674–82.

29. Compare with recurring myth motif in Sigmund Freud, "Moses ein Aeypter," *Imago* 23 (1937): 5–13.

30. Graillot, *Le Cult de Cybèle*, p. 149.

der Germanen und ihrer Nachbarvölker and in *Antike Wald- und Feldkulten.*[31]

Followers who wished to enter the order of serving priests, the Galloi, identified themselves with the dying god, in order to dedicate themselves completely to the goddess. They worked themselves into a state of frenzy near unconsciousness by means of dizzy swirling dances with excessive contortions of the body, accompanied by the violent stimulation of the rhythm of monotonous mourning music. Piercing cries were mixed with the shrill notes of Phrygian flutes, the droning of bronze cymbals (cymbalon) and the dull beat of the hand drum (tympanon). Lucretius describes how this music overpowered the senses and brought on the ecstasy of the Mystes, in which they felt no more pain. They inflicted wounds on themselves in the sword dance and castigated themselves with ankle whips made of leather and bone, sprinkling the altar of the goddess with their blood. This continued until at the peak of exaltation on "dies sanguinis," March 24, every one of the Galloi voluntarily castrated himself, cutting off the entire genitals with a consecrated stone knife (acuto silice) or a fragment of pottery. The use of bronze or iron was forbidden for this act. Women who dedicated themselves to the goddess in like manner cut off one or both breasts.[32]

The celebration on March 24 reminds one of the orgiastic feasts of Dionysus or the Sabazios mysteries of Thrace, the home of the Phrygians. Most authors (Graillot, Hepding) believe, however, that the Phrygians took over these savage acts of self-multilation from neighboring semitic peoples, among whom the sacrifice of the genitals had been moderated in the course of time to circumcision. Eduard Meyer on the other hand, assumes that the custom originated from older previous dwellers in Asia Minor. The instrument of the Stone Age testifies to the great age of the cult.

31. Wilhelm Mannhardt, *Der Baumkultus der Germanen und ihrer Nachbarstämme* (Berlin: Gebrüder Borntraeger, 1875) and *Antike Wald- und Feldkults* (Berlin: Gebrüder Borntraeger, 1877).

32. Graillot, *Le Cult de Cybèle*, pp. 256, 296, 293. It is to be noted that March 24 is the Phrygian "Holy Friday."

Lucian[33] describes how the Dea Syria Mâ was worshipped later in Kappadocia, adjacent to Phrygia. The Bellonarians, who corresponded to the Galloi, held similar orgiastic feasts in spring. Here, according to his report, the flood of orgiastic emotion even spread to the onlookers and they, too, castrated themselves. With their genitals in their hands, the worshippers ran through the streets and threw them into some house, from which they then received women's clothing, according to custom. In spite of cauterisation with boiling oil, many died of the castration wounds. The victims were carried outside the city and covered with stones. The bearers of the bodies were considered unclean for seven days.

According to Phrygian custom, the sacrificed genitals and the masculine clothing of the Galloi were carried into the innermost shrine, the bridal chamber of Cybele, where they were washed, annointed, and possibly guilded, then ceremoniously buried. According to another version, they played a part in the mystery cult in the Kernophorie, when the "Kernos" or offering vessel containing the consecrated genitals was carried in solemn procession on the heads of the priestesses.

The Galloi henceforth wore only women's clothing, richly decorated with pictures of the gods. They were carefully anointed; they wore long hair, which they offered to the goddess from time to time. Their bodies were freed of hair and rouged like a woman's, often tatooed. Latin and Greek writers usually speak of the Galloi in the feminine.[34] They often wandered through the country as begging monks, performing their ecstatic dances and scourgings, and breaking into prophecy in their ecstasy. The onlookers gave them presents and fed them. From this form of religious exercise, arose the concept of fanaticism (from fanum—sanctuary). These "fanatici" of Cybele were in the thralls of the goddess, her "famuli," they were excluded from the masculine struggle for life. To be filled with the Great Mother, to be possessed by her, was the only form of life they desired.

33. See Cumont's article on the Galli in the Pauly-Wissowas *Realencyklopädie der Altertumswissenschaft* 8:679–82.

34. Gaius Valerius Catullus, *Catulli Carmini*, 63. 12: "Agite ite ad alta, Gallae, Cybeles nemor simul."

The sacrifice of human castration in the mystery religions was gradually replaced by the offering of a steer or male sheep, the taurobolium or criobolium, an offering taking place in other mysteries as well. Clemens Alexandrinus, who was initiated into the Phrygian mysteries before he became a Christian, writes in a characteristic manner of this matter: "Zeus tore out the vires of a sheep and threw them into the lap of his mother Dea, under the false pretense of punishing himself for his passionate embraces, and acting as though he had castrated himself."[35] Celibacy among priests is apparently also a substitute for castration. The mystery cult necessitated a priesthood of various ranks as well as numerous cult servants. Priestesses also played an important role though a subordinate one. The leadership lay in the hands of the Archigalles, of whom several Latin writers, Firmicus Maternus, Prudentius and Servius declare that they themselves were eunuchs even at times when they enjoyed Roman rights of hospitality.[36] At any rate, the barbaric custom of self-multilation appears to have broken out time and again in late Roman times. A castrated Phrygian, who had become converted to Christianity, founded the sect of montanism, which carried on the heritage of the Phrygian cult in rigorous ascetic sexual morals and ecstatic readiness for martydom. Mohammedanism carries on the ecstatic tradition in the dancing Dervishes.[37] The Russian sect of the Scoptzes introduced ceremonial castration in their religious rites as late as the eighteenth century.[38]

THE MYSTERY CULTS

The peculiarities of the Cybele mystery are apparently difficult to separate from the confusion of syncretic fusions with other antique mysteries, even for the specialist. Into all these mysteries had penetrated the orphic-pythagoric teachings of a half-philo-

35. Eusebius Pamphili, *Evangelicae Praeperationis*, 2. 2. Cited in Graillot, p. 156.

36. Julius Firmicus Maternus, *Matheseos*, 3. 6. 22; Prudentius, *Contra Symmachi Orationem*, 2. 51; Servius, *Ad Aeneide*, 9. 115. Cited in Graillot, p. 231.

37. Erwin Rohde, *Psyche*, vol. 2 (Tübingen: J. C. B. Mohre, 1921), p. 27.

38. Marc Lanval, *Les Mutilations sexuelles* (Paris: Le Rouge et le Noir; Brussels: LeLaurier, 1936), p. 137 ff.

sophical, half-theosophical belief in the reincarnation of the soul. The deep secrecy surrounding the cult and the teachings of the mysteries makes it hard for later generations to form a clear picture of these matters.[39] The metric bible of the neoplatonist Proklos has not been preserved to us. The semi-pedantic, semi-fantastic work of Julian Apostata on the magna mater does not reveal the secret of the mystery cult. We must therefore rely for our information on Firmicus Maternus and Clemens of Alexandria, who from their Christian standpoint could hardly do the mysteries justice.[40]

The Oriental mysteries were "different from the closed cult brotherhoods of Hellas, into which one had to be born as citizen of a city, or member of a phratry, to share in their blessings."[41] Strangers to the tribe could be taken into the cult of Cybele and that of Isis by adoption by the Great Mother. These strangers found in the other members of the cult a new family. In the worship of the magna mater, we see the longing of the worshipper to make certain of his relationship to a parent, to become by sacramental act the child of this Great Mother for the after life.[42]

The requirement for admission to the initiations into the mysteries was ritual purity. In the Attis mysteries this was attained above all by refraining from eating foods prepared from seeds. Rubbing with bran or clay was part of the purification. In both rites, the connection with mother earth and her fruits is clear. These preparations preceded the lower initiations, consisting of ceremonial eating and drinking. The cult musical instruments, the tympanon and the cymbalon, contained the food and drink of the sacrament. The taking of this sacramental nourishment was the first act in the cult drama of the union of the worshipper with the maternal deity. In the Eleusinian mysteries, the quaffing of the kykeon, a spiritous liquor made of barley corn, turned mourning

39. See Graillot, Le Cult de Cybèle, pp. 150 ff., and Hepding, "Attis," pp. 155 ff. for description of the Mystery Cults.

40. Julius Firmicus Maternus, De Errore pro profanorum Religionem, Hahn Edition, chap. 3; Clemens Alexandrinus, Protrept. 2. 15 (Dindorf).

41. Rohde, Psyche, vol. 1 (Tübingen: J. C. B. Mohre, 1921), p. 287.

42. Albrecht Dieterich, Mutter Erde, p. 91, and Albrecht Dieterich, Eine Mithrasliturgie, ed. Otto Weinreich (Leipzig and Berlin: B. G. Teubner, 1923), p. 146.

into joy, the pain of parting into the joy of reunion. The initiate of Attis spoke these words:

> I have eaten from the tympanon,
> I have drunk from the cymbalon,
> I am the initiate of Attis.

This mystery verse served the worshipper as "signum ut in interioribus partibus homo moriturus possit admitti."—Firmicus.[43] Thereafter, the initiate might be admitted to the temple's holy of holies, which was underground like the old cave sanctuaries. Here, in the bridal chamber of the goddess, he underwent the most sacred consecration. The climax of the initiation into almost all mysteries was a marriage with the deity. But this symbolic marriage involved no love relationship. The initiate entered into the wedding chamber of the goddess as one about to die. Darkness surrounded him, and the ghostly flicker of torches. He was actually buried—he had to go down into his grave. The wailing for the dead rumbled in his ears. True, Attis was mourned, not he, but the initiate might well think the latter was the case. Over his grave, the "taurobolium" or "criobolium" was performed, and he was soaked with the blood of the animal whose genitals were offered to the goddess in place of his own. Out of the tension between fear of death and anticipation of bliss, he might say with Apuleius, one of the followers of Isis, "I have touched the shores of death, I have rested my foot upon the land of Proserpine, I have passed through all the elements and have returned from thence, in the underworld, I have seen the sun dazzling with purity. I have seen the high gods and the low and have worshipped them near at hand."[44] The following is from the ritual of a Lower Italian mystery religion: "I have entered into the lap of the queen of the underworld."[45] The sacred wedding which is here celebrated is death. Dieterich is of the opinion that in some mysteries the union with the deity was

43. Julius Firmicus Maternus 18. 1, 2.

44. Apuleius, *Metamorphoses* 11. 23, Accessi confinium mortis et calcato Proserpinae limine per omnia uectus elementa remenaui; nocte media uidi solem candido coruscantem lumine; deos inferos et deos superos accessi coram et adoraui de proxumo.

45. Fritz Kern, *Orphicorum Fragmenta* (Berlin, 1922), frag. 32, par. c, v. 8.

carried out in the form of a more or less symbolic coitus. Thus, in the Sabazios mysteries, "the snake was drawn across the lap of the initiate." "The rite can have no other meaning than that of a sexual union of the deity with the initiate." Dieterich gives a similar interpretation to the synthema of Clemens Alexandrinus, described by Arnobius: "Ieiunavi atque ebibi cyceonem; ex cista sumpsi et in calathum misi, accepi rursus in cistulam transtuli." Dieterich's interpretation is a follows, "A pudendum must be meant, in this rite. . . . In believing as I do that a phallus was taken from the chest, that something was done with it, that it was then laid in the basket and later taken out of it and put back into the chest, in believing that what was done with the phallus corresponded with that done with the snake in the above ritual, it seems to me that I am only giving voice to a rather probable surmise." Dieterich gives as a further basis for his theory: "the deity is always the masculine element, with whom humans unite physically."[46] Piccard assumes that the chest contained a phallus, and the basket a cunneus, and that the initiate took them and put the one in the place of the other as a symbol of sexual intercourse.[47] Wehrli bases his explanation on the myth of the union of Demeter and Jason in the plowed field, and of the birth of Pluto. He believes that in the mysterious Eleusinian rite, two events were acted out together, a sacrificial marriage *hieros gamos* and the experience of birth.[48]

We see from this difference of opinion how well the equivocal formula of the cult hides its secret. It might occur to a psychoanalyst that in the dark secret which aroused fear and bliss in the initiate, no rationally defined episode of adult sexual life is depicted, but that in this climax of the cult drama, which was designated as "looking on," the initiate relived the fears of early childhood as he looked upon the parents and experienced their

---

46. Dieterich, *Eine Mithrasliturgie*, pp. 123–24; Arnobius, *Adversus Nationes* 5:26.

47. Martin P. Nilsson, "Die Eleusinischen Gottheiten," *Archiv für Religionswissenschaft* 32 (1935): 79–141. See in particular p. 121 where the author refers to Picard, "L'Episode de baulo dans les mystères d'Eleusis," *Revue de l'Histoire des religion* 95 (1927): 220 ff.

48. Fritz Wehrli, "Die Mysterien von Eleusis," *Archiv für Religionswissenschaft* 31 (1934): 77–104.

incompletely understood and variously interpreted adult sexual life, so familiar and yet so strange and awful. The initiate might thus be freed of his childish fears and his capacity for love and for religious bliss increased. The above digression contains a mere conjecture as to the meaning of the Cybele mystery and is not intended to anticipate the explanation in a later section. Let us now return to the description of the mystery of Cybele. The followers of Attis were also delivered from the fear of death caused by their descent into the Chthonic sanctuary, and by the animal sacrifice. A light dispelled their fears, accompanied by a proclamation of ascension; the initiate was feted as one "reborn into eternity."[49] He was given milk and honey, like a newborn babe. At the same time, he experienced the hieros gamos with the Great Mother; he was enthroned beside her image, invested with the insignia of the god Attis, and worshipped by the multitude of the faithful.

This return to intimate nearness to the mother, as in earliest childhood, together with the idea of the most intimate sexual relationship with her is one of the deepest wish fantasies of mankind. The clearly sexual character of this wish apparently became more and more manifest in the course of development or decadence of the faith. Augustine describes the feast of the lavatio, the washing of the image of the goddess, which followed the hilaria —the feast of ascension of Attis—after a day of rest. In the feast of the lavatio, the marriage of Cybele and Attis was celebrated in liturgy and song in none too chaste words.[50] The Roman feast of hilaria ended in wild masquerades, and their usual accompaniment of sexual freedom.

The tendency to disclose the secret of incest, which was only hinted at in the myths, appears to be a later phase of the cult, one which is designated in the study of the neuroses as the return of the inhibited material from repression. The bacchanalia which were celebrated in the second century B.C. at Rome caused such a scandal, according to Livius, because of their "shamelessness" that the senate repressed these mystery feasts by force. Cumont however considers the accusations, which even rose to hinting at ritual

---

49. Cumont, *Die orientalischen Religionen,* p. 63.
50. Aurelius Augustinus, *De Civitate Dei* 2. 4.

murder and omophagia, as ill-founded. But the drunken orgies of these nightly feasts, uniting the two sexes in the cult of the phallus, could not help but offend the "frosty morality" of the senate. Similar "disgraceful scenes in the Sabazios mystery cults" led half a century later to their suppression, as well. When later centuries raised the ban, the tendency to lay aside the inhibitions must have become even more pronounced. Philosophical and theosophical speculation had, indeed, read into the mystery of Cybele and Attis the deliverance of the soul from the bonds of matter. A defender of this faith even found it possible to say of the Gallos Pileatus, bedecked with the Phrygian cap, "Et ipse Phileatus Christianus est."[51] But the laying aside of the inhibitions, at first felt as a certain release of the individual from religious fears, must have caused qualms of conscience, with the further advance of this development, and this paved the way for Christianity's conquest over the mystery religions.

THE CYBELE AND ATTIS MYTHS

In order to understand the peculiar rite of sacrificial castration of the Phrygian Galloi and its later forms of development, we must consider the myths which surrounded this ritual. These myths, as indicated above, appear to supplement the cult in much the same way associations supplement the manifest dream.

There are numerous Attis myths, of two principal versions, a Lydian and a Phrygian, the former with strong similarities to the myths of Adonis, in which Attis is killed by a boar, and the latter with the fatal castration of Attis as the climax. The Phrygian form predominated, in time, over the Lydian.

The Phrygian myth has been handed down to us by Timotheus of the Eleusinian order of priests, the Eumolpides, who strove to have the Serapis cult introduced into Alexandria under Ptolemy I. The works of Timotheus are not extant, but Arnobius and Pausanias used his works as their source.[52] Arnobius contaminated this

---

51. Aurelius Augustinus, *In Johannis Evangelicus Tractatus* 2. 1, 6.
52. Arnobius, *Adversus Nationes* 5. 5 ff.; Pausanias, 7. 17.

with another work; Hepding has isolated the two. From this source, we learn of the following myth of Timotheus:

Zeus attempted unsuccessfully to rape the Great Mother in her sleep. His seed was spilled upon the earth, and brought forth a dreadful hermaphrodite, Agdistis—one of the auxiliary names of the magna mater. This monster of two sexes obeyed neither god nor man, but destroyed all in his wantonness. Bacchus got the better of it on the advice of the gods, by a trick. He filled Agdistis' well with very strong wine, and when he had fallen into a drunken sleep, Bacchus fastened the male genitals of the hermaphrodite with a lasso[53] to a tree, so that Agdistis, springing up from his sleep, castrated himself. The blood which flowed from the severed penis soaked into the earth, and a pomegranate tree grew from it. Nana, the daughter of the River Sangarios—also a manifestation of the nature goddess of Asia Minor—put one of the fruits of the tree in her lap, and became pregnant from it. She was condemned to death by hunger by her father, as a maid disgraced. She was rescued by the gods, and bore a son, Attis, whom Sangarios put out to die, and who was in turn rescued by a goat, which gave him to suck. (Arnobius considers the etymology of the name Attis to be either from the word goat, or from the Lydian term for "darling.") Agdistis loved the beautiful Attis, as he grew; she made him her lover, and gave him gifts of game. Attis boasted that he had brought down the game himself, and betrayed Agdistis' love in his cups. King Midas of Pessinus wanted to marry Attis to his daughter. Agdistis appeared at the marriage feast in a fury, and caused all the guests to go mad. The king castrated himself. Attis tore the syrinx (flute) from Agdistis' clutches and ran in bacchanalian rage through the forests, threw himself under a pine tree, and killed himself by cutting off his genitals. Filled with remorse, Agdistis begged Zeus to bring Attis back to life. But Zeus granted only that his body should not decay, that his hair should continue to grow, and that his little finger should remain alive and move. Agdistis buried Attis in Pessimus, and founded his cult.

53. "Lasso" equates with *bolus* in Latin, which is to be found again in the Latin *taurobolium*, the sacrifice of a steer.

In the second source used by Arnobius, the Great Mother is born from one of the stones which Deukalion and Pyrrha threw behind them after the great flood, in order to create men. She loves Attis in his beauty, and knows that it is his fate to live only as long as he knows no woman. She tries to break up his marriage with the daughter of King Midas by breaking down the walls of the city, closed for the wedding feast, with her head. When Attis sees her, he goes mad, and cuts off his genitals under a spruce tree. The Great Mother washes and anoints the penis, wraps it in a cloth and buries it. Violets spring up from the blood and the penis, surrounding the spruce tree with their beauty. Attis' bride mourns him with the Great Mother, swathes him in soft woolen wrappings, and kills herself by cutting off her breasts. An almond tree grows up on her burial mound.

In the form in which Ovid hands down the myth, Cybele binds Attis in chaste love, and makes him promise to remain untouched. When Attis falls in love with a nymph and breaks his promise, the nymph is killed by the magna mater, Attis goes mad, hacks at his body, and castrates himself with the words, "Pereant partes quae nocuere mihi." Arnobius, in his version, gives the words of Attis as follows: "There, take these genitals—you caused trouble enough on their account." In the metamorphosis of Ovid, Attis is changed into a pine tree.[54]

In the version of Servius, the high priest of Cybele, Attis is pursued by the homosexual love of the King of Phrygia. As he flees before him, he and the king both castrate and kill each other.[55]

In the hymns of Hippolytus, which have been interpreted by the gnostic sect of the Naassenians, Attis is a shepherd, born from an almond tree. He is the lover of the Great Mother and castrated by her.[56]

The Lydian myth of Attis is much similar to that of Adonis of Byblos, the beloved of Baalat, and to that of the Babylonian Tam-

---

54. Ovid, *Fastorum*, Merkel edition 4. 179 ff., and Ovid, *Metamorphoses*, A. Riese edition 10. 103–05.

55. Servius, *Ad Aeneide*, Thile and Hagen edition 9. 115.

56. Hippolytus, *Refutatio Omnium Naeres*, Duncker et Schneidewin edition 5. 7. 138.

muz, beloved of Istar. Both myths attribute plant nature to Attis. Adonis springs from the myrtle; Tammuz from the tamarisk. Both commit the sin of Oedipus—they love the mother of the gods. Adonis is torn to pieces by the angry father of the gods, called Ares or Hephaestos according to the Greek version, in the form of a boar, like the Lydian Attis. The boar is also connected with the foe of Osiris, Set-Typhon, the strange Egyptian god borrowed from the Hyksos conquerors.[57]

In the myths as well as in the cult, the joy of resurrection is everywhere of less significance than the mourning over the death of the young god, and in the Tammuz myth, it does not appear at all. The ressurection thought seems to have been introduced into the myths later.

SURVEY OF THE INTERPRETATIONS OF CULT AND MYTHS

The confusion of many ceremonies and saga elements originating at various times and places, in the cult and myths of Cybele and Attis, makes it very difficult to find an interpretation; some authors even doubt that such a myth is capable of interpretation.[58] It is a fact that attempts at interpretation have brought forth very contradictory results, both in olden and in recent times.

The mythologists who interpret Attis as the sun god, in accordance with Macrobius, have arrived at this interpretation from the syncretic sun worship of late heathen times; they have wandered far from the origins of the cult. The ruling explanation today has its source in the "interpretatio physiologica" of Porphyrius.[59] The Attis myth is considered to depict the life of nature, and Attis and other young gods who die and rise again represent the "spirit of vegetation." This interpretation is based on Mannhardt's *Antike Wald- und Feldkulte* and on the large amount of comparative material which Frazer has brought together in his work on this subject.[60] Cumont also interprets according to the vegetation cult: "Attis

57. Baudissin, *Adonis und Esmun,* pp. 94, 138, 155, 136.

58. Hepding, "Attis," p. 213.

59. Macrobius, *Saturnalia,* Eyssenhardt edition 1. 21. 7–11; Porphyrius, according to Augustinus, *De Civitate Dei* 7. 25.

60. Frazer, *The Golden Bough,* in particular pt. 5, vols. 1 & 2, "Adonis, Attis, Osiris."

personifie probablement la végétation brûlée par les ardeurs de l'été avant d'avoir atteint sa maturité et qui durant l'hiver paraît s'affaiblir et pour ainsi dire perdre sa virilité, puis mourir pour renaître au printemps avec un nouvel éclat."[61] Rapp's explanation is similar. He goes further into the details of the myth: "Agdistis, the mother of earth, in order to bring forth nature's forms from the fulness of her own strength, unites the creative power of both sexes, but these two forces soon separate. . . . Out of the unity of life force, the mother (Cybele), vegetative life springs, as the son (Attis). . . . Creative force, in the beginning unbounded, experiences a sudden halt, vegetation dies, Attis castrates himself!"[62]

In Asia Minor, the death of spring vegetation under the glow of the summer sun is indeed a very impressive sight, but if this impression alone were the origin of the spring rites, why should men mourn so deeply over the death of vegetation just when it is in its first green beauty, in spring? This mood would be better suited to July, the time of the Adonis feast, and to the quick wilting of his gardens at that time. But here, the joy of resurrection which follows immediately would be inappropriate. Robertson Smith's idea is that a human being was offered as a sacrifice each year and that this is the basis of the myth of the death of the god.[63] But this brings up the question as to the reason for this sacrifice. The utilitarian motive ascribed by Frazer for the castration of priests, that this was to assure the fertility of the earth is not very satisfactory.[64] Walter F. Otto, in his description of the Dionysus cult, which is closely related to that of Attis, points out how unsuitable is the utilitarian motivation of modern rationalistic thought in explaining the creative forces active in the production of a cult. The tragic fate expressed in the cruel rites of the cults of Dionysus and Attis spurn all harmless interpretations.[65]

61. Hepding, "Attis," p. 129. See mention in Cumont, *Extrait du Bulletin de l'institut archéologique Liegeois* 39 (1909): 5.

62. Rapp, *Lexikon der Mythologie* 2 (Roscher): 1048 ff.

63. William Robertson Smith, *Religionen der Semiten*, trans. Stübe (Friedburg, 1899) p. 316.

64. Frazer, *The Golden Bough*, "Adonis, Attis, Osiris," 1:283.

65. Walter F. Otto, *Dionysus, Mythos und Kultus* (Frankfurt am Main: V. Klostermann, 1933), pp. 23 ff.

The psychoanalyst Lorenz, in his article on chaos and rite, also draws attention to the insufficiency of typical explanations of the "spirit of vegetation." Why this marked ambivalence in relation to this beneficient spirit of vegetable growth, who had to die cruelly before he rose again? Lorenz connects the yearly sacrifice of the youthful god of vegetation with an annual penance for the sin of Oedipus committed against the primal father, inasmuch as the guilt due to this crime threatened to lame man's procreative and productive powers.[66] This interpretation is much more in accord with the emotional violence of the rites of the cult, for desires to murder the father are no distant, mythical matter of the long-forgotten past, but for each successive generation, a conflictful situation forcing its way anew into consciousness. We saw in the development of the Attis cult that the incest thought almost broke into consciousness, and this is still clearer in the Adonis cult. The explanation that the sacrifice of the darling of the mother of the gods was a penance for the sin of Oedipus is therefore a natural one.

Reik in his monograph, *Die Pubertätsriten der Wilden* describes how the sufferings of the son-god are to be considered as penance for the murder of the primal father and how the initiation customs of primitive peoples re-act this penance, in order to free the initiate from his childish tie to his mother sufficiently so that the homosexual relationship to his male tribal companions which replace the former may be strong enough to make him a socially useful representative and protector of the tribal traditions.[67] The cult of Attis has much in common with these initiation customs of the totemistic cults, nor are totemistic features lacking in the myth. But the initiate of the Great Mother does not attain release from her; he rather strengthens and deepens the mother-child tie. Attis and the related son gods lack all heroic traits to make a struggle against the father successful, distorted as the father is to villainy, as Rank points out

---

66. Emil Lorenz, "Chaos und Ritos. Ueber Herkunft der Vegetationskulte," *Imago* 17 (1931): 434–94.

67. Theodor Reik, "Das Ritual," in *Die Pubertätsriten der Wilden, Probleme der Religionspsychologie* (Leipzig and Vienna: Internationaler Psychoanalytischer Verlag, 1919), pt. 1, pp. 58 ff.

in his outline of myths *Von der Geburt des Helden*. In some versions of the Attis myth, the father figure does indeed suffer castration and death. The repression of the father in other Attis myths can probably be explained as Jones does: the denial of procreative fatherhood in matriarchal societies is due to the tendency to avoid the rivalry of father and son in the Oedipus conflict.[68] The cult and myth of Attis are indeed attempts to master the Oedipus conflict. The failure of this attempt results in a regression. The attitude of Attis negates every tendency to successful rivalry with the father. This fundamental attitude of the son-god, repellent to masculine pride, allows the conjecture that the interpretation of myth and cult may give opportunity for penetration into the deeper psychic layers, which in the development of the individual precede the full experience of the Oedipus conflict, and which represent a regressive stage in relation to it. The myth, as well as the dream, is overdetermined, and its possibilities are not exhausted with one interpretation.

Even for the Adonis myth, in the most usual form of which the father-son conflict is so clearly manifested in the killing by the boar, representing the offended father-god, the interpretation by means of the Oedipus conflict does not exhaust the possibilities. Baudissin has demonstrated that an older form of the myth preceded the familiar one. According to the former, handed down by Panyasis (died 460 B.C.) Aphrodite gives the beautiful boy over into the keeping of the underworld goddess Persephone, in a chest. Persephone refuses to give him back. Aphrodite mourns him.[69] In this form of the myth, the conflict with the father seems to have disappeared, and in its place, the mother-son conflict is the keener. The mother goddess is divided into two figures, Aphrodite and Persephone, the good and the bad mother. The ambivalence conflict between son and mother in the mother relationships in the early childhood of depressive patients manifests itself similarly in the division into a fostering and an avenging mother image, which the child cannot fuse into one because his feelings are so

68. Ernest Jones, "Das Mutterrecht und die sexuelle Unwissenheit der Wilden," *Imago* 13 (1927): 199–222.
69. Panyasis *Bibliotheca Apollodoris* 1. 3. 14. 4.

divided. To such a deeply ambivalent relation to the mother goddess, the castration motive seems closely related.

Nock in *Eunuchs in Ancient Religions* finds the motive of self-castration in the desire for a purity which ancient peoples apparently could attain only in this way, and in the wish to be like a child or a virgin, so as to be better able to serve the deity, especially the feminine goddess. Nock also finds the idea prevalent that castration, the relinquishment of the individual's own genital satisfaction, is supposed to increase the fertility of the earth.[70] Eduard Meyer expresses a similar thought in relation to the Attis cult: "Castration is the supreme sacrifice, by means of which to enter into relationship with the deity; castration allows man to approach as near as possible to the nature of the goddess."[71]

This desire to be like the female deity or the ideal of virginity brings up the question as to whether in the religions of mother worship, the ego ideal and the superego formations have feminine character? Roheim reports on the matrilinear, omophagous Papuans, whom he studied from the standpoint of psychoanalysis that their group ideal, the "tonisagari," the generous giver of feasts, is the ideal of a fostering and nourishing mother. The superego of these plutocratic planters has the following motif: "there are no fathers, only mothers. I am one of the mothers, not a father. . . . There are no fathers, no one who will eat you up, there are only mothers, who can be eaten."[72] (To make this motive clear, the explanation should be added that the fathers, deprived of their rights in matriarchal Papua, are rather sadistic in their care of the children—they suck their penes). One can indeed see the beginning of a superego in this readiness to take the mother by force, to get her possessions, her riches, in order to shine with her wealth before others as a generous feast-giver. The superego arises from the introjection of the mother, from the identification with her bounty. This is indeed only the beginning of superego formation,

---

70. Arthur Darby Nock, "Eunuchs in Ancient Religions," *Archiv für Religionswissenschaft* 23 (1925): 25–33.

71. Meyer, *Geschichte des Altertums*, pp. 649 ff.

72. Géza Róheim, "Die Psychoanalyse primitiver Kulturen," *Imago* 18 (1932): 547 ff.

serving the domination of fear. This fear is indeed far from a pronounced sense of guilt, as found in the true building of conscience
in the superego.

In the religion of the Great Mother, the creative sense, which
Freud and Reik have placed at the beginning of human morality
and religion, appears to me to be still weak.[73] Even in the highly
developed mystery religions, ethical elements are in the background.[74] The fasts and purifying ceremonies do not spring from
ethical ideals and duties, they are rather of apotropaic character,
they serve to keep off spirits and bad gods, and to overcome fear.
The concept of sin—through Orphism, even the idea of original
sin was incorporated into the mystery religion—is less moral than
religious. Sin is absence from god, which can be converted into the
saving presence of the deity, not by morally acceptable actions,
but by taking part in ritual. This religious attitude corresponds to
the early stages of superego development in the individual before
the mastery of the Oedipus complex, this is, in general, before the
sixth or seventh year. Before this time, the child still acts according
to the magic point of view, copying the mighty adults around him.
He strives to convert the bad or angry mother into the good
mother, as primitive peoples tried to convert a bad spirit into a
good one, or as the monotheist desires to convert the terrifying
distance from God into blissful nearness to him.

Here, however, there seems to be a fundamental difference between the religions which have nearness to a father god as their
central point, and those whose chief object of worship is a mother
goddess.

Baudissin found in the peoples of Anterior Asia where both
father and mother gods are worshipped that national and ethical
ideas are developed with reference to the masculine deity. The
mother deity, on the other hand, remains morally indifferent. She
is the representative of life and death, of fecundity, of the repro-
ductive and destructive forces of nature. The feminine deity is often represented naked and with marked sexual characteristics. A

73. Freud, "Totem und Tabu," pp. 176, 191; Reik, *Die Pubertätsriten der
Wilden*, p. 131.
74. Rohde, *Psyche* 2:74 ff.

phallic cult is often combined with the mother religion. Cult customs in regard to the origin and destruction of life have been preserved in dependence on the maternal deity with rare persistence.[75]

The idol of fecund maternity, pregnant and often with many voluptuous breasts, with emphasis on the sexual organs, a hint of which can be seen in the Venus de Medici, can be followed in Anterior Asia back to the Ice Age, with the aid of archaeological excavations.[76]

EXCURSIONS INTO PREHISTORIC TIMES

If we desire to follow back the roots of the maternal religion, we must call upon the material of the science of prehistoric times. The religious philosopher Usener says: "All popular religions of which we possess more extensive information are accomplished at the time the peoples are first mentioned in authentic history. They bring their gods and their sagas with them into their historical existence as their ancestral heritage. All that can be determined from authentic sources is the history of the decline of gods and sagas; their rise and development lies beyond the bounds of history."[77]

In this era "beyond the bounds of history," which is inaccessible to human consciousness, like the events of early childhood in the life of the individual, there has been an important reorientation in the last few decades. In 1930, Menghin finished his epochal work on the Stone Age. Even earlier, in accord with Menghin's ideas, the Bonn school of Gräbner and the Viennese school of Pater Wilhelm Schmidt created "the theory of the cultural groups" in connection with ethnological, anthropological, archaeological and historical research, which appears to gain predominance over the evolutional conception of ethnology, as represented by Bastian, Tylor, and Frazer.[78] Without attempting to judge the value of this

75. Baudissin, *Adonis und Esmun,* pp. 19 ff.

76. Leonhard Franz, "Die Muttergottin in vorderen Orient und in Europa," *Der Alte Orient* 35 (1937): 3.

77. Herman Usener, "Mythologie," *Archiv für Religionswissenschaft* 7 (1904): 7.

78. Pater Wilhelm Schmidt has been attacked from many sides. He has been heatedly accused of a subjectively hostile attitude to the sexual life of primitive peoples by an author with closely related philosophy, Josef Winthuis, *Einführung in die*

reorientation, one may say that psychoanalysis cannot afford to ignore this new conception, especially in any attempt at shedding light on the open question of the maternal goddesses, which is so patently connected with the matriarchal cultural groups of the early and later planters.

Kern, who in his survey, *Die Anfänge der Weltgeschichte* takes a position in favour of Menghin, says: "The cult of the magna mater, *'Ammas'* appears to have spread through the world for the first time as a great religion about the middle of the second ten thousand years B.C."[79] According to Kern, Asia Minor was still in protoneolithic times (8000 to 5000 B.C.) the domain of planter culture, whereas in Europe, the three deep cultures, the hunter, the planter, and the shepherd cultures, had already mixed.[80] According to the theory of cultural areas or groups, the group of the planters, of those who cultivated with the hoe or the sharp stick, was the first group who displaced the *acquisitive* by the *cultivative* form of management. How far pure forms of these cultural groups are still extant today, spread as they were for thousands of years over the earth, and later united with other cultures, appears still to be an open ethnological question.[81] To the cultural group of the totemistic hunters, the cultural group of the early planters is in antithetical contrast. Early planter culture is characterised by the matriarchal forms in contrast to totemistic patriarchal rights, moon mythology instead of the sun mythology prevalent among the totemists, weapons for cutting among the planters, weapons for thrusting among the hunters, the quadrangular gabled house among the planters, the conical hut among the hunters. The magna mater and fecundity cult arose among the early planters, and was passed on

---

Vorstellungswelt primitiver Völker (Leipzig: C. L. Hirschfield, 1931). If these accusations be true, the loss to the research interests of psychoanalysis is great. But even so, the great services of this research worker remain a fact, based as they are on his ingenious amassing of an enormous amount of material.

79. Fritz Kern, *Die Anfänge der Weltgeschichte* (Leipzig and Berlin: B. G. Teubner, 1933), p. 61.

80. Ibid., pp. 81 ff.

81. Wilhelm Schmidt and W. Koppers, *Der Mensch aller Zeiten* (Regensburg: Joseph Habbel 1924), pp. 257 ff. The following material is taken principally from this work and from Kern, *Die Anfänge der Weltgeschichte*.

to later mixed cultures. Orgies seem to have been especially developed in connection with the display of the charms of fecundity, in the totemistic-matriarchal mixed culture, which has its ethnological parallel in the Australian natives of today.[82]

If we ask how it happened that there was this antithetic development of the totemistic culture on the one hand and the matriarchal culture on the other, in the mielithicum, that is, in the late Ice Age, we must turn for the answer to the antecedents of these deep cultures, which Menghin has termed the "fundamental cultures." They extend into the protolithicum, into the beginnings of the Ice Age and the tertiary epoch, they are much freer of the antithetical contrasts of the deep cultures, and persisted in their stability according to Kern's estimate, for hundreds of thousands of years. Uninfluenced by other cultures, these game-hunting fundamental cultures are to be found even today, though sparsely, for example, among pygmies and semi-pygmy races. Their stability appears to be due to the harmonious division of work between man and woman among the game-hunters. The man provides food by hunting and the woman by gathering plants. Every want can be supplied by these primitive all-sufficient activities of the two sexes. No hunger occurs, which could only be satisfied by greatly specialised work. Man and woman are in large measure equal on the basis of common effort, family life is monogamous and relatively free of irritation. The relationship to the offspring is predominantly a happy one, and the children are brought up without instilling much fear in them, and without intimidation. The rites of puberty are much simpler than among the later totemists. They are confined to fasting and breaking out a tooth, that is, to the oral sphere, whereas the initiation customs of the totemists are concentrated on the phallic sphere (circumcision and subincision). The organization of society, which is not yet developed from individual and tribe totemism to the characteristic group totemism of the totemistic cultural groups, hardly extends beyond the family. The men of the fundamental cultures are not cannibals, they are not warlike. Fear reactions and aggressive instincts are in great measure

82. Kern, p. 81.

absorbed in the effort at mastery of animals and things. Due to this diversion of his aggressions the tolerance of early man seems to have been much greater than that of later cultures. The peaceful relation of men to each other is reflected in the confidential relation to the "supreme being," in early "primal monotheism." The right to call these primitive forms of religion "primal monotheism" has been disputed often enough in the literature of religious philosophy, but never, the relative freedom from fear as a characteristic of this relationship. If this early epoch of man's development were to be compared with a phase in individual development, as the psychoanalysts see it, one would think of the preambivalent early stage of development of the satisfied infant.[83] To support this view of the fundamental cultures, P. W. Schmidt has brought together a large quantity of material in the third edition of his work *Familie und Staat auf der Urstufe*. This has of course aroused much opposition because it is employed as argument against the evolutionary conception of human development. It contradicts only the idea of a development from a low moral standard to a very high one, which one may doubt on other grounds than those of prehistoric times alone. It does not contradict, however, the idea of a development from comprehensive and understandable simplicity to a complexity that can no longer be mastered by mankind.

In the cultural group of the totemists as well as that of the planters, the balance of the sexes is much more labile. The totemistic hunter, who settled in zones with plenty of game, developed hunting to such a pitch that the whole working capacity of a man was no longer absorbed, as in the fundamental cultures, in the struggle for the preservation of the individual and the family. The surplus productive energy of the man brings about a development in division of work and artistic achievement almost equal to that of the later city cultures. But the totemistic culture is founded on the one-sided preponderance of the man. His constructive, state-building powers produce the complicated social structures, the age classes, the totem and marriage classes. The educational founda-

83. Karl Abraham, *Versuch einer Entwicklungsgeschichte der Libido* (Leipzig: Internationaler Psychoanalytischer Verlag, 1924), p. 90.

tions of this form of society are the strict and cruel rites of puberty, which tear the youth from his mother-tie and introduce the terrified boy into the men's group, the clue to which is the active and passive experience of force. Only the man-to-man relation, not the man-to-woman relation, profits by the sublimation of the incestuous mother tie. Family interests are entirely subordinate to the interests of the tribe, and these latter are the concern solely of the men. This one-sidedness of the totemistic cultural groups of necessity produces the typical cultural defects of a one-sided masculine form of society.[84]

The one-sided economic predominance of the woman in the matriarchal cultural group of the planters also led of necessity to similar cultural defects, due to the tension of ambivalence. In zones where there was not so much game, and which were at the same time more favourable for plant growth (tropical alluvial valleys), the original gathering of plants had been converted by the initiative of the woman into productive cultivation. That led to settling down in one place. It is possible that the strong inimical ambivalent tension between the growing girl and the mother gave her, in anxiety for her own children, the idea of driving into mother earth with the hoe and wringing fertility from her. At any rate, primitive agriculture remained in the hands of the woman, she was the driving force in the sublimation of anal instincts, the human powers which, arising from the production of the body's waste, strives to convert other earthly material and to pile up possessions. The aim is to taste the elixir of power, even though in its most abstract form, the amassing of achievements, or the possession of money. In the matriarchal cultural group, the private ownership of land was introduced for the first time by the woman.[85] Pottery, the spiral roll technique of plaiting, and weaving, are all her inventions. The fact that the planter settled down in one place, led to a fear-inspiring ancestor cult, as he could not leave his dead behind, as did the nomad or the hunter. Among the planters, the dead were buried in a squatting position in the communities of the

84. Schmidt and Koppers, pp. 225 ff.
85. Kern, pp. 50 ff.; Schmidt and Koppers, pp. 256, 539.

living. In the matriarchal cultural group, money was invented. Marketing was in the hands of the woman. On this basis of management, the matriarchate in the early stages of planter culture rose to gynecocracy, but not without arousing violent envy in the man. The one-sided dependence of the household existence on the woman must have been hard for the man to bear, and must have made the conditions for the mastery of the Oedipus conflict unfavorable, this conflict which is so important for human development. It was Abraham's discovery that the fixation of the boy on his mother in the transition period from the oral to the anal phase, that is, in the transition from the purely receptive interests of the child to his first productive efforts, may have a fatal outcome; it may leave behind a disposition to manic-depressive affections.[86] Matriarchal planter culture appears not to have overcome this difficulty of development completely. Masculine development did not detach itself from the nourishing mother. The ideal of the fecund mother goddess, the cults of fecundity indicate constant anxiety as to fertility, similar to the fear of starvation in depressive patients. Matriarchal planter culture is the home of cannibalism. Narcotics (betel, banana beer, palm wine) are unknown to the fundamental and patriarchal cultures; they make their first appearance among the planters. A deep dissatisfaction in the oral instinctual sphere is to be seen in these innovations, due in part to the preponderance of vegetable nourishment over meat, in part, doubtless, to the limitation of the expansive instincts of the man, used to hunting, and to his dependence on the woman.

Matriarchal planter culture is connected with most sanguinary human sacrifices, found repeatedly in all fertility cults. It is hard to understand why human sacrifice as such should be supposed to increase the fertility of the earth. Reik[87] has pointed out that the custom of offering up the firstborn contradicts any rational relation between sacrifice and concern for sufficiency of food; such anxiety would rather appear with the birth of later offspring. But possibly both, the concern as to fertility, and human sacrifice, are the result

86. Abraham, pp. 48 ff.
87. Reik, *Die Pubertätsriten der Wilden*, pt. 1, p. 42.

of an unbroken mother tie, which increases the danger of castration, the result of a general manic-depressive disposition. Then human sacrifice in the matriarchal society would correspond to the elementary suicidal tendency of the melancholic. Reik attributes the sacrificing of a child principally to the fear of the avenging fathers, as the man sees in the children avengers of his father's generation. I do not wish to minimize this important reason for sacrifice of children, but it is of interest that these sacrifices are neither of very great age nor very general. They are rather a local transfer of the primal offering of plants and animals to the human firstborn, which was later confined again to animals. Human sacrifice is found especially in matriarchal cultures. The development of the form of society cannot be without influence on the Oedipus conflict. In the matriarchal family, the insignificance of the father compels a regressive transfer of the conflict tension between father and son to an increased ambivalent tension in the mother-child relationship, just as the too great enhancement of the father's significance in the patriarchal-totemistic family increases the son's castration fear of the father. The negative side of the ambivalence tension in the mother-son relationship is felt not only as a castration threat, but as a threat to life itself, because in the dependence of early infancy, maternal love is essential to the child's welfare. Joan Riviere has shown in her article on "The Genesis of Psychical Conflict in Earliest Infancy" that the lack of mother love revealed when the child experiences hunger is not yet understood by the infant as a *threat to life* but is indeed felt as *fear of death*.[88] Melanie Klein attributes the manic-depressive psychoses to this primal fear.[89] The offering of a child is an ethnological manifestation of the lack of parent love, the sign of increased ambivalence in the parent-child relationship, unknown to the fundamental cultures. In the concern for fertility, we see manifested the fixation on the fear with which this ambivalent tension, this threat to life, pursues many generations.

88. Joan Riviere, "On the Genesis of Psychical Conflicts in Earliest Infancy," *International Journal of Psycho-Analysis* 17 (1936): 401.

89. Melanie Klein, "A Contribution to the Psychogenesis of Manic-Depressive States," ibid. 16 (1935): 145–74.

Bachofen's conception that the matriarchate developed from a period of indiscriminate promiscuity, from a time of "hetaeric swamp procreation" has not been verified by later research.[90] But the paradisical fantasies of an early time of unchecked fertility, corresponding with the unbound care given the infant, are comprehensible as reaction under the heavy burden of concern as to fertility which the fixation on the nourishing mother cannot relinquish.

I am far from considering the matriarchal culture as a paradise for women and feminists, as is often the case. On the contrary, I shall show how envy and hate reactions of the man brought woman's work progressively into slavish dependence. First, the economic predominance of the woman and the matriarchal customs arising therefrom demand of the man the mastery of serious injuries to his pride. The initiation of the male youth, which in the fundamental cultures was not strongly developed, and which was to gain primary significance among the patriarchal totemists, disintegrates in matriarchal planter culture. The initiation of the girl, on the other hand, comes to the front, with ceremonies at her first menstruation, the token of the fecundity of the mother-to-be. The loneliness and seclusion to which the young girl was banned at this time has been traced back as early as Frazer to primitive man's deep-rooted fear of menstrual blood.[91] This ceremony was confined to the individual family, showing the woman's lack of state-building powers in that her libidinous interests do not extend beyond the home. These families unite loosely into villages of democratic character, in contrast to the strict masculine forms of society of the paternal totemists. Amazonian states never did exist, except as a myth born of the fantasy of male Greeks.[92]

The custom of the couvade of the man, which is associated with the second matriarchal cultural group, late planter culture, allows the man to share magic-wise in the labor pains of the woman. This "pseudomaternal couvade" has been attributed by Reik to man's unconscious enmity to the woman and to his masochistic reactions

90. Bachofen, *Urreligion und Antike Symbole.*
91. Compare Daly, "Der Kern des Odipuskomplexes."
92. Schmidt and Koppers, p. 273.

arising from feelings of guilt.[93] It seems possible that "envy of childbearing" also might have a part in the man's enmity to the woman in a culture which so stresses the prestige of the fecund female. This is forced into the background in the paternal cultures by "penis envy," here more important. This "envy of childbearing" however can be demonstrated even in our present-day civilization with the help of analysis.

There are various indications found in everyday habits of a tendency in the matriarchate for female conduct to be accepted as the ideal for the man as well. For example, Herodotus testifies that the men, among the Egyptians, urinated in the female squatting position.[94] In Egypt, many a matriarchal custom was long preserved, such as the beardlessness of the man, whereas the beard worn by the king can be traced to paternal influences.

A further proof of the man's tendency in matriarchal cultures to follow a feminine ideal is recorded in a sentence of P. W. Schmidt in his estimate of the matriarchate in the history of civilization. "How far the self-destructive tendencies of the man may go in matriarchal groups can be seen in the fact that the Indian Schiva-Schakti faith with the worship of the tripurasundari, not only teaches that the deity is a woman, but every true worshipper is accustomed as part of his religious exercises to think of himself as a woman, and his highest aim is to become one."[95]

This form of religious introjection too, belongs in my estimate to the initial stages of superego formation. This must be very detrimental to the consolidation of the masculine ego, and must increase fear of castration, whereas penis envy, on the other hand, is very disturbing to the development of feminine individuality. Envy of childbearing as well as penis envy are signs of high ambivalent tension between the sexes.

The lack of knowledge of primitive man as to male procreation, as often found in matrilinear inheritance, is not considered by Jones as actual ignorance, but as the result of inhibition, to avoid the father-son hatred arising from the Oedipus conflict, just as is

93. Reik, p. 58.
94. Herodotus 2. 35. 3.
95. Schmidt and Koppers, p. 291.

the whole institution of the matriarchate.[96] It appears to me that a tendency to inhibition, to ward off the knowledge of fatherhood, might make the discovery of the actual, complicated relations very difficult. In any case, the denial of fatherhood in the matriarchal family isolated the man greatly, especially when marriage was conducted matrilocally. The share of the man in the care of the children, as observed by Malinowski among the present-day Trobrianders, and by Roheim among present-day Papuans, corrects this isolation somewhat through identification of the man with the mother ideal. But if we follow the development of the man within the matriarchal group, we must come to the conclusion that his economic dependence and isolation in the family force him into reactive opposition, which results in enmity to the woman. The man manifestly has not enough outlet for his dammed up libidinal energy.

This hostile attitude of the man manifests itself in the gradual reformation found in the service marriage, where the man wins the woman by labor (compare Jacob's years of labor for Leah and Rachel) and in the buying of a wife, where the man then employs the services of the woman he buys like those of a slave. The woman is given some protection against this exploitation in the later stages of the matriarchate in the support of her family by her brother. On the grounds of the necessity of such protection, Gutmann explains the growth of exogamy in the matriarchal group, where endogamy is supposed to have been the original form.[97] "The energy with which marriage with a relation was spurned makes it plain that this was once the custom." Originally, there seems also to have been no check on sexual relations between father and daughter, in matriarchal cultural groups.[98] Possibly the denial of fatherhood has a bearing on this one-sided incestuous freedom. But the woman who married into her own group of relations "had no blood aven-

96. Jones, "Das Mutterrecht," p. 199.

97. Bruno Gutmann, *Das Recht der Dschagga* (Munich: C. H. Beck'sche, 1926). There is a reference to this work in an article by Thornwald on the Matriarchate in *Reallexikon der Vorgeschichte*, ed. Max Ebert 8:360.

98. Max Ebert, *Reallexikon der Vorgeschichte*, 15 vols. (Berlin: W. de Gruyter, 1924–32), 8:361.

ger, she was at the mercy of her husband's whim." She herself was also "freer to do harm, to kill her husband or children," when not held back by relatives vouching for her. This picture of the matriarchal family reveals the high ambivalent tension in the relation of the sexes. According to Gutmann's conception, the position of power and protection of the mother's brother arose after the renunciation of incest between brother and sister. The brother then had the right to protect the interests of his sister and her children as their blood avenger, and in this way, to check the unbearable flood of ambivalent tension in the sexual relation of man and woman. In this role of the mother's brother, it is again the man who is the bearer of tribal tradition.

Tribal tradition and ancestor worship were further practiced in the secret societies of the men, which according to Schmidt's ideas, also sprang from masculine opposition to the economic predominance of the woman. These secret societies, in which among many an Indian tribe manifest pederasty was practised, exclude the women from their meetings, on penalty of death. The men, in their secret groups, develop magic arts, by means of which to terrify the women. They make rain and weather spells, and cause the dead to rise again by means of hypnotic and narcotic practices. In contrast to the totemistic age classes, open to all male members of the tribe, here there were requirements for admission into these secret societies. Rank was apportioned according to riches and possessions. Here, the men administer the law, and in the later stages of the matriarchate, they seize the political power. A certain compensation for the envy of childbearing, aroused by the fecundity and economic predominance of the woman, may perhaps be seen in this magic and plutocratic sphere of power of the men's societies.

There remains, however, a dangerous element of restlessness attached to the cultural groups of the early and late planters, which springs from the unbound libidinal and destructive energies of the man. Their primitive agriculture is carried on by the woman, and hunting is limited where the planter settles down in one place. As a result, the man stresses the importance of war and the business of robbery. Headhunting spreads widely especially in the later free-matriarchal cultural groups.

We find the cultural circle of the matriarchal planter as well as of the patriarchal totemistic hunter thus overburdened with destructive instinctual forces, which seem to be due to the unequal part of the two sexes in the duties of self- and family preservation. This disturbs strong family ties and peace within the family, as found in the fundamental cultures in the relations between marriage partners and between parents and children, and also in the monogamous family life of near-human monkeys, according to the description of animal sociology given by Alverdes.[99] Among the totemists, and reactionally, among the planters as well, the emphasis is shifted from the positive tie between man and woman to that between man and man. The steady balance of the positive affectionate tie between mother and son, between man and woman is forced into the background by the overheated orgies of the fecundity cults, which, like the forced sensuousness of the modern neurotic, spring not so much from genital needs as from an unsuccessful attempt to drown the fears caused by the dreadful ambivalent tension between man and woman.

A certain compensation arose where planter cultures were overlaid by conquering shepherd folk. These shepherds form the third of the deep cultures which developed simultaneously. According to the theory of cultural groups, these nomadic shepherds affiliated themselves most closely with the older fundamental cultures, whose father-god they preserved. Family ties are stronger than tribal ties, as shown in the lack of initiation celebrations. In their symbiosis with the herd animals of the Asiatic steppes, the shepherds developed from the very beginning a much more rational relationship to the animal than that of the totemistic hunters, who transfer their irrational fears and latent homosexual father and ancestor ties to the animal, feared by the hunter, and desired as well. As man's activity is the foundation of animal breeding as well as hunting, the original equality of the woman is replaced by the unlimited patria potestas of the man, the head of the great family, in the societies of the shepherds. Due to their riches in constantly

99. Friedrich Alverdes, "Research on Folk Psychology and Sociology," in *Tiersoziologie,* vol. 1 (Leipzig: C. L. Hirschfeld, 1925), p. 31.

increasing herds and to their capacity as riders, the shepherds acquire dominion over planters and hunters, which makes them conquerors of the cultures with a settled home from the end of the Ice Age on. The overlaying of the planter cultures by the shepherd cultures makes plowing possible, as well as more intensive cultivation of the fields, and breeding of cattle, preparing the way for the multiplicity of forms of the high cultures. The patriarchally organized shepherds remained the feudal lords in these mixed cultures. Patriarchal religiousness and a masculine ethos are characteristic of the high cultures to which totemism and the fecundity cults yielded.

The mighty god of the ancient Hebrews, and the pre-Mohammedan Allah of the Arabians, are hardly affected, according to Baudissin's description, by the fecundity concepts, by the contrast between life and death. This patriarchal god belongs to the tribal gods who know no death and no resurrection, only continuous life. In the service of the unlimited authority of this tribal god, the man frees himself from his mother tie sufficiently so that the rivalry between man and man within the tribe is silenced to a considerable extent. The tribal god is the representative of conscience, of the superego, he embodies the national ethos. Baudissin describes further with what energy the Hebrews banned the naturalistic and the mythical from their religion in the name of Jehovah, and under the leadership of great men with the gift of prophecy. But the tendency to call upon the goddess of female fecundity in idols of Ashera broke out ever and again among the soil-tilling Israelites. Reik shows that there are also traces of totemism to be found in the religion of Jehovah.[100]

The psychoanalyst gains the impression from the theory of the cultural groups that in the high cultures the oral tendencies of the fundamental cultures which were carried on by the conquering and exploiting shepherds are fused to a unit with the anal tendencies of the matriarchate and the phallic tendencies of totemism, producing the manifold possibilities of sublimation corresponding to the genital stage of development of the individual. The stability

100. Reik, pt. 1, "Das Schofar," p. 178.

of this fusion product is however far below that of the preambivalent fundamental cultures. In the headlong haste of development of the high cultures, now this element reminiscent of previous times gains ascendency, now another, burdening these cultures with the tensions of mass madness, comparable with the neurotic and psychotic breakdown of the individual.

As long as pride in the national ethos, the tie to the traditions of the fathers, dominates the individual and contents him, the specifically religious concepts of salvation and resurrection hardly come to the surface of consciousness. The belief in salvation and resurrection springs from the fecundity cultures of the maternal religions. The sacrament, the token of rebirth, representing the mystic incorporation of the deity, comparable with the desire of the child to unite with the mother, was annexed to the paternal religions secondarily, according to Dieterich.[101] The assertion that there were totemistic communion celebrations, often repeated since Robertson Smith, is refuted forever by Beth.[102]

In Asia Minor, the maternal religion persisted in unusual purity despite Greek, Persian, and Roman settlements. We may expect to find that in this religion the dangers persist which were inherent in the anal matriarchal culture for the unsatisfied instincts of the man. From Asia Minor, the maternal religion spread in Roman times together with other mystery religions to all the politically dissatisfied, as I pointed out earlier.

ATTEMPT AT A PSYCHOLOGICAL INTERPRETATION OF
THE CULT AND MYTHOLOGY OF THE GREAT MOTHER

After the excursion into the past, let us return to the interpretation of the cult and mythology of the Great Mother of Asia Minor. The comparison of the matriarchal cultures with others shows us the dangerous ambivalence of the man in his relation to the wife and mother as the result of his economic dependence on her. Some cultural manifestations of the matriarchate show the negative side of this ambivalence, the aggressive, oppositional and divisional

101. Dieterich, *Mutter Erde*, p. 191.
102. Karl Beth, *Religion und Magie* (Leipzig and Berlin: B. G. Teubner, 1927), p. 318.

tendencies in the men's societies arising from this dependence, so galling to masculine pride. We may expect that the maternal religion also conserves the positive side of this dependence. When the father is thrust into the background in family life, and all the ambivalence of infantile emotional life is concentrated on the mighty mother, there is no other outlet than self-destruction for the aggressive and destructive tendencies of the man, who remains bound in infantile fixation on the mother, or regresses to this stage. The greater stability of the family life of the fundamental cultures I think I could show to be due to the equality of man and woman, which provides much more favorable conditions for the mastery of the Oedipus complex than the economic inequality between man and woman of later cultures.

I have pointed out that the organization of the matriarchate appears to bring danger of a developmental retardation to the man in the transition from receptive orality to productive anality. We can best understand the character of this retardation by comparison with a typical individual neurosis which often occurs in our civilization due to the one-sided preponderance of the mother's influence in the development of the child, whether the child is left entirely to the mother or mother representatives due to the early death of the father, or for reasons of persistent early fixations.

A well-balanced family life, in which the mother is principally the allowing member and the father, the forbidding, has for the son the advantage that he can love and desire the mother wholeheartedly, and just as whole-heartedly oppose the father as rival and foe. That is, he can develop a predominantly positive Oedipus complex, which requires only enough curtailing of instincts so that the enmity to the father may be mitigated to competitive identification with him, and love of the mother to tenderness, with the original sexual aim deflected. In this case, the transfer of libidinal and aggressive desires to the outside world is possible without severe restrictions and distortions of the instincts. If both roles in the child's rearing, the allowing and the forbidding, are united in one person, the two dangerous extremes of rearing, spoiling and repression, are very much harder to avoid.

If the mother alone is the allower and the forbidder, the child's ambivalence to her is increased. It loves the allowing, and hates the forbidding mother, and dares not hate her, on the other hand, for fear of losing her altogether. The fear of loss enhances love to fixation, and the aggression, which the child dare not turn outward, for fear of provoking loss of love, is turned inward. In accepting punishment, the child seeks to secure the love of the strict mother as well, it identifies itself with the bad mother who punishes. Thus the masochistic mechanism of depression begins, a mechanism that can go so far that the child dare not love actively, in order not to lose. There results the measureless, passive demand for love, which can only take, and not give—characteristic of the narcissistic neurosis. This narcissistic development retardation conserves the dependence on the mother, and provides very poor conditions for the mastery of the Oedipus complex. A genital love, which can bear the ebb and flow of desire and fulfillment, of loneliness and union, is often not attained at all, or it is regressively denied and the punishment of castration accepted. The narcissistically retarded individual aims in his libidinal desires at perpetual unalterable possession of his love object, as found in introjection, an aim which is unattainable.

This aim, which is no longer useful as the child grows, is strengthened when he sees the mother often pregnant and in confinement, when he envies the closer bond between the younger child and the mother, and is thereby still more deterred in his striving for independence. The child longs to return to the mother's breast and to the womb, on the one hand; on the other, he himself wishes to be the pregnant mother who, according to the child's theories of pregnancy, has taken the baby into her body as a secure possession, like food eaten. But these enormous instinctual demands of the child are immediately followed by fear of punishment. The desire to return to the womb arouses fear of being eaten, the oft-recurring motive of fairy tales. The desire to take the mother into his body, as the infant does the mother's milk, or the pregnant woman the infant, arouses the fear that the bad mother as the powerful foe, may become the all-conquering inner danger, so that the child is forced to tear this all too close dependence asunder, to wrench out the bad mother like a foreign body, to cast her out, even though he bleed to death himself in the act. These regressive forms of castration fear concentrated on the mother assume such awful proportions because the one-sided dependence on the powerful mother leads to an insoluble conflict between the desires of love and the interests of self-preservation. The depressive patient does not want to eat, nor to take in anything intellectually, because he is completely absorbed and possessed by the too-powerful mother within him.

We know how fundamentally the melancholic is attracted by suicide. His whole fear-ridden aggression is turned against the inner foe, the loved and hated love object, within his body, to which he is indissolubly bound, so that he cannot part with it without killing himself. After an unsuccessful attempt at suicide or even after a certain period of masochistic self-torture, there may be a relaxation of the deep depression, when the patient is successful in tearing himself away from the intense fixation. The reintegration of the ego crippled by the act of freeing itself, may even lead to an ecstasy of freedom, expressed in mania, in which the freed ego, with desire renewed, turns again to the outer world. The enormous intensity with which the manic does this betrays the fact that the new object ties are not so much genital as oral and introjective in character, so that they lead again inevitably to melancholic jeopardy of the ego.

This short, typical description of the melancholic taken from Freud's and Abraham's discussion of this subject,[103] and from my own clinical experience, allows us to see that the mythology of Attis describes a manic-depressive individual, unable to free himself of his one-sided mother fixation. Abraham found in every analysis of a male melancholic that the castration complex is predominantly connected with the mother. I myself have found in my psychiatric work that there is really a disturbance of the family balance in the early history of many manic-depressive patients, an important role being played by the predominance of an injurious maternal influence. The additional effect of constitutional factors cannot be denied. In favorable cases, these injurious factors in the

103. Sigmund Freud, "Trauer und Melancholie," in *Gesammelte Schriften,* vol. 5 (1924), pp. 535–53.

family constellation can be overcome, but in unfavorable cases, the individual cannot hold his own against this danger, even in small doses.

The constitutional factor has often been called upon to explain the Attis cult. Cumont says: "The trend toward passionate ecstasy was long an endemic disease in Phrygia."[104] The discovery of a constitutional factor alone cannot satisfy the etiological questioning of psychoanalysis. But the knowledge that this endemic disease, a manic-depressive disposition, is an inherited burden from matriarchal conflicts, will clear up many a puzzling characteristic of the cult as well as of the mythology.

Attis is a beautiful, narcissistic youth, who hardly attains the maturity of a genital love relationship. It is his fate to be one of those who "die when they love." He is the spoiled darling of the Great Mother. He himself does not love others, he only allows them to love him. The oral form of overindulgence is expressed in the myth in the gifts of game and in the scenes of drunkenness. The boy boasts of the love of the mother and of the gifts which he, in his idleness, allows her to give him, to increase his own self-esteem.

Oral indulgence arouses fear of being forsaken by the fostering mother. This dependence is expressed in the myth motive by the danger of starvation and the miraculous rescue of the pregnant woman and the newborn infant. As so often in fairy tales and in children's fancy, impregnation is treated the same as the act of eating or that of sowing and planting in mother earth. This form of procreation, excluding the father, emphasizes the deep-rooted bond between mother and child, and makes the birth of an individual dependent on a cruel act of force: biting, tearing away, or castration. This concept of procreation and birth, moreover, involves a doubt as to the possibility of separating mother and child. In the myth, the procreation of Attis is ascribed to the fastening and tearing out of the penis of Agdistis, and in another version, to a woman picking up a fruit grown from the blood of the penis soaked into the earth. Agdistis in one form of the myth derived from the Deukalion and Pyrrha saga, is procreated by an anal act,

104. Cumont, *Die orientalischen Religionen,* p. 47.

symbolised by their throwing stones behind them; in another form, by the moistening of the earth with the seminal fluid of Zeus, which is followed by birth as a tearing apart of the earth.

The repression of the procreating father, who is a mere shadow in the background in all these forms of the myth, is in accord with the androgynous concept of the mother which we meet in the fantasy life of children living under the one-sided influence of an overpowerful mother, or who are able to repress the forbidding power of the father for some reason or other. Such unbalanced power in the hands of the mother may retard the productive independence of the child, and keep him in receptive dependence. The child conceives of himself as a mere adjunct, as a part of his mother; in his unconscious fantasy he may see himself as the mother's penis.

All these mythical pictures of a vegetative connection between mother and child deny a separation of the love and self-preservative instincts, in accord with individual development. Does not this extreme dependence, which denies individuality, remind one of one side of religious life, the side which Schleiermacher calls "absolute dependence"? This bond extending beyond the individual himself is wonderfully comforting for the childishness in man, and at the same time, a fearful danger to the development of the ego. It is similar to the fascination for the individual of being submerged in a crowd. I have called attention variously to the strong ambivalence in the descriptions of the Great Mother, to the fact that the qualities of "fascinans" and "tremendum" stand side by side.

For Attis and his followers, Cybele is at once the high and holy goddess in her chastity, and the fearful temptress. Agdistis, the hermaphroditic monster, who allows himself all instinctual freedom, reminds one of the concept of witches in which the male of the Middle Ages clothed his fear of the female temptress. Attis also feels his ambivalent tie to the Great Mother as an intense threat to his ego. He feels himself pursued by the jealous goddess and when he sees her maddened by love, his own excitement breaks forth. He projects his own love onto the goddess. He is a helpless child, she is the instigator. The fantasy of pursuit by the goddess is only his denial of his own desire for close union with the mother, his denial of the introjection. The pursuit motif is likewise a denial of the possibility of losing the mother, an assurance of the strength of her love. The paranoid psychotic defends himself similarly in his mania of persecution and pursuit by a lover, when the relation to him becomes a threat to his ego, with certain set denials, as Freud has shown in the case of paranoia taken from the patient's autobiography.[105] The pursuit fantasy is the melancholic's attempt at self-cure, since he is in great danger from the introjected love object within him, which he fears to love. The enthusiasm, the feeling of being filled with God, is not only the height of bliss for him possessed of God, it is also a shattering threat of danger. The sense of being filled with the deity, and the ecstasy, the feeling of being out of one's self, the destruction of the personality, these are closely related dangers in the manic-depressive psychosis.

The whirlwind dance numbing consciousness, the exciting rhythms of the mourning music, the bloodthirsty acts of cutting into one's own flesh, all these are means to a mystic union with the deity. "He who knows the strength of the whirlwind dance, lives in God, for he knows how love destroys," says Dscheladdin Rumi, called by Erwin Rohde the most daring of all the mystics.[106] But these acts signify not only a death in God, they are also the beginning of resurrection in their satisfaction of the artistic needs. They are the only active attempts of Attis and his followers to give expression to their inner madness in creative liberation, and to free themselves of it. These acts are born out of a storm of uncoordinated movements, out of the plaintive cry of the child, afraid for his life, in danger of the mother's wrath.[107] But the angry mother is an inexorable inner foe, who cannot be driven out by exorcism of self-punishment. Out of the desire for expiation and for reconciliation stem the worshipper's masochistic acts of cutting into his own

---

105. Sigmund Freud, "Ueber einen Autobiographisch beschriebenen Fall von Paranoia," in *Gesammelte Schriften*, vol. 8 (1924), pp. 355–435.

106. Rohde, *Psyche*, 2:27.

107. Joan Riviere in "On the Genesis of Psychical Conflicts" has shown how the violence of the discharge brings the forsaken, desperate child to the very brink of the experience of death.

flesh. We are shaken by this fear-driven race between erotic and destructive instincts, between life and death, in the cult and myths, and as we live them through with the patient in the tortured final struggles of a melancholic psychosis. The destructive instinct conquers in the act of suicidal castration.

This final conflict of the religious drama comes in springtime, the time of heightened libido in all mankind, comparable with the heat of animals. Even in our time, spring brings the highest number of melancholic affections and the maximum of suicides. Attis is the type of youth in puberty in whom all the libidinous forces are overstrong and concentrated on the phallic aim of deciding to be a man. The myth shows Attis at his marriage feast. But the paralyzing fascination emanating from the Great Mother, the youth's childish fear of the all-devouring power of the mother, causes him to start back in terror before his own phallic activity as well as before his mad love projected onto the goddess. Because he desires to remain the child bound irrevocably to the mother, because he fears the passion of union as well as the separation that follows, he hates his own independent procreative power. In order to turn the terrible, passionate woman back into the tender, good mother who cannot be lost in order to pacify her angry jealousy, the reflection of his own disavowed passion, Attis and his followers cast away the organ of procreation, they sacrifice it to the mother, as though that were her command. They identify themselves with the strict, angry mother, and cast all chances of active love behind them, in order that they may possess the mother forever in passive dependence. She alone shall remain the phallic mother, the desire of childish fantasy, to whom the boy stands in the relation of receptivity to the giver of all things. Thus the follower of Attis, in the thralls of the Great Mother, renounces his own individuality, he returns to the lap of the mother, who is reconciled by his self-punishment, he returns to a plant-like feminine-childish dependence on her. As the castrated youth, he resembles the feminine deity; in his conversion into a tree, he is the symbolic penis of mother earth, which draws its strength from her alone.[108] The surviving Cybele worshipper

108. Compare Otto Fenichel, "Die symbolische Gleichung: Mädchen-Phallus," *Internationale Zeitschrift für Psychoanalyse* 22 (1936): 299–314.

withdrew from masculine rivalry. From that time on, he led the childishly protected life of the Metrargyrtes, the begging monks.

The doctrine of resurrection is closely connected with expiation and reconciliation with the mother. It is a denial of the possibility of losing the mother. In mythology, this faith has common, naturalistic forms. The sacrificed procreative power proves immortal through sacrifice. The indestructibility of the body of Attis, the growth of the hair, the motility of the little finger signify in symbolic reference to other organs that the castration is rescinded. The sacrifice is a blow to the fecund mother, and spurs her on to new fertility, to rebirth. Thus the manic experiences the enormous restorative power of Eros, the synthetic forces of the ego, when he has passed through the door of death, in the shattering asunder of his individuality. It is like a new birth, as though man's envy of childbearing had brought him to this desired end. In the mystic union with the fruitful mother, he has given rebirth to himself.

This appears to be the explanation for the rationally incomprehensible connection between the fecundity cult and human sacrifice in the maternal religion. The anxiety as to fertility in matriarchal planter culture is not alone a rational, justifiable anxiety as to the food supply, it is reenforced by the unconscious, melancholic dependence on the nourishing mother, by a tendency to be like her, out of envy of her childbearing properties. This especially endangers the individuality of the man, whereas the comparable fault of development in the woman arising from penis envy leads to Amazonian aping of the man. The suicidal threat to the individuality is deflected outward in the offering of other beings, whether animals or humans. The sacrifice of the firstborn is next to suicide and self-castration. The latter appears to have sprung up at a time when animistic religion, which freed men from inner conflicts by projection outwards, began to defeat its goal and the religious process of introjection had not yet been converted into ethical elaboration. In the martyrdom of later forms of religion, we see the continuation of religious self-destruction.

In this connection, it is interesting that W. Koppers considers cult castration as a derivative of "the myths of cutting and tearing to pieces" which arose among Indogermanic shepherd folk in touch with the matriarchal fecundity magic of south Asiatic folk around the Pacific Coast. These typical dismemberment myths attribute the beginning of the world to the tearing apart of a primal being—a primal father, the moon, a primal cow, according to whether the matriarchal or patriarchal element predominated. From the torn members of this being, the world is supposed to have been made.[109]

In the development of the individual, Melanie Klein calls attention to the fear of dismemberment of the love object and of the ego in early infancy, laying the foundation for later melancholic danger.[110] Just as the individual defends himself against the melancholic danger of dismemberment by means of the paranoic projection mechanism, or a manic urge toward healing, there is a similar desire for projection and healing in whole groups of people, who feel themselves torn by melancholic fears, expressed in myths of the beginning of the world and in faith in rebirth.

AN ATTEMPTED INTERPRETATION OF THE MYSTERIES

The naturalistic form of the Phrygian myths and cult is indeed terrifying because it portrays an extreme, psychotic development, which was only realized in individual cases. But this development is nevertheless deeply rooted in mental laws, which shine forth in different creative forms. On the basis of this general human potentiality, a highly differentiated mystery religion developed, the symbolic performance of the human "die or live." The rebirth experience of this mystery religion, which is attained by mastery of fear of castration and death, is entirely comprehensible to modern religious persons. The dramatic performance of the mystery, the Greek tragedy, and the sacrifice of the Mass in the Christian church are the human acts of sublimation of artistic and religious nature which free men from the psychotic disposition dangerous to his individuality. Ella Freeman Sharpe, in her article on sublimation and the formation of delusions, distinguishes an introjective

109. W. Koppers, "Pferdeopfer und Pferdekult der Indogermanen," in *Wiener Beiträge zur Kulturgeschichte und Linguistics* vol. 4 (1936), p. 287.

110. Klein, "Psychogenesis of Manic-Depressive States."

and a projective phase in artistic sublimation.[111] We shall rediscover these same phases in religious sublimations.

In the mystery religion of the Great Mother, the first act of the Dromenon, the lower consecration of the mystics, was an act of sacramental eating and drinking, the oral conception or introjection of the deity. The fascination of the sacred image lures the believer on to letting himself be completely penetrated by the all-powerful one, to allowing himself to be filled to drunkenness with the deity. This Eucharist is similar to the conceptional stage of artistic creation. It is no accident that the experience of artistic creation is ever and again compared with that of pregnancy and birth. Just as conception begins as an internal process, which of necessity ends with an act of separation and birth, just as the food taken into the body is separated by assimilatory forces and those of destruction, in the same fashion, mental conception, introjection, initiates a "separation of erotic and destructive instinctual forces."[112] In the introjective phase, libidinal forces are utilized for self-preservation and ego enrichment, renouncing their genital instinctual aim. But at the same time, the explosive force of destructive powers makes itself felt within the artist, the creative man, and this force strains outward, toward creation, toward forming the world anew.

The religious individual does not form the outer world, at least it is not a primary aim. His new creation is in the inner world of the ego. The religious man may remain stationary in the introjective phase of the mystic conception of God, of joy in Him. The narcotic effect of religions has been pointed out, and every psychiatrist is familiar with forms of religious mania, where the danger of destruction is not less than that of suicide among narcotic addicts. In the "absolute dependence" of the religious experience, all personal active possibilities of creative work may go down before the overpowering grace of heavenly intuition. Wallowing

111. Ella Freeman Sharpe, "Certain Aspects of Sublimation and Delusion," *International Journal of Psycho-Analysis* 11 (1930): 12–23.

112. Sigmund Freud, "Das Ich und Das Es," in *Gesammelte Schriften*, vol. 6 (1925), p. 384. For the English translation see *The Ego and the Id* (London: Hogarth, 1927).

in the bliss of the introjective phase does not lead to a desexualisation process of introverted instinctual aims, as does the normal process of sublimation. The religious addict desires only to attain the introverted instinctual end by extragenital means.

Josine Müller has shown from detailed case histories how some narcissistic neurotics have a fixation on an image of the deity, usually hermaphroditic, corresponding to the two introjected parents.[113] This imago comes from the stage of transference from orality to anality, the development danger point at the transition from infantile receptivity to productivity. Through persistence in the lustful introjection of the imago, the self-preservative functions of the organism are flooded with nondesexualized libido, and thus overburdened, so that they are hardly in a position to ward off the danger of physical or mental illness. The introverted image of the deity, which promises the height of bliss and joy, and at the same time threatens the ego with destruction, causes a conflict within the patient between love and hate, which is the more dangerous, the more he lacks opportunities for discharge in the outer world. The epileptic fit is an extreme type of destructive discharge. According to Reich's psychoanalytical conception, it is brought on by introjection of desexualized libidinal energies, which have taken possession of the ego functions, of the muscle system, and produce an equivalent for the genital discharge, by means of tonic-clonic convulsions of the extragenital motile apparatus.[114]

Religious and political enthusiasms are far behind artistic or scientific production in their achievement of desexualization, but they are far ahead of these in their bliss-giving and dangerous dynamics. The more primitive the form of religion the more incomplete is the desexualization. In the consciousness of this dangerous tension in the progressive spiritualization of religion, the struggle for purity, for banning of aggressions, is never silenced. In the mystery religions, sexual abstinence of the priests takes the place of the castration of the Galloi. The believer who experiences his own

113. Josine Müller, "Die Erforschung der infantilen Weiblichkeit aus der Erkrankung Narzisstischer Personen" (unpublished).

114. Wilhelm Reich, "Ueber den Epileptischen Anfall," *Internationale Zeitschrift für Psychoanalyse* 17 (1931): 263–75.

subservience to the sexual instincts, demands that the priest, the intermediary between God and man, live independent of instinctual life, as an example for him. The naturalistic phallic cult is degraded in Christianity to devil service. The sacrifice of the immediate genital satisfaction is supposed to seal the perpetual mother-child relation to the deity. When in the course of religious development, the return of the inhibited material from inhibition causes the late Roman hilaria feast to be degraded into a carnivalistic debauch of freedom, during which in unveiled form the marriage of the magna mater with Attis is celebrated, that must signify a loosening of the bond to the maternal religion, and as a result, paternal religion triumphs easily over it.

The first act in the Dromenon of the mystery religion represents sacred conception; the second act of the higher dedication causes the mystic to live through birth in shattering reality. The religious experience is intensified to mania, to morbus sacer, to an experience of rebirth which endangers existence itself. The destructive, expansive forces, which in artistic creation are deflected directly to the outer world, expend their entire force on the ego of the religious individual. The mystic experience is converted into prophesy. The religious psychologist William James portrays in his book, *The Varieties of Religious Experience,* how the critical experience of a religious conversion may cause the unconscious to break through in an act of surrender of the actual personality, though this outburst is usually prepared long before.[115] In the mystery religions, this expansion of the personality discharges itself in manic prophesy. Sacrificial castration, or the taurobolium which takes its place, kindles ecstatic prophesy. He who had passed through the taurobolium was worshipped by the multitude of the faithful. The deity breaks forth from the mouth of the prophet.

I do not know to what extent Paul, the great missionary of Christianity in Asia Minor, was influenced by the mystery religion of the Great Mother. His faith, which he acquired in an experience of conversion similar to death itself, an epileptic attack, is primarily

---

115. William James, *The Varieties of Religious Experience.*

in contrast to the Jewish faith of laws. Paul's experience was one of rebirth, in which he acquired the conviction that God lives in the man who passes through death, and that in the degree to which the Christian dies with God, God lives in him. "I am crucified with Christ, nevertheless I live; yet not I, but Christ liveth in me" (Gal. 3:20).

In the belief in rebirth, there often appears an idea that the reborn, like the castrated Galloi, is able to lead from then on an angelic, asexual existence, or like the Great Mother, a hermaphroditic existence without genital cravings. In this idea, there is reflected the regression of religious experience from the genital to the oral-anal stage of organization of the instinctual life.

The religion of the Great Mother has few prophetic characteristics. The mystical experience of being filled with the deity remains in the foreground of religious experience. But it is an easy step to the assumption that in the time of syncretism, the father religions and their ethos, driving the believer on to activity, had also taken hold upon the mother religion of Asia Minor or, more exactly, that it had awakened the repressed conflict with the father. The Mithras mysteries, this religion of men's secret societies of soldiers, who excluded the woman entirely from the cult life, arose in Asia Minor, and was well fitted to complement the deficiencies of the mother religion. The Mithras religion reached its climax, as does later Christianity, in the proclamation of the unity of father and son; Helios and Mithras are one. The ethos built on the solidarity of the men's societies consisted entirely of fighting—the struggle between good and bad spirits. The obedient subservience to the good father, also an act of introjection which of necessity released destructive forces, gave the believer permission to pursue and destroy the bad father in the form of wicked spirits. Immortality here was not alone due to the grace of the deity, it was a boon won and ratified in the court of the world, it was an active victory in the name of the sol invictus.[116]

The feminizing cult of Attis was the more intensely spurned among the patriarchally organized peoples, the more the ethos of

116. Graillot, *Le Cult de Cybèle*, p. 123.

their men's societies, similar to a compulsion neurosis, was endangered by the temptations of the maternal religion of grace, with its disuniting forces. The Greeks were especially disdainful of the Attis cult. Yet their sagas relate that even the Greek national hero, Hercules, was in danger of falling under the sway of a woman, of going into the service of the Queen of Asia Minor, Omphale, who compelled him to put on women's clothing and to do women's work. But Hercules freed himself from this "shameful" serfdom. He is the conqueror of the Amazons. Bachofen was the first to show the misogynous character in the heroic overemphasis of his masculinity.[117]

Abraham demonstrated the close kinship between compulsion neurosis and manic-depressive affections.[118] In the field of the perversions, which are the negative of the neuroses, the compulsion neurosis is comparable to active, and the manic-depressive illnesses, to passive homoeroticism (Ferenczi). The manic-depressive patient is distinguished from the compulsive neurotic by a periodically recurring step in his regression from the anal to the oral stage, whereas in the free intervals, between phases of his illness, he is a compulsive neurotic. Mette has disclosed the struggle of manic-depressive and compulsion neurotic dispositions in the contest between the dionysic and the appolinic principles in Hellas.[119] There is many a parallel between the Dionysos Zagreus, who was torn by beasts and then rose again, and the Phrygian Attis.

The archeologist Hans von Prott believed, even before the publishing of Dieterich's "Mutter Erde" and independent of Bachofen's findings that "he had discovered one of the main roots of Greek religion in the religion of Meter." In his aphorisms, he named the Greek saga of the heroes "the great purgatory, by means of which the Greeks freed themselves from the torturing concepts of the maternal religion and group marriage." Prott was not able to complete these studies. In the opinion of his friends, he came

117. Bachofen, *Urreligion und Antike Symbole.*
118. Abraham, *Versuch einer Entwicklungsgeschichte der Libido*, pp. 1 ff.
119. Alexander Mette, "Zur psychologie des Dionysischen," *Imago* 20 (1934): 191–218.

upon this theme under the influence of symbolic and psychological ideas which later led to his suicide.[120]

With reference to Bachofen's thesis of "promiscuity and hetarical swamp vegetation" in early Greece, I have pointed out above that this thesis has not been verified. The matriarchal forms of society are universally monogamous. Sagas which bring up such "painful memories" testify to a conflict with the overstrong mother tie which the Greek, like men of other cultures, wards off in that he sees in the mother the holy one whom he worships, and at the same time, the witch or prostitute. There is a close connection between the concern as to fecundity found in the maternal religion, and still manifest in the Demeter mystery, and the phallic mother concepts and autochthonic birth sagas which were later repressed in the olympic father religion.

Not only in hero worship, however, did the Greek free himself from the mother religion. His very heroes, even according to Rohde, still bore many chthonic traits.[121] But the Greek was still further freed from the maternal religion by his artistic creative faculty, which shielded him against a passive surrender to the mother. The Orpheus saga which is also connected with the coast of Asia Minor, is characteristic of this turning to freedom, though Orpheus also has many a trait in common with Attis. It is his fate that he cannot detach himself from the woman he has lost, he is torn by furious maenads, and the head of the dying Orpheus is carried on, still living, like that of Osiris; he lives beyond his death like the evergreen spruce tree of Attis. But what lifts the Greek out of the paralyzing sphere of suffering of the followers of Cybele is the birth of immortal, all-powerful song, which gives life to the lifeless, which causes stones to skip. In the Attis cult, music and dance remain on a low level of artistic development; they are principally narcotic in their effect. Characteristic of the fact that music here was principally receptive as a narcissistic instrument of pleasure and a narcotic, is the peculiar custom that the cult

120. Hans Prott, "MHTHP, Brückstück sur Griechischen Religionsgeschichte," *Archiv für Religionswissenschaft* 9 (1906): 87–94; Carl Albrecht Bernouilli, "Foreword" to Bachofen, *Urreligion und Antike Symbole*, vol. 2 (Leipzig: Philipp Reclam Jun., 1926).

121. Rohde, *Psyche* 1:146 ff.

musical instruments contain the sacrament by means of which the mystic takes into his body the maternal grace.

There is a faith in rebirth connected with the name of Orpheus, which led to the giving up of human sacrifice. We have already seen that this introjection of religion resulted in danger of self-injury for the individual because it swamped the organism with libidinal and destructive instinctual forces, which clamoured for freeing action and discharge to the outer world. Animistic forms of religion gave the outer world souls, and primitive sacrificial rites freed the individual possessed by the tremendum of religion. The damming up of the libido, arising from introjection of religion, led among the Jews principally to creative prophesy, among the Greeks, to artistic creation.

The mystery religions were increasingly individualistic in comparison with older forms of religion. They were carried on by individuals, who were no longer inevitably embedded in collectivity, and this allowed widening of the personality in the religious group. The introjected, individualistic religion of the mysteries fights against the dangerous damming of libido which threatens to destroy the individual. The degradation of outer world relationships drives the mystic into psychosis. Mystic religion is to a great degree amoral. Freud has shown that the mastery of the Oedipus conflict leads to an introjection of the images of the parents, and thus creates a representative of society within the individual, which makes it possible for him to act ethically in the outer world, even when away from the influence of society and dependent on himself alone.

We saw that religious experience in the religion of the Great Mother extends as far as the Oedipus conflict, but there it shrinks back and does not master it, due to the fears of the melancholic disposition. They are expressed in concern as to fecundity; they seek refuge regressively in an infantile mother tie. Here, we can expect no individual morality, the prerequisites of which are laws introjected and made accessible to the demands of reality.

The maternal deities are amoral. Confession of sin, however, is not absent in the mystery religion.[122] These are the cathartic acts

122. Raffaele Pettazoni, "Confession of Sins and the Classics," *Harvard Theological Review*, vol. 30 (1927).

which usher in the initiation. But these beginnings of a *feeling of guilt* involve no individual judgment in this pre-Oedipal stage of development, no *knowledge of sin*. These acts arise rather from fear of the image of the deity, fear of being forsaken by the deity. The longing for perpetual possession of the mother is what determines this act of converting the angry mother into a good mother by magic means. The little child and the human being in the pre-Oedipal stage of development lack the reservoir of narcissistic power to bridge over a period of emptiness, forsaken by the deity. The mature adult experiences this narcissistic assurance in the agreement of his ego with the demands of his superego. The religious individual can experience it, aside from these moral possibilities, in the experience which he calls trust in God. The little child is swamped with a flood of destructive instinctual forces at every pang of hunger, or whenever he feels himself deserted. This is manifested outwardly by cries for help, and inwardly by suffering. Similarly, the childish individual is completely shaken by the feeling of guilt, which he experiences as a feeling of being deserted by the deity. His magic attitudes, his dances, his music are like the cry of the hungering, forsaken child for the help of the mother. The destructive instincts of the individual driven to despair by the damming up of the libido, may also turn inward, and self-punishment, self-wounding, or even self-destruction is perpetrated in order to propitiate the mother goddess, and at the same time, to punish the bad mother. In this phase of the mother religion, the actual outer world relationships play only a slight role; the damming up of the libido makes itself felt principally in the inner world.

The masculine authority of the paternal deity, on the other hand, forces the men of the tribe, chiefly, to come to terms with society, to master the Oedipus complex. The worship of a father god may lead to extreme developments, just as it is true of the mother religion. In the monotheistic faith of the Hebrews, the maternal deity is suppressed, at the expenditure of no small amount of force, as is the case with the paternal deity in the religion of the Great Mother. Nöldeke, stimulated by Dieterich's work, *Mutter Erde,* also found in the Semitic religion traces of the fixation on mother earth.[123] Above all, we find here the feminine attitude of humans, men as well as women, to their god. The strict ethical orientation to the paternal deity, demanded of the Jews a great act of renunciation, which was intensified by the loss of their homeland. This renunciation could only be upheld by strong restrictions, like those of a compulsion neurosis, inasmuch as there was no relieving dualism such as that of the Persian religion, separating the good god from the bad, and giving the latter over to be the prey of destructive human instincts. The national ethos of Jewry has ever aroused admiration and fear in the world, and the fear is always the greater, the less vent the homeless Jews could find for their aggressive forces, of necessity freed by the introjection of strict laws in the outer world.

If the development of morality, as Baudissin has shown, is principally due to the authority of the paternal god, nevertheless in the ethically indifferent maternal religion there are independent strains of a religious nature, which also may be found in the forms of piety in which the mother tie has become an anonymous deep layer of religious experience.

Even Lutheranism, which deprived the believer of the merciful mother of heaven, expects salvation solely from the receptive attitude toward heavenly grace. By faith alone, Luther hoped to attain grace. He had little respect for the active strivings of a faith based on good works, in comparison with the efficiency of a grace at once perilous and blissful, which reached down into the deep layers of the unconscious, and brought about a rebirth of the personality there, far exceeding the reaches of man's conscious powers. The image of the deity which accords with this faith in rebirth will always combine maternal with paternal traits.

Even where the longing for rebirth is hardly aware of its religious origin, in the desire of Peer Gynt, for example, to be eaten over again, in the desire of the sick person for healing, or even of a well person for analytic treatment, today, man is driven to descend to the mothers. This "die and live" does not come about in a single, sudden experience of conversion. In this descent, man encounters

123. Theodor Nöldeke, "Mutter Erde und Verwandtes bei den Semiten," *Archiv für Religionswissenschaft* 8 (1905), 161–66.

the inner instinctual conflicts from a time when he felt himself delivered in infantile helplessness to all-powerful forces, in fear and longing. No atheistic emancipation can disavow this child in man. Going through the shattering danger of rebirth which leads the ego down into the depths of the fear of castration, desertion, and death, a healing of the instinctual conflicts, a rebirth may occur, in which the ordered instinctual forces may operate in a widened and firmly established personality; following their own inner law, they may then conquer a portion of the outer world for their own. The ego of the religious person may likewise become a prophecy of that which mortal man feels to be everlasting, through a rebirth which is experienced as a divine dispensation. In view of the universal law of tragedy of religious experience, which wrestles with the melancholic disposition deeply rooted in man, many a one will think this view far too optimistic. I may refer to Dostoevski, a poet who knows all the dregs of the human soul, and who has set at the beginning of his realistic yet deeply religious novel, *The Brothers Karamazov* a quotation from the gospel of John, which testifies to his belief in rebirth: *Verily, verily I say unto you; except a corn of wheat fall into the ground and die, it abideth alone: but if it die, it bringeth forth much fruit.*

Existentialism and Its Relations
to Psychotherapy

In Central European psychotherapy, as in this country, there are a variety of approaches and a certain diversity of concepts. But the greater pressure of totalitarianism—which, according to its nature, is hostile to any psychotherapy because it believes only in drill, the leadership principle, extinction of the "unfit"—has pushed different psychotherapeutic schools into a common defense against this pressure. There seems to be on the whole mutual exchange, tolerance, respect, and understanding among them.

There is also a great concern for philosophic orientation in Central European psychotherapy. Leading psychiatrists are philosophers, for example, the German Karl Jaspers and the Swiss Ludwig Binswanger, to mention the most outstanding names. In a largely secularized culture, such as ours, which lacks the bonds of generally accepted institutionalized religion, philosophy seeks to coordinate the variety of scientific disciplines by finding the basic trends which characterize the culture. Scientific specialties which lose these philosophic moorings are likely to become scientific techniques. On the other hand specialties which deal with human beings on the basis of a restricting philosophy are endangered by sectarianism, dogmatism, intolerance, and, in extreme cases, even fanaticism. To the true philosopher however—I quote Whitehead[1] —"the clash of doctrines is not a disaster, it is an opportunity"—an opportunity for broadening mutual understanding.

Reprinted by permission from *Psychiatry: Journal for the Study of Interpersonal Processes* 12 (1949): 399–412. Copyright 1949 by the William Alanson White Psychiatric Foundation, Inc.

1. Alfred North Whitehead, *Science and the Modern World* (Cambridge University Press, 1947).

The philosophy in which Central European culture of our day finds its most significant self-expression is existentialism. I shall try to give a necessarily sketchy picture of some main trends in existentialism, particularly some which seem to me to have some similarities with the psychiatry of interpersonal relations in this country.

European philosophers of the last hundred years have shown an increasing interest in psychological phenomena and a tendency towards self-expression in inspired poetry: Nietzsche was a poet; Jean-Paul Sartre is a novelist and playwright. Existentialism or ontology (science of being) goes back a hundred years to the Dane Sören Kierkegaard, a very sensitive literary and philosophic genius with surprising psychological insights, gained from his struggle with passions, anxieties, and indecisions. By his daring leap into the pathos of renunciation he lighted up anew problems of human existence. While Kierkegaard's existentialism had a religious connotation, generally the present-day existentialists, for instance, the German Heidegger and the Frenchman Sartre, are decided atheists. Karl Jaspers, however, though far removed from institutionalized religion, sees in the philosophic elucidation of existence a fundamentally religious function.

I base my presentation mainly on information gathered from Ludwig Binswanger's work *Grundformen und Erkenntnis menschlichen Daseins* (Basic Forms and Understanding of Human Existence).[2] As a psychiatrist he is a student of Bleuler; as a philosopher, a disciple of Heidegger, from whom he has parted in his main idea. Heidegger first presented existentialism in his work *Being and Time* (1927), which is difficult to study[3] Jean-Paul Sartre spread the existentialist ideas, but the popular movement that began with Sartre has lost some of Heidegger's depth.

The existentialist philosophy according to Binswanger turns its back on idealistic as well as positivistic philosophies of the past. It reverses Descartes' phrase, "Cogito ergo sum." We cannot under-

2. Zurich: Max Niehans Verlag, 1942. This book is out of print; a copy was at my disposal for only a limited time, so that I cannot give specific references.

3. Binswanger in his book has extensively expounded Heidegger's ideas, and I base my references on Binswanger's review.

stand thought processes if we do not first understand human existence. Existentialism strives for a pre- or extrascientific grasp of naive, spontaneous experience (*Erlebnis*). In such experience there are no separate entities, individuals, egos. The separation of subject and object, the division of spirit, mind and body are artificial scientific operations. The individual existence is not enclosed in the boundaries of a man's skin. In his actions, feelings, intentions, thoughts, memories, the individual reaches beyond himself into the surrounding world, and the world reaches into his existence. Existence is always with others. Even Robinson Crusoe, marooned on an island, is still with others, even if they are not present at the moment. Existence is being-in-the-world. This being-in-the-world, though interwoven with others, is yet experienced as mine, yours, his, hers. Being-in-the-world is limited in time, it has a beginning and an end. Being-in-the-world is existence towards death. As soon as the infant is born, he is old enough to die. It is characteristic of the existence of man, this "metaphysical or ontological animal," that in being there is concern about his own being. This concern, this anxiety, is a fundamental mode of existence. Heidegger calls it *Sorge*. William Barrett, an American interpreter of Heidegger, has translated Sorge as "care."[4] But this does not give the full meaning of the German word Sorge—it is care fraught with anxiety. It is not fear: fear is definitely directed towards something. Anxiety is indefinite: it belongs to being-in-the-world. In psychoanalytic literature it has been called "free-floating anxiety."

Binswanger postulates two modes of existence, care and love. In the definition of care he follows closely Heidegger's lead. I will try first to describe the existential mode of care, as Binswanger sees it.

Being-in-the-world is always existence with others. Existence without relatedness to someone or something is, in Binswanger's terms, "naked horror." If I exist only unrelatedly, I am absolutely helpless, I cannot be helped, I cannot help myself, no God can help me. In naked horror existence loses even the sense of selfhood.

4. William Barrett, *What Is Existentialism?* (New York: Partisan Review Series, no. 2, 1947).

It is not beside itself, as it is in the rages of passion, although intense passion theatens existence with horror, or the loss of self. Fear of death is still fear of something. If anything like death can still have a meaning to the existence in horror, it can have only the meaning of salvation. Therefore, a not yet complete naked horror leads almost inevitably to suicide. The existence of the psychotic, although it totters at times on the verge of horror, is still most of the time a being-in-the-world, however delusionally distorted this world may be.

Binswanger's description of "naked horror" brings to mind the world catastrophe (*Weltuntergang*) experienced in a schizophrenic psychosis, which Freud interpreted as a total withdrawal of object libido.[5] This catastrophe—the horror of nonexistence—is mostly followed by typical psychotic symptom formation, delusions, which according to Freud are attempts at restitution, primitive forms of relatedness. Also Sullivan, though he does not use the libido concept, considers the loss of relatedness, which "actually menaces one's survival," the core of schizophrenia—"the structure of his world was torn apart."[6] From this horror Sullivan, too, sees the psychotic return to "being-in-the-world" by patching up relations with the help of schizophrenic symptomatology.

From these extreme borderlines of human experience, let me return to Binswanger's and Heidegger's ideas about care.

In everyday living, anxiety, not to speak of horror, is scarcely visible, since everyday being-in-the-world is a mode of living of human beings in which existence and its finite boundaries, the abyss of nothingness which surrounds existence, is kept in forgetfulness. The Who of the everyday being-in-the-world is according to Heidegger (in German) *man*, (in French) *tout-le-monde*, (in English) one. It is everybody, anybody. It is the One of public life, of the plural mode of existence, the One of banalities and trivialities. It is the One of conventionality who tells us what one does, or

---

5. Sigmund Freud, "Psycho-Analytic Notes upon an Autobiographical Account of a Case of Paranoia" (1911), in *Collected Papers*, vol. 3 (London: Hogarth, 1942), pp. 390–470.

6. Harry Stack Sullivan, *Conceptions of Modern Psychiatry* (Washington: The William Alanson White Psychiatric Foundation, 1947).

what one does not do, how one behaves under given circumstances. The One is a busybody, constantly busy to distract himself from his own existence. The One is related to others, but the relations are thin and widespread, based on curiosity and inquisitiveness. The One is a taskmaster at adjustment in the sense of agility and adaptation. The One is dependent on whatever is at hand, he is driven, thrown into existence, without awareness of its futility and its lack of freedom. Speech is a fundamental trait of everyday being-in-the-world. Speech is partially self-expression, but largely determined by the surrounding world. The speech of the One is chatter, small talk, gossip and ambiguities; his speech disguises more than it reveals. The One avoids making choices, decisions, commitments, taking a stand. Characteristic is the attitude of the One towards death. He chatters glibly: "Everybody must die one day," but *everybody* is not me and one day is not now, it is far off. Death in everyday being-in-the-world is covered over by rituals and ceremonies; it becomes a public event. The One escapes from tragedy. Psychoanalytically speaking, death succumbs to a generally accepted repression.

According to the existentialists, death permeates being-in-the-world. Facing death, freeing oneself for one's own death is the first step in the philosophical labor of salvaging the authentic self from the accidental dependencies of the One. In facing death and more than death, the nothingness that surrounds being-in-the-world, existence braces itself for the willingness to experience and accept anxiety and therewith to surmount the helpless submission to the automatic rulings of care. The psychiatrist would call this process the growing awareness of resistance, of the automatic defenses against anxiety.

Being-in-the-world is fundamentally not only anxious, but, also guilty. Guilt in Heidegger's terms—Erich Fromm in *Man for Himself: An Inquiry into the Psychology of Ethics*,[7] is here in agreement with him—means the inescapable incompletion, imperfection which leaves existence always behind the full development of its potentialities. The phenomenon of conscience is a result of this

7. New York: Rinehart and Co., 1947.

fundamentally guilty character of existence. Being-in-the-world is fundamentally unfree, it means being thrown without choice into and out of existence. One cannot help being reminded here of Kafka's novels.

In the heroic acceptance and endurance of this lack of freedom from guilt and anxiety, in the resolute anticipation of death and nothingness, existence dares to arrive at a relative freedom of decision for what in a given, limited life situation is most essential for the optimal development of the potentialities of the Self; existence dares to take a stand, to make choices, to make commitments. Existence opens up to the opportunities of fate and dares to swing into action, to get involved without the fear of losing the authenticity of the Self. Fate becomes opportunity for the development of maturity. Existence arrives at a relative mastery of fate. Selfhood makes out of the impersonal One, a personality who has a history.

Selfhood opens up existence for the dignity of caring for other existences in friendship and love. "Only since existence as such is determined by selfhood can an I-myself relate to a You-yourself" (Heidegger). The One, as Heidegger has described him, the borderline existence of extreme evasion of anxiety, is completely preoccupied with keeping anxiety out of sight, out of experience. The endurance of anxiety opens existence up for other existences, not from the viewpoint of making use of the other in the sense of escape from anxiety, which is the secret viewpoint of the One in his impotent struggle with anxiety, but for a real concern for the other fellow's existence, for the optimal development of his selfhood.

The One driven by anxiety and the Self enduring and surmounting anxiety are dialectically related to each other, they are extreme trends of existence. Nobody is only One, nobody is only Self in his being-in-the-world. Daring to face anxiety, guilt, lack of freedom and nonexistence need not lead to a religious or philosophic withdrawal from the world. The most authentic self is still being-in-the-world. But the reference to the very basis of existence as nothingness permeates the existence of the self, as a spice, with essential meaningfulness. From the psychoanalytic viewpoint the resolute confrontation with those most discomforting aspects of existence implies the surrender of the deepest-rooted, universally cherished illusions of unlimited freedom, perfection, absolute security, and grandiosity. Heidegger is here very close to Kierkegaard's heroic renunciation. The nothingness as the very basis of existence, as Heidegger sees it, seems identical with the "all encompassing," the inaccessible "horizon of all horizons," which Jaspers refers to as God;[8] Jaspers, however, makes no attempt to touch this *mysterium tremendum* with any rational concepts, from which it necessarily recoils into further absolute inaccessibility. In most institutionalized religions there is a tendency to transform the horror of nonexistence, the *mysterium tremendum,* into an accessible, comforting deity.

Jaspers and Binswanger have described another mode of living —dialectically different from the existential mode of care—the mode of love, the intimate togetherness of the *you* and the *I* in the experience (Erlebnis) of *we-ness,* which gets little mention in Heidegger's work. Heidegger's heroic resoluteness which transcends anxiety, even where it approaches friendship, love, concern, and care for another existence, stays rather cool and aloof, remains basically within the realm of care. But since care fills the foreground of existence with so much noise, let us first dwell a while on the descriptive manifestations of care in order to work out more clearly its contradistinctions from the "existential" love, which is so much more silent that total cultural epochs have almost lost sight of it.

Sartre characterizes dealings in the world of care as sadomasochistic with the exception of the expression of love-free-from-purpose (*la caresse*).[9] Sartre has taken over the term sadomasochism which is used in psychoanalytic theory where sadomasochism characterizes an immature stage of development or neurotic or psychotic regression. Sartre uses this term in a broader sense. Throughout the world of so-called "normal adults" care sets the principle of competition in space and time. To quote Binswanger, the imperative of daily living is "Ôte-toi, que je m'y mette" (Get

8. Karl Jaspers, *Von der Wahrheit* (Munich: R. Piper, 1947).

9. Herbert Marcuse, "Existentialism: Remarks on Jean-Paul Sartre's *L'Etre et le néant,*" *Philosophy and Phenomenological Research* 8 (1948): 309–36.

out of my way, so that I can take your place). Being-in-the-world means being with others, but as far as care is concerned this is not the closeness of *you* and *me:* it is the relation of *one* to *another.* The one and the other are not really together, they are opposed to each other, hold each other at arm's length, even if they make reasonable concessions to each other, even if they meet each other halfway. They have the tendency to use or manipulate each other. One becomes for the other usable material for the sake of career, for the sake of comfort, for the sake of political or educational interests, basically for the sake of care, which rules the struggle for existence. Relation to material, to things, is relatively uncomplicated, to wit the remarkable development of human techniques. Though things are resistive they don't run away. Plants, animals, human beings are along this scale increasingly difficult to handle. In the realm of care, transcendence of existence has the tendency toward instrumentalization of existence, and this implies a loss of mutual respect and consequently a loss of self-respect. Existence in every day living is always in danger of sinking from the level of respecting Selves to the level of doomed and drifting Ones. This instrumentalization of existence is called in psychiatric terms "security operation."

Binswanger tries to characterize the sociological structures of being-in-the-world with others in the realm of care by the principle of "taking someone by something": Taking someone by his ear, by his word, by his honor, by his weakness, by his passion, taking someone like a steer by the horns, taking someone by surprise, taking someone for a ride—that is, by his stupidity—taking someone for a sucker. The centuries-old wisdom of speech in such slogans shows a prescientific understanding of persons and their dealings with each other.

The organs by which material or persons used as material are taken, manipulated, directed, appropriated are originally the sucking, biting mouth, later mainly the grabbing, grasping, groping hands. The mastery of manipulation is supported, elaborated, and refined by sight, hearing, locomotion, speech, recall and foresight, rational calculation. Man is distinguished from animals in that he tends to take his life, his fate, into his hands and to use his fellows

365

as instruments of his plans. Being passively taken in by others for any purpose known or unknown to the victim is also a maneuver for the sake of care. Success or failure in these operations is likely to decrease or increase manifest or latent anxieties.

By the principle of taking someone by something Binswanger tries to clarify social complexities such as leadership, education, combat, seduction, punishment, and so on. The "taking someone by something" may work with brutal force, Machiavellian cleverness, plausible rationality, organizational skill, or impressive facility of speech. Social institutions—such as family, school, church, state, police, army—all handle, manipulate, master, and take care of their members or dependents, and vice versa. Submission and rebellion are part of these power operations, which create a variety of distances, sometimes an oppressive closeness. The closeness of love is fundamentally different. Love is neither forceful, nor clever. "Love can never be made into an institution" (Nietzsche). Love does not impress, oppress, or manipulate, nor can love be impressed, oppressed, or manipulated; love is absolutely outside of these power operations. But sexuality without love definitely belongs in the realm of care and its power operations. Sexual partners who do not love each other, who are more or less accidentally accessible to each other, actually use each other or take advantage of each other for the sake of lust or other profitable purposes. Binswanger quotes one of Fontenelle's dialogues in which a lady of the world says: "Qu'on me donne l'homme le plus imperieux, je ferai de lui tout ce que je veux, pourvu que j'ai beaucoup d'esprit, assez de beauté et peu d'amour" (Give me the most domineering man and I shall make of him all I want, under the condition that I have much intellect, enough beauty, and little love).

In the realm of care people meet each other in a variety of roles and "take" each other by these roles: father and son, master and servant, husband and wife, seller and buyer, doctor and patient, teacher and pupil, one playmate and another, one colleague and another, and so on. These roles determine not only action, but already perception of a situation. "Perceptions are opportunities for action according to roles" (Binswanger). In the situation of a car accident the victim, the driver, a relative, a bystander, a doctor, a

lawyer perceive and act differently. Success in a role means prestige, failure makes one lose face. Reputation, fame, or prestige are
magic garments by which persons take hold of each other; if this
hold is an attack, anxiety is aroused. The roles are disguises for the
real Self. C. G. Jung calls the role *persona* (mask). If a person plays
different roles, this may throw him into the turmoil of neurotic
conflicts. Since he takes hold of himself by the role, inward doubts
or external threats to a role seem to endanger the Self. Binswanger
understands the hearing of voices in a psychotic as a sort of "name
calling," an attack on one of the patient's roles, in a state where his
roles are falling apart.

The tension between the two existential poles of the One and
Self permeate all of the social conditions which Binswanger has
described as manifestations of the principle of taking someone by
something. In the sphere of ethics—taking someone by his word,
his obligation—the Self prevails over the One. True ethics are never
determined only by care, but also by love. Taking or being taken
by a promise or a duty presupposes a high degree of respect, mutual respect as well as self-respect, loyalty, truthfulness to one's
own existence. Respect is inseparable from love. Ethical relations
move from closeness to distance along a scale marked by confidence, with trust at one pole and distrust and suspicion at the
other. Cautiousness exaggerated into suspiciousness, a preventive
defense against disappointment, belongs definitely within the
realm of care fighting off anxiety. Distrust and suspicion cling to
past experience, shut out new experience, and thus sterilize existence. Realistically oriented confidence progresses by broadening,
maturing experience. But ethical behavior can deteriorate into le-
galistic formalities; promises, duties, obligations may become
forceful weapons in an argumentative battle to maintain overpowering righteousness and to put the opponent in the wrong, a
battle which belongs primarily within the realm of care.

Everyday existence constantly offers possibilities of getting lost
or thrown into the impersonal, unscrupulous dependencies of the
One, of getting lost in empty chatter or in distracting pursuits, of
grasping indiscriminately for success or for possessions, and of being tossed around by a variety of opinions for the sake of momen-

tary reassurance. In the turmoil of everyday living, existence is never able fully to maintain the integrity of the self, true to its very own potentialities. Existence progresses step by step, from situation to situation, selecting, deciding, forming opinions, taking a stand true to the relative freedom of the self, never lulled into stagnating complacency, in all situations alert to new possibilities of integration with the surrounding world. Existence in action—in the broadest sense of the word—is neither quite lost, dependent on the world, nor fully self-sufficient, independent in the sense of the Self of philosophic existence. Between the One and the authentic Self moves the self of personality-in-action, developing its own history in the process of maturing by experience.

After this sketchily descriptive excursion through the everyday manifestations of being-in-the-world as care, let me return to the completely different mode of existence, which Binswanger calls love. If the existence of the One is called the plural mode of being-in-the-world, and the existence of the Self the singular mode, then love is the dual mode of existence. This separation in the service of clarification of existence is naturally artificial, for existence is never that of One only, nor that of Self in isolation: it is never exclusively determined by either care or love. In real existence there is a constant tension between the dialectic poles and an endless scale of possibilities of interaction.

We must recognize that it takes a certain audacity on the part of the philosopher-psychologist to talk about love. In everyday living love is disguised, transformed, distorted by the constant impact with care. There is a confusion of concepts. If somebody says, "All's fair in love and war," he does not mean love, but sexual passion. One talks about love when one really means romance or sentimentality or mystic contemplation, comforting dependency, more or less hypocritical kindness or altruism, the latter being an ethical phenomenon. All this is not love. Love is so much pushed into the background by the noisy preeminence of care that many people do not believe in the true existence of love, or consider it to be only a comforting illusion of poetry. I have spoken before of the universal repression of death; the same holds true for love—the fear of death and the fear of love are frequently compared in poetry, understandably so, since in the struggle for existence in a world ruled by anxiety and care, the surrender to the existential experience of love appears softening and therefore weakening. Nobody wants to be taken for a sucker or to be considered a weakling. Certainly there is a widespread yearning for love, but this frequently does not develop further than a quest for dependency or comforting reassurance, which means that it does not transcend care. There is a deeply ingrained embarrassment or shame even in admitting a sincere yearning for love. In our present-day culture there is no great difficulty in talking about sexuality, particularly if it is considered as successful performance, if it provides prestige. One can also bring people to confess their so-called "perverted" sexual inclinations, even their hateful, revengeful, ambitious, envious, jealous, or murderous tendencies. But love is deeply taboo. Love is spontaneous, beyond willpower control, and this arouses fears. Therefore Binswanger does not draw on sources of information in everyday living, where the yearning for love is hidden in so many disguises or remains inarticulate. In order to develop the phenomenology of love, Binswanger uses the documents of poets, artists, the great lovers that mankind has produced.

The existentialist refuses to interpret love as nothing but the more or less sublimated product of sexual biology. It is too narrow an approach to treat an existential phenomenon like love only by one sector of science, to force it into the boundaries of biology. It is true that love finds its most perfect expression in the union of the sexes, because in this experience (*Erlebnis*) even the barriers of bodily separation are surmounted, swept away by the intensity of the experience. The possibility of impregnation, the anticipated union of sperm and ovum may add a taste of life's creative permanance. But the biological act by itself is not essential. I have pointed out above that sex without love belongs in the sphere of power operations dictated by anxiety. According to Binswanger love as anxiety is an irreducible "existential." Essential is the living experience of togetherness, of *we-ness*, the complete transformation of being-in-the-world by this dual mode of existence. Here is no longer the *I* threatened by the loss of self in the struggle for existence, nor the *you* endangered by isolation: *I* and *you* are merged in the *we*, togetherness. This *we-ness* is experienced as the most triumphant security and certainty of existence there is. The transcendence of love is much more complete than any transcendence in the realm of care, where the reaching out from one existence into another is always ambiguous, ambivalent, vacillating between the danger of losing the Self and the threat of isolation in the movement of withdrawal. In the transcendence of love there is no anxiety nor struggle for self-assertion, for in the *we-ness* the Self is received as a gift of grace.

The phenomenology of love is principally different from that of care. Being-in-the-world in its relation to space and time is differently experienced. I referred above to the imperative of daily living: "Ôte-toi, que je m'y mette." Being-in-the-world as care creates an oppressive closeness, concessions are made by force or by prudence. Loving togetherness is without pressure, force, or control; the natural gesture of love is the embrace, *la caresse* (Sartre). The fight for right, entitlement, for one's place in the sun becomes superfluous, for existence as love experiences space as bountiful, infinite, without being anxiously lost in it. This very infinity of space is home, ours, the home of togetherness. There is a security of closeness even in spatial separation. Rilke says: "Home and heaven disappear, only where you are, there is my place." Shakespeare's Juliet expresses the boundless generosity of love:

> My bounty is as boundless as the sea,
> My love as deep; the more I give to thee,
> The more I have, for both are infinite.

In the realm of care, closeness and distance are determined by the circumspect, prudent choice of accessibility. In the sphere of love closeness is determined by the yearning for union, totality, fullness of existence. Lovers open up to each other horizons which had not been dreamed of before and they give each other a freedom that no calculating impartiality could ever provide, the freedom of unpremeditated spontaneity.

Time experienced in the existential mode of love is also specifically different from that of care. It is not the carefully planned time of appointments, schedules, and itineraries. If space in the dual mode of existence is infinite and home, time is experienced as eternity and simultaneously as the moment in its richness and fullness (Bergson: *le temps vécu*). Eternity and infinity must not be understood as a stretching out of time and space by the yardsticks of the world of care. Love experiences infinity as home and eternity as moment of fulfillment, where care recoils from uncanny nothingness. Shakespeare, who certainly is not estranged from life's realties, says in one of his sonnets: "Love's not time's fool" and "Eternal love in love's fresh case weighs not the dust and injury of age." And so certain is he of his everlasting ability to love that he ends the sonnet with the words: "If this be error and upon me proved, I never writ and no man ever loved." The aspect of eternity is a structural element of this dual mode of existence. Elizabeth Barrett Browning speaks of love that endures and life that disappears. Aristophanes in Plato's *Symposion* says: "Love must see eternity behind and before it." Lovers feel that they have known each other forever. Robert Browning: "My soul is full, overfilled, I believe it must have been ever this way," and Elizabeth Barrett Browning: "Certainly have I loved you unawares in the idea of you all my life."

The everlastingness of love is experienced in the present moment as an opening up of existence for the bounty of unlimited potentialities. Love is not an invention to ease the hardships of existence. By its very nature love transcends restricting anxieties. Love does not worry, is not conscientious nor unscrupulous, does not fear nor hope. Fear and hope belong within the realm of care. Love has arrived at the security of home. Love is outside the categories of cause and effect and is experienced as an inexplicable miracle. It is a mysterium how *I* and *you* become transparent to each other in the *we-ness*. This mutual understanding does not stem from the intellectual grasp but from the revelation of the heart. A person who is unable to love cannot reveal himself. The existential security of togetherness provides a faith which transcends rational as well as intuitive knowledge. Only passion is blind; love is intensely seeing and looks into the hidden potentialities, stimulating their development, molds and transforms a human being, as can no educational process or transmittance of knowledge. *Eros héauton auxon*—that is, the self-increasing, ever-productive Eros—opens up the sources of creative imagination and inner truthfulness.

But Eros does not withdraw the lovers into a sterile seclusion from the world. When lovers isolate themselves from the surrounding world, they do so upon the promptings of anxiety and care. The invasion of overwhelming care may cause the decay of love. *Eros héauton auxon* opens up wider horizons beyond the togetherness of *you* and *me*. Robert Browning said to his beloved that his heart went out to her not as to one person, no, as to all that he called goodness. The creative imagination visualizes in the personal *you* all which can ever become *you* to *me*. And this is not idealization or deification, produced and driven by anxiety. The genuine togetherness, the very reality of the *we* sets natural boundaries to the creative imagination. Fantastic falsifications, illusions, and deceptions do not grow in the climate of love. They are necessities in the atmosphere of care. The reality of the we frees you as well as me to find our selves. The greater the reality of the we the greater the independence of you and me. And the greater the independence of you and me, the greater are the potentialities of the we-ness. "As you are true to yourself, so you are true to me," says Thekla to her lover in Schiller's "Wallenstein."

In Binswanger's clarification of love as the dual mode of existence, we encounter a concept of selfhood different from the one developed in the survey of Heidegger's existentialistic ideas. There, selfhood was gained in a heroic struggle, facing the uncanny nothingness, enduring anxiety, guilt, death, the limitations of human freedom, withdrawing resolutely from the drifting, dependent existence of the One. Here the living experience of *we-ness*, togetherness in unquestioning generosity, endows you and me with selfhood without any struggle to overcome the helplessness of isolating anxiety. I repeat a quotation from Heidegger: "Only since existence as such is determined by selfhood, can an I-myself relate to a you-yourself," to which Binswanger responds: "Love and yearning would not be possible, if existence were only determined by selfhood, if existence were not fundamentally determined by We-ness." Love does not strive for self-perfection, for powerful mastery over anxiety. I-myself and you-yourself exist by the grace of the *we*, the self is revealed by the *we*. I give myself to you and receive myself back as a gift of the *we*, as you give and receive yourself in the *we*.

Love cannot be without solitude. There is a dialectic rhythm between duality or togetherness and solitude. And the more real the togetherness, the more meaningful is the solitude and vice versa. Solitude is not loneliness in the sense of isolation. Solitude is carried by the creative imagination of the Eros héauton auxon, by the security in the fullness of existence. Neither solitude nor selfhood can take anything away from this certainty of togetherness. Love that cannot stand solitude is dependency, belongs within the sphere of care. The extreme escape from solitude, the compulsive rush from one love object to another (Don Juanism) approaches the pathology of the manic, while the loneliness which does not dare to respond to the yearning of Eros leads into depression.

The existential certainty of love triumphs even over death. Not that it takes anything away from the intensity of grief. But there is not the bitterness which follows the ultimate termination of an ambivalent relation, the ambivalence being due to the involvement with anxiety and care in the sense of dependency, exploitation, possessiveness, and so on. In "Mourning and Melancholia," Freud described the labor of mourning in ambivalent relations first as a period of idealization of the lost love object at the expense of the bereaved person, followed by a period of gradual devaluation of the lost object and final acceptance of reality for the sake of the premium of survival. Love does not need and does not want to forget or devaluate. Love does not need the cult of the dead nor the escape into comforting speculations about immortality, which stem from the sphere of care. Eros transcends the contrast of presence and absence. The nature of love is above all separations, since the selfhood of you is so deeply imprinted in me, just as mine is in yours, that the security of we-ness endures. Only an individual can die, the we-ness remains intact. This we-evidence meets life with that "deep serenity, which dwells at the bottom of the unextinguishable grief" (Jaspers).

While the speech of ethical existence is confession, testimony of the authentic Self, the speech of love is silence. It is trusting surrender, which burns even the bridges of communication behind it. Love does not need verbal communication, it expresses itself in looks, gesture, embrace, often in overwhelming intensity. Anxiety about and care for love make the lovers talk and their communication may express a most valuable integration of love and care. But love as existence of security and fulfillment is beyond doubts and questions. The harmonies of music touch most closely on the harmony of we-ness. The esthetic transcendence and the transcendence of love are tuned together in the love poem. Robert Browning: "No artist lives that longs not once and once only and for one only (ah the prize) to find his love a language fit and fair and simple and sufficient."

Love is never without care. Love proves itself in the world of care, in friendship, marriage, in any meaningful, close relations which are distinguished by different shades of integration of love and care. Love has a widening and broadening influence on personality development and permeates the daily living of anxiety and care with the spirit of creativeness. Love deepens the busy pursuits of daily living by the weight of its fulfilled restfulness, it stimulates the productivity of competition and adds to the ambitions of worldly success the steady, unanxious outlook into infinity. Care alone uses men and material for the purpose of surmounting anxiety; love transforms useful occupation into meaningful work. The visions and Gestalten of art are born out of the spirit of love, the Eros héauton auxon, the yearning for eternal, infinite *we-ness*. Religious creations at their best, living religiosity which has not been ritualized by the pressure of anxiety and care, stem from being-in-the-world as love. Binswanger, in his descriptions of transcendence, never loses the ground of realistic existence under his feet, but he points out that a psychology which cannot embrace in its understanding the experiences of art and religion remains too narrow. If love experienced in existence as togetherness turns to the self, it creates a form of self-love—very different from narcissism or autism, which are characterized by self-deception and by absorption in role playing and are threatened by the loss of self in the One. Binswanger has pointed at the philautia of ancient Greece

—the friendship with oneself—and the religious *amor sui* of Augustine as forms of self-love, in which the conflicts of the self and the One are surmounted in creativity and self-esteem.

Existence as love is delicately structured and therefore constantly in danger of breaking down under the impact of anxiety. We-ness may get lost in the distractions of the One, or in the escape into isolating, self-sufficient independence. The lovers may lose themselves to each other in clinging dependency, in blind passion, fanaticism, mystic deification of the you, rebellion against the imprisonment by each other, if the lovers have lost the respect of each other. Without respect love deteriorates, love turns into hatred. In these shipwrecks of love, the self is deeply humiliated and may drift dangerously close to the experience of futility and nothingness. But such deterioration is never irreparable. Love has unlimited healing creativeness and potentialities of reconciliation.

I do not want to leave this description of being-in-the-world in the mode of love, in which I have tried to condense in the main Binswanger's ideas, without mentioning his concept of the vocation of the psychotherapist. Binswanger sees the psychotherapist as a scientist and artist in one, integrating in his personality the needs of care and the potentialities of love. As a scientist he collects facts and data, searches for cause and effect, motivation and purpose in careful rational procedures. This part of his task is a dignified pursuit which he owes to existence as care. But he would remain an intellectual technician, if that were all, if he were not also an artist, open to visions of togetherness, totality ,to existence as love, to the healing potentialities of the creative Eros.

I have presented some ideas of existentialism, particularly in Binswanger's version, as an attempt at a contribution to the multi-disciplined thinking for which Harry Stack Sullivan so warmly pleaded in his lifetime. There are some parallels between existentialist and psychotherapeutic thinking, but also obvious discrepancies in the approach to human beings. Psychotherapy in all variations fundamentally based on Freud's psychoanalysis studies the dynamics of human behavior in individual developmental histories, seeking for the causes of psychopathology. Existentialism is not interested in individual psychopathology; it describes certain basic irreducible dialectic trends like One and Self, care and love, which determine existence in our culture. The psychotherapist looks at trees, the existentialist at the forest as a whole, but not so much in sociological as in philosophical terms.

Existentialism has something in common with the psychiatry of interpersonal relations. Even more radically than the latter, existentialism surmounts the scientific split between subject and object, points at the interwoven transcendence of existence. The psychiatry of interpersonal relations has shown the deep interdependence of human existence and the dangers for the self that arise from the disjunctive effect of anxiety in relations of interdependence. Anxiety is also at the core of Heidegger's philosophy. He does not consider anxiety as a result of early individual experience, but as a constituent factor of being-in-the-world; and the One is its victim. The One is a prototype of that dependency which Erich Fromm has described as "escape from freedom."

The concept of self is differently used in psychiatry than in existentialistic terminology. Sullivan's concept of self-system implies the conditioning by more or less crippling experiences of anxiety in relation to early significant persons. Sullivan sees the individual rise above his anxieties by careful exploration of the defensive self-system, gradually dissolving its rigidities in interpersonal understanding and consensual validation. Heidegger defines the self as the authenticity of personality, towards which existence is directed in shaking off the dependencies of the One, facing death, enduring inevitable anxiety, guilt, restrictions of freedom, and loneliness. A psychiatrist may feel that there is something unconvincing in this heroic power operation, the isolated transcendence of fundamental human helplessness. It sounds like a "schizoid maneuver" (Silverberg).[10] Perhaps it is not accidental that Heidegger in contradistinction to all other existentialists has compromised himself by leaning towards national-socialism. Sullivan is closer to the psychiatrist-philosopher, Binswanger, who sees selfhood as a natural endowment by the grace of we-ness and love, the security and certainty of which triumph over all manipulations and opera-

10. William V. Silverberg, "The Schizoid Maneuver," *Psychiatry* 10 (1947): 383–93.

tions of Care. For comparison I may mention here a passage from Sullivan's *Conceptions of Modern Psychiatry:* "The relatively uncomplicated experience of love is entirely ennobling. Sympathy flows from it. Tolerance as a respect for people—not as an intellectual detachment from prejudice—follows it like a bright shadow."[11] Since the existentialist considers anxiety as a constituent factor of being-in-the-world, all security operations which the psychiatrist describes, neurotic and not neurotic ones, are dictated by the necessities of care from the existentialist point of view. Operations which attain ambitions, accumulate wealth, and achieve power positions guarantee a certain degree of freedom of movement, but leave existence fundamentally threatened by nonexistence and the human yearning for security unfulfilled. Binswanger sees this yearning for security fulfilled only to the degree that existence is open to love, to creativity. The existentialist's recommendation to the psychotherapist seems to be to sort out with his patient which part of his security operations is directed towards a reasonable, situationally limited stabilization of his existence, and which part is a misled, misunderstood and therefore ineffective yearning for spontaneous, creative self-expression of love.

The existentialist on the other hand might be able to learn from a psychoanalytically trained psychiatrist to substantiate the generalities of his existentialist system by a more detailed study of human interaction and a more pragmatic understanding of individual developmental history.

Freud in his writings repeatedly rejected philosophic concerns. The philosopher, he thought, is whistling in the dark and avoids the hard facts of natural science. However, in some of his later writings he became a philosopher himself. In his paper *Beyond the Pleasure Principle*[12] he presented the dialectic poles of human existence in the contrast between Eros and the death instinct. In terms of instincts he pointed here to the same dialectic relation that the existentialist sees between existence as anxiety—care—and existence as love. In Freud's interpretation of Eros he used Plato's

11. Sullivan, p. 26.
12. London: Hogarth, 1922.

myth about the origin of Eros presented by Aristophanes in the *Symposion:* Human beings were originally androgyne until Zeus split them in two. From then on individuals, thus split, were in eternal search of the partners from whom they were separated, yearning and longing for the original completeness. Freud visualized in this paper the infinitely integrating possibilities of Eros which creates ever new forms of life, counteracting the resistance of the death instinct.

In practical psychoanalytic work this dialectic polarity hinges upon the phenomena of transference and resistance. Transference, whether positive, negative, or ambivalent, in spite of all counteracting resistance—defenses against anxiety—aims at the collaborative integration of the curative work. In existentialistic terms, psychoanalysis gives an opportunity to experience the duality of existence, not as love, since doctor and patient are bound to existence as care: the patient using the doctor, the doctor taking care of the patient in the frame of a contract with appointments and fees. But the dual experience of analysis works to remove the obstacles, to free the patient for the experience of love. A patient who is really able to love—that is, able to integrate the yearning for love into an existence determined by care—no longer needs an analyst.

Existentialism has criticized in psychoanalysis the one-sided adherence to biology. But in this criticism existentialism does not stand alone. In a recent paper "A Neglected Boundary of Psychoanalysis," a disciple of Freud, Fritz Wittels, criticizes psychoanalysis for neglecting the attention due to the primal phenomenon, the *Erlebnis*.[13] He acknowledges that Freud has succeeded in his personality to integrate the scientist and the artist, but he speaks of the pupils of Freud, who "present us with a dry, almost unreadable jugglery of so-called Freudian mechanisms." The *Erlebnis* that is most neglected in psychoanalytic literature is the phenomenon of love which is much broader than orgastic potency or genital maturity. The psychoanalyst in his daily work sees so much of the productions of anxiety, of care—mostly distortions and in-

13. See *Psychoanalytic Quarterly* 18 (1949): 44–59.

hibitions of love—that he might be inclined to dismiss the real manifestations of love as unrealistic poetry.

This oversight might also concern the manifestations of Eros in childhood. Does the phenomenon of love really not appear earlier than with sexual maturity or, as Sullivan has seen it, in preadolescence? Freud has shown us that sexuality has its roots in early childhood, and it is clear that the more the existence of a child is loaded with anxiety, the more drastic are the manifestations of sexuality and its perversions. The infant is born with all the apparent symptoms of anxiety, but the child is also born into a very intimate form of we-ness, that of mother and infant. These facts make plausible the existentialist's thesis that both anxiety and love are constituent factors of existence.

This thesis is debatable. It implies that anxiety (care) and love are irreducible "existentials," inborn propensities which never appear isolated, but in a variety of shades of integration. Translated into Freudian terminology, these irreducible factors are instincts, Eros and death instinct, which do not appear pure, but in a scale of states of "fusion" and "defusion." The term "existentials" is obviously more vague, less committed to biology than the term "instincts," but both terms refer to an inborn quality.

Not all psychotherapists have accepted Freud's latest dialectic instinct theory. Jung has always denied the dualism of instincts. Fenichel doubts the usefulness and necessity of the concept "death instinct."[14] "For a better classification of instincts," he said, "we shall have to wait until physiology develops more valuable theses about instinct sources."

We are obviously on hypothetical grounds when we speak of "birth anxiety," interpreting the signs of distress in the newborn infant as an anxiety response to the threat to survival in the beginning battle between Eros and death instinct. We have no valid memories or means of communication with the infant. Descriptively similar distress in later life is experienced as a "danger signal" (Freud), an upsurge of intensified physiological functions,

14. Otto Fenichel, *The Psychoanalytic Theory of Neurosis* (New York: W. W. Norton, 1945).

accompanied by anxiety, which mobilizes more or less practical, integrating defenses.

In psychoanalytic practice we have learned to understand impractical defenses against anxiety which threaten the patient with states of "defusion," more or less dangerous to his survival, more or less incapacitating him for the experience of love. On this basis we can help the patient towards a state of improved integration. But even when we succeed in revealing the environmental factors which mobilize anxiety or those which most usefully check anxiety, we do not yet know anything about the ultimate origin of anxiety or love. We observe that the infant by empathy participates in the mother's anxiety and her love. This pushes the question of the origin of anxiety and love one generation back. If a patient harps on the idea: "I am doomed forever to remain the victim of anxiety because of my parents' anxiety," we recognize this as an expression of impractical defense. "The greatest danger in therapy is the possibility of confusing the original drive with the covering defense mechanism" (Edmund Bergler).[15] Theory is also hampered by such confusion.

In spite of anxiety-mobilizing pain and present experiences, neurotic and even psychotic patients do become able to master anxiety effectively and to experience love—though not always and not to perfection—when the catalytic intensification of life experience by the psychoanalytic process "working through" insight dissolves the faulty integrations and opens the road to spontaneous development. But the very term spontaneity points at inborn sources that are tapped. There are no "techniques" of being loving or integrative mastery of anxiety that can be learned by rote. It happens—frequently with the connotation of surprise.[16]

The assumption of innate resources or the admission of ignorance as to the ultimate origin of anxiety (care) or love does not seem to be an unproductive attitude in our scientific striving. On the contrary, if we cover this ignorance with a pseudoknowledge

15. Edmund Bergler, *The Basic Neurosis* (New York: Grune and Stratton, 1949).

16. Theodor Reik, *Listening with the Third Ear* (New York: Farrar, Straus and Co., 1949).

we are in danger of getting into dogmatic argumentations between scientists who "believe in" instincts and philosophers who "believe in" existentials, a definitely unproductive preoccupation.

I mentioned above the phenomena of love seem to appear earlier than in adolescence or preadolescence. In early childhood there are expressions of tenderness, budding manifestations of Eros, or yearning for love, so intense, so genuine, so spontaneous, that the more conventionalized adult may blush at his own comparative emptiness. There is no doubt that parental and particularly maternal over-anxiety has a paralyzing, crippling effect on the child's spontaneous development and that parental love is helpful to his integrative growth. But, taking the existentialistic view in consideration, not all anxiety stems from the past. The world of adults, into which the adolescent enters, is full of anxieties, the main preoccupation of adults being, according to Sartre, a sadomasochistic struggle for existence in the name of care. If we tear the opportunistic, hypocritical mask of the One from the competition of adults, it appears more relentless and cruel than the competition of juveniles, who are more frank in their fistfights, but also more ready to be friends again. In the child who is not seriously intimidated there is more sparkling spontaneity and more creative potentialities of the Eros héauton auxon than in the adult, who has become "adjusted" to the world of care. The most severe psychotic catastrophes occur when the adolescent enters into the world of adults. The most gifted youngsters are frequently the most endangered ones who may break down or withdraw into a shell. The more sensitively structured, the more potentially loving or yearning for love and existence is, the more frightening is the impact of and the involvement with the world of care. Frieda Fromm-Reichmann has pointed out the close relation between artistic endowment and schizophrenia, in "Remarks on the Philosophy of Mental Disorder."[17] The psychoanalyst knows how difficult it is to melt the "psychosclerotic" armor of the One, the shell of conventionality, that surrounds the neurotic adult who comes for help in his conflicts. In order to cure psychoneurotic conflicts it is not only necessary to

17. See *Psychiatry* 9 (1946): 293–308.

help the patient to face and endure anxiety, but also to free the childhood sources of spontaneity and creativity, which have become obstructed by care.

Western culture looked at with the eyes of the European existentialist does not present a flattering picture. Even if the existentialist may not have much to contribute to a greater understanding of individual psychopathology or therapy, he affords us a profound insight into the pathology of the culture as a whole. Indeed his gloomy picture of the culture has been influenced by the disillusionment of totalitarianism and war, which destroyed many ideals and values of the past. However, out of the deep European misery, there rises a revaluation, not a mystical movement, not the recognition of one value among others, but of *the* value, the triumphant security and creativity of human love.

Psychotherapy and Existential Philosophy

In the course of the past decades, psychiatry and philosophy have moved toward common meeting grounds. Psychiatry is, and remains, a branch of medicine concerned with the observation, understanding, and treatment of the deranged human mind. The interdisciplinary approach has enabled psychiatry to assemble biological, physiological, pathological, psychological, sociological, and anthropological facts and data, but the psychiatrist must seek a basic philosophic orientation in this confusing multitude of aspects. The question looms up: What is man in his totality? This totality, this wholeness, is more or less deranged in mental illness. The psychiatrist turns to philosophical anthropology for an answer to the question: What is man?

PHILOSOPHICAL ANTHROPOLOGY: A PHENOMENOLOGICAL AND EXISTENTIAL APPROACH

In modern times this anthropology is frequently called existential philosophy. Colin Wilson views existentialism as a revolt against mere logic and reason.[1] It is a plea for intuition and vision; it is a plea for recognizing oneself as being involved in the problems of existence as a participant, not just as a spectator. The search for truth in existential philosophy breaks away from conventional language. Since traditional words and concepts are loaded with traditional prejudices, the existentialist's language—

Reprinted by permission from *The Journal of Religious Thought* 19, no. 2 (1962/63): 129–40.

1. Colin Wilson, *The Outsider* (Boston: Houghton Mifflin, 1956).

particularly that of Heidegger—creates new concepts and verbal neologisms. Not easily accessible in the original language of the author, they become almost untranslatable into English.

To understand existential philosophy one must first of all understand its methodology, which is the methodology worked out by the German philosopher, Edmund Husserl, called phenomenology. Husserl's phenomenology does not merely represent another philosophical system; primarily it is a methodology that aims at arriving at an exact intuition of reality. Husserl was an adversary of psychological theories one-sidedly influenced by natural science. His phenomenology has become a method of rethinking traditional concepts as to the relation of the perceiving subject and the perceived object. The phenomenological method deals with the intentional acts of consciousness and strips them from all presuppositions. Objects of sensory perception are always perceived incompletely like the moon; they are seen only from one side, as it were. Objects in our reach can be turned around, seen, or touched from every angle. Additional experiences and memories supplement what we see, hear, and touch, so that we become able to grasp an object intuitively in its totality. Consciousness is directed not only toward objects of sensory perception, but also toward memories, imaginations, emotions, and values. Tangible objects as well as nontangible objects make up the reality world in which man's existence is rooted. Previous to all reflection, man intuitively grasps the objects that pass through consciousness as a stream of appearances, aspects, or phenomena. The phenomenological method limits experience to this intuitive content of consciousness that precedes reflection and theory formation. The strict discipline of this method permits a fresh look and a rethinking of traditional concepts, applicable to all branches of science.[2]

Heidegger, the German philosopher, and Ortega y Gasset, the Spanish author, reflect the phenomenological method in their philosophical orientation. Both philosophers try to arrive at the radical realities of human life. Philosophy, they say, is more basic than all

2. Edmund Husserl, *Phenomenology*, ed. Joseph J. Kockelmans (Garden City: Doubleday, Anchor Books, 1967).

sciences.[3] Ortega observes that science is only one of the countless activities, actions, operations that man practices all his life. We begin to practice science after we are already living in the world and hence, when the world is already for us this that it is.

According to Heidegger, man is thrown into existence. From the very beginning, existence is my, your, his, or her existence. Other people's lives, the life of a friend, a mate, is for me a mere spectacle. I cannot really enter into the other's pains, joys, thoughts, and impulses. My neighbor's toothache is, strictly speaking, a supposition, a presumption. I see signs that indicate the toothache: his facial muscles are contracted, he covers his jaw with his hands, or he groans and complains in words. But I cannot even be sure whether he does not pretend. The pain of the other is not a radical reality for me. My pain is my pain alone. Life is not transferable; each man has to live his own life. Only in solitude are we our truth. And only in moments of contemplation, when we withdraw from the activities of every day living, do we become aware of this solitude and gain perspective for our actions. According to Ortega we do not live in order to think, but we think in order to succeed in subsisting or surviving.

Being thrown into existence means, in the language of Heidegger, "being-in-the-world." That is, from the very beginning, previous to all reflection, the world is always there. Man's world is different from the environment of the animal that reacts to selective factors of his environment according to innate instinctual behavior patterns. Man is not a passive victim of fate. Being-in-the world means being in a constant flux of action and reaction, being exposed to potential danger situations which man tries to master by premeditation or by voluntary efforts directed toward his survival. Being thrown into existence, man tries to make sense of the situations that he encounters. They offer him choice and he is forced to be free. Even when he does not decide, he has chosen nondecision. Man has the ability to take the facticity of his exist-

3. Martin Heidegger, *Being and Time,* trans. John Macquarrie and Edward Robinson (New York: Harper and Row, 1962); Jose Ortega y Gasset, *The Modern Theme* (New York: Harper & Brothers, Harper Torchbook, 1961).

ence upon him and to transcend his present existence by foresight into the future.

Heidegger says: "The human being is a being that, in being, is concerned about his being."[4] Man is the only animal who knows about death. He knows that life is limited and that death is inevitable. This danger does not always enter into full awareness, but it gives rise to the danger signal of anxiety. Man's freedom saddles his being-in-the-world with responsibility. His existence is directed towards the optimal fulfillment of his potentialities. This goal also is not always in full awareness. But lagging behind this goal of existence, the fulfillment of potentialities or self-realization, gives rise to the danger signal of guilt. Man is the guardian of his existence. Heidegger expresses this aspect of being-in-the-world by the German term, *Sorge,* which can be translated as "care" or "concern." Being-in-the-world in the form of care, man encounters things that have no being of their own, but lend themselves to the purposes of care. For example, food, shelter, tools, or weapons may become means for the purposes of care.

In its basic structure, being-in-the-world is always being-with-others. This implies danger. Things that are part of the forces of nature, as storms, floods, fires, can become dangerous opponents of care, but they can become largely predictable and therewith increasingly manageable. Living creatures, plants, and animals are also, on the basis of increasing knowledge, predictable and therewith serviceable. Being with other men is more dangerous though man as a natural organism has many predictable features. But on the basis of human freedom, man is fundamentally not predictable, therefore being-with-others is loaded with greater dangers than being-with-things. When you meet a stranger the question arises as to whether he is for you or against you. My care for my existence may collide with his care for his existence. If the other one is not for you, that means strife in violent or in civilized form. Conventionalities and ceremonials of courtesy and politeness are used in interpersonal encounters to cushion potential blows. Men become known to each other by trial and error.

4. Heidegger, p. 231.

From the very beginning of life, and to a certain degree through-out the span of life, the human being cannot take care of his exist-ence alone. The infant needs the care of his parents in order to develop his potentialities to take care of himself. Caring for another being implies an intuitive understanding of his needs and poten-tialties of freedom for self-realization. The potentialities of freedom grow only slowly in the dependent human infant, but they grow only when they are cared for. Out of the original symbiosis with his mother the child's ego develops as separate self-consciousness. The integrative function of intuitive understanding grows only in the atmosphere of trust. Mutual trust, the infant's trust in his mother and the mother's trust in her child's developing freedom, opens up the potentialities of coexistence in ever changing new situations. Anxieties can be understood as warning signals of dan-ger, while guilt indicates inhibition of development. Overwhelming anxieties and guilt feelings confuse and becloud the light of mutual understanding. Care transcends each given situation in the direc-tion of the future, if possible, shaping chaos into cosmos.

If man stops caring, chaos overtakes him. Being-in-the-world is more than living. The Swiss psychiatrist Ludwig Binswanger ob-serves that mere living, existing without aim and direction, is sub-jectively experienced as "naked horror."[5] One who lives in this way deteriorates. He cannot help himself, he cannot appeal for help, and he cannot accept the help of others. Death could be aimed at as a salvation from horror, but suicide still implies some degree of decision and therefore aim-directed action. If man does not care any more, even this way out is barred. It is man's misery that he can be lost in his existence; it is his glory that he can find himself again.

Being-in-the-world is opened up in the subjective experience of moods, emotions, affects. At one end of the scale—in horror, despair and panic—the world appears impenetrably chaotic; at the other end of the scale being-in-the -world is lightened by joy, hope, trust, and the world is opened to desire, intention, achievement, integrat-

5. Ludwig Binswanger, *Grundformen und Erkenntnis Menschlichen Daseins* (Zurich: Niehans, 1953), pp. 445–48, 475, 596, 643.

ing mastery. It is meaningful to live, not only in the moment of fulfillment, but also in the opening up of potentialities, in the mastery of adversities, in the directedness toward the future. Between the two ends of the scale of emotions lies the zone of indifference, boredom, and carelessness in which the individual, buffeted around by fate, more or less passively yields to the world, overtaken by the anonymous, inauthentic existence of "the one."

"The one" is a translation of Heidegger's German term, *man*, the impersonal pronoun, that can be everybody and anybody. "The one" drifts without decisions from pillar to post, distracted by distractions, with no goal of his own. His communications deteriorate into chatter and gossip, impoverished of meaning. In psychoanalytic terms we speak of this as weakness in the ego synthesis. But in Heidegger's terms the ego is never without his world. In the structure of "the one's" being-in-the-world, the pole of the world is topheavy; "the one" is more or less lost or drowned in his world. He depends on the world's fashions and standards, on public opinion. In this inauthentic existence "the one" may drift dangerously close to the brink of despair and horror, hiding this danger from his awareness.

PSYCHOTHERAPY: AN EXISTENTIALIST AND PHENOMENOLOGICAL
ORIENTATION

In psychopathology the application of the phenomenological method has stimulated renewed, unprejudiced descriptions of data of observation that have been explained traditionally according to various presupposed methods of interpretation. Phenomenologically oriented psychopathology encourages the psychiatrist to enter into the subjective experience of his patient without premeditated attempts to reduce the unknown to familar concepts. He tries to look into the patient and share his experience. In each single experience the unique person reveals himself with the whole background of his individual development. But the uniqueness of this revelation cannot be grasped in an intuitive act if the observer jumps to conclusions. The phenomenologist does not depreciate the validity of explanatory theories but he postpones them in order to free himself for a fresh look. The intuitive encounter is disturbed by emotional involvement as well as by preconceived expectations. Thus the phenomenological method imposes a strict discipline on the psychiatrist. The physiognomic impressions and the verbal reports of the patient are necessarily incomplete. Yet the psychiatrist stays with the patient's subjective experience. The doctor does not seek to convince the patient of his theoretical interpretations, but to enter as realistically as possible into the patient's subjective experience.

What the existentialist and the phenomenologically oriented psychiatrist calls "the authenticity of existence," "the aim of active interest," "concern" or "care" approaches what the psychoanalyst calls "ego strength." The synthetic function of the ego is at work from the very beginning of existence. Even before the dawn of self-consciousness the infant fits into his world. Early adaptations are automatic, but seldom chaotic. Similarly, the animal fits automatically into its environment as the fruit fits into its skin. The animal's adaptations remain automatic throughout his life; there is no freedom for conscious, aim-directed experimentation. Its actions and reactions are determined by instinct. Man gains a limited freedom of decision through the faculties of consciousness. The optimum of clarified consciousness is obtained by active interest. It is periodically lost in deep sleep and is only dimly lighted in dreams and twilight states. In a state of depersonalization a patient feels unfree, like an automaton. Consciousness is partially beclouded by moods which render impressions deceptive. The individual is lost in his world. Clarity of consciousness and relative freedom of decision are almost completely extinguished in states of excessive anxiety in which being-in-the-world is reduced to chaos.

In a psychotic collapse the two poles of being-in-the-world, self-expression and the intuitive understanding of the self-expression of others, are simultaneously deranged. Both are based on trust. Trust in oneself and trust in one's world are inseparable. Trust is the inner attitude that gives a unity of meaning to the psychomotoric manifestations of self-expression and aim-directed action and enables the individual to receive in his intuition the totality of meaningful messages in the encounter with the other and to respond appropriately in a given situation. This ability to trust gives the maximum freedom for action. Psychotherapy of schizophrenia tries to retrieve this ability to trust, to reestablish the broken bridges of communication. Since the patient has lost his own boundaries and his own freedom and is passively exposed to a dangerously intruding world, the therapist has to take over the care which the patient is no longer able to handle. Beyond that, the psychotherapist tries to help the patient to retrieve his authenticity, to understand himself and his whole life history in order to give him the chance for a new start. But this is only possible when the frozen attitudes of defense can be melted and when the patient can face his anguish and isolation together with a therapist whose communications can become meaningful to him.

In psychopathology we see morbid preoccupation with death as well as defiant denial of human mortality by individuals who consciously or unconsciously are courting danger. Human mortality is a severe blow to man's narcissism, and religious cultures frequently nourish a comforting belief in immortality. On the other hand, the curse of not being able to die is expressed in some legends, as in that of Ahasuerus, the eternal Jew, or that of the Flying Dutchman. The psychotherapist is sometimes helpless if his patient is struck by a fatal disease. But even in relation to a patient in a state of reasonable physical health, the theme of death should not be avoided, for psychotherapy has the goal of supporting the maturing process, of overcoming narcissistic illusions, and of achieving the acceptance of mortality. The mature person comes to terms with the universal fear of death. The finitude of existence pervades daily living. The yesterday must die so that the tomorrow can live. An anxious or defensive dependency on the past prevents the spontaneous openness for the future. Goethe expressed this thought in the words: "As long as you do not have the freedom to die and to become, you are only a shadowy guest on this earth."[6]

The problem of man's limited freedom arises from the fact that, reaching into the future, the human being becomes aware both of his capacity for self-realization and his inability to fulfill his poten-

6. Wolfgang Goethe, "West-östlicher Divan," "Selige Sehnsucht" in *Sämtliche Werke* (Leipzig: Tempel Verlag, n.d.), pp. 361–62.

tialities. Subjectively, he experiences this incompleteness as unfulfilled responsibility or guilt. Thus in psychotherapy, we frequently find patients haunted by false guilt feelings which arise out of fantastic expectations, exaggerated aspirations, and ambitions that do not grow out of the patient's identity with himself, but out of invidious comparisons or other-directed influences. The psychotherapist may sometimes, together with his patient, lose the sober foresight of what he can be. A superego grows out of parental prescriptions, environmental expectations, and adaptations to external standards in which the authenticity of one's own conscience is silenced. As a result one does not direct his existence toward aims that are his own and toward what he can be. The lack of authenticity leads to a drifting, anonymous existence. Only a sound sense of guilt, willingness to accept responsibility, and a realistic appraisal of one's potentialities make it possible for one to accept and to live with his limited freedom.

PSYCHOTHERAPY AS LOVING CARE

Existential philosophy not only helps the psychiatrist better to understand the derangement of man in mental illness; it also points the way to the restoration of the mentally ill to wholeness. Existential philosophy is most suggestive in this connection in its understanding of man as a creature of relationship. Heidegger, for example, holds the point of view that the individual, as long as he is alive, is never a single one. Existence is always with others. Even if one is shipwrecked on a solitary island, he reaches out, he hopes and plans for a future of reunion. Even though a paranoid patient's world is darkened by the horrors of persecution, he still hopes to free himself from his enemies, to clear his world so that it may ultimately confirm his existence.

Creature of relationship that he is, how does man overcome the anguish and loneliness of existence and realize most fully the life of relationship? As suggested earlier, human care or concern, directed into the future and toward the goal of self-realization, is of fundamental importance in this quest. But care by itself is not enough. If care is to function most satisfactorily it must be set in a context of love. In a word, the life of relationship is fully experienced through loving care.

Where there is loving care, two persons encounter each other, according to the Jewish philosopher Martin Buber, as I and Thou, and both experience a trust that does not need to conceal anything from each other.[7] Where there is loving care the I and the Thou become transparent to each other. Such self-revelation and intuitive understanding on both sides grant freedom. I and Thou are open to each other spontaneously, without forcing or being forced. In their being-we-together, I and Thou are open to the potentialities of a creative communion. By this opening of potentialities the horizon of their world is widened and clarified, yet in this broadened world both are firmly at home with each other. In the revelation of I and Thou, both find themselves confirmed by each other's trust. When lovers have nothing to conceal from each other, their looks, their greetings, their embrace, their sexual union—any form of shared intimacy—become deeply meaningful. When the moment is filled with meaning, it has subjectively an eternal value. The lovers need not cling to the moment's fulfillment since trust makes the moment in its fullness unlosable. Even the grief of separation cannot extinguish the light of their communion. Grief becomes intolerable only by the remorse of missed potentialities. In genuine love the anxiety of loss and separation is reduced. Furthermore, trust eliminates the anxiety of being exploited. Love is generous without reckoning.

Since love grants such freedom of spontaneous development and such deep meaning of fulfillment, it is the goal of yearning, consciously and unconsciously, in every human being. But in the every day experiences of interpersonal relations we seldom meet such deeply founded trust or such self-transcending enthusiasm in the care of one for another. Sullivan, in contrast to Freud, distinguishes between love and lust.[8] Sullivan thought that human

7. Martin Buber, *I and Thou*, trans. Ronald Gregor Smith (New York: Scribners, 1937.
8. Harry Stack Sullivan, "Conceptions of Modern Psychiatry" (The First William Alanson White Memorial Lectures), *Psychiatry* 3 (February 1940) and 8 (May 1945).

up unrealistic ideals of isolated self-perfection. His precarious equilibrium breaks down when such grandiose ideals of self-perfection are challenged by realistic adversities. A superficial opportunistic or hypocritical conformity leaves the individual fundamentally lonely and insecure. The isolated person misses the corrective experience of spontaneous I-Thou relations which convey acceptance and confirmation of his very existence. Even a hypocritical adjustment may reveal the deep-seated longing for meaningful interpersonal relations.

Frequently without understanding their need in full awareness, patients want to express their own love, to open the more or less blocked resources of active loving care which saves them from the loneliness and meaninglessness of existence. But, on the other hand, the yearning for active love may be experienced as extreme danger, particularly by those patients in whom the basis of trust was shattered early in their existence. This very yearning threatens to reduce them to infantile dependency and helplessness—as if they would become clay in the hands of the molding therapist—an It, a thing without selfhood. In masochistic self-denial the patient may appeal to the therapist's urge to take over, as if he wanted forever to get away from the promptings of his own care. In other cases, the patient fights bitterly against being taken over.

It is not enough that the therapist knows about the development of instincts and the typical structures of defense. It is important for the therapist to be at home in the world of care. Imperfect as it may be, care lightens the therapist's own world as well as the patient's world to him. Without forcing psychological concepts and hypotheses on the patient, the therapist's loving care establishes the rapport of true intuition. Intuitive understanding is made possible by the trust of the patient in the doctor as well as the trust of the doctor in the patient. This trust can err, but, through trial and error, the I and the Thou may touch each other and elicit a spontaneous response. It is true that the psychotherapist cannot work without theories and hypotheses to verify and compare his observations. But it is important that he take the detached look of the phenomenologist so that he may be open to the fresh experience of the unprejudiced observer. The fresh look can stimulate loving care in him, which is easily inhibited by foregone conclusions and presuppositions.

Loving care and creative imagination are closely related. They open the horizon for all that the I and Thou can have in common and that is much more than the solitary individual can visualize. Loving care is not free from anxieties on the part of the patient or the therapist. Trust is daring and the possibility of failure can never be excluded. This is a reason why therapist and patient are inclined to cling to theories and technical rules. The therapist may seek guidance by the scientific absolutes of his profession. But the real situations may make him anxious and guilty. Anxiety and guilt feelings separate him from spontaneous exchange with his patient, particularly when the therapist is one-sidedly preoccupied with his reputation. The spontaneous impulses of loving care in psychotherapy are not simply sweetness and light. The therapist has to be acquainted with the danger zones of anxiety and he must know how to stand his own anxieties. The longing for meaningful communication on the part of both therapist and patient helps to forego transient, illusory comforts and reassurances. Trust takes transient anxieties and frustrations in stride, since the subjective experience of wholeness that corresponds to the synthetic function of the ego is the most urgent concern of every patient. This search for understanding need not be forced on a patient, for he is reaching out to obtain the freedom for such understanding.

Thus I have presented my conception of the phenomenological and existentialist approach to psychopathology. The central problem, as I see it, is the intuitive understanding of the totality of human existence by what Sullivan calls participant observation. The psychiatrist tries, as far as possible, to enter into the subjective experience of the patient. He describes the changes of consciousness, the various degrees of clarity that elucidate his being-in-the-world, and the influence of moods and emotions on the state of consciousness. The greatest clarity of consciousness represents the individual's optimum of freedom to make his decisions, to find his place in his world, to master the situations into which he is thrown, and to transcend them in the choice of self-expression and aim-directed action. Overwhelming emotions and habitually rigid attitudes of defense interfere with the optimal function of care. The individual may become engulfed in his world as a passive victim of external stimuli and disorganizing emotions. Denial of the past by repression or dissociation, as well as rejection of the limitations in the future, lead to distortions of being-in-the-world and to segmentation of the total personality. Man often misunderstands and sometimes misuses his fellows. This elicits guilt. But man also learns to meet the challenges of his existence, to take hold of the things in his world, and to use them for the purposes of his subsistence. Man represents to man his greatest danger and challenge because of his unpredictability. But since we are all fundamentally human, there is the possibility of intuitive understanding which arises from the basis of trust. Trust is not an emotion. It is a responsive, flexible attitude. Established in the self-confidence of his own being-in-the-world, man arrives at the decision as to whom, where, and when he is able to trust. He extends his care to those whom he trusts, not only using them for gratification and security, but granting them and caring for the freedom of their authentic development towards self-realization. The highest degree of integrative understanding is reached in the relation of loving care which does not only gratify instinctual needs but opens the ingenuity of intuitive understanding and the spontaneous resources of creativity. Psychotherapy at its best is a function of loving care. Though it is limited in gratifications and doomed to failure when there is distrust on either side, psychotherapy can rise to an intuitive understanding and, in creative collaboration, help the patient in the meaningful reintegration of his existence.

Søren Kierkegaard's Mood Swings

Kierkegaard was a forerunner of existential philosophy (Husserl, Jaspers, Heidegger, Sartre) as well as of modern psychoanalytical psychology. His psychology was that of a poet and philosopher, not that of a scientist. It grew out of his self-observations. He expressed the most delicate nuances of his emotional experiences in his diaries, and his poetic-philosophical writings represent a veiled, yet most intimate autobiographical confession. There exists a vast literature on Kierkegaard in Danish and other languages. For my limited purposes I found particularly useful the Danish biographer of Kierkegaard, Johannes Hohlenberg, and a German psychoanalytic study of Kierkegaard by Fanny Lowtzky[1] Fanny Lowtzky describes how close Kierkegaard came to discovering his Oedipus conflict and how he tried to solve it in philosophical and religious terms. Since this publication in 1935 we have gained a deeper understanding of psychoanalytic ego-psychology. Ernst Kris has shed light on the process of creative sublimations in his *Psychoanalytic Explorations of Art,* Lawrence Kubie has described the contribution of preconscious processes to creativity depending "upon freedom in gathering, assembling, comparing and reshuffling of ideas." This creativity is according to Kubie as universal as the neurotic process that hampers creativity.[2] Phyllis Greenacre has

Reprinted by permission from *The International Journal of Psycho-Analysis* 41, pts. 4–5, pp. 521–25.

1. Johannes Hohlenberg, *Sören Kierkegaard,* trans. T. H. Croxall (New York: Pantheon, 1954); Fanny Lowtzky, *Sören Kierkegaard: Das subjective Erlebnis und die religiöse Offenbarung: eine psychoanalytische Studie einer Fast-Selbstanalyse* (Leipsig: Internationaler Psychoanalytischer Verlag, 1935).

2. Ernst Kris, *Psychoanalytic Explorations in Art* (New York: International Universities Press, 1952); Lawrence Kubie, *Neurotic Distortion of the Creative Process* (Lawrence: University of Kansas Press, 1958).

developed "collective alternates" in "The Family Romance of the Artist," and Erik H. Erikson in his book *Young Man Luther* has brought to life the inner revolutions of another religious genius who, like Søren Kierkegaard, suffered from manic-depressive mood swings.[3]

We hesitate to apply a psychiatric classification to a genius. But there is no doubt that Kierkegaard's mood swings reached extremes, in which, corresponding to Edith Jacobson's article on "Normal and Pathological Moods: Their Nature and Functions," the subject as well as the entire object world appears unpleasantly or pleasantly transformed.[4] Two examples may illustrate Kierkegaard's extreme moods. In 1839 he wrote in his *Journals:*

> The whole of existence frightens me, from the smallest fly to the mystery of the Incarnation; everything is unintelligible to me, most of all myself; the whole of existence is poisoned in my sight, particularly myself. Great is my sorrow and without bounds; no man knows it, only God in Heaven, and he will not console me; no man can console me, only God in Heaven and he will not have mercy upon me.[5]

In an "Attempt in Experimental Psychology" called *Repetition,* published in 1843, he wrote:

> I was at the highest peak and surmised the dizzy maximum which is not indicated on any scale of well-being, not even on the poetical thermometer. The body had lost all its earthly heaviness, it was as though I had no body . . . every function enjoyed its completest satisfaction, every nerve tingled with delight . . . every thought proffered itself with festal gladness and solemnity, the silliest conceit not less than the richest idea. . . . The whole of existence seemed to be, as it were, in love

---

3. Phyllis Greenacre, "The Family Romance of the Artist," in *Psychoanalytic Study of the Child,* vol. 13 (New York: International Universities Press, 1958); Erik Erikson, *Young Man Luther* (New York: Norton, 1958).

4. Edith Jacobson, "Normal and Pathological Moods: Their Nature and Functions," in *Psychoanalytic Study of the Child* 12 (1957): 72–113.

5. Sören Kierkegaard, *The Journals* (London: Oxford University Press, 1938), no. 275.

with me, and everything vibrated in preordained rapport with my being.[6]

Kierkegaard was aware that his melancholy had its roots in his childhood. He wrote in his *Journals* that sorrow in adulthood can depress the conscious mind, but "the terrible thing is when a man's consciousness is subjected to such pressure from childhood up that not even the elasticity of the soul, not all the energy of freedom can rid him of it, [of] something which lies as it were beyond the conscious itself."[7]

It is remarkable that Kierkegaard never mentioned his mother in his writings. She was, according to Hohlenberg, "a good-natured housewife, a mother hen to her chickens who could not accompany them on their flight."[8] If there had been a strong early tie between this mother and Søren, her youngest child, it was soon replaced by a tie of intense identification between father and son. The father was a gifted, melancholy man tormented by religious scruples. As a poor, lonely, starving, and freezing shepherd boy he had cursed God for neglecting him, but he had worked his way up and had become a wealthy merchant. His first beloved wife died childless. Since he had impregnated a relative, working as servant in his household, he felt obliged to marry her still in the year of mourning. But he never loved her. Søren suspected from the father's veiled intimations his guilt due to loveless sexual greed. The father was 57 at Søren's birth, and Søren was the last of seven children. The old man experienced his wealth and success as a curse. His second wife and five of his children died before him. Søren was a hunch-backed, precocious child with a rich intellectual and emotional endowment. Outlandishly dressed, without physical strength, he defended himself against ridicule with his keen wit and sharp argumentativeness, which gave him the nickname "the fork." He, too, expected an early death. The father saw in him a sacrificial lamb, destined to expiate his guilt. Søren shared the father's "silent

6. Søren Kierkegaard, *Repetition*, Introduction and notes by Walter Lowrie (Princeton: Princeton University Press, 1941), pp. 74–75.

7. *The Journals*, no. 420.

8. Hohlenberg, *Sören Kierkegaard*, p. 42.

despair" and his daydreams.[9] The father retired early from business and dedicated himself to the youngest, favorite son. He took him on long exhausting walks through the rooms of their house, visiting foreign countries in their imagination, talking with imaginary people, and arguing about the gloomy aspects of religion. On the other hand, the father was given to frightening outbreaks of rage which reduced the child to guilt, despair, and spiritual impotence.

We cannot exclude a hereditary factor in Kierkegaard's mood swings, but, in addition, the symbiotic identification with a melancholy father must have intensified the son's suffering. Freud in a footnote to *The Ego and the Id* mentioned "borrowed guilt feelings" related to melancholia.[10] Fenichel took over this concept in his paper on "Identification."[11] Identification is a stage preliminary to object love, characterized by ambivalence, empathic emotional contamination; at this stage the primary process of emotional orientation is not yet mastered by rational understanding. There is a yearning for the primary union of trust and absolute security, but a persisting overprotective symbiosis by which Therese Benedek characterizes the "depressive constellation" smothers and misdirects the child's own instinctual impulses. He develops a defensive secondary narcissism reinforced later by the messianic ego-ideal to become the depressed parent's savior, an aim of superb grandiosity, an all-or-none alternative, doomed to annihilating failure again and again.[12] The young Kierkegaard was not fully able to discriminate the lonely, unique *I* from the engulfing *you*. The symbiotic identification with a father who could not confirm the positive values of life, who was torn by a rift between sacred and profane love, made the son doubt his own sexual role as a male. He described in *Stages of Life's Way* the reproduction of a primal scene as "Solomon's Dream."[13] "The son was blissful in his devotion

9. *The Journals*, no. 483.

10. Sigmund Freud, *The Ego and the Id* (London: Hogarth, 1927).

11. Otto Fenichel, "Identification," *Internationale Zeitschrift für Psychoanalyse* 12 (1926: 318.

12. Therese Benedek, "Toward the Biology of the Depressive Constellation," *Journal of the American Psychoanalytic Association* 3 (1956): 389–427.

13. Sören Kierkegaard, *Stages on Life's Way*, trans. Walter Lowrie (Princeton: Princeton University Press, 1940), pp. 236–37.

to his father," he wrote. In the night Solomon sneaked into his royal father David's bedroom, frightened by the idea of a murderous raid. He found the old hero prostrate in despair with the bitterest accusations of remorse about his sexual greed. The son recognized in trepidation that "one must be an ungodly man to be God's elect." "If there is any pang of sympathy, it is that of having to be ashamed of one's father, of him whom one loves above all." And "Solomon's spine was broken" by too heavy a load (an allusion to Søren's hunchback and a symbolic expression of his castration anxiety).[14]

The burden of borrowed guilt feelings prevented a full consolidation of Kierkegaard's ego. His superego was split up into many ego ideals eliciting in a prolonged adolescence the stormy crises of identity that Erikson describes in Luther's adolescence. Submitting to the father's wish Kierkegaard studied theology, but he soon turned in rebellion to aesthetic interests, romantic poetry. He became a leader in debating clubs. He passed the nights in coffee houses, theaters, and elegant restaurants. He spent the money of his inconsistently indulgent father lavishly. According to family standards he led a dissolute life. Only after the father's death he finished his theological studies without sidestepping, but he did not become a cleric.

One year before the father's death he met Regine Olsen, then 14 years old, ten years younger than Søren. He fell in love with her at first sight. Regine was the girl of his erotic dreams; he carried his dreams in him for three years. After he passed his examinations, he declared his love to her. He was intensely persuasive in his passion. He overcame her hesitation and became engaged to her. But as soon as he had made this commitment, the image of his fervent hopes changed into the pale image of his memories. Søren became the victim of doubts. Could he, burdened by depressive mood swings, carry the responsibility of this commitment, would the rift between his erotic ecstasies and the obligations of conjugal love ever heal? Was he not going to destroy her and himself? Was he

14. Søren Kierkegaard, *Stadien auf dem Lebensweg*, trans. Christoph Schrempf (Jena: E. Diederichs, 1922), p. 227.

not a frivolous seducer, a Faust, a Don Juan, or Ahasuerus, the eternally wandering Jew? Was it not selfish to ask for salvation through love? Could he trust like Sara, the bride of Tobias in the biblical legend, the woman whose six previous bridegrooms were killed by a demon on the wedding night and who nevertheless accepted Tobias' love and trusted to be healed by it? He saw himself in the role of Hamlet or of Richard III. This flood of male and female self-images indicates the anxiety that foreshadows the dangers of ego disintegration. Kierkegaard wrote: "The misfortune really is that no sooner has one evolved something, than one becomes it oneself. I told you the other day about an idea for a Faust. I only now feel, it was myself I was describing; I have hardly read or thought about an illness before I have it."[15]

For one year Kierkegaard tried to play the part of the considerate conventional fiancé. He tried to convince Regine that he was unworthy. He was deeply distressed by her clinging attachment. His conflict was a double bind: "Do it and you will regret it. Do it not and you will regret it, too."[16] At last he broke the engagement, deeply humiliated by his defeat, Regine's misery, and the accusations of public opinion.

He saved himself from disintegration by a fever of creative writing, in a kind of manic mood. He wrote to find himself, to explain himself to Regine, to win her back, not as a wife, but as the muse of his creativity. He wrote under an array of pseudonyms: Victor Eremita, Constantin Constantius, Johannes de Silentio, Frater Taciturnus, the Quidam of a psychological experiment, etc. By the pseudonyms he concealed himself in shame, and yet he was bursting out in defiant self-revelation. The pseudonyms indicate his various self-images, ego ideals which he tried on for size in order to collect different aspects of reality. Kierkegaard's Socratic self-irony played with these various roles sometimes like a child, yet deeply serious in his search for integration. In his inward trial "Guilty?/Not guilty" he raged with the indignation of a Job against whom God had conspired with the devil to take away all he loved

15. *The Journals*, no. 90.
16. Hohlenberg, p. 91.

to test his faith. Was he, Søren, not also innocent? Was there still any hope that would reorganize his future or was he entering the Inferno where hope and love are dead?[17]

He rephrased the myth of Antigone to explain his secret destiny to Regine: Antigone has discovered the secret crime in the life of Oedipus, her father, and that she is the fruit of an ill-fated incestuous bond. Her father dies without sharing his secret with her or with any one. Antigone does not dare to accept the wooing of a lover to whom she is deeply attracted, since she cannot betray her dead father's secret; she is bound by filial duty and is free to love only when she dies.[18]

Kierkegaard repeated the theme of the Oedipus conflict in many variations. In the variation of Periander, Tyrant of Corinth, he described the contradictions in his father's character. Periander spoke as a God-fearing wise, and generous man, but he acted like a madman. He had had an incestuous relation to his mother and murdered his wife; the son rebelled against him but then forgave him.[19] In these variations of the Oedipal theme it is significant that always the father is guilty and the child borrows the guilt. The Antigone variation indicates Søren's feminine identification and the homoerotic aspects of his tie to the father.

In his prodigious writings Kierkegaard gradually reconciled the dialectic tensions that had torn his soul. His bisexual endowment, his masculine and feminine identifications, his active and passive ego ideals slowly reached the stage of ego integration and superego consolidation. Kierkegaard never had to beg his muse for inspiration. He was flooded with ideas. And what he passively and gratefully received as inspiration he actively and forcefully elaborated into his own convictions.

His first book *Either/Or* presents the battle between sensuous aesthetic immediacy and endless ethical reflections in Kierkegaard. In analytic terms the contradictions between the id and the super-

17. *Stages on Life's Way.*

18. Søren Kierkegaard, *Either/Or*, trans. David F. Swenson and Lilian Marvin Svenson (Princeton: Princeton University Press, 1944), pp. 125–33.

19. *Stages on Life's Way*, pp. 298–302.

ego appeared still irreconcilable. But he divines a solution of the conflict on a religious plane.

In *Fear and Trembling* he approaches a solution of his conflict by rephrasing the story of Abraham and Isaac in his own terms. Abraham was willing to sacrifice his only beloved son, his hope for the future, to the will of God, as he understood it, all alone without any assent of other human beings. He achieved the "movement of infinite resignation," he faced the nothingness that surrounds human existence, he accepted destiny as a free agent and herewith he transcended its frustrations, and the son was given back to Abraham, not in a life after death, but here and now, by "the movement of infinite faith." Owing to the *credo quia absurdum* he received the son in a new trust, no longer as a selfish personal possession in his own limited existence. The *species aeternitatis* was opened to him, through the leap into faith, into the forever impredictable future.[20] Kubie speaks of the "leap into the dark of the genius."[21] The legend of Abraham and Isaac reminds us that Søren's father had chosen the favorite son as sacrificial lamb for the expiation of his guilt. The legend of the Bible laid the foundation for the Jewish covenant with God and the custom of circumcision. Borrowed guilt feelings descending from father to son gave rise to the dogma of original sin, the damnation of a narcissistic asocial sexuality and the dogma of expiation of sin by a sacrificial death. The self-revelation in *Fear and Trembling* indicates that Kierkegaard was freeing himself from the selfish appropriation by and identification with his father. And to the degree he was freeing himself of this dependence, the chains of his own defensive narcissism, his arrogance, ambition, and possessiveness gradually dropped away. After a long search for identity he was finding himself, he recovered from what he called the "Sickness unto Death" in which he had "desperately tried to be himself and yet also tried desperately not to be himself."[22] He searched for "the knight of faith" in once-

20. Søren Kierkegaard, *Fear and Trembling* (Princeton: Princeton University Press, 1941), pp. 65 ff.

21. Kubie, *Neurotic Distortion.*

22. Sören Kierkegaard, *The Sickness Unto Death*, trans. Walter Lowrie (Princeton: Princeton University Press, 1940), p. 44.

born individuals who simply trust the immediacy in living, while others twice-born, like himself, can only by the leap into faith return to this basic trust.[23] And this leap is more than a rational yielding to the necessities of reality. Says Kierkegaard:

> The thing is to find a truth which is true for *me*, to find the idea for which I can live and die. . . . What good would it do me, if truth stood before me, cold and naked, not caring whether I recognized her or not, and producing in me a shudder of fear rather than a trusting devotion?[24]

On this basis he built his own subjective philosophy and religion. He protested against the system-building philosophy of Hegel which encompasses the universe of man's cognitive potentialities. Kierkegaard had certainly learned much from Hegel's dialectic thinking. He emphasized the "either/or" of decision versus the "and/and" of synthesizing thought processes, religiosity versus philosophic speculation. Kierkegaard's concern was the individual, his subjective needs and passions and his dread of disintegration in the dialectical tension between his passions and the prohibitions imposed by reality. He saw the human being in a process of becoming a self, the courage of becoming conscious, transparent to himself in a struggle against the forces of self-concealment, seclusion, and illusion. Kierkegaard therewith ploughed the field for discoveries that were made in psychoanalysis a century later. I do not enter into Kierkegaard's religion and philosophy. I wanted only to give a sketch of his personal development. Kierkegaard succeeded in trusting his own spiritual potency, and in this trust he reached the experience of subjective freedom that united his will with his destiny. He had experienced his symbiotic identification with the father and the repetition compulsion of a defensive narcissism as "original sin"; the integration of his ego, the creative liberation came to him as a gift of divine grace.

Until his early death at the age of not yet 45 Kierkegaard remained a polemic fighter, as if he had to reinforce the boundaries of a hard-won ego strength against the intrusion of a hostile world

23. *Fear and Trembling.*
24. *The Journals*, no. 90.

and hostile father-images. He fought against the anonymous corruption of journalism, and his sensitivity had to endure bitter counterattacks in the *Corsaire,* the Danish *Punch.* He fought against the lack of authenticity of the individual who loses his subjective freedom and personal responsibility doomed by the more or less hypocritical adjustment to the currents of a mass society. He fought against the compromising, unserious complacency of modern institutionalized Christianity and did not mince words in his attacks. He fought valiantly, but in fighting he had found the personal relation to the God of Love. He did not pile up financial gains. At his death there was only money left for the funeral. He did not gather glory in his lifetime. But he had the conviction that his ideas would reach future generations.

Just when he had finished the last pages of his last book *The Instant,*[25] Kierkegaard fell from his sofa unconscious and was taken to the hospital, where he died after a month. He presented in his last book the pregnant instant in which Time touches Eternity and demands a personal decision. In contrast to the rationalists' idea of the identity of subject and object, the unity of thought and being, Kierkegaard says "Man is a synthesis of the infinite and the finite," but this synthesis is just the opposite of identity. It is the basis of existential despair, it separates subject from object, thought from being, it reveals the dynamic insecurity of the spirit.[26]

In the last weeks of Kierkegaard's life his friends and relatives saw him free from anxiety, though he was fully aware of his closeness to death. Unanimously, his physician, nurse, and visitors experienced a radiant serenity in the dying man, "heart-felt love, a blessed, released sorrow, penetrating clarity and a playful smile."[27] The words of Bertrand Russell are applicable to Kierkegaard's life and development:

> Except for those rare spirits that are born without sin, there is a cavern of darkness to be traversed before that temple can

25. Søren Kierkegaard, *Der Augenblick* (*The Instant*) (Jena: E. Diederichs, 1923).
26. *The Sickness Unto Death.*
27. Hohlenberg, p. 268.

be entered. The gate of the cavern is despair, and its floor is paved with gravestones of abandoned hopes. There Self must die; there the eagerness, the greed of untamed desire must be slain, for only so can the soul be freed from the empire of Fate. But out of the cavern the Gate of Renunciation leads again to the daylight of wisdom, by whose radiance a new insight, a new joy, a new tenderness, shine forth to gladden the pilgrim's heart.[28]

Kierkegaard had to overcome severe obstacles in his rich but tragic endowment: his physical handicap, the burden of borrowed guilt feelings in his prolonged symbiotic identification with a melancholy father who indulged and tormented him and was unable to offer him the image of self-assertive maleness to emulate. Søren Kierkegaard suffered from the ambivalence in this relation, from the dialectical tensions of bisexuality, in the stormy identity crises of a prolonged adolescence. He could not eradicate what he called "the thorn in his flesh," the rift between erotic passion and the yearning for conjugal love. But his regressive tendencies entered into the service of ego integration and of the creative sublimations of the artist as Ernst Kris has described them.[29] Kierkegaard mastered the dialectical tensions of bisexuality. As an adult he worked through his unsolved Oedipus conflict. He accepted his ego boundaries, renounced the overcompensations of a defensive, secondary narcissism, and in a renewal of basic trust he transcended the limitations of his individual existence. Like Luther before him and Freud after him, and other men of genius, he took the risk of nonbeing implied in the rejection by his contemporaries and entrusted his ideas to future generations.

28. Bertrand Russell, *Mysticism and Logic* (London: Allen and Unwin, 1929).
29. Kris, *Psychoanalytic Explorations in Art.*

Index

Abraham, Karl, 68, 137, 176, 177, 341, 352
Adaptability, 5
Adler, Alfred
  compared with Jung, 210–11, 216, 217
  dissenter from Freud, 220–21
  on ego psychology, 205–06
  on individual psychology in treatment, 208–09
  on neurosis, 207–08
  overemphasis on love, 210
  on patient-therapist relation, 208–09
  on reality adjustment, 206
  terminology, 209–10
Affective psychoses. *See* Manic-depressive psychoses
Alexander, Franz, 226, 261, 265
Alverdes, Friedrich, 336
Analysand, attitude toward therapist, 21–22
Animal behavior
  appetitive behavior concept and consummatory acts, 289–90
  applications of ethology to man, 291 ff.
    acquirement of tools, 295
    consciousness of freedom, 296–98
    decay of sublimations, 296
    disintegration from failing inhibitions, 296
    infantile sexuality as appetitive

Animal behavior (*cont.*)
    behavior, 294
    integration of needs, 297
  compared with human behavior re freedom to evaluate, 285–86
  in conflict situations, 286
  displacement action, 287–89
  innate releasing mechanism for blockage of motor patterns, 287
  instinct as working hypothesis, 286
Anxiety, xv, xvi
  castration, 57
  in childhood, 7, 16
  as danger signal, 7, 55, 122
  defense against loneliness, 54
  definitions, 84
  detrimental effects, 7–8
  Freud's categories, 54–55
  from instinctual impulses, 54
  parental, effects of, 9–12
  superego, 58–61
Apollonius Rhodius, 305
Arrested emotional development in childhood, 20

Bachofen, Johann Jakob, 305, 332, 353
Balint, Michael, 93, 121, 264, 272, 274, 275
Bally, Gustav, 285, 294, 295
Barrett, William, 360
Barth, Karl, 299
Bastian, Adolf, 325

Index